The Cassa per il Mezzogiorno, the World Bank and the Model for Italian Economic Development

The Cassa per il Mezzogiorno, the World Bank and the Model for Italian Economic Development

By

Amedeo Lepore

Cambridge Scholars Publishing

The Cassa per il Mezzogiorno, the World Bank and the Model for Italian Economic Development

By Amedeo Lepore

This book first published 2023

Cambridge Scholars Publishing

Lady Stephenson Library, Newcastle upon Tyne, NE6 2PA, UK

British Library Cataloguing in Publication Data
A catalogue record for this book is available from the British Library

ISBN (10): 1-5275-3768-4
ISBN (13): 978-1-5275-3768-2

to Federico Lepore and Antonio Di Vittorio

"The Governor envisioned – and the times allowed that back then – that the unbound stance of the Cassa, together with its seriousness, reliability and efficiency, […] made it the most suitable tool for attracting the most significant intervention (300 million dollars) the World Bank had ever made in Europe; such a relevant commitment was obtained by Menichella from the President of the World Bank himself in Paris in 1952. […] The World Bank, following a suggestion by the Governor, shifted the focus from granting loans to individual projects – which referred to single plants – to rather broad sectors targeting a whole territory. […] This made the intervention model of the Cassa an exemplary case for the implementation of development policies in economically depressed areas all over the word. Hence the worldwide interest for the action of the Cassa […] which Menichella then leveraged to propel this institution into the sector of private financing"

(G. Pescatore, *Menichella, l'intervento per il Mezzogiorno e la Banca Mondiale*, in D. Menichella, *Testimonianze e studi raccolti dalla Banca d'Italia*, Rome-Bari, Laterza, 1986, p. 139)

"*Sviluppo* is a policy of development planned by those Italians who are concerned not merely with improving the standard of living of the Southern peasant, but also with raising the economic level of the whole of Italy by making the South a reasonably prosperous partner in the Italian economy contributing to a steadily growing national wealth, instead of being a burden which can only be regarded with shame by a Western European country"

(M. Carlyle, *The Awakening of Southern Italy*, London, Oxford University Press, 1962, p. 44)

TABLE OF CONTENTS

The Appendix is available on the SVIMEZ website (http://win.svimez.info/cassa/index.html) and on the Historical Archive of the Italian State website (https://aset.acs.beniculturali.it/aset-web/info/documentazioneIBRD).

This book includes references to IBRD internal-use reports and reports by the IBRD Presidents, as well as to other documents and materials concerning the Cassa per il Mezzogiorno. All the IBRD materials have been made available by the World Bank upon their public disclosure.

ITALY
The Mezzogiorno: Abruzzo, Molise, Campania, Puglia, Basilicata, Calabria, Sicily, and Sardinia regions.
SWITZERLAND
AUSTRIA
HUNGARY
SLOVENIA
CROATIA
FRANCE
PIEDMONT
LOMBARDY
VENETO
LIGURIA
EMILIA-ROMAGNA
TUSCANY
UMBRIA
MARCHE
LAZIO
Rome
ABRUZZO
MOLISE
CAMPANIA
PUGLIA
BASILICATA
CALABRIA
SICILIA
SARDEGNA
Ligurian Sea
Corsica (FR.)
Sardinia
Adriatic Sea
Tyrrhenian Sea
Ionian Sea
Mediterranean Sea
Mediterranean Sea
Sicily
Tunis
ALGERIA
TUNISIA
MALTA
Valletta

Main Abbreviations

ACS	Archivio Centrale dello Stato, the main Historical Archive of the Italian State
ASBI	Archivio Storico della Banca d'Italia, the Historical Archive of the Banca d'Italia, the Italian Central Bank
ASS	Archivio Storico della SVIMEZ, the Historical Archive of SVIMEZ
BIRS	Banca Internazionale per la Ricostruzione e lo Sviluppo (see IBRD)
CASMEZ	Cassa per il Mezzogiorno
CICR	Comitato Interministeriale per il Credito e il Risparmio, an Italian Interministerial Commitee focused on top-tier vigilance on the protection of savings and credit-related activities
CIS	Credito Industriale Sardo, a special credit institution focused on financing industry in Sardinia
CNRN	Comitato Nazionale per le Ricerche Nucleari, the Italian National Committee for Nuclear Researches
ECA	Economic Cooperation Administration
EFIM	Ente partecipazioni e Finanziamento Industria Manifatturiera, a State-owned financial institution focused on industrial participations and investments
EIB	European Investment Bank
ENEL	Ente Nazionale per l'Energia Elettrica, historically the main Italian electric power company
ENI	Ente Nazionale Idrocarburi, historically the main Italian hydrocarbons company
ENSI	Energia Nucleare Sud Italia, the project that led to the construction of the Garigliano nuclear power plant
EPU	European Payments Union
ERP	European Recovery Program

FINSARDA	Società Finanziaria Sarda, a financial institution established to promote investments in Sardinia
IASM	Istituto per l'Assistenza allo Sviluppo del Mezzogiorno, a body which provided technical assistance and promoted the localization of new businesses in Southern Italy
IBRD	International Bank for Reconstruction and Development
IDA	International Development Association
IMI	Istituto Mobiliare Italiano, a self-managed public law entity created to promote the recapitalization of Italian industry, which managed the Marshall Plan funds
INSUD	Nuove Iniziative per il Sud, a development finance body controlled by the Cassa per il Mezzogiorno
IRFIS	Istituto Regionale per il Finanziamento alle Industrie in Sicilia, a special credit institution focused on financing industry in Sicily
IRI	Istituto per la Ricostruzione Industriale, the institution established for the reorganization of the Italian banking and industrial system, involved in post-war industrial reconstruction and in interventions to develop the Southern regions
ISAP	Istituto per lo Sviluppo delle Attività Produttive, a public body to promote development in Southern Italy
ISVEIMER	Istituto per lo Sviluppo Economico dell'Italia Meridionale, a special credit institution focused on financing industry in Southern Italy
ISTAT	Istituto Nazionale di Statistica, the Italian National Institute of Statistics
MSA	Mutual Security Agency
MW	Megawatt
OECD	Organization for Economic Cooperation and Development
SENN	Società Elettronucleare Nazionale, an Italian public company building nuclear power plants

SME	Società Meridionale di Elettricità, a Southern Italy-based company created to build and operate hydroelectric plants
SOFIS	Società Finanziaria Siciliana di Investimenti Industriali, a Sicilian public finance institution aimed at supporting companies which experienced economic downturns
SVIMEZ	Associazione per lo sviluppo dell'industria nel Mezzogiorno, the main Association concerned with industrial development in Southern Italy, which promoted the establishment of the Cassa per il Mezzogiorno
TVA	Tennessee Valley Authority

Currency equivalencies

1 US$ = 625 Lit.
Lit. 1 = 0.0016 US$
Lit. 1,000,000 = 1,600 US$
Lit. 1 billion = 1.6 million US$

INTRODUCTION

The extraordinary intervention in Southern Italy has been mostly analyzed by the literature with a focus on the reasons, origins, evolution and outcomes of such a policy. The usual perspective considers this one among the hypotheses that have been proposed over time to solve the main contradiction of the Italian national development, i.e., the "Southern Question", meaning the historical gap in both economic and social conditions between the Northern and Southern areas of the country. The Italian economic dualism and its long-term evolution during more than a century and a half of national unity has indeed stimulated a prolific literature on these matters, which tends to consider the Cassa per il Mezzogiorno as the most important tool deployed to solve the internal contradiction of an advanced country with a large backward area. Reconstructing these events, that affected Italian economic policies for almost all the second half of the 1900s, does still require a demanding, long-lasting research effort, in consideration of the availability of vast, in scope and size, and still-untapped primary sources at the national level, which are currently located in the Central State Archive (ACS, *Archivi dello Sviluppo Economico Territoriale*, <https://aset.acs.beniculturali.it/aset-web/>), but also in many other places which are not always easily accessible for researchers. Moreover, their uncovering opens new opportunities for more precise statistical analysis, adding to the other sources, making up a significant ensemble of materials needing to be studied and understood.

However, the primary sources that have recently been made available within the ample and significant internal documentation produced by the World Bank – whose public disclosure and consultation was authorized only a few years ago – are an invaluable trove of information. These documents concern the evaluations that the Bank's Presidents and its main departments carried out on the Cassa per il Mezzogiorno and on the economic development of Southern Italy, as well as other various aspects related to the loans requested to the World Bank and the public investments carried out in Italy. Such valuable sources are useful not only to achieve a better understanding of the significance of the extraordinary intervention and its trends during at least 15 years, but also to provide an original viewpoint on the matter. Studying the extraordinary intervention through the lens of the World Bank can indeed widen the scope of the analysis and show the Italian development policies within an international context. To summarize, the reports and the other papers issued by the International Bank for Reconstruction and Development (IBRD) open up a new frontier for the research on the Cassa and the economic growth of Southern Italy during the propelling phase of the Italian "golden age". These documents prove the "double paternity" of the extraordinary intervention: it emerges from studying them that such a policy was not only the product of a farsighted and serious national reflection, but also depended on the involvement of several institutions and economic entities abroad. Therefore, by means of such a rich array of primary sources containing data, evaluations and proposals, it is now possible to reconstruct an overall profile of a crucial period, i.e., the one going from the end of the postwar reconstruction to the key moments of the Italian "economic miracle". Furthermore, through the study of the IBRD documents, it becomes possible to substantiate a methodological approach which goes beyond the idea that the Southern Question concerned only the relationship between Northern and Southern Italy. Instead, this analysis suggests the development of a much wider perspective, within which to frame and explain the backwardness of Southern Italy, including its evolution and the opportunities to find a solution for it in an international setting. In so doing, after an oblivion having lasted for more than two decades, a significant contribution is given to a new meridionalist perspective, one which would not simply retrace past interpretations, but rather, identify in the scenario of international integration new tools to interpret the backwardness of Southern Italy and propose possible answers to the need for an economic recovery and a productivity acceleration for both the Mezzogiorno and the country as a whole.

On the other hand, when assessing the Cassa's experience, one cannot overlook the evaluations of a certain historiography which shares with the common sense and the prevailing political sentiment a negative outlook on the extraordinary intervention. Such views have tended to underestimate, criticize or disrepute the general fabric of the extraordinary intervention as a whole or for a large part. The overall negative judgment passed down on this experience depended on several reasons, ranging from the lack of consideration for the extraordinary intervention as a general strategy, to the preference for the promotion of local development policies. However, the choice of denying nationwide strategies led to the fragmentation of the Italian national interest, as well as to a waste of public resources by the local institutions, and to the eschewing of a unitary vision for the two macro-areas of Italy. Nevertheless, considering also the documents and the information made available by the World Bank, it is possible to expose the ideological bias characterizing some of the more destructive interpretations on the matter, and to reconsider this prevailing but erroneous approach. As a matter of fact, if one looks at history without prejudice, it may be observed how the Cassa per il Mezzogiorno was, up until the early 1970s, an undoubtedly successful initiative which proved itself greatly useful to the Italian economic progress. It was only with the end of the "golden age" and the onset of more invasive policies, especially after the establishment of the Italian Regions, that the extraordinary intervention definitively lost its character of crucial tool for the productive modernization of Southern Italy, and instead turned it more and more into a "routine" practice, mostly plagued by excessive forms of assistance.

After all, the controversy surrounding the so-called policy choice between "*macchine o maccheroni*" ("machinery or macaroni") – itself a staple of the phase preceding the establishment of the Cassa – was to appear again and again, until more recent times. With the expression mentioned above, Minister Roberto Tremelloni defined the two alternative views that shaped the discussion on the Italian economic policy since the end of WWII. In 1950, in an article titled "*Tempi Lunghi*" ("Long Terms"), Luigi Einaudi argued that hastily encouraging the industrialization of the South, rather than focusing the intervention on building physical and civic infrastructure as a priority to strengthen its economic fabric, would have been a grave mistake. On this idea, Guido Carli aptly remarked, with an extraordinary, way ahead, but controversial statement, that: «Developing the ideas of Giustino Fortunato, Einaudi argued that the development process could not be promoted in the absence of a higher level of education and civics, and therefore of a more direct participation in managing local administrations. The Italian State had to build the State where it was chronically absent» (G. Carli, *Cinquant'anni di vita italiana*, in cooperation with P. Peluffo, Rome-Bari, Laterza, 1996, p. 126). Against such an inflexible stance, the government led by Prime Minister Alcide De Gasperi chose to establish the Cassa. Probably, this decision was also suggested by the favorable opinions of international partners, who leaned in favor of expansive economic policies in Southern Italy. However, the most bitter confrontation of ideas happened between those who, like Donato Menichella, would have rather used the aid provided by the Marshall Plan to strengthen currency reserves, covering the deficit in the balance of payments through the supply of foodstuffs and consumer goods, and those who, as it was the case with Giovanni Malagodi, deemed that investments in industrial initiatives, by buying capital goods, were the best way to restart a virtuous development process of the Italian economy in its entirety.

As it was pointed out when explaining a parliamentary motion concerning the use of European Recovery Program funds: «It came a time when the Council of Ministers [...] faced such a problem: whether the choice was to import machinery or macaroni. That was to say, to choose if raw materials were to be imported, which would immediately provide for the creation of a dedicated lire fund, and therefore the means to invest in the Mezzogiorno, or if, on the other hand, the choice was to import machinery. And Hon. Tremelloni chose the latter, precisely at that moment. But why did he choose the machinery import program? Because we were no longer able to import goods and raw materials. And why was that so? Because we had hoarded the famous dollar fund that Minister Lombardo strives to spend nowadays, and to do so rapidly. The issue had these exact features and it was an overall problem, which affected the structure and the core of Italian economy deeply» (Atti Parlamentari, Camera dei Deputati, *Discussioni*, Afternoon assembly of May 17, 1950, Intervention by M. Zagari, p. 18310). A similar general value characterized the decision to intervene in favor of the most backward area of Italy, not only through internal funds and wit the realization of gradual steps within the design of the extraordinary intervention, but also through the recurse to "impact loans", that is to say a particular form of loans provided by the International Bank for Reconstruction and Development, which would impact on the economy as a whole and not on specific projects. However, the radical contrast of approaches over which economic strategy should be implemented – which culminated in the aforementioned diatribe between "machinery or macaroni" – lost some steam and eventually disappeared. An original solution was finally found which, as it will be shown in this volume, rested on the pragmatic amalgamation of objectives that was realized in the experience of the Cassa per il Mezzogiorno, and was grounded on the complementarity between the two strategic directions and endowments of financial resources for the South, which referred respectively to the Italian State and to the World Bank. As it was noted: «The controversy over "machinery or macaroni" was in the end resolved in a peculiar way, which characterized Italy's emergence from the political and economic throes of postwar reconstruction. The role of the World Bank was crucial in this contest, as it presented an acceptable compromise (considering not only the program, but also the institutions) both for the "Keynesians" overseas and the Italian "conservatives" at home» (L. Paganetto, P.L. Scandizzo, *La Banca mondiale e l'Italia: dalla ricostruzione allo sviluppo*, Bologna, il Mulino, 2000, p. 95).

Moreover, the long-term commitment towards the economic and social development in the Mezzogiorno created the need for an articulate and innovative model. The result was born out of the opportunities offered by fostering growth in a rapidly changing context, rather than arising from the theories and cultures which faced off during the postwar reconstruction era. In particular, the model was founded on the joint initiatives carried out by the national institutions and international organizations. Their cooperation was based on three kinds of opportunities, namely the opportunity to act in the interest of Southern Italy and to tackle the territorial gap; the opportunity of sustaining productive modernization and competitiveness for Italy as a whole; the opportunity to abide by the guiding role of the overseas allies and the advantage their economy would have acquired from widespread economic development in Europe. Hence, the relationship between public intervention and market initiative in Italy did not follow the usual rules of the past but pursued instead a novel path. In a contribution that is still very important in order to understand the essential features of the Southern question, Adriano Giannola and Alfredo Del Monte, recalling the viewpoints of the "new meridionalism" of Pasquale Saraceno and Rodolfo Morandi, noted that «the role of the State should not substitute private initiative in Southern Italy, but should rather help and support it, in order to overcome some initial disadvantages», and that «the Italian State had to create and activate those "agglomeration factors" useful in triggering a spontaneous flow of private savings to be invested in productive activities»; anyway: «Direct State intervention in the industrialization of Southern Italy was excluded» (A. Del Monte, A. Giannola, *Il Mezzogiorno nell'economia italiana*, Bologna, il Mulino, 1978, p. 121). This volume may help understand how much of the original core of meridionalist thought was made a reality, and what other kinds of conditions and choices contributed to that, beginning with the implementation of the agreements struck with the International Bank for Reconstruction and Development in building a model for the economic development of Italy.

The main themes connected with the evolution of the "Southern Question" – i.e., of the gap between Northern and Southern Italy from its inception to the current times, of the trends in the expenses for the extraordinary intervention and of the development policies, as well as of the evaluation of the action of the Cassa and the strategic role of this entity in favor of Italian economy – have already been described in detail in previous works. Much care was taken to offer a unitary representation of this historical experience, for it not to lose itself in the plethora of single episodes of the whole design for such a unique policy in the history of Southern Italy. These works have shown the worth of such an original model, which empowered the economic development of Southern Italy during twenty-five years, substantially contributing to bridging the gap with the rest of the country. Hence, the main goal of this new work on the Cassa per il Mezzogiorno and the World Bank is to shed light on a significantly wider scenario and on the strategic connections between one of the international organizations established by the Bretton Woods agreements and the events of the Italian economic dualism. Therefore, because of the wealth of information they contain, the IBRD documents have been considered in their chronological progression and without systematic links with other similar sources, be they national or foreign. The critical evaluation of these sources has allowed to examine and interpret unique materials, that will certainly be of interest to all researchers that have been analyzing – as some have done in similar or comparable directions – the relationship between the Cassa and the international organizations, as well as Italy and its overseas partners, during a new era of economic and social development, started right in the most backward Italian territory, i.e., the Mezzogiorno.

The four chapters of this volume follow a path going from the examination of the role of the World Bank during the first phase of the extraordinary intervention, to the analysis of the evolution of the financing the World Bank made available for the economic and social development of Southern Italy, up to the evaluation of the period of greater flowering of the IBRD initiative, corresponding with more significant dynamism in the economy of Southern Italy, and finally, to the observation of the last funding phase carried out by the World Bank and the outcomes of such a "systemic" intervention in Southern Italy. Furthermore, an extensive appendix to this volume, featuring the primary sources and the documents used for research, has been made available on the SVIMEZ and the Historical Archive of the Italian State websites. To the achievement of such a challenging level of research contributed, besides a few experts, several people from both the SVIMEZ and the field of Economic History, to whom the Author would like to extend his deeper and heartfelt gratitude. It goes without saying that the mistakes and the limits that may be contained in this book are due to the Author, as he is the sole responsible of the ideas, the elaborations and the other contents of this volume.

The Author wishes to thank Adriano Giannola, President of the SVIMEZ, renowned economist and scholar, who offered his precious advice for the research. The late Nino Novacco, former President Emeritus of the SVIMEZ, generously spurred and helped such efforts by the Author, discussing them in depth and offering constant indications and wise suggestions, until the end of his days. Riccardo Padovani was generous both during our interactions, especially on industrial policy issues, and with his organizational support. Luca Bianchi provided very interesting hints for reflection and food for thought. The research and operational structure of the SVIMEZ, to the entirety of which the Author would like to express his gratitude, were very close to him in the persons of: Susanna Greco, who provided precious materials and bibliographical references; Agnese Claroni, who accompanied the verification of some parts of this work with her usual kindness; Sandro Gattei who, together with Alessandra Stanca, contributed to the first editorial setup phase of this volume; Fabrizio Greggi for the predisposition of the appendix in electronic format, including the documents used for research; Delio Miotti, Grazia Servidio, Stefano Prezioso, Franca Moro, Giuseppe Goffredo and the late Gianni Comodi, who gave, by a different degree, but all with the same availability, an important contribution and invaluable elements for discussion, starting with the statistical elaborations on the Northern-Southern Italy divide, which were published on the occasion of the 150 years of Italian unification. The author would also like to express his hearty friendship to all the SVIMEZ Board members, for all the feedback and dialogue on meridionalist themes and the initiatives espousing further study which have been promoted during these years.

An especially grateful thought goes to the late Antonio Di Vittorio, my mentor and former President, then President Emeritus of the Società Italiana degli Storici Economici (SISE), the Italian scientific association of the Economic Historians, for his patient and farsighted guidance on the complex paths of the Economic History, as well as for the invaluable spur and advice in completing this work, by means of his usual closeness and priceless teachings. Claudio De Vincenti shared with the author the passions and themes of the history of the South as the worthy economist he is. Leandra D'Antone allowed to clarify some key points by means of her works on "extraordinary interests" for the Mezzogiorno. Andrea Pomella, Valentina Sgro, and Keti Lelo effectively and kindly cooperated in revising this text. Andrea Ramazzotti gave a generous and intense contribution by re-reading and checking the whole text. Erika Basile accompanied and helped this book since its beginning, with both expertise and fondness. Furthermore, the Author would like to extend his special thanks to Elisa Liberatori Prati, Chief Archivist of the World Bank Group during the writing of this book, for her kind availability, and to Sherrine M. Thompson, archivist at the World Bank, for her indications on the available documents. Last but not least, Antonio Enrico Buonocore translated, with a particular narrative taste, and proof-read the final text in English. To everyone mentioned, as well as to those which might have been forgotten, the Author would like to express his deepest gratitude.

Naples, July 15, 2023
Amedeo Lepore

PREMISE

THE MAIN SOURCES FOR THE STUDY OF THE EXTRAORDINARY INTERVENTION IN SOUTHERN ITALY: THE DOCUMENTS ISSUED BY THE WORLD BANK

The documents concerning the credit lines bestowed upon Italy that the World Bank has made available in the past few years – and with greater availability since 2010 – are a very important legacy when revisiting the years straddling between postwar reconstruction and the Italian "economic miracle", which featured a "double convergence", never achieved before. During that era, for the first and only time in the history of unified Italy, a course of events began which was able to thrust Italy towards the most economically advanced areas in Europe, and the same time allowed Southern Italy to grow faster than the rest of the country, thus reducing the structural gap between Northern and Southern Italy, which had been the cornerstone feature of the "Southern Question" in the previous decades and was to be the case again after the crisis of the 1970s and the end of Fordism. The extraordinary intervention and the Cassa per il Mezzogiorno, its most important and useful tool for about 25 years, became a paradigmatic initiative, helpful not only for the area it was focused on, i.e., the one undergoing reforms from 1950 onward[1], but also as a general model for development.

---

[1] The two most important laws to develop Southern Italy, which came into force upon the end of the reconstruction were the agrarian reform (the so-called "excerpt law") of October 21, 1950, no. 841, following the Italian law of May 12, 1950, no. 230 (the so-called "Sila law"), having the objective to expropriate privately held land in order for it to be divided up amongst farmers, as well as the law of August 10, 1950, no. 646, establishing the Cassa per il Mezzogiorno and foreseeing a general plan, initially featuring a ten-year span, to carry out extraordinary works in order to usher in the economic and social advancement of the regions in Southern Italy.

Southern Italy was doubtlessly favored by that strategy, itself opening the path towards significant financial resources (initially, 1,000 billion lire within a decade[2]) in order to speed up the creation of infrastructure supporting agricultural production and civic growth during the first seven years of the program, and to promote a broader industrialization, starting from 1957 onwards. Therefore, Southern Italy became the protagonist of a steady modernization of its production facilities, succeeding in making the first steps on the path of economic development. However, the choices made at that time, within a framework completely favorable to economically expansive policies, did not grace just a part of Italy. As a matter of fact, it was the whole of the country which experienced a period of deep and fruitful prosperity, based on the reciprocity of the market and production relationships established within its main areas. The ultimate drive towards this significant phenomenon of economic transformation arose from several favorable circumstances and purposeful actions, both at the national and the international level, all of them connected to the redeeming capacity of Southern Italy as well.

According to Pasquale Saraceno, the extraordinary intervention responded to «the need of making industrialization in Southern Italy possible; as this process had started later in that area, compared with the rest of Italy, the three following conditions were required: quicker procedures than those envisioned by ordinary administration, an allocation of funding longer than the annual period of the Italian state budget, accompanied by a series of activities to be carried out in a coordinated way, within different programs and fields. These were all activities that could not be entrusted to the ordinary administration of the State, due to its binding regulatory system [...]. Therefore, [...], the operational entity chosen to resolve those issues, namely the Cassa per il Mezzogiorno, had to be a public law institution; the cornerstone of its autonomy must be found in a somewhat special instance of Italian administrative law, especially when we consider the powers of its

[2] By means of the Italian law of July 25, 1952, no. 949, the overall duration of the extraordinary intervention was extended to 12 years, raising the spending forecast to 1,280 billion. Through the Italian law of July 29, 1957, no. 634, advancing industrial initiatives first and foremost, the duration of the plan was extended to 15 years and the available budget grew up to 2,040 billion lire. In 1964, the budget availability of the Cassa per il Mezzogiorno reached the significant amount of 2,227.6 billion lire.

Board of Directors and the controls by the Italian Superior Council of Public Works and the Italian Court of Auditors»[3].

By the end of the first 15 years of activity by the Cassa per il Mezzogiorno the picture was rich, especially concerning investments in Southern Italy (see Table 1a and Table 1b). Indeed, considering the actions up to December 31, 1965, infrastructure built directly by the Cassa amounted to 1,560.7 billion lire (33.4% of overall investments), while private initiatives supported with the incentives of the Cassa amounted to 2,973.6 billion (63.6% of overall investments) and the other investments (programs supporting the city of Naples, its surroundings and province, school buildings, vocational training and contributions towards social activities) amounted to 142.3 billion (i.e., 3% of overall investments). All in all, the interventions reached the significant amount of 4,676.6 billion lire[4].

Considering the international milieu, the analysis and the elaborations first, and then the financing provided by the World Bank – which at the time was called the International Bank for Reconstruction and Development (IBRD) – were the main external impulse towards beginning the extraordinary intervention, implementing those special resources which came straight from Washington. The idea of "impact loans"[5] – i.e., a form of loans granted by the International Bank for Reconstruction and Development, acting on the economy as a whole, and not on single projects – was established on the basis of the "Big Push" theory, a brainchild of Paul

---

[3] P. Saraceno, *Gli interventi del primo IRI: dallo smobilizzo delle grandi Banche alla proposta di legge bancaria, 1933-1936*, in "Banca, borsa e titoli di credito", year XLIV, New Series, XXXIV, folio III, 1981, p. 302.

[4] See Camera dei Deputati, *Relazione sulla attività di coordinamento (ai sensi delle leggi 18 marzo 1959, no. 101 e 26 giugno 1965, no. 717) depositata dal Ministro per gli Interventi Straordinari nel Mezzogiorno*, Rome, Istituto Poligrafico dello Stato, 1966, p. 9.

[5] The model of the "impact loans", the one explicitly chosen for the first financing lines to develop Southern Italy, did not intend to support specific actions, but rather supported overall interventions able to reverberate on the whole economy of Italy, by providing foreign currency loans useful to bridge those gaps within the balance of payments due to the effects of investments.

Table 1a. *Investments carried out by the Cassa up to December 31, 1965 (in billions of lire)*

	Infrastrutture								
		Servizi civili						Totale	
Esercizi finanziari	Bonifiche, sistemazioni montane e riforma fondiaria (a)	Viabilità ordinaria	Acquedotti e fognature (b)	Opere ferroviarie e marittime	Diverse	Totale	Opere d'interesse turistico	Valori assoluti	Incidenza sull'esercizio %
1950–51	3,0	0,1	0,8	–	–	0,9	–	3,9	*97,5*
1951–52	22,3	14,9	3,2	–	–	18,1	0,5	40,9	*80,0*
1952–53	59,0	24,3	9,1	–	–	33,4	1,7	94,1	*78,2*
1953–54	85,9	20,6	13,9	2,6	–	37,1	2,2	125,2	*78,8*
1954–55	100,4	12,2	13,9	11,9	–	38,0	2,5	140,9	*75,1*
1955–56	80,8	7,7	13,3	14,9	–	35,9	2,6	119,3	*58,2*
1956–57	67,3	7,1	14,6	12,2	–	33,9	3,5	104,7	*50,9*
1957–58	56,6	4,8	15,1	2,6	–	22,5	2,4	81,5	*42,5*
1958–59	66,8	9,8	21,5	15,5	–	46,8	1,2	114,8	*43,1*
1959–60	50,9	11,4	18,6	12,3	–	42,3	2,3	95,5	*32,3*
1960–61	53,6	13,6	21,1	9,6	–	44,3	5,2	103,1	*28,7*
1961–62	56,9	16,2	30,5	12,7	–	59,4	4,3	120,6	*26,4*
1962–63	69,8	7,7	43,5	5,5	7,2	63,9	5,2	138,9	*23,4*
1963–64	70,8	10,2	38,8	2,4	2,2	53,6	4,3	128,7	*20,1*
1964–65	50,1	15,1	29,5	1,8	4,5	50,9	5,8	106,8	*17,2*
1° luglio – 31 dicembre 1965	17,5	7,8	13,1	1,0	1,6	23,5	0,8	41,8	*13,0*
Totale ...	911,7	183,5	300,5	105,0	15,5	604,5	44,5	1.560,7	*33,4*

Source: Cassa per il Mezzogiorno, in Camera dei Deputati, *Relazione sulla attività di coordinamento (ai sensi delle leggi 18 marzo 1959, n. 101 e 26 giugno 1965, n. 717) depositata dal Ministro per gli Interventi Straordinari nel Mezzogiorno*, Rome, Istituto Poligrafico dello Stato, 1966, p. 8.

Table 1b. *Investments promoted by the Cassa and totals up to December 31, 1965 (in billions of lire)*

Investimenti privati sostenuti da incentivi					Altri investimenti				Totale generale		
			Totale				Totale				
Miglioramenti fondiari (c)	Iniziative industriali (d)	Pesca e artigianato	Valori assoluti	Incidenza sull'esercizio %	Edilizia scolastica, istruzione professionale e contributi per attività sociali	Provvedimenti a favore della città e della provincia di Napoli	Valori assoluti	Incidenza sull'esercizio %	Valori assoluti	Incidenza sull'esercizio %	Incidenza sul totale %
0,1	—	—	0,1	*2,5*	—	—	—	—	4,0	*100,0*	*0,1*
9,4	0,8	—	10,2	*20,0*	—	—	—	—	51,1	*100,0*	*1,1*
18,4	7,8	—	26,2	*21,8*	—	—	—	—	120,3	*100,0*	*2,6*
20,3	13,3	—	33,6	*21,2*	—	—	—	—	158,8	*100,0*	*3,4*
24,6	21,1	—	45,7	*24,3*	—	1,1	1,1	*0,6*	187,7	*100,0*	*4,0*
32,6	51,8	—	84,4	*41,1*	0,2	1,3	1,5	*0,7*	205,2	*100,0*	*4,4*
30,6	68,5	—	99,1	*48,2*	0,8	1,1	1,9	*0,9*	205,7	*100,0*	*4,4*
38,3	63,1	—	101,4	*52,8*	2,1	6,9	9,0	*4,7*	191,9	*100,0*	*4,1*
43,6	95,6	0,9	140,1	*52,6*	6,9	4,6	11,5	*4,3*	266,4	*100,0*	*5,7*
47,5	133,3	6,7	187,5	*63,3*	7,7	5,2	12,9	*4,4*	295,9	*100,0*	*6,3*
49,1	182,1	10,5	241,7	*67,3*	12,4	2,1	14,5	*4,0*	359,3	*100,0*	*7,7*
47,4	251,5	16,7	315,6	*69,2*	13,4	6,6	20,0	*4,4*	456,2	*100,0*	*9,7*
40,3	378,7	15,8	434,8	*73,3*	16,5	3,1	19,6	*3,3*	593,3	*100,0*	*12,7*
20,1	456,5	21,4	498,0	*77,9*	11,8	1,2	13,0	*2,0*	639,7	*100,0*	*13,7*
30,0	441,6	20,0	491,6	*79,3*	20,0	1,4	21,4	*3,5*	619,8	*100,0*	*13,2*
12,0	230,0	21,6	263,6	*82,0*	15,5	0,4	15,9	*5,0*	321,3	*100,0*	*6,9*
464,3	2.395,7	113,6	2.973,6	*63,6*	107,3	35,0	142,3	*3,0*	4.676,6	*100,0*	*100,0*

Source: Cassa per il Mezzogiorno, in Camera dei Deputati, *Relazione sulla attività di coordinamento (ai sensi delle leggi 18 marzo 1959, n. 101 e 26 giugno 1965, n. 717) depositata dal Ministro per gli Interventi Straordinari nel Mezzogiorno*, Rome, Istituto Poligrafico dello Stato, 1966, p. 9.

Rosenstein-Rodan[6], who suggested the adoption of non-fragmented interventions, themselves able, through their unitary impact, to provide, within a reasonable timeframe, the big push onwards needed in order to kickstart the policies for the development of Southern Italy. The loans granted by the World Bank, themselves subdivided into eight different tranches from 1951 to 1965, amounted to about 400 million dollars and played no secondary role in starting the productive take-off of Southern Italy, concerning both their size and quality. The development model adopted in Italy with the crucial intervention of the World Bank was based on the roles played both by the State and the relevant international institutions, which did not pursue the mere growth of aggregate demand, but rather strove to promote productive investment towards modernizing the economic and social system of Southern Italy by using a logic of "supply-side Keynesianism"[7].

A source which proved to be critical towards fully understanding the worth of the extraordinary intervention carried out in Southern Italy and the role of the World Bank in supporting the most backward area of Italy, as well as in further studying the overseas analyses concerning Italy, is the sizable hoard of documents the World Bank issued through its departments and restricted to internal use alone. These documents have been opened to public research. This documentation is subdivided into two specific series featuring, on one side, the reports involving the analysis and evaluation on several issues concerning the development program on behalf of Southern Italy, the Italian projects on industry, irrigation and power, the Cassa per il

---

[6] See P.N. Rosenstein-Rodan, *Problems of Industrialisation of Eastern and South-Eastern Europe*, in "The Economic Journal", vol. 53, no. 210-211, 1943, <http://la.utexas.edu/users/hcleaver/368/368rroneseetable.pdf>; Id., *The international development of economically backward areas*, in "International Affairs", vol. 20, no. 2, 1944; Id., *Notes on the theory of the big push*, in H. Ellis, H.C. Wallich (eds.), *Economic development for Latin America*, New York (NY), St. Martin's Press, 1961; Id. (ed.), *Capital formation and economic development*, London, Allen & Unwin, 1964; The World Bank/IFC Archives, *Oral History Program*, *Transcript of the Interview with Paul Rosenstein-Rodan*, by R. Oliver, New York (NY), Columbia University, Oral History Research Office, August 14, 1961, <https://oralhistory.worldbank.org/transcripts/transcript-oral-history-interview-paul-rosenstein-rodan-held-august-14-1961>, <http://oralhistoryportal.cul.columbia.edu/document.php?id=ldpd_4072948>.

[7] Pasquale Saraceno, in particular, thought to the need of achieving capital accumulation as an engine of development for Southern Italy, therefore enabling the productivist vocation of the area (see P. Saraceno, *Politica Keynesiana e Mezzogiorno*, in "Informazioni SVIMEZ", no. 11, 1976, pp. 540-541; also published in "Rinascita", no. 21, 1976, p. 23).

Mezzogiorno, as well as the activities supporting the growth of the regions of Southern Italy. On the other side, the reports issued by the President of the International Bank for Reconstruction and Development, themselves bent towards informing the Bank's executive directors on the requests by the Cassa, the financial resources proposed towards the development of Southern Italy, as well as on the results achieved by the relevant loans and the Italian economic conditions as a whole. The latter element, assessing the condition of the Italian national economy, was considered crucial towards the granting of loans, as one of the earliest contributions noted by showing the existence of an "extraordinary" kind of interest towards Southern Italy in conjunction with the initiatives carried out by the World Bank[8].

The papers produced by the International Bank for Reconstruction and Development are a source of primary importance for a detailed reconstruction of the assessment performed on both Southern Italy and on the country as a whole by the representatives of the Bank (established in Bretton Woods in 1944), parting the veil of diplomatic relationships and official negotiation. The official documents issued by this institution were addressed to a much wider and more diverse audience. The internal papers, instead, helped setting up, without possibility of mistakes, the decisions on the loans to be granted in order to develop a markedly backwards area. Through the documents issued by the World Bank, it is also possible to notice, from an "objective" and geographically distant point of view, the overall worth of the extraordinary intervention, albeit by verifying the effective outcome of each and every credit line. Therefore, the documents by the IBRD, originally intended for internal use within the Bank's management, have become the main tiles useful in completing the mosaic reflecting an overall brand new image of the initiatives carried out by the Cassa per il Mezzogiorno, of its establishment and activities, themselves all peculiar features within the framework of the Italian productive development and economic modernization.

Gabriele Pescatore, who was the President of the Cassa per il Mezzogiorno from 1955 until 1976, effectively summarized the motivations underlying the interventions carried out by the World Bank, following the viewpoint held by Donato Menichella: «The Governor envisioned – and the times allowed that back then – that the unbound stance of the Cassa, together with its seriousness, reliability and efficiency, […] made it the most suitable tool for attracting the most significant intervention (300 million dollars) the World Bank had ever made in Europe; such a relevant commitment was

---

[8] See L. D'Antone, *L'«interesse straordinario» per il Mezzogiorno (1943-1960)*, in "Meridiana", no. 24, 1995; now published in Id. (ed.), *Radici storiche ed esperienza dell'intervento straordinario nel Mezzogiorno*, Naples, Bibliopolis, 1996.

obtained by Menichella from the President of the World Bank himself in Paris in 1952. […] The World Bank, following a suggestion by the Governor, shifted the focus from granting loans to individual projects – which referred to single plants – to rather broad sectors targeting a whole territory. […] This made the intervention model of the Cassa an exemplary case for the implementation of development policies in economically depressed areas all over the word. Hence the worldwide interest for the action of the Cassa […] which Menichella then leveraged to propel this institution into the sector of private financing»[9].

From a previously unpublished report, set up by Paul Rosenstein-Rodan for the Economics Department of the International Bank for Reconstruction and Development on July 7, 1950[10], several interesting elements emerge, and they confirm the unique extent of a significant set of documents. The "Preliminary report on the development program of Southern Italy" began with a summary pointing out that Italy deserved credit for loans amounting up to 20-25 million dollars per year[11]. This part of the document featured also an important note, especially at that time: it stated that the main danger to government stability was not the political tensions or the risk of Communism, but rather the absence of a sound program of economic development[12]. Furthermore, the document noted that the program to

[9] G. Pescatore, *Menichella, l'intervento per il Mezzogiorno e la Banca Mondiale*, in D. Menichella, *Testimonianze e studi raccolti dalla Banca d'Italia*, Rome-Bari, Laterza, 1986, p. 139.

[10] See P.N. Rosenstein-Rodan, *Preliminary report on the development program of Southern Italy*, Economic Department Report, no. E98, Washington (DC), The World Bank, 1950, <https://documents.worldbank.org/en/publication/documents-reports/documentdetail/792731468262476081/preliminary-report-on-the-development-program-of-Southern-italy>.

[11] The document started like this: «The examination of Italy's creditworthiness leads to the conclusion that, under reasonably optimistic assumptions, Italy would appear to be creditworthy for an additional dollar debt burden represented by a series of annual loans of $ 20 to 25 million per annum. The loans envisaged for the development of the South are well within this limit. In fact, they only absorb about one-half of the "reasonably optimistic" credit ceiling. Even under less optimistic assumptions, loans envisaged at an annual rate of $ 10 million could just be serviced by Italy» (P.N. Rosenstein-Rodan, *Preliminary report on the development program of Southern Italy*, cit., p. 1).

[12] The text contained the following passage: «The maintenance of a stable Government seems probable in spite of high political tension both on the Left and on the Right. Centrifugal tendencies within the anti-Communist majority are rather a symptom of a smaller immediate danger of Communism than of any weakening of the anti-Communist front. While there might be reshuffles in the Cabinet, for instance, a movement within the present majority parties to the Right in the short-

develop Southern Italy was a well-built and coherent one, being a priority within the Italian investment policy[13]. The interventions foreseen for Southern Italy, according to the note by Rosenstein-Rodan, was the biggest project for regional development in the world and was to be financed by 90% with local capital and only by 10% through foreign loans: Italy was deemed fit to support such investments, which were to finance agricultural land reclamation and irrigation, aqueducts, roads, public works, enhancing tourism and agricultural processing facilities, without jeopardizing the country's monetary stability[14].

The institution chosen to channel such interventions (the Cassa per il Mezzogiorno) – itself the object of a draft bill, still not approved by the Parliament at the time – was considered feasible and, furthermore, suitable to make these development policies a reality. There was also the wish for it to remain «relatively a-political»[15], i.e., a tool bereft of those heavy conditionings, typical of those policies being focused merely on managing financial resources, such as those responsible for turning the positive features of the extraordinary intervention upside down during the 1970s. The enactment of the former strategy would have achieved important results, involving also some tangible effects on the Italian trade balance and on the availability of foreign currency: «The realization of the investment program will provide for productive employment of an additional 250,000 to 300,000 unemployed workers. These workers consume at present 300 to 400 lire per day and will earn, when employed, 1,000 to 1,100 lire per day; they will thus consume 600 to 700 lire more a day than hitherto. Since Italy lacks vital foodstuffs (wheat and fats and raw materials) a proportion of the newly employed workers' additional expenditure will lead to a demand for additional imports. An analysis of the Southern Italian family workers' budgets and of the raw materials required by Italian manufacturers for the investment program leads to the conclusion that the equivalent of $ 100

---

run and to the Left in a somewhat longer-run, the main danger to political stability would be the absence of a large economic development program» (P.N. Rosenstein-Rodan, *Preliminary report on the development program of Southern Italy*, cit., p. 1).

[13] See *Ibidem*.

[14] The document featured the following indications: «For the first two years, about 43 billion lire per annum and about 25 billion lire in the third year of the program will be financed from the lire counterpart fund so that only 57 billion lire in the first two years and 75 billion lire in the third year will form additional investments. From the fourth year onwards, the whole of the 100 billion lire will represent additional investment» (P.N. Rosenstein-Rodan, *Preliminary report on the development program of Southern Italy*, cit., p. 2).

[15] *Ibidem*.

million investments per annum will cause additional dollar imports of around $ 10 to 12 million per annum, while the expected increase in dollar exports is small. The foreign exchange needs other than dollars amount to the equivalent of about $ 40 million per annum, i.e: four times the amount of the dollar requirements»[16].

The aim of the loan granted by the World Bank was twofold: on one hand, it had to cover the additional imports in dollars following the enactment of the plan for Southern Italy, without denting the Italian currency reserves; on the other hand, it had to provide an equivalent amount of additional currency to finance the program[17]. Furthermore, the currency equivalent in lire of the credit line bestowed by the IBRD upon the Cassa per il Mezzogiorno was to be invested in specific supplementary projects[18], further enriching the overall investment program[19]. At the end of the summary,

---

[16] *Ivi*, pp. 2-3. The document featured an additional assessment of the possible impact of the investment program in Southern Italy: «Increased income from investments will begin to flow in four to six years time, since it takes so long for most land reclamation and irrigation schemes (which form two-thirds of the whole program) to bear fruit. The increase in production of grains, milk and meat, fruit and vegetables will not only save some imports but will also increase exports to the non-dollar areas. Foreign exchange receipts from the increased exports are expected to cover the bulk of the indirect foreign exchange requirements at the end of the program. "Local currency loans" thus only advance subsistence funds over a transition period after which the higher level of production can be maintained without the continuation of additional lending. For the same reason, the Italian Government can advance the non-dollar foreign exchange requirements out of its own present reserves without danger to its long-run balance of payments position. [...] When after the first two years, the additional investment caused by the plan will rise from $ 100 to $ 120 million in the third year and then to $ 160 million per annum from the fourth year onwards, it is probable that some dollar imports may be substituted by non-dollar imports and may thus represent a smaller proportion of the indirect foreign exchange requirements of the plan. Italy may also then be able to finance out of its own reserves one part of the indirect dollar requirements of the plan besides providing for all non-dollar foreign exchange requirements. If neither of the two possibilities obtained, the case for raising somewhat the dollar financing by the Bank might be considered for future tranches of the loans after 1953 or 1954» (P.N. Rosenstein-Rodan, *Preliminary report on the development program of Southern Italy*, cit., pp. 3-4).

[17] See *Ivi*, pp. 4-5.

[18] See *Ivi*, p. 5.

[19] The report highlighted such a procedure, stating that: «It would thus, incidentally, raise the total amount of additional investment in Italy from $ 100 million to the equivalent of at least $ 110 million per annum. In practice, however, it would raise the investment to the equivalent of at least $ 120 million, since the lire counterpart

a positive assessment for the development plan for Southern Italy was expressed, as such a plan could have been «a turning point in Italian economic history», and a conclusive evaluation on the interventions carried out by the International Bank for Reconstruction and Development was given: «Italy has unused manpower and a good machine industry but it lacks foodstuffs and raw materials. Development of unused resources would be impossible without additional imports of foodstuffs and raw materials. Loans to provide these indirect foreign exchange requirements are therefore the most efficacious way to contribute to the solution of Italy's fundamental economic and social problem. Such loans will not create a permanent need for credits to finance a higher standard of living but will only be required during a transition period of seven to eight years, after which the productive results of the development program could suffice to maintain a higher standard of living without further credits»[20].

The second part of this document, more analytical in nature, was called "Notes on Development Program of Southern Italy" and was focused on some particularly relevant themes, such as the economy of Southern Italy, the priority of that region in the whole of the Italian economy, the overall goals of the plan, the agrarian problems, the investment program and the financing of the plan through the Cassa per il Mezzogiorno[21]. Economically speaking, Southern Italy was considered as an underdeveloped area within a developed country, with its own unique features: «It has all the characteristic features of an underdeveloped country: an agrarian surplus population, open and disguised unemployment, a low income per head ($ 150 per annum as against the Italian average of $ 212 and the Northern Italian average of $ 240) and a rate of progress lower than the rest of the country. But it has also assets which other underdeveloped countries lack: availability of administrative managerial and technical know-how, a potential supply of additional skilled and semi-skilled workers from the North and a local capital supply which, though not sufficient, may be larger

---

of the Bank's dollars will be used as a loan to companies which will provide at least 50% of their own capital not much of which might have been otherwise invested for investment in specific projects. The Bank's loan of $ 10 million per annum would be an essential element in a flow of additional investment in Italy of $ 110 to $ 120 million per annum. The collaboration and consultation in the whole field of the development program will give the Bank an influence and a vital part in an investment more than ten times as large as the amount of its loans» (P.N. Rosenstein-Rodan, *Preliminary report on the development program of Southern Italy*, cit., p. 5).

[20] *Ivi*, pp. 5-6.

[21] See *Ivi*, p. 7.

than the supply in most other underdeveloped countries»[22]. From these notes emerged the fact that Southern Italy was not condemned to be less advanced than its Northern counterpart. However, the Italian Unification, despite its undoubted importance and positive effects for the South as well, had not brought about the necessary economic integration between the two halves of the country and the following industrialization had favored only the Northern areas, gradually widening the gap in economic development and *per capita* income, and structurally increasing both unemployment and emigration[23].

Considering the priorities of the Italian politics at the time, the "Southern problem" was not only a regional issue, something that had already been acknowledged since a long time, but rather required a nationwide commitment, to be deployed on four economic and one social theme[24]. Given the ample supply of unused land and labor, it would have been both safer and more economical to employ the rural workers on the lands present in the areas where they lived in; the development program for Southern Italy was not to be limited to spur employment locally, but was also to advantage industry in the North; while Southern Italy experienced preliminary activity to

---

[22] *Ibidem*. The passage went on further clarifying the following: «The economic resources of the South consist mainly in good, cheap and adaptable manpower, in land which although on the whole poor, is capable of considerable improvement and development, and, last not least, of some social overhead capital in railroads, roads, and public utilities, which is considerably better than that obtaining in other underdeveloped countries. There should be, therefore, better prospects of success for a development program in the South of Italy than almost anywhere else in the world» (P.N. Rosenstein-Rodan, *Preliminary report on the development program of Southern Italy*, cit., p. 7).

[23] See *Ivi*, pp. 7-8. More precisely (p. 8), the document stated that: «Out of the total increase of population in the South, between 1861 and 1936 of 9.4 million persons, only 0.2 million found productive employment in the South; 4.1 million swelled the ranks of the unproductive or unemployed people; 1.3 million was the increase in the number of children, while fully 3.8 million people emigrated either to the North or abroad. Only about 5% of the increase in population found productive living in the South, while 95% had either to emigrate or to remain unemployed. It may be noted that more than half of the increase in population remained unemployed while less than half succeeded in migrating. The situation threatens to become even worse at present because the possibility of absorbing emigrants from the South is very much diminished in the North of Italy. The emigration abroad, while vitally important, cannot possibly provide a sufficient outlet for the increase in population in the South».

[24] See P.N. Rosenstein-Rodan, *Preliminary report on the development program of Southern Italy*, cit., pp. 8-10.

manage investment and their related projects, Northern Italy did not[25]: the lower wages were not enough of an incentive towards investing in Southern Italy; the economic framework was to be modified in order to ensure an inflow of long-term capital and avoid the loss of a production base for all of Italy. Furthermore, without a specific program for Southern Italy, there was the risk of a "social explosion", liable to unsettle the stability of the whole Italian economy[26]. According to a more general point of view: «The task of the development program in the South is primarily to employ productively unused resources and to create a changed economic structure which once achieved would attract spontaneously a flow of private capital sufficient to secure a higher standard of living in the South and a more balanced economy for the whole of Italy. The achievement of such a program requires a certain minimum quantum of investments in the area for a number of years. A minimum size and continuity of investments of several years are accordingly the basic features of the program envisaged at present. Such investments will lead to a fuller utilization of the existing unused capacity [...], will induce a modernization of the existing industry and will lead to the creation of additional industries operating on an optimum scale. It is thus not only the direct profits accruing from the investment but also substantial indirect profits and the new investment opportunities created which must be taken into account»[27].

[25] On this, the text of the notes is worth reporting, as it appears notably up-to-date: «While there are single projects in the North of Italy which might be directly more profitable, not a sufficient amount of them exists to provide a minimum size of investment which would acquire the proper momentum of creating a new economic structure in Italy through a further industrialization of the North. It is quite true that it is not only the lack of capital which is an obstacle to economic development but also the lack of the "organization of investment", ie: the successful preparation of all the projects required. The activities of the Svimez (Society for the Development of the South) over the past three years provided a stock of studies and projects without which the development plan for the South could not possibly start. These studies exist for the South but not for the North and that in itself is an additional reason why a large industrialization program in the North could not start at present» (P.N. Rosenstein-Rodan, *Preliminary report on the development program of Southern Italy*, cit., pp. 9-10).

[26] See *Ivi*, pp. 8-10.

[27] *Ivi*, pp. 10-11. The passage focusing on the priorities of Italian economic policies went on, ending as follows: «The new investment opportunities will only emerge after the first phase of the program has been successfully achieved in four to six years time. In a way, therefore, the whole of investment over the first phase may be considered as foregoing somewhat higher profits in the short-run for the sake of securing more profits in the longer-run. It is thus quite true that there are presumably

Considering its objectives, the development program for Southern Italy was a typical pre-industrialization initiative, focused on creating an additional market and a context within which a true industrialization could then be achieved: according to Rosenstein-Rodan, this plan – based on enhancing agriculture (to which the two thirds of the overall investment were allocated), infrastructure, services and the processing of agricultural products – was sound, coherent and fit to receive banking credit lines[28].

When considering the issues of the Italian agriculture, after a description of the structures and state of the art within the different areas of Italy[29], the document tackled the agrarian reform in particular, stating that such reform could not achieve, on its own and considering its strictly redistributive features, the longed-for solution towards a modern development of this economic sector, also due to the scarcity of land available. The "notes" deemed necessary further studies on new crop rotations, training for farmers and preliminary investment in agriculture: while the activities of land recovery and irrigation were able to favor a growth in both agricultural

many single projects which might yield profits of well over 25% from capital invested, while the plan, as a whole, can be expected to produce a direct return in terms of increased national income of only about 10 to 12% per annum. But besides these direct returns of 10 to 12%, the development plan would produce many additional investment opportunities which in the long-run would raise the national income above the level which other single projects could secure even though these other projects yield in the short-run higher direct profits».

[28] See P.N. Rosenstein-Rodan, *Preliminary report on the development program of Southern Italy*, cit., pp. 11-12.

[29] The situation of agriculture in Southern Italy was effectively summarized as follows: «The worst agrarian problem exists in the South. Only one-tenth of the area is intensively cultivated, along the coast largely in small holdings. This one-tenth of the acreage supports half the peasant population and is more than seven times as productive as the rest of the land. The irrigated area is only 12% of the irrigated area of Italy. It amounts to only 5.5% of the acreage in the South (compared with 26.5% in the North) and can be increased to 8.8%. Almost nine-tenths are extensively cultivated areas, of which a) 5 million acres in latifundia (large estates), and b) several more million acres in very small holdings owned by several hundreds of thousands of peasants. Peasants frequently own several widely separated patches of land, renting few from large estate owners. The latifundia are therefore frequently atomised into thousands of unrelated pieces of land, without a common plan of production. Both large and small holdings constitute a problem in the South. The integration of small units is as important and even more difficult than a redistribution of the large ones» (P.N. Rosenstein-Rodan, *Preliminary report on the development program of Southern Italy*, cit., p. 14).

employment and production, the so-called "agrarian pacts" could regulate the price of land leases, usually too steep[30].

Concerning the investment plan, the papers detailed the two cornerstones of the initiatives it foresaw: those projects wholly financed by the Cassa per il Mezzogiorno and the connected industrial projects, partly financed by private firm capital and partly by the Cassa itself[31]. The overall investment shouldered by the Cassa (land reclamation and improvement, speeding up the European Recovery Program, supporting the building of aqueducts and streets, supporting tourism and other public works) was to amount to more than 1,150 billion lire; the investments concerning the "connected projects" (such as collection centers for fruit and vegetables; facilities for the processing of olive oil; hydroelectric plants; the nitrogen plant in Bagnoli; a plant producing vegetal fiber panels), were to reach, during the first four years of the plan, an amount of about 52 billion lire[32]. The detailed investment forecast for this can be found in Table 2, below.

---

[30] See *Ivi*, pp. 14-16.

[31] See *Ivi*, p. 16.

[32] See *Ivi*, pp. 16-17. In the footnotes it was specified that: «*Irrigation projects* are very well worked out, refer to seven different districts covering an area of 185,000 hectares. The average increase of production per hectare after six to ten years amounts to 250%. The increase in net income produced per hectare amounts to 122,000 lire. The total investment foreseen is 135 billion lire and is expected to yield after six to ten years about 15%. Additional employment provided amounts to over 50,000 people. *Land Reclamation* [...]. This program will conclude 240 reclamation projects which are expected to raise production by about 30% in the areas concerned. The reclamation works in the plan will increase production on the average by about one-third and will provide work for 175,000 to 200,000 people. [...] The reclamation work will use materials which Italy can supply while direct import requirements are negligible. In consequence, the investments do not imply the use of many scarce factors or any choice between alternative outlays and are capable of increases in income which are technically possible, but would not otherwise be achieved. *Aqueduct projects* are very well worked out. In Southern Italy, 20% of the population is without water. The aqueducts program represents a concentration of effort which will make possible a more rational administration and better maintenance of aqueducts. They will take from three to six years to construct and will provide on the average employment for 28,000 people. The connected projects will raise substantially the value added by processing agricultural products of the South. Among them, the fruit collecting centers will increase considerably the value added in fruit and vegetables which represent 25 to 30% of value of the agricultural output of the South. Olive oil crushing and refining will improve the value added of olive oil which represents 10% of the value of the agricultural output in the South» (P.N. Rosenstein-Rodan, *Preliminary report on the development program of Southern Italy*, cit., p. 17 and pp. 20-21).

Table 2. *Projected Investment in the Ten-Year Development Program for Southern Italy, including Sicily and Sardinia (in billions of lire)*

Projects	Total investment (10 yrs)	Investment in 1st year (1950)	Investment in 2nd year (1951)	Investment in 3rd year (1952)	Investment in 4th year (1953)
Plan proper					
Irrigation 1/					
Public investment	87.1	10.6	23.0	20.2	14.4
Private investment	47.7	0.1	2.2	3.9	5.7
Land reclamation and improvement					
Accelerated program using ERP counterpart funds	160.3	54.1	51.2	29.8	
Supplement to accelerated program					
Public investment	257.1	4/	4/	4/	4/
Private investment	249.3	4/	4/	4/	4/
Aqueducts	106.8	17.1	34.1	34.1	10.7
Roads (mainly secondary) 2/	100	(10) 3/	(10) 3/	(10) 3/	(10) 3/
Tourism (private investment)	50	(5) 3/	(5) 3/	(5) 3/	(5) 3/
Other public works	100	(10) 3/	(10) 3/	(10) 3/	(10) 3/
Total: Plan proper	1,158.3	106.9	135.5	113.0	
Connected projects					
Fruit and vegetable collecting centers 1/	15.9	2.9	2.9	-	-
Olive oil industry 1/	10.0	0.8	0.8	0.8	1.0
Hydro-electric plants 1/	20.9	1.6	4.0	6.8	8.4
Nitrogen plant (Bagnoli) 1/	4.3	1.0	2.5	0.8	-
Fiberboard plant 1/	0.7	0.7	-	-	-
GRAND TOTAL	1,219.1	113.9	145.7	121.4	

Source: P.N. Rosenstein-Rodan, *Preliminary report on the development program of Southern Italy*, Economic Department Report, no. E98, Washington (DC), The World Bank, 1950, p. 18, <https://documents.worldbank.org/en/publication/documents-reports/documentdetail/792731468262476081/preliminary-report-on-the-development-program-of-southern-italy>.

According to the assessment carried out by Paul Rosenstein-Rodan, the development program for Southern Italy was to favor the growth of total investment by about 10% and an increase in the national income of between 2% and 4%. Such a situation was to advantage those industries based both in the North and in the South, achieving external economies both at the regional and extra-regional level. Furthermore, after the first part of this project was carried out, it was possible to foresee a spontaneous influx of private investment in Southern Italy: such "catalytic effects" of this plan were to represent the ultimate result of its success[33].

In the end, concerning the credit lines activated for the program as a whole, this document pointed to the "State owned" company called the C.O.S.P.I.M. (Cassa per Opere Straordinarie di Publico Interesse nell'Italia Meridionale)[34], with the duty of enacting the plan and making it a reality: «As an investment authority for the South, the Cassa will be the main administrative and financing instrument of the plan. [...] The Cassa has to prepare, coordinate and finance a program which is additional to the normal public works in the South of Italy in the fields of land reclamation, irrigation, agricultural improvement, secondary roads, aqueducts – all these also where they are connected with the agrarian reform – as well as establishments for processing of agricultural products and investments connected with tourism»[35]. Having detailed the main content of the law establishing it as proposed by the Italian Government, the notes highlighted the authorization bestowed upon the Cassa, within the very same law, to take out foreign loans, guaranteed by the Italian State, in every section of its activity; therefore, the credit lines of the International Bank for Reconstruction and Development were not to be ratified by the Italian Parliament[36]. The Cassa per il Mezzogiorno, exactly because of its "functional" features, being both autonomous and politically neutral, could have been fit to reach its particular goals[37]. Its opponents belonged to the following three main categories: public bureaucracy, who saw it as a threat to its power, the Italian MPs, who did not want to lose their powers of control, and some representatives of the entrepreneurial world, who hoped they would not have to reimburse their loans guaranteed by the Government and that saw they had to repay the Cassa instead[38]. In every case, the fulfillment of the

---

[33] See *Ivi*, p. 21.

[34] This was the early name of the Cassa per il Mezzogiorno.

[35] P.N. Rosenstein-Rodan, *Preliminary report on the development program of Southern Italy*, cit., p. 22.

[36] See *Ivi*, pp. 25-26.

[37] See *Ivi*, p. 26.

[38] See *Ibidem*.

development program for Southern Italy was to be decided by the technical conditions of the extraordinary intervention and, even if the Cassa was not to reach its intended spending goals, it was to significantly augment its investment capacity and was to fully rise to the challenge[39].

The final part of the document examined highlighted how Italy had then the very same *per capita* income it had at the beginning of the 1900s: «Like Alice in Wonderland, Italy had to run very fast in order to stand still. Gross investment amounted to 15 - 16% of gross national product, which is a very high proportion on that low level of income. The rising unemployment eats into the vital savings of the country. The unemployed receive very low unemployment benefits over a short period only. Family feeling takes in Italy the place of the Welfare State. The unemployed are supported by close and even distant relatives on the land and consume without producing resources a large part of which could otherwise be invested. Open and disguised unemployment in Italy may be estimated at around 4 million people. Over 2.5 of them are in the South. If there were any likelihood of a United States of Europe and freedom not only of trade but also of movement of population, there might be some doubt about the appropriateness of a large scale regional development in the South. As it is there can be none»[40].

Alice (i.e Italy, in this case) – by means of the farsighted initiatives carried out by the International Bank for Reconstruction and Development and thanks to the opening of a new era of global economic changes – could, unlike the character in the tale by Lewis Carroll, take the Red Queen behind the looking glass as a reality and run at least twice quicker than the usual, leaving every kind of stasis behind and running towards a time of development and prosperity, succeeding in achieving a twofold convergence, involving Southern Italy moving towards the Northern half and Italy as a whole going towards the most advanced countries, both in Europe and all around the world:

> Alice looked round her in great surprise. "Why, I do believe we've been under this tree the whole time! Everything's just as it was!"
>
> "Of course it is," said the Queen. "What would you have it?"
>
> "Well, in *our* country," said Alice, still panting a little, "you'd generally get to somewhere else – if you ran very fast for a long time as we've been doing."

---

[39] See *Ibidem*.

[40] *Ivi*, p. 27.

> "A slow sort of country!" said the Queen. "Now, *here*, you see, it takes all the running *you* can do, to keep in the same place. If you want to get somewhere else, you must run at least twice as fast as that!"[41].

As the unpublished IBRD document states, international institutions pushed to go beyond the phase of mere postwar reconstruction, towards a dynamic path of economic growth. Without the strategy carried out by the World Bank, strongly supported by both Eugene Robert Black[42], its President, and by an economist such Paul Rosenstein-Rodan, Italy would, probably, never have succeeded in setting itself free from an economic policy focused mainly on achieving monetary stability and would have never been touched by those expansive choices able to quickly make its "economic miracle" a reality. The documents issued by the International Bank for Reconstruction and Development bear extraordinary witness of those times when the economic unification was a more tangible goal, as Saraceno intended it, and of the effort carried out to modernize production in Italy. These documents are an invaluable source, due also to the fact that they keep growing in both size and scope, online as well. They also allow us to consider a part of Italian national history from a different, wider point of view. Therefore, they can be an important starting point towards re-evaluating the "infancy" of economic history in post-war Italy. An overhaul and a widening of our research horizons may also give several indications useful for the current situation in Italy, as the country is called yet again to join its North and Southern halves in order to leave the significant crisis it is in behind. Locating common interests for both areas of Italy may also trigger changes at the European level, turning the need for a new phase of economic development into a reality.

---

[41] L. Carroll, *Through the Looking-Glass, and What Alice Found There*, New York, The Macmillan Company, 1907, p. 42; originally published in London, by Macmillan & Co., Christmas 1871 (although post-dated 1872 on its frontispiece). The sequel of *Alice's Adventures in Wonderland*, titled *Through the Looking Glass and What Alice Found There*, contained the passage this note refers to, itself a good metaphor for what we intend to prove.

[42] See The World Bank, Archives, *Eugene R. Black*, <https://www.worldbank.org/en/about/archives/history/past-presidents/eugene-robert-black>.

CHAPTER ONE

THE ROLE OF THE WORLD BANK DURING THE STARTING PHASE OF THE EXTRAORDINARY INTERVENTION

1.1 The World Bank and the beginning of the extraordinary intervention in Southern Italy: the internal documents

The International Bank for Reconstruction and Development (IBRD), better known as the World Bank[43], was conceived in July 1944 within the Bretton Woods agreements to support the European countries in their postwar reconstruction. However, such initial mission changed in the face of the significantly wider and deeper kind of intervention foreseen by the Marshall Plan[44]. Hence, the original mission of the Bank was soon

[43] Michele Alacevich made clear that: «The "World Bank" locution was born as a media-friendly definition upon the birth of this institution in 1944. Its correct name was, however, International Bank for Reconstruction and Development (IBRD). When the IBRD was joined by its first affiliates, i.e. the International Finance Corporation (IFC, born in 1956) and the International Development Association (IDA, established in 1960), the expression "The World Bank" became officially used to jointly indicate the IBRD and the IDA (but not also the IFC), while the entire group (i.e. IBRD plus IDA plus IFC, to which later on also the ICSID – International Centre for the Settlement of Investment Disputes – in 1966, and the MIGA – Multilateral Investment Guarantee Agency – in 1988 were added) has been called "The World Bank Group"» (M. Alacevich, *Le origini della Banca Mondiale. Una deriva conservatrice*, Milan, Bruno Mondadori, 2007, p. XIII).

[44] As it was indicated: «The International Bank for Reconstruction and Development (IBRD) – since its beginnings known as the World Bank – was instituted at the 1944 Bretton Woods Conference with the principal purpose of aiding European reconstruction after World War II. The abrupt deterioration of international relations, the onset of the Cold War and the concomitant direct intervention by the US in European reconstruction with the Marshall Plan, made the World Bank loans to European countries redundant – in fact useless – principally because of the much

superseded by the most challenging one of promoting development in economically backward areas. Southern Italy was among these, although with some peculiar features. As a matter of fact – as it has been pointed out elsewhere – unlike underdeveloped countries, this part of Italy was «endowed with local capital, services, know-how and unused labor and productive resources»[45]. In an internal document of the IBRD, titled *Creditworthiness of Italy*, specific attention was given to such a theme. As it analyzed the situation of the country as a whole and the main reasons behind a general change of opinion towards the regions of Southern Italy, the document explained:

> The Italian national income fell to catastrophically low levels during and immediately after World War II. It is estimated that in 1945 it was only about half as great as before the war. Aided by foreign relief and reconstruction grants, however, the economy recovered very rapidly, and by 1950 the national income sufficiently exceeded the prewar level to offset the growth in population and to provide a real income per head at least equivalent to that of 1938. There were further increases in real national income of roughly 5% in 1951 and 2 – 3% in 1952. Although the Italian income per head remains among the lowest in Western Europe – roughly equivalent to $ 300 at the current rate of exchange – and leaves much room for improvement, the postwar performance of the Italian economy demonstrates its basic vitality and holds out promise of further growth, provided that favorable domestic and international conditions prevail. […] Until very recently, the principal aims of Italian investment policy have been to reconstruct the productive plant destroyed or damaged by the war end expand basic industries. With these objectives virtually achieved, the primary emphasis has now shifted to the development of underdeveloped areas and the creation of additional employment opportunities. In both these fields, the program of the Cassa per il Mezzogiorno plays a key role. The continued maintenance of adequate levels of private and public investment

greater magnitude of the US commitment: while the Bank's loans in 1947 totaled less than half a million dollars, the Marshall Plan brought to Europe around four billions dollars per year» (M. Alacevich, *The World Bank's Early Reflections on Development: A Development Institution or a Bank?*, in "Review of Political Economy", vol. 21, no. 2, 2009, p. 227, <http://www.tandfonline.com/doi/abs/10.1080/09538250902834046#preview>).

45 L. D'Antone, *«Straordinarietà» e Stato ordinario*, in F. Barca (ed.), *Storia del capitalismo italiano dal dopoguerra a oggi*, Rome, Donzelli, 1997, p. 600.

is a basic prerequisite for the future growth of the Italian economy and for the solution of its major structural problem of unemployment[46].

The overall decision of spreading the process of economic growth into depressed areas marked – as a consequence – the shift from short-term projects to longer interventions. Although this created a discontinuity between the reconstruction and development phases, a strong methodological and operational link remained between the two. Indeed, there was a true interconnection between the two main moments of the activities carried out by the World Bank[47]. In the beginning, especially in 1947-1948, the Bank experienced ample internal discussions about the nature of its objectives, tools and activities. Eventually, the internal discussions led the Bank to take a precise role, which was considered conservative in nature and which it would keep until the second half of the 1960s[48].

---

46 International Bank for Reconstruction and Development, Department of Operations Europe, Africa and Australasia, *Creditworthiness of Italy*, E.A.–25a/Restricted, September 28, 1953, pp. 1-2, <https://documents.worldbank.org/en/publication/documents-reports/documentdetail/515851468253816376/italy-creditworthiness-of-italy>.

47 See M. Alacevich, *Loan Interruptus: The World Bank, Reconstruction and Development in Italy, 1947-53*, New York (NY), The Italian Academy for Advanced Studies in America at Columbia University, Working paper prepared for the Italian Academy Seminar Series, February 2010, <https://academiccommons.columbia.edu/doi/10.7916/D87S7V3G>.

48 On this subject, it appears noteworthy to point out the content of a recent doctorate thesis, which further studied several very interesting themes concerning the primary years of the IBRD (See A. Guelfi, *La Banca Mondiale fra ricostruzione e sviluppo: il caso del primo prestito all'Italia, 1947-1951*, a doctorate thesis in "History and Theory of Economic Development", Rome, Luiss, 2012). Alacevich, on his part, noted that: «The internal debates within development economics, their echoes and particular reception at the Bank, […] as well as the overall international context, are the main elements to understand the cultural, economic and political influences which spurred the Bank to hold its role as a rigid and shut-in, conservative in nature, financial institution, actually refusing the suggestions from its own inner core towards a more articulate and inclusive approach for the definition of its intervention policies, may be understood. The Bank kept such a position at least until the second half of the 1960s, when the ever-greater disappointments felt by many in the field of development economics concerning the development model which was still dominant at the time (and that the Bank had adopted with conviction), compelled it to a change of heart» (M. Alacevich, *Le origini della Banca Mondiale. Una deriva conservatrice*, cit., p. XX). However, the choices taken by the World Bank with the Italian case, featuring the loans in support of the extraordinary intervention in Southern Italy, may, if not wholly overturn such an evaluation, contribute to mitigate

Such an effort in defining strategies and their implementation concerned also the hypotheses of initiatives that would use two different forms of loans: "impact loans" and "social loans"[49]. The former type of intervention – which eventually became the first to be chosen for financing the development of the Mezzogiorno – focused on supporting not a specific project, but rather the overall impact for the economy of the whole country. It involved making a loan to the government in a foreign currency in order to correct the imbalances in the balance of payments provoked by the effects of the investments.

The latter type of intervention was focused on tackling social themes instead, by providing specific loans to solve other issues, which were not directly related to productivity concerns, but which were nevertheless essential when an extended vision of the accumulation process and its premises were considered. The first type of loans was traced back to the «positions which were merged under the approach which was defined "structuralist", opposed to the "monetarist" one. The latter approach did not trace back the issues within the balance of payments and the inflation of many developing countries to squandering fiscal and monetary policies enacted by governments, but rather to the structural imbalances inevitably arising from supply bottlenecks during the development process»[50].

The discussion on "impact loans" began after an analysis carried out by Paul Rosenstein-Rodan, the Assistant Director of the Bank's economic department[51], concerning the request of a credit line carried out by the

---

it and open an observation field on an intervention mode which was innovative since the 1950s.

[49] See M. Alacevich, *The World Bank's Early Reflections on Development: A Development Institution or a Bank?*, cit.; M. Alacevich, *Le origini della Banca Mondiale. Una deriva conservatrice*, cit., pp. 201 and following.

[50] *Ivi*, p. 202.

[51] Rosenstein-Rodan had this job from 1947 to 1953 (see The World Bank, Archives, *Rosenstein-Rodan, Paul N.*, <https://oralhistory.worldbank.org/person/rosenstein-rodan-paul-n>). His role was crucial during these years: «Rosenstein-Rodan gave birth to the concept of "impact loan", itself flying in the face of many of those rules and procedures the Bank had built during its still short life in full synergy with the conservative and banking vision which had held sway within the IBRD up to that point, focused on the concept of "specific projects". […] The impact loan drawn up for Italy was not actually tied to the completion of predetermined series of specific projects – even if, from an operational point of view, a focus on selecting some investment projects was carried out nevertheless, in order to allocate, albeit indirectly, the overall sums […] – but it all was ideally paired with the achievement of the national development plan in its entirety. […] Since it was a multiyear investment plan, Rodan's idea was to provide a consecutive series of loans, which,

Italian government during the final months of 1948[52]. On this, he later recalled that: «if Italy tried to solve a problem which is a long-drawn structural problem and a problem which can be solved only beyond the time limits of the Marshall Plan, a long time action program, for instance, in the development of the South, which for 80 years or 90 years of Italian existence was not solved, and if Italy conceived a long-drawn development program – perhaps seven years or ten years, investing, say, $ 100 million of their own – into a coherent, thought-out, long-run plan of development in the south of Italy, then the Bank, [...] would have spent favorably for a whole consistent program going beyond the time limits of the Marshall Plan [...] and which presumably would amount in total to ten times the amount that the Italian government asked»[53].

Indeed, after joining the International Bank for Reconstruction and Development in 1947[54], Italy intended to start a significant investment

---

albeit each modest in amount when taken singularly, would have ensured, as a whole, a crucial support to the long-term development program». (A. Guelfi, *La Banca Mondiale fra ricostruzione e sviluppo: il caso del primo prestito all'Italia, 1947-1951*, cit., p. 148 and p. 115).

[52] See The World Bank/IFC Archives, *Oral History Program*, *Transcript of the Interview with Paul Rosenstein-Rodan*, cit., pp. 10-16. In the same interview (pp. 15-16), Paul Rosenstein-Rodan explained that: «The loan device was then a kind of economist's loan based upon a multiplier formula whereby an additional investment, which the Italian government obligates research to do, will, via its multiplier effect, increase income. This increased income will result in increased demand, and part of this increased demand will cause either an increase in demand for imports or a fall in the supply of exports, which has to be compensated by a loan. This was the formula which was accepted for the Italian loan, which means it is not tied; it finances the impact of an investment program which the Italian government undertakes; it is not tied to imports of equipment from abroad – in this respect it's quite different from the normal loans –; it's intended to be for many operations. And it was accepted after a long discussion. Certain, how shall I say, reservation clauses or certain covering of the retreat were provided that this near equivalent of this dollar should be attached to some additional projects, which would be supervised by the Bank. But it was still secondary and, as such probably unnecessary, but on the whole it was progress. I once considered this an important prototype of a type of lending policy much broader, which I hoped would be not only for Italy, but that Italy would pave the way in point of fact».

[53] The World Bank/IFC Archives, *Oral History Program*, *Transcript of the Interview with Paul Rosenstein-Rodan*, cit., pp. 11-12.

[54] See The World Bank, *Italy and the World Bank*, <https://www.worldbank.org/en/country/italy>. As it was reminded: «Italy joined the IBRD in March 1947. The following August a loan request for $ 250 million was submitted. In September, a delegation of the Bank arrived in Italy to gather

program using internal capital, although the country had not enough reserves of foreign currencies to be used in tackling the inflationary pressure to follow. Therefore, the commitment through which the Bank would have been financing the majority of the impact of the Italian investment program consisted then in the supply of foreign currencies in greater amounts, so that the country could resist their erosion. Thus, the important figure of the Poland-born economist fully emerged since this very phase, especially for his direct link with the IBRD and the modernization work carried out in Southern Italy. As it was pointed out in a volume concerning the history of this international financial institution, «Rosenstein-Rodan's involvement produced an innovative loan design, the "impact loan", especially in its program character and regional poverty focus»[55].

The role of the World Bank in support of the Italian development strategies has been described and summarized in another work by Michele Alacevich, which can be useful to quote: «From 1951 and during the whole of the 1950s, Italy became the most important European borrower from the World Bank. A number of reasons explain the centrality of Italy for the World Bank's development policies in Europe: Southern Italy was the largest underdeveloped area in Europe. At the same time, the Italian political and financial institutions were well developed and sophisticated, and the Bank could thus easily enter into a productive dialogue with them. For this reason, among others, the Bank became deeply involved in the design and implementation of the development plan for the Italian Mezzogiorno, which became a pilot project for the World Bank itself. Southern Italy even became a playground for development economists and social scientists. Finally, the development of Italy, and the bringing up to

---

information on the imports deemed necessary to implement a reconstruction program. […] When it became known that in bestowing Marshall aid the quantity of currency held by the beneficiary States would have been a factor and the Bank resources were limited, a significant loan, fit to the scope and the complexity of the general reconstruction plan, had to be forfeited; negotiations then continued only concerning the financing of single projects. Nevertheless, Menichella kept in mind the idea that it would have paid to be prepared; as soon as further opportunities for international loans would have been available, they had to be used to finance development programs he saw, even then, as to be made available to Southern Italy» (S. Cafiero, *Storia dell'intervento straordinario nel Mezzogiorno (1950-1993)*, Manduria-Bari-Rome, Lacaita, 2000, p. 17).

55 D. Kapur, J.P. Lewis, R.C. Webb (eds.), *The World Bank: History*, vol. 1, *The World Bank: Its First Half Century*, Washington (DC), Brookings Institution Press, 1997, p. 134, <http://documents.worldbank.org/curated/en/313081468322727631/pdf/578750PUB0v10W10Box353775B01PUBLIC1.pdf>.

speed of its less advanced regions, was essential for the country's political stability and crucial to the integrity of the Western bloc during the Cold War. The Bank of Italy, the Cassa per il Mezzogiorno (the Italian regional development agency), and research institutions such as Svimez, all agreed that Italy's main economic goal should be the territorial expansion of the industry to include less developed regions, for which catching up with the rest of the country was essential. Reconstruction and development should go hand in hand, and the World Bank became the principal counterpart that helped Italy in its efforts toward this goal. Between 1951 and 1965 Italy received eight loans from the World Bank, totaling almost US$ 400 million, the largest amount lent (and the one disbursed over the longest period of time) by the Bank to a European country»[56].

In a volume by Edward Sagendorph Mason and Robert Eller Asher, titled *The World Bank since Bretton Woods*, a direct reference was made to the earlier amongst the eight loans the International Bank for Reconstruction and Development made to Italy between 1950 and 1965[57]. The authors

---

[56] M. Alacevich, *The World Bank loans to Italy and the history of postwar development policies*, Working paper, New York (NY), Columbia University, 2009, p. 1, <http://academiccommons.columbia.edu/catalog/ac:130387>. For example, a World Bank document contains the first loan granted to Italy, with an indication of supporting a development project:

> Loan of $ 10 million made to Cassa per il Mezzogiorno of Italy (another of the Bank's "impact" loans). The purpose of the loan was to develop the land of southern Italy, Sicily, Sardinia and Elba, to employ unused manpower, and to create a sound basis for industrialization. About one-half of the project funds were for reclamation and irrigation of land along the coast and in the river valleys, for reforestation of mountain areas, and for farm improvements. One-quarter of the project expense was to finance the settlement of land distributed under Italy's land reform program, while the rest of the funds were used for the construction of aqueducts, the construction and rehabilitation of provincial roads, and to develop tourist facilities

(The World Bank, Archives, *First funding for Italy: Loan 0050 – Equipment for Development Project*, October 10, 1951, p. 39, <http://docshare02.docshare.tips/files/26751/267519895.pdf>).

[57] On this, in the Archivio Storico degli Economisti, i.e., the historical archive of Italian economists, references can be found to a file folder «concerning the negotiations held between Italy and the World Bank during the December 1947 and June 1948 period about the possibility of a loan by this multilateral organization on behalf of our country. Such documents bear witness to the request of $ 250 million by Italy and to the following negotiations concerning the sectors to be financed and the effective amount of the loan» (Archivio Storico degli Economisti, <http://www.sie-ase.it/>, Fonds: *WB IBRD/IDA 01 Country Operational Files*,

noted that: «the IBRD undertook in the 1950s a series of loans of a type it has been loath to consider in recent years. The lending in question included [...] two loans totaling $ 20 million to the Italian Cassa per il Mezzogiorno in 1952 and 1954»[58]. Furthermore, the volume offered a concise description of the institution and of its early activity, stating that: «The Cassa was a public corporation established and financed by the Italian government to advance the development of southern Italy. It operated through hundreds of contractors, who engaged in particular projects and who were, of course, paid in lire. The dollars provided by the Bank loans were sold by the Cassa to the Italian government for lire. The dollars then disappeared from the Bank's purview and were used by the government for current imports and additions to its monetary reserves. The lire were credited to a special account by the Cassa and used for projects in the selection and supervision of which the Bank played a role. This role, however, was rather tenous.

Series: *WB IBRD/IDA 01 Country Operational Files – Italy*, File no. 6434). Furthermore, the whole series gathers documentation and information concerning the eight loans given by the World Bank:

> For each loan, the documentation is organized into folders which concern the preparatory negotiations and the following administration of the loan. The documents mostly consist of correspondence with the top management of the Cassa per il Mezzogiorno, which in turn is the direct beneficiary of the loans, and of documents and internal correspondence of the World Bank on the matter. The reports the World Bank prepared for internal use, concerning the economic conditions of Italy during that period and the social and political evaluations supporting the policies of the World Bank in Italy, result particularly interesting

(Archivio Storico degli Economisti, Fonds: *WB IBRD/IDA 01 Country Operational Files*, Series: *WB IBRD/IDA 01 Country Operational Files - Italy*, File: no. 6425).

[58] E.S. Mason, R.E. Asher, *The World Bank since Bretton Woods: the origins, policies, operations, and impact of the International Bank for Reconstruction and Development and the other members of the World Bank group: the International Finance Corporation, the International Development Association [and] the International Centre for Settlement of Investment Disputes*, Washington (DC), Brookings Institution Press, 1973, p. 269, <http://documents.worldbank.org/curated/en/306851505231641661/The-World-Bank-since-Bretton-Woods-the-origins-policies-operations-and-impact-of-the-International-Bank-for-Reconstruction-and-Development-and-the-other-members-of-the-World-Bank-Group>. On a later page (p. 271), it was highlighted that: «The second set of impact loans made by the Bank were the two loans of $ 10 million each to the Cassa per il Mezzogiorno in 1952 and 1954. After this the term "impact loan" disappeared from the Bank's lexicon. So also, except for minor aberrations, did the practice of making program loans without reaching an agreement with the borrower as to what imports were to be financed».

Disbursement of the loan was to be proportional to the Cassa's expenditures on the development program»[59].

Along with financing the loans, from 1954 to 1960 the World Bank also organized fifteen operations in conjunction with the private sector, acting as some sort of underwriter in favor of investors that would loan directly to government institutions, an activity which meant to strengthen the attractiveness of market solutions. In making these loans, the World Bank certified both the creditworthiness of the borrower and the soundness of the project for which the money was requested. Table 1.1 below presents information on the whole series of operations, more than half of which were carried out on the private investment market. As it can be observed, Italy was included in these joint initiatives between the World Bank and private investors as well, and the financing that resulted was bestowed entirely on the Cassa per il Mezzogiorno.

---

[59] E.S. Mason, R.E. Asher, *The World Bank since Bretton Woods: the origins, policies, operations, and impact of the International Bank for Reconstruction and Development and the other members of the World Bank group: the International Finance Corporation, the International Development Association [and] the International Centre for Settlement of Investment Disputes*, cit., p. 271. Both within that same page and the following one, the authors went on, noting that: «But as the responsible staff officer said to the executive directors,

> We cannot supervise the plan through the disbursement procedure. We will supervise the plan through the normal means of receiving progress reports, going over these and having a look at the development once in a while, but, most particularly, by close contact with the Italian Government and with the Cassa, and every indication has been given us of a cordial welcome when we go.

Again the directors offered no objection to the first Italian loan. Indeed one of the most prominent among them remarked,

> I am quite sure that we all feel great satisfaction that the solution has been found to make it possible for us to participate in a very important and interesting scheme without being hampered in that by misunderstood orthodoxies about what we should or shouldn't do. … I see this control on the spending of the counterpart lire more as a form of cooperation between the Cassa and ourselves than as a sort of supervision.

The only difference the second Italian loan introduced was the dropping of the special account for projects in which the Bank had some rights of supervision and selection. The Bank's only role now was to receive reports about, and to inspect from time to time, the progress of the general development program. But […] these Italian loans probably represented the furthest the Bank has been able to advance (retreat) from orthodoxy, and the advance (retreat) was of relatively short duration».

Table 1.1 *Joint operations of the World Bank and Private Investment Market, 1954-1960 (in thousands of dollars)*

Year	Country	World Bank loan	Bond or note issue	Total financing
1954	Belgium	20,000	30,000	50,000
1955	Norway	25,000	15,000	40,000
1955	South Africa	25,200	25,000	50,200
1956	Australia (Qantas Airline)	9,230	17,770	27,000
1957	Air India International	5,600	11,200	16,800
1957	Belgium	10,000	30,000	40,000
1957	South Africa	25,000	35,000	60,000
1958	Rhodesia and Nyasaland	19,000	6,000	25,000
1958	South Africa	25,000	25,000	50,000
1958	Austria	25,000	25,000	50,000
1959	Japan	10,000	30,000	40,000
1959	Denmark	20,000	20,000	40,000
1959	Italy (Cassa per il Mezzogiorno)	20,000	30,000	50,000
1960	Japan Development Bank and Kawasaki Steel Corporation	6,000	4,000	10,000
1960	Japan Development Bank and Sumitomo Metal Industries	7,000	5,800	12,800
	Total	252,030	309,770	561,800

Source: International Bank for Reconstruction and Development, *Treasurer's Department*, now present in E.S. Mason, R.E. Asher, *The World Bank since Bretton Woods*, Washington (DC), Brookings Institution Press, 1973, p. 343, <http://documents.worldbank.org/curated/en/306851505231641661/The-World-Bank-since-Bretton-Woods-the-origins-policies-operations-and-impact-of-the-International-Bank-for-Reconstruction-and-Development-and-the-other-members-of-the-World-Bank-Group>; the table originally appeared in International Bank for Reconstruction and Development, *Policies and Operations of the WORLD BANK, IFC and IDA*, Washington (DC), Report no. 11116, 1962-1963, p. 95.

Considering the main tasks of the International Bank for Reconstruction and Development, i.e., supporting development programs in all the relevant backwards areas, it is possible to build up a synoptic table of the amount of the eight loans this international institution provided to Italy between 1951 and 1965. Table 1.2 below considers them both overall and one by one, and it is compiled both by using the database and consulting the *Statement of Loans* by the World Bank. Despite the vast availability of analyses on the Bank's activities, particularly concerning Southern Italy, just a few elaborations currently exist that offer a compact but complete view of all the loans, with their individual description and duration. Because of this, it seems fit to begin our description of the IBRD's work to reduce Italy's regional gap by providing a comprehensive overview of the credit lines activated towards this goal.

Table 1.2 *Loans granted by the World Bank (IBRD) to Italy, 1951-1965 (in dollars)*

Dates of loan approval and maturity, loan number and description	Amount of the loan by the World Bank (*The amount that has been disbursed from a loan commitment in equivalent US dollars calculated at the exchange rate on the value date of the individual disbursements*)
I. 10/10/1951 – 1/11/1976 (*Loan no. 00500 – Equipment for Development Projects. Loan made to Cassa per il Mezzogiorno of Italy – "impact loan"*)	10,000,000.00
II. 06/10/1953 – 01/11/1978 (*Loan no. 00880 – Equipment for Development Project. Cassa per il Mezzogiorno – Second Cassa*)	10,000,000.00
III. 31/05/1955 – 15/07/1975 (*Loan 01170 – Cassa per il Mezzogiorno – Loan to Italy for projects to increase agricultural production, industrial output, and electric power service in Southern Italy*)	68,400,000.00 (70,000,000.00)

IV. 11/10/1956 – 01/09/1976 (*Loan no. 01500 – Cassa per il Mezzogiorno – Southern Italy development – Power, Agriculture & Industry*)	74,628,000.00
V. 26/02/1958 – 15/02/1978 (*Loan no. 01890 – Cassa per il Mezzogiorno – Southern Italy development – Power, Agriculture & Industry*)	75,000,000.00
VI. 20/04/1959 – 01/01/1979 (*Loan no. 02240 – Cassa per il Mezzogiorno – Southern Italy development – Power & Industry*)	20,000,000.00
VII. 14/09/1959 – 15/08/1979 (*Loan no. 02350 – Cassa per il Mezzogiorno – SENN Nuclear power*)	40,000,000.00
VIII. 22/06/1965 – 01/07/1980 (*Loan no. 04190 – Cassa per il Mezzogiorno – Southern Italy industrial*)	100,000,000.00
Total (*The original US dollar amount of the loan(s) committed and approved*)	399,628,000.00
Total (*The amount disbursed from a loan commitment in equivalent US dollars calculated at the exchange rate on the value date of the individual disbursements*)	398,028,000.00

Source: Author's own elaboration based on the data contained in International Bank for Reconstruction and Development, *IBRD Statement of Loans*, <https://finances.worldbank.org/Loans-and-Credits/IBRD-Statement-Of-Loans-Historical-Data/zucq-nrc3>, <https://documents.worldbank.org/en/publication/documents-reports/documentdetail/139951468336683147/europe-and-central-asia-and-middle-east-and-north-africa>.

As it can be inferred by examining Table 1.2 above, despite the diversity in the aims and the amounts of each loan, the Cassa per il Mezzogiorno was constantly the cornerstone institution and the structure responsible for financing, under the cover of the warrant given by the Italian State to international partners as well. The situation that emerges from the loans provided by the IBRD confirms, even chronologically – as the time window considered, between the grant of the first loan and the expiration of the effects of the last one, coincides exactly with that of greater operational capacity and importance, i.e., the golden age of the Cassa – the fundamental importance that the Bank acknowledged about the extraordinary intervention within the framework of globally-relevant development strategies. It also clearly attested the Bank's commitment, as well as the significant endowment of resources to be used in rebalancing Southern Italy[60].

In order to understand the role played by the World Bank in supporting the development of the most backward areas in Italy, as well as to reach a deeper knowledge of the considerations and the evaluation carried out on the other side of the Atlantic on the Italian economy, a very interesting and useful source can be found in the materials the Bank reserved to its internal use[61], and which have been made available to the general public in their

---

[60] Within the specific box of the "Projects & Operations" section of the web portal of the World Bank, the summary data of the eight loans granted to Italy are presented overall.

Country Lending Summaries – Italy – Loans/Credits/Grants Summary in USD Equivalent

	IBRD	IDA Credits	IDA Grants	Total
Original Principal	399,628,000.00	00.00	00.00	399,628,000.00
Cancellations	1,600,000.00	00.00	00.00	1,600,000.00
Disbursed	398,028,000.00	00.00	00.00	398,028,000.00
Undisbursed	00.00	00.00	00.00	00.00
Repaid	132,316,815.68	00.00	00.00	132,316,815.68
Repaid third party	265,711,184.32	00.00	00.00	265,711,184.32

Source: The World Bank, *Projects & Operations*, *Country Lending Summaries*, <https://projects.worldbank.org/en/projects-operations/projects-home>, <https://datacatalog.worldbank.org/dataset/world-bank-projects-operations>.

Compared with the original table, the lines detailing Due, Exchange Adjustment and Borrower Obligation, presenting zero values, have been eliminated, while the columns concerning IDA Credits and IDA Grants have been kept in order to offer a complete overview.

[61] Each one of these documents features on its front the following printing «This report is restricted to use within the Bank», besides the report number, position and

entirety only a short while ago. These documents generally fall into one of two categories. On the one hand, we have the reports and summaries evaluating several issues of the development program for Southern Italy, the Italian projects for industry, irrigation and energy, the Cassa per il Mezzogiorno and the promotional and financing activities geared towards growth in Southern regions. On the other hand, there were the reports and recommendations by the President of the International Bank for Reconstruction and Development informing the executive managers of the Bank in a confidential way about the requests made by the Cassa per il Mezzogiorno on the proposed financing tools for the development of Southern Italy and the effects of the relevant loans, on the trends in their use as well as on the economic conditions of Italy. In fact, a fundamental prerequisite for a loan was a positive judgment on the conditions of the national economy, as it was pointed out by what can be considered as the most accurate study on the relation between the so-called "extraordinary commitment" towards Southern Italy and the initiatives carried out by the IBRD: «To establish the form and amount of financial contributions, the International Bank carefully evaluated the economic and financial situation in Italy, the solvency of the country compared to its debts and the specific investment program»[62].

Hence, the documents issued for internal use by the International Bank for Reconstruction and Development have proven to be an invaluable resource for a more articulate knowledge of the opinion of international actors interacting with Italy, absent the veil of diplomatic relationships and the need to attenuate judgments, as it is the case in official documents. The latter were aimed towards a wider and much more heterogeneous audience, thus a different one compared with the people allowed to read the internal reports, which represented essential tools to reach decisions about the loans to be granted to the Cassa per il Mezzogiorno. Furthermore, by means of such a documentation starting from an "objective" – even if geographically far – point of view (something different from the more traditional sources usually limited to Italy alone) it is possible to contribute towards a balanced evaluation of the extraordinary intervention as a whole, effectively verifying the forecasts and outcomes of every specific financing activity. Therefore, the IBRD materials, intended in the beginning for the closed management circle of the bank, become the essential tiles to complete an original mosaic,

---

publication date. Furthermore, along its left margin the «Public Disclosure Authorized» indication can be seen, as it was added after the publication of such documents was authorized.

[62] L. D'Antone, *L'«interesse straordinario» per il Mezzogiorno (1943-1960)*, cit.; now published in Id. (ed.), *Radici storiche ed esperienza dell'intervento straordinario nel Mezzogiorno*, cit., p. 55.

which gives us a lively and active image of the Cassa per il Mezzogiorno, its premises, role and unique experience within the context of the productive development and modernization of the Italian economy.

1.2 The strategies of the World Bank and the contribution by Paul Rosenstein-Rodan to the development of Southern Italy

The primary sources, i.e., the documents issued by the World Bank, allow to verify the degree of participation by international institutions in creating the Cassa per il Mezzogiorno, and the evolution thereof. Within such a framework, it becomes possible to appraise the role in "connecting" several kinds of experience and expertise – as well as the two sides of the Atlantic – played by personalities such as the development economist Paul Rosenstein-Rodan, who was the leader of the experts at the International Bank for Reconstruction and Development[63] and carried out his function as the manager of the Bank's economic department whilst being part of the SVIMEZ Board of Directors, where he remained for twelve years[64]. He did

---

[63] On this topic, it was pointed out that, since its inception, financing the extraordinary intervention in Southern Italy directly involved the IBRD and its experts: «Besides the meetings held at the Washington premises, this issue was tackled during the several missions to Italy, led by the Bank's economic manager, Paul Rosenstein Rodan. This famous development economist was given the task to personally verify the importance of the Southern regions in the Italian economy, the actual existence of alternative plans, whether investing in Southern Italy could be more promising than elsewhere in the country, if the plan was well worked up, if the Italian financial situation allowed to hold the weight of the agrarian reform and whether the entrepreneurial milieus in Milan and Turin where against such a program. [...] The several meetings held, more and more after the end of 1949, between representatives of the Bank, led by Paul Rosenstein Rodan, and those of the Italian government amongst which the governor of the Bank of Italy, Donato Menichella, was present, were instrumental towards formulating the law establishing the Cassa per il Mezzogiorno and in shaping the American decisions, which, far from being regulated by the criteria held by this international financial institution, took the form and follow the times and the needs of the monetary and economic Italian authorities, as well as the programs followed by the meridionalists within the SVIMEZ» (L. D'Antone, *L'«interesse straordinario» per il Mezzogiorno (1943-1960)*, cit., p. 55 and p. 82).

[64] See L. D'Antone, *«Straordinarietà» e Stato ordinario*, cit., pp. 603-604. Paul Rosenstein-Rodan, amongst other things, contributed to the Centro per gli studi sullo sviluppo economico, a center of study in economic development, established at the SVIMEZ, holding lessons and conferences between 1958 and 1962, on themes

remark the absolute importance of the strategy underlining the extraordinary intervention for Southern Italy, an issue that, according to what Leandra D'Antone reported, was placed «within the virtuous circle of American support to the reconstruction and modernization of Italian economy» and represented the «bigger and more attractive plan of regional development in the world»[65]. The possibility that the IBRD – after the presentation of a document titled *Financing of Economic Development of Southern Italy* by Francesco Giordani[66], in October 1949 – could finance «an organic program of public interventions», rather than specific single projects in favor of the Mezzogiorno, was substantially due to the actions by Rosenstein-Rodan[67],

---

concerning economic development theory and the need of capitals for development, as well as its provision, developed areas and development plans. To the activity of such center several scholars took part, such as Giuseppe di Nardi, Evsey David Domar, Augusto Graziani, Oskar Lange, Gaetano Stammati and Paolo Sylos Labini. As it has been pointed out:

> The Centro was born on July 1, 1957 with the main objective of further studying, by means of operational researches, the main themes of economic development and train scholars and officers over the words to be inserted in the words of research in public administration most of all. In order to achieve these goals, an institute for young scholars was established, financed by the Ford Foundation, by the intercession of Paul Rosenstein Rodan. The courses of such a school have been carried out up to 1969, featuring a significant attendance of professors and pupils, which then became good economists: a significant role in managing its activities fell on the shoulders of Pasquale Saraceno and Claudio Napoleoni

(Archivio Storico degli Economisti, Fonds: *Centro per gli studi sullo sviluppo economico - [Istituto: Associazione per lo sviluppo dell'industria nel Mezzogiorno - Svimez]*, File: no. 2301).

[65] L. D'Antone, *L'«interesse straordinario» per il Mezzogiorno (1943-1960)*, cit., p. 84. In another work of hers, the Author clarified that: «The IBRD would have been involved to finance in dollars those industrial projects included in the program, or the supporting and ancillary ones. It was also assured that no double instances would have been created in financing industries in the concerned areas. All of this entailed a relatively modest commitment by the financing parties, while achieving more favorable results than in any other backwards area in the world. Therefore they joined a program which, if "properly planned" would have become "milestone in the social and economic development of Italy, and a monument to the activity of this bank"» (L. D'Antone, *«Straordinarietà» e Stato ordinario*, cit., p. 600).

[66] Francesco Giordani, as it has been reminded, was the «*alternate* for the Italian Director at the World bank», i.e., a vice executive director of della IBRD (L. D'Antone, *«Straordinarietà» e Stato ordinario*, cit., p. 599).

[67] On this specific issue it has been observed that: «Paul Rosenstein-Rodan, then the most important economic theoretician at the Bank, opposed the institution's increasing propensity towards financing of individual projects. Specifically,

«who theorized a supply/demand balanced "Big Push" as a good tool to restart a backward economy»[68].

In his volume concerning the World Bank's economic policies, Michele Alacevich has in fact stressed, time and again, the importance of the study set up by Rosenstein-Rodan «concerning the loan request made to the bank by the Italian government during the end of 1948»[69] for the start of the financing to the Mezzogiorno. Furthermore, Alacevich clarified that: «The Italian government had the means to start an investment program with mostly internal capital, but it was lacking adequate reserves of foreign currencies. In such a situation – this was the prediction by Rosenstein-Rodan – the greater income resulting from the investment program would have generated an increase in the overall internal demand, which would have triggered an additional demand for imports in turn. In both cases, the country would have been subjected to inflationary pressure and would have needed further currency reserves. Therefore, the Bank would make these further reserves of foreign currencies available. The loan would then finance "the impact of an investment program carried out by the Italian government"»[70].

In his famous essay published in 1943 and titled *Problems of Industrialisation of Eastern and South-Eastern Europe*[71], the development economist had argued that, at the international level, the decision to industrialize depressed areas was not only in the interest of those countries grappling with economic growth problems, but also in that of the whole world. It was, therefore, also a way to attain «a more equal distribution of

---

Rostenstein-Rodan maintained that linking a loan to a single, well-defined project was chimerical. He claimed that single-project loans would end up financing the *marginal* project that the beneficiary country would have abandoned had it not obtained a line of credit from the Bank. In other words, these funds would finance a project that a country would have probably accomplished anyway» (M. Alacevich, *Early Development Economics Debates Revisited*, in "Policy Research Working Paper", The World Bank, World Bank Archives and Development Economics Vice Presidency, no 4441, 2007, p. 7, <https://documents.worldbank.org/en/publication/documents-reports/documentdetail/980951468338671925/early-development-economics-debates-revisited>).

[68] S. Cafiero, *Storia dell'intervento straordinario nel Mezzogiorno (1950-1993)*, cit., p. 22.

[69] M. Alacevich, *Le origini della Banca Mondiale. Una deriva conservatrice*, cit., p. 202.

[70] *Ibidem*.

[71] See P.N. Rosenstein-Rodan, *Problems of Industrialisation of Eastern and South-Eastern Europe*, cit., pp. 202-211.

income between different areas of the world by raising incomes in depressed areas at a higher rate than in the rich areas»[72]. Furthermore, Rosenstein-Rodan put the limelight on the need to focus, first and foremost, on building an adequate, modern production apparatus in backwards areas. Such a structure had to be created through an integrated, constant intervention, itself based on a series of evaluations and cornerstone goals, which may be inferred by some pieces of his essay: «In order to reach an "optimum size" of the industrial enterprises, the area of industrialisation must be sufficiently large. This fact [...] make it imperative to aim at an economic unit comprising the whole area between Germany, Russia and Italy. There are two fundamentally different ways of industrialisation of that area: (i) That Eastern and South-Eastern Europe should industrialise on its own, on the "Russian model" [...], aiming at self-sufficiency, without international investment. [...] (ii) The alternative way of industrialisation would fit Eastern and South-Eastern Europe into the world economy, which would preserve the advantages of an international division of labour, and would therefore in the end produce more wealth for everybody. It would be based on substantial international investment or capital lending. [...] Complementarity of different industries provides the most important set of arguments in favour of a large-scale planned industrialisation. [...] Two [...] types of "external economies" will arise when a system of different industries is created. First, the strictly Marshallian economies external to a firm within a growing industry. The same applies, however (secondly), to economies external to one industry due to the growth of other industries. [...] If the industrialisation of international depressed areas were to rely entirely on the normal incentive of private entrepreneurs, the process would not only be very much slower, the rate of investment smaller and (consequently) the national income lower, but the whole economic structure of the region would be different. [...] If we create a sufficiently large investment unit by including all the new industries of the region, external economies will become internal profits out of which dividends may be paid easily. [...] Industrialization of international depressed areas, once it is accomplished, may create an equilibrium, from which onwards normal private incentives may operate successfully. But it seems hopeless to rely on them before that point is reached»[73]. In the years following the publication of this analysis, once postwar reconstruction was underway, Paul Rosenstein-Rodan's vision was to be made a reality in his contribution to the action of the International Bank for Reconstruction and Development

---

[72] *Ivi*, p. 202.

[73] *Ivi*, pp. 202-203, p. 205, pp. 206-207, p. 208.

and, in particular, concerning intervention in those cases deemed particularly interesting because of the dual structure of their economy, such as the Italian one.

This phase, itself very complex but rich in brand-new themes, was described in a rare testimony by Sydney R. Cope[74]. This testimony allows to correctly frame the choices made by Rosenstein-Rodan and their overall influence on the strategies of the World Bank for Italy, during an age of wide intellectual breadth, as well as of theoretic confrontation on the cornerstones of development economics, of construction of a unitary perspective towards progress of the Western world, and farsighted action towards modernizing backward areas. The testimony recounted that: «Dr. Rosenstein-Rodan had been interested in the early days of the Bank in the development of Italy as an intellectual exercise. It was fairly early in the history of the Bank, in fact, that the Italians asked us for a loan. Italy was one of the many countries who filed applications with the Bank in the first year of its activities, but for a variety of reasons nothing much happened. There was no formulation of projects or definition of a program in the first approach. In 1948 they did put up a few specific projects and, indeed, we sent a mission to Italy to look at these projects. They didn't come back with anything that the Bank regarded as acceptable, one of the reasons being that the projects that they had seen to be important were those requiring a great deal of local expenditure. It was about this time that Professor Rosenstein-Rodan came up with the idea that it would not be a bad plan for the Bank to give assistance to Italy in financing the general development of the south of Italy. That was sometime in 1949. The Italian Government at the time were working out a very large program involving the investment in the south of Italy of something like a thousand billion lire and were thinking of setting up a special body to handle it, a body which was eventually set up under the name of Cassa per il Mezzogiorno»[75].

---

[74] Sydney R. Cope was a member of the Loan Department at the World Bank, from 1947 to 1949; he became a loan officer for the European division of this department, from 1949 to 1952; he then was assistant director of the Department of Operations for Europe, Africa and Australasia, from 1952 to 1955; then he became director of the department, from 1955 to 1972; in the end, he was deputy chairman del Loan Committee, during the whole period from 1947 to 1972.

[75] The World Bank/IFC Archives, *Oral History Program*, *Transcript of the Interview with Sydney Cope*, by R. Oliver, New York (NY), Columbia University, Oral History Research Office, August 9, 1961, p. 17, <https://oralhistory.worldbank.org/transcripts/transcript-oral-history-interview-sydney-cope-held-august-9-1961-main-report>, <http://oralhistoryportal.cul.columbia.edu/document.php?id=ldpd_4074072>.

As Cope recalls, after a long discussion within the Bank the management of the IBRD made the idea of defining the development program for southern Italy as a crucial element for the granting of loans to the Italian government: «Mr. Black decided to approach this question very cautiously and the initial loan was small – it amounted only to 10 million dollars. This decision was made [...] in the course of 1949, and Mr. Black visited Italy in April, 1950 to talk with the people on the spot. He came back rather enthusiastic about the potentialities for raising the standard of living in the South, and later that year, later in 1950, we accepted the idea that we would envisage a continuing relationship with Italy in helping them develop the south and that we would envisage lending foreign exchange for local expenditure»[76]. The Cassa per il Mezzogiorno was established during that very same year, but it was only in October 1951 that the Bank carried out its first loan amounting to $10 million, to be granted at the rate of a dollar for each 10,000 Italian lire invested in the initiatives featured by the program. On this, Cope shared the concern on giving the public correct information about the destinations and use of the invested money, clarifying that: «The device was accordingly adopted of setting up a counterpart fund created by the sale of the foreign exchange by the Cassa to the Banca d'Italia, and this counterpart fund was to be used for so-called supplementary projects in the industrial sector which were to be agreed with the Cassa people»[77].

After recalling the main uses of such a loan and their offset, Sydney R. Cope expressed his satisfaction for the reaction caused by the commitment of the Bank towards the development of Southern Italy, and explained the reasons behind a greater ease in implementing the second loan, amounting to $10 million, and effectively granted two years later. However, by then a confrontation opened within the Bank regarding the theoretical basis of the first loans, particularly concerning their "impact"[78]. On such a dispute, he believed that older loans granted by the International Bank for Reconstruction and Development involved some "impact lending" and that, therefore, the true distinction was not to be made between the "impact loans" and the other kinds of loans, but rather between their direct impact,

[76] *Ivi*, p. 18.

[77] *Ibidem*.

[78] As Cope himself affirmed: «The impact argument is a familiar one to economists. It runs that expenditure within a country which is not completely covered by increased savings has an inflationary impact because it increases the demand for imports directly or indirectly and that therefore one is justified in providing foreign exchange in respect of local expenditure» (The World Bank/IFC Archives, *Oral History Program*, *Transcript of the Interview with Sydney Cope*, cit., p. 19).

itself the "orthodox" form to grant imports-linked financing, and the indirect one, represented by the Italian case[79]. However, Cope further elaborated on the issue: «The idea of impact [...] was found to be rather theoretical; some people didn't like it very much, and towards the end of the year it was decided by the management to tacitly drop the impact justification. We had many meetings in the course of 1953 at which were arranged on one side the theoretically minded people and on the one side people [...] who had practical considerations very much in mind and wanted to limit as far as possible the Bank's activities in financing local expenditure»[80].

Two years after the second loan, the Bank's policymakers opened up to a broader approach, looking, as proposed by Rosenstein-Rodan, not at single interventions in backward areas, but rather at a series of consecutive loans, which were able to support a transformation program for those areas, through a repeated and increasing availability of external resources to be implemented for a longer phase. As Cope pointed out: «In 1954 Mr. Black went over to Italy to review the progress of the Cassa program in which he'd been interested right from the start, and after a meeting with Mr. Vanoni, who was then the Minister of the Budget, and with Menichella, who was governor of the Banca d'Italia, he indicated that, subject to working out of satisfactory loans and approval of the Bank's Executive Directors, that he would be prepared to envisage an amount of 200 million dollars of lending

---

[79] See *Ibidem*.

[80] *Ivi*, p. 20. In the two following pages, Cope went explaining the problem, noticing that: «Although the impact justification was officially abandoned in 1953, there was no intention of abandoning the idea of making loans for local expenditure. But we rather tended to shift our ground and to justify them on the basis of there being a need on the part of a borrower carrying out a high priority project for money which he could not raise in his own market. It was perhaps a part in the growing emphasis in the Bank on the project as the basis for the Bank's lending as opposed to the need for foreign exchange on the part of the country as a whole. [...] the Bank started off in 1947 by making loans which were not related to projects at all. They were loans whose justification was the general need for foreign exchange on the part of the borrowing countries. And that thought dominated our lending in the early years; even though we moved over to projects we tended to be presented with projects whose real *raison d'être* was not so much the priority of the project but was the need on the part of the economy's problem for foreign exchange. As conditions in Europe and in the world generally as far as exchange shortages changed as conditions improved generally, thinking in the Bank, I think quite unconsciously, moved too in the direction of giving greater weight to projects and less weight to the need for foreign exchange on the part of the economy».

to Italy over a period of years»[81]. Following the 1955 loan, the procedures of the first phase were overcome and the financing model was definitely established, leading on to other loans which followed the same setup: «under the 1955 loan we did not attempt to calculate the impact and we made no reference to it and we justified on the grounds of the necessity to provide capital for Italian enterprises to move south, and so set up businesses and help industrialize the area. We justified it on the need to help carry out infrastructure. We justified it on the basis of the need to provide irrigation, to facilitate the settlement of farmers in the poorer areas of the south»[82]. Therefore, the orientation of the IBRD loans and their non-episodic contribution to the development of Southern Italy was made clear.

1.3 The initial phase of the loans provided by the World Bank to Italy and the status of the economy in its Southern regions

The first loans granted by the International Bank for Reconstruction and Development were based on the evaluation of their usefulness for the whole of the country, given their destination to the Mezzogiorno, as well as on the necessity of a sustained continuity – beyond the amount of each loan – in

---

[81] The World Bank/IFC Archives, *Oral History Program*, *Transcript of the Interview with Sydney Cope*, cit., p. 23. In this very page, Cope went on noting that: «This loan, unlike the first two loans, was not disbursed on the basis of a formula. It wasn't disbursed on the basis of a relationship between expenditure on the plan as a whole and the disbursement of the loaned monies. Instead we concentrated on the projects which came within the Cassa program. These were not necessarily projects being carried out by the Cassa itself; these expenditures were very largely for infrastructure. But this loan was to be used in part for industrial enterprises put up by private capital but enterprises which needed the inducement of loan money from the Bank in order to encourage them to make investments in the south. It was one thing, said the Cassa, to put in infrastructure; it was another thing to get Italian industry to move south. And the use of the counterpart of the Bank loans was regarded as an important element in the industrialization of the South».

[82] The World Bank/IFC Archives, *Oral History Program*, *Transcript of the Interview with Sydney Cope*, cit., pp. 24-25. Cope, in the second of the two pages indicated, he concluded the part of his interview dedicated to Italy, adding that: «I think what was of key importance was that Mr. Black himself was very much sold on the idea of helping the development of the south. I think it was also true that the individual project examination and the concentration of the counterpart of these loans on industrial projects and infrastructure projects, which the Bank had examined and felt were good for the economic point of view, was thought to take a good deal of the sting out of the objections to the local expenditure».

the impulse to the Italian economy. It has been as a matter of fact noted that, at the beginning of the 1950s: «the Bank ventured into an explicit and dramatic effort to address poverty through regional allocation, in southern Italy. A modest, first loan of $ 10 million in 1951 to the Cassa per il Mezzogiorno was followed by six [seven] additional loans between 1953 and 1959 [1965]. [...] Receiving the proposal for the first of these loans, the Board was told that regional trickle-down was ineffective in Italy: industrialization in the north would benefit only the north, with very little positive effect for the south»[83]. Therefore, the new interventions had to be localized in the Mezzogiorno, for at least three good reasons: to bridge the gap between Northern and Southern Italy and begin a wide action of productive modernization; to stimulate demand growth – by means of the investments activated in the Mezzogiorno – which would have given a wider market base to the main industrial productions in Northern Italy; and to bring about the conditions for financial stability, towards which the international loan would have contributed, within the framework of the coordinate development between the two sides of the Atlantic and the respective interests.

The International Bank for Reconstruction and Development took a full and active part in creating opportunities for the Mezzogiorno. These were to be a prelude to an unmatched and lasting "golden age", by means of the Bank's financing initiatives, which are reconstructed in detail within this book, making use of the internal documents, as well as by consulting the well-known official ones. The first of the internal documents was a report issued on July 31, 1951, titled *An Appraisal of the Development Program for South Italy*, whose open disclosure was authorized only on April 16, 2010[84]. This report was dedicated to the "Southern Italy Development Project", i.e., the first concrete form of execution for the decade-long program for economic development in Southern Italy. The project concerned the building of highways, an element deemed able to ensure new

[83] D. Kapur, J.P. Lewis, R.C. Webb (eds.), *The World Bank: History*, vol. I, *The World Bank: Its First Half Century*, cit., p. 134. In the note linked to the passage reported, on the same page, it was specified that: «Paul Rosenstein-Rodan argued, however, that the failure of income to spread was not symmetrical; though income would not spread from north to south, it would flow in the opposite direction, from south to north, as investment in the south created purchasing power and demand for goods from the north».

[84] See International Bank for Reconstruction and Development, Loan Department, *An Appraisal of the Development Program for South Italy*, L133/ Restricted, Archives/Records Center, Room HB1–001, Box 254–22, Nus Location 065–3–1, July 31, 1951, <https://documents.worldbank.org/en/publication/documents-reports/documentdetail/429011468044151649/italy-an-appraisal-of-the-southern-italy-development-project>.

employment in critical areas; the buildup of waterworks, facilities and sewers, in order to give adequate utilities to Municipalities; the implementation of new land improvements and irrigation, responsible for significant effects on income and employment; flood control for erosion-plagued lands and forests; the transformation and colonization of agricultural terrains; the promotion of tourism towards Southern Italy at the national and international level; and the activation of industrial projects, but only concerning plants dedicated to preservation and processing of agricultural products[85]. The report, signed by E. Wayne Rembert, was limited to an evaluation of the program of public works the Cassa per il Mezzogiorno was called to implement in the ten-year period following July 1, 1950, for other aspects of the interventions had been tackled in previous reports by the Bank's Loan Department and Economic Department (*Report of the Italian Working Party on the Program for the Development of Southern Italy and Possible Method of Bank Financing*, issued in July 27, 1950; *The Creditworthiness of Italy*, set up by Alexander Stevenson, issued on August 15, 1950; *Italy's Economic Policy and Prospects*, set up by Alexander Stevenson, on June 21, 1951; *Report on the Development Program of Southern Italy*, set up by Paul Narcyz Rosenstein-Rodan, issued on May 21, 1951)[86].

The part of the document concerning the detailed explanation of the main features of the development program mentioned the SVIMEZ, because this institute carried out activities connected with selecting and coordinating the projects. The institute acted as «an independent organization supported largely by the contributions of private enterprise, since 1947», and the document maintained that the program on the Cassa was widely based on elaborations carried out by the SVIMEZ itself, «with some minor changes and additions resulting generally from political considerations»[87]. Furthermore, the goals of the Cassa were detailed schematically, as follows:

> The Cassa was created as an autonomous agency in order to guarantee the availability of funds on a fixed schedule and to expedite the program to the

---

[85] See *Ibidem*.

[86] See *Ivi*, p. 1. In this very same page, it has been pointed out that: «This report is based on numerous discussions with various representatives of the Cassa and other Government agencies, documents submitted by them, and field observations by a Bank mission which was in Italy during March and April, 1951. The information which is available is not complete for the purpose of a comprehensive technical and financial appraisal, but it is considered adequate to allow the Bank to reach a decision regarding the suitability of the public works program as a basis for Bank participation to the extent which is contemplated».

[87] International Bank for Reconstruction and Development, Loan Department, *An Appraisal of the Development Program for South Italy*, cit., p. 2.

> maximum extent possible within the means available to it. In the Cassa law an attempt is made to eliminate bureaucratic and other delays in the execution of the works. Funds for the Cassa operations are derived from the counterpart of U.S. aid programs and from the ordinary budget[88].

In another part of the same report, the organization and management of the Cassa were described in greater detail:

> The Cassa Law [...] established a Committee of Ministers to formulate a general program for the improvement of economic and social conditions in southern Italy to run over a period of 10 years [...]. The Committee is designated as "The Committee of Ministers for the South". The Law establishes the chairman of the Ministerial Committee as the supervisor of the administration of the Cassa. [...] The management of the Cassa is the responsibility of a Board of Directors selected for a term of four years. It is composed of a chairman appointed by the President of the Republic on the recommendation of the Prime Minister, two vice-chairmen, and ten members appointed by the Prime Minister after consultation with the Cabinet. Actual operations of the Cassa are in the hands of a Director General and a small staff of technical experts. At the present time, three divisions are in operation, namely, (1) land reclamation, irrigation, and land improvement; (2) aqueducts and sewers; and (3) accounting and disbursements. An Office of Roads to formulate and supervise the Road Program has also been established. A fourth division to deal with credit, industrial development, and the promotion of tourism is being formed[89].

Furthermore, indications were also provided about the staff of this Entity – amounting to about 200 employees, «which is not excessive for the work involved in this operation»[90] –, and on the controls to be carried out on the activities of the Cassa, in order to prevent the misuse of its funds or the

---

[88] *Ivi*, p. 3.

[89] *Ivi*, pp. 24-25. In the first of the two aforementioned pages, it was also specified that:

> Minister Campilli has formed a technical secretariat for the Committee, consisting of seven men selected by him. This secretariat, while not definitely authorized by the Law, is typical of the organizations used by Minister Campilli during the early stages of any new position which he has acquired in the past. The members act as advisors to him and as a channel through which the Committee now transmits its directives to the Cassa. On the basis of past experience with Campilli organizations of this type, it is to be expected that this secretariat will be disbanded as soon as the Cassa is operating effectively.

[90] International Bank for Reconstruction and Development, Loan Department, *An Appraisal of the Development Program for South Italy*, cit., p. 25.

insertion of useless and excessively expensive projects within its program[91]. The document listed all the specific initiatives envisaged by the Cassa's program, with a detailed amount of information and relevant tables that were attached at the end of the report[92]. Remarkably, it is worth mentioning a note which, in reference to the industrial program, presented some new elements that are worthy of consideration, despite the thinness of the interventions reserved to this aspect among the initiatives for Southern Italy.

> The law as presently interpreted, obviously does not permit the Cassa to participate in any substantial industrial development of the South. It was thought, at the time the law was formulated, that such participation would not be required since it was expected that after the public works program had progressed sufficiently, private capital for industrial investment would be attracted in sufficient amounts without government assistance. Within recent months, however, it has been decided to accelerate industrial development in the South through investments by or credits available through the Cassa. An amendment to the Cassa law has been presented to Parliament which will permit borrowing from domestic and foreign sources by the Cassa for such financing. It is in this field that the IBRD proposes to participate, along with private capital, by means of loans to firms desiring to establish industrial enterprises in the South and on the islands[93].

---

[91] It has been in fact underlined that:

> 1. All programs and program changes require approval of the Committee of Ministers for the South and must be reported to Parliament.
> 2. Before authorizing the preparation of any suggested project, or approving the execution of projects already prepared and costing over L. 100 million, the Cassa must consult with a sub-committee of the High Council of Public Works.
> 3. A Board of Auditors is established by the Cassa Law, under the chairmanship of a councillor of the Court of Accounts. This Board has the responsibility of determining the regularity of the Cassa accounts; auditing of its expenditures; reviewing documentary proof of such expenditures; and ensuring proper implementation of the law by the Board of Directors.
> 4. A new advisory committee has been formed which will be responsible for the study and the preparatory work necessary for the comprehensive overall program. This Committee at present consists of six men under the chairmanship of Professor Pasquale Saraceno, Director General of IRI, an outstanding economist who has been very close to the formulation of the development program for the South in his past position as Director General of SVIMEZ

(International Bank for Reconstruction and Development, Loan Department, *An Appraisal of the Development Program for South Italy*, cit., p. 25).

[92] See *Ivi*, pp. 3-18.

[93] *Ivi*, pp. 17-18.

However, it was in the section dedicated to the "Financial Requirements and Sources of Funds" that the summary data on the financing of Southern Italy were recalled, along with a further analysis – typical of this early phase – of the entwining between the resources given by the plans of the European Recovery Program (ERP) – in particular, those managed by the Economic Cooperation Administration (ECA) – and the economic endowment for the activities of the Cassa, something that relied on the counterpart funds of American aid[94]. As it has been pointed out about a report by the chief of the

---

[94] See *Ivi*, pp. 18-21. In particular, concerning the financing by the ECA, the following was pointed out (p. 20): «The greater part of the dollar loans, while made in lire, are designated by the Government as a part of the overall ECA loan to Italy and the repayments will be used to service this loan. The lire loans are repayable in lire to the Italian Government, and it is expected that service payments will be credited by the Government to the Cassa although ECA has not yet agreed formally to this plan». Furthermore, the sources and the amount of financing punctually indicated, in the document by the IBRD: «The sources of funds vary by years through the period of ERP operations and have been definitely established in the law as follows»,

In the fiscal year 1950-51

(a) 42.6 billion lire from the ERP counterpart lire fund
(b) 23.8 billion lire from the U.S. Interim Aid counterpart lire account on the books of the Bank of Italy
(c) 33.6 billion lire from the budget of the Ministry of the Treasury

In the fiscal year 1951-52

(a) 18 billion lire from the U.S. Interim Aid counterpart lire account on the books of the Bank of Italy
(b) 82 billion lire from the budget of the Ministry of the Treasury, of which 50 billion lire from amounts accruing in that fiscal year to the ERP counterpart lire fund

In the fiscal years 1952-53 through 1959-60

(a) 80 billion lire from the budget of the Ministry of the Treasury
(b) Principal of and interest on loans, made by Istituto Mobiliare Italiano (IMI) for industrial re-equipment from funds allocated for this purpose by ECA and repayable to the Italian Government
(c) One half of moneys accruing to the ERP counterpart lire fund after June 30, 1952 and until the end of ECA operations in Italy

Source: International Bank for Reconstruction and Development, Loan Department, *An Appraisal of the Development Program for South Italy*, L133/ Restricted, Archives/Records Center, Room HB1–001, Box 254–22, Nus Location 065–3–1, July 31, 1951, p. 19, <https://documents.worldbank.org/en/publication/documents-reports/documentdetail/429011468044151649/italy-an-appraisal-of-the-southern-italy-development-project>.

ECA mission, Leon Dayton, titled *Program Plans for Cassa – Fund for South*[95], and concerned the activation of the agreements between the Economic Cooperation Administration and the Cassa: «the choice on the transfers of funding from the 1950-1951 Counterpart Fund to the Cassa per il Mezzogiorno was compliant with the goals of the Cassa, as it was originally stated by the ECA and offered the contribution to realize long-term (namely decade-long) programs»[96].

The final evaluations contained in the IBRD document, then, pointed out the positive aspects of the opening moments of the extraordinary intervention:

> The development program for southern Italy, as presently conceived, involves a large group of public works and agricultural development projects, most of which have been planned for many years, and a large number of which are in the course of execution. These projects are, in general, well studied and engineered and construction can be rapidly undertaken. [...] Assuming no serious deterioration of the international situation, it is probable that the program [...] can be executed within the 10 year period established by law and within the amount of L 1,000 billion which has been allocated to it over this period[97].

Anyway, this specific part of the document took also the problems which came up in the beginning phase into consideration, such as, for example, those due to the lack of credit sources for private investment in the agricultural sector, coupled with some evident lacks in both the management of the industrial and the tourism programs[98]. The report concluded with an

---

[95] See NARA, *Program Plans for Cassa – Fund for South. I-a 1950/51 Land Reclamation Program for Southern Italy*, from ECA Special Mission to Italy – to ECA Washington and OSR Paris, Despatch number D-157, 28 June 1958, RG. 469, Box 34, F. 8.

[96] M. Gesummaria, *Piano Marshall e Mezzogiorno*, Atripalda, Mephite, 2003, p. 161. This volume (pp. 149-180), contains two very interesting paragraphs, useful to clarify the more complex parts linked to the beginning of the extraordinary intervention; these paragraphs are titled: *Il ruolo dell'ECA nell'istituzione della Cassa per il Mezzogiorno* e *Le raccomandazioni americane e le "regole del gioco" per l'utilizzo dei fondi ERP da parte della Cassa per il Mezzogiorno*.

[97] International Bank for Reconstruction and Development, Loan Department, *An Appraisal of the Development Program for South Italy*, cit., pp. 25-26.

[98] See *Ivi*, p. 26. As it has been observed in this very page:

> The administrative and technical personnel of the Cassa are believed to be competent and fully qualified for the direction of the program with the exception of those concerned with the industrial and touristic programs where some re-staffing is believed to be required. [...] The greatest deterrent

indication that, while confirming the assent to the loans on the IBRD's part, any further commitments were to be linked to an accurate verification of the activity of the Cassa per il Mezzogiorno on a yearly basis:

> The development program has no aspects at the present time which should prevent the Bank from participating along the lines that are contemplated, that is, the granting of a series of loans to cover the dollar impact of the program on the Italian economy. The operations of the Cassa will, however, require careful review each year before additional commitments are made[99].

Another paper, issued on October 5, 1951 and titled *Report and Recommendations of the President to the Executive Directors on the Proposed Loan for the Development of Southern Italy*, was authorized for open disclosure on June 24, 2010. This report – which came from the President of the International Bank for Reconstruction and Development, Eugene Robert Black and on whose first page the "Confidential" sign was well evident – was followed by an appendix, containing some drafts for internal use[100]. This report was divided into eight parts and explained the granting procedures of the first $10 million loan to Italy. One of the first indications concerned the show of interest for the Southern Italy-based

---

to the realization of the final results of the program will probably be the lack of credit for private investment in agriculture. It is likely that the Cassa will find it necessary to provide such credit in substantial amounts from its own resources in order to facilitate final settlement of reclaimed areas and lands distributed to small farmers under the system of land reform.

[99] International Bank for Reconstruction and Development, Loan Department, *An Appraisal of the Development Program for South Italy*, cit., p. 26.

[100] See International Bank for Reconstruction and Development, *Report and Recommendations of the President to the Executive Directors on the Proposed Loan for the Development of Southern Italy*, P–22/Restricted, Archives/Records Center, Room HB1–001, Box 935–01, Nus Location 099–1–2, October 5, 1951, <https://documents.worldbank.org/en/publication/documents-reports/documentdetail/846541468042537580/italy-southern-italy-development-project>.
The attached drafts concerned the following documents: *Loan Agreement between the Bank and the Cassa*; *Guarantee Agreement between the Republic of Italy and the Bank*; *Report of Loan Committee under Article III, Section 4(iii), of the Articles of Agreement on the proposed loan to Cassa per il Mezzogiorno*; *Approval of recommendations of the President that the Bank grant a loan to the Cassa per il Mezzogiorno in the amount of $ 10,000,000, to be guaranteed by Republic of Italy: authorization to President or Vice President or Assistant to the President or Loan Director or Treasurer to execute Loan Agreement, Guarantee Agreement and other documents relating thereto.*

development plan, considered in its entirety, by the International Bank for Reconstruction and Development, as stated in a letter sent to the Governor of the Bank of Italy:

> A letter from the Bank to the Governor of the Bank of Italy, dated August 21, 1950, has provided the basis for all subsequent discussions. It stated that the Bank's interest would lie in the development plan as a whole; a figure of $ 10 million was mentioned as possible participation by the Bank corresponding to the dollar impact of expenditure of the first annual appropriation for the Plan; it implied that the Bank would have a continuing interest over the life of the Plan; stated that the extent of the full Bank participation over a period of years would depend upon the general evolution of the Italian economy and on satisfactory progress of the development plan; and expressed the Bank's wish to select representative projects for financing in part through the lira counterpart of the loan[101].

The report followed through with a reference to the financing proposal, identifying the receiver of the loan as the «Cassa per Opere Straordinarie di Pubblico Interesse nell'Italia Meridionale, more familiarly known as the Cassa per il Mezzogiorno, a governmental authority which administers the Plan»[102]. Its guarantor was the Italian state, itself a member of the Bank. The report also identified the proposed amount, its conditions and its main goals. The terms were very clear:

> The loan would be amortized by semi-annual payments, on the basis of equal payments of principal and interest combined, the first of the principal payments being due on November 1, 1956 (5 year period of grace), and the last on November 1, 1976 (25 year maturity). [...] The loan would bear interest, including 1% commission, at the rate of 4½% per annum. The first interest payment date would be May 1, 1952. A commitment charge of 3/4% per annum has been provided for, accruing from December 31, 1951, whether or not the loan becomes effective by that date[103].

The purpose of the loan was extensively described, the precise explanation of its function perfecting the cornerstone economic design at the base of the extraordinary intervention:

> The Plan is noteworthy in that it seeks to develop an underdeveloped area in a country which already possesses important industrial facilities. The

---

[101] International Bank for Reconstruction and Development, *Report and Recommendations of the President to the Executive Directors on the Proposed Loan for the Development of Southern Italy*, cit., p. 1.
[102] *Ivi*, p. 2.
[103] *Ibidem*.

> Plan is very large in relation to Italy's resources and will have a measurable impact on the country's balance of payments. Italy depends to a considerable extent on imports of fuel, vital foodstuffs (wheat and fats) and raw materials. Some increased imports will be required to carry out the Plan itself, but more importantly, the Plan will provide increased employment and income for a substantial number of workers whose larger consumption will in part be translated into a higher demand for imports of consumer goods. It has been estimated that expenditure of the first 100 billion lire annual appropriation for the Plan will create a demand for additional dollar imports of all kinds amounting to about $ 10 million. The direct purpose of the Bank's loan would be to meet the dollar impact of the initial stages of the Plan. [...] The impact is of course felt by the whole economy and not by the Cassa. The Bank of Italy would buy the dollars from the Cassa, against lire. When the whole loan is disbursed the Cassa would have obtained 6.25 billion lire (the equivalent of $ 10 million). In the circumstances the Bank felt it should have a voice as to the uses of the counterpart. Accordingly it has been agreed that the Cassa would lend the counterpart to private companies for the financing of industrial projects which are supplementary to the Plan. These supplementary projects are connected with the Plan but they would not be financed from the Cassa's governmental appropriation because the Cassa is confining itself to basic works of a public character such as roads, irrigation, and land reclamation. Thus, as with the loans the Bank has made in the past, the proposed loan would be directed primarily towards meeting needs in foreign exchange. As a second step the Bank would concern itself with the use of the local currency counterpart. Hence separate arrangements have to be made for disbursement of the dollars and of the lire equivalent, and for the control of their use[104].

In the part of the report detailing the development plan for Southern Italy both a definition of the Cassa[105] and an explanation of the plan itself were

---

[104] *Ivi*, pp. 2-3.

[105] According to the indication contained in the report:

> The Cassa is a government agency, established for the purpose of administering the Plan by virtue of a law of August 10, 1950, and possessing independent juridical status. It operates under the supervision of a special Cabinet Committee composed of the Ministers of Agriculture, Treasury, Industry and Trade, Public Works and Labor and Social Security. The management of the Cassa is in the hands of a Board of Directors, to whom the General Manager is responsible. [...] The organization is relatively small. It will have the ultimate responsibility for the execution of the Plan which, however, will be carried out through regional and local agencies both within and without the government

(International Bank for Reconstruction and Development, *Report and Recommendations of the President to the Executive Directors on the Proposed Loan for the Development of Southern Italy*, cit., pp. 3-4).

given[106]. Furthermore, the established procedure for the effective grant by the IBRD was described as follows:

> Since it would be the purpose of the loan to meet the impact of expenditures distributed over a wide area, a "list of goods" would not be appropriate. The basis for withdrawals would be expenditures incurred on the Plan as a whole, as reported to the Bank in summary accounting statements. Withdrawals would be at a rate that would see the $ 10 million disbursed when 100 billion lire had been expended[107].

This part of the document, by Eugene Robert Black, included the evaluation of the development plan which, besides considering those other elements useful in raising the standard of living in the Mezzogiorno, was ahead of its time in tackling the issue of creating industry in the area and underlined the objective of improving the overall economic and social conditions in Italy:

> The Plan to which the proposed loan would lend aid is a realistic attempt to come to grips with a basic Italian problem – the low standard of living in the South. As a result of the Plan agricultural output should eventually increase and the better grading and processing facilities provided should make the area's products more marketable. Development of the basic facilities provided by the Plan, and the increase in purchasing power, should lead also to the establishment of industries in the area, including the industrial enterprises which would be financed in part by the lira counterpart of the proposed loan. Although the loan in itself is not likely to strengthen Italy's dollar position, it should eventually improve her overall balance of payments by saving imports and increasing exports. It will, I believe, bring added employment and help to stabilize economic and social conditions, not

---

[106] The description of the ten years' development plan was put in an extremely concise form:

> The 1000 billion lire ($ 1.6 billion) expenditure to be made over ten years is for the depressed part of the country to the south of a line drawn across the middle of the peninsula from a point between Rome and Naples, and including the islands of Sicily, Sardinia and Elba. This area is 40% of the area of the country. The Plan aims at the development of agriculture through reclamation, irrigation and improvement of land, and at investment in public utilities, such as aqueducts and roads. A limited investment is planned in tourist facilities and installations for storing and processing agricultural products

(International Bank for Reconstruction and Development, *Report and Recommendations of the President to the Executive Directors on the Proposed Loan for the Development of Southern Italy*, cit., p. 4).

[107] *Ibidem*.

only in the south, but in the member country as a whole, all at a dollar cost small in relation to the size of the Plan and to Italy's balance of payments[108].

The final part of that report was focused on evaluating the Italian economic situation, during its difficult postwar recovery phase. However, the emerging picture coincided with the positive effort the country was undertaking in order to rise from its ruins and pointed towards a future of progress and welfare, thus favoring positive judgment by international financial authorities and moving towards the confirmation of the $ 10 million loan by the IBRD, as the President of the Bank himself declared:

Despite formidable obstacles, the Italian economy has shown a steady improvement in the years since the end of the war. After a severe inflation in the early postwar years, internal financial conditions have remained fairly stable. Increases in output, particularly in industry, have brought income and consumption per head at least to prewar levels and have enabled investment to go forward at a substantial rate. The rising trend should continue, though at a modest rate in view of the rapid growth of population and the added burden of rearmament. [...] The severe disequilibrium which appeared in the Italian balance of payments after the war has been substantially reduced. The current account deficit, which was equivalent to about $ 700 million in 1947, was almost eliminated last year. There was still a deficit of around $ 200 million with the dollar area which was met, as in earlier postwar years, by financial assistance from the U.S. Government. This deficit, however, was only half as large as it had been in 1948, and was almost completely offset by a surplus with other countries, particularly in

---

[108] *Ivi*, p. 5. In the very same page, the "Supplementary Projects" were recalled:

One result of expending large sums of public monies in the area should be that private capital is attracted to the South. To accelerate the process, the Cassa will be authorized to borrow funds from foreign sources and to lend the counterpart to private companies whose activity would advance the general purposes of the Plan. The lire equivalent of the proposed Bank loan would be Cassa funds supplemental to regular appropriated funds, to be lent for projects supplementary to the Plan. [...] Supplementary projects satisfactory to the Bank and the Cassa have been tentatively approved, final approval being subject to negotiation of loan contracts between the Cassa and the private companies. These loan contracts would in their general terms be subject to approval by the Bank. Private capital would participate substantially in each project; in the aggregate, participation by the Cassa and the private companies would be about equal. The total amount to be invested in each project has been discussed by the Bank and the Cassa and the maximum amount which the Cassa would advance to each has been agreed. The Cassa could propose substitutions of other projects for those that have been agreed.

Europe. [...] Nevertheless the international economic position of Italy remains basically vulnerable since, broadly speaking, she imports essentials and exports non-essentials. Her major markets are in Europe whereas particularly since the war she has been heavily dependent on imports from the Western Hemisphere. After Korea, reflecting a shift in pattern of trade and deterioration of terms of trade, an overall deficit on current account reappeared, and the deficit with the dollar area increased somewhat. [...] It is still reasonable for Italy, at her present stage of development, to import capital. Consequently, her balance of payments could be said to be in equilibrium if there were a moderate inflow of long term capital to offset the current account deficit. With some further U.S. assistance, especially to cushion the impact of rearmament on the balance of payments, Italy should be able to achieve overall equilibrium in this sense, in her international accounts, in the next few years. This equilibrium may well continue to involve deficits with the dollar area balanced by surpluses with other areas, notably Europe. While the speedy resumption of full convertibility of European currencies cannot be safely assumed, there is reason to hope that such a dollar problem as may then arise could be resolved, under a healthily functioning system of international payments. [...] The external debt owed or guaranteed by the Italian Government amounts to the equivalent of about $ 500 million, practically all payable in U.S. dollars. If the service payments on this debt were not so largely in dollars, they would cause little difficulty, since such service amounts to only about 2% of the country's external earnings in all currencies. Since it can not be assumed that Italy will be able to convert her surpluses in other currencies into dollars, some risk attaches to lending to Italy in dollars. Nevertheless new obligations which are so small in relation to existing dollar service charges should not be beyond Italy's capacity to bear. [...] Italy's record of service on external debt is good. Already by 1947, and on Italian initiative, a settlement had been reached on the major portion of the dollar bonds and on the small amount of sterling bonds outstanding, on which service was suspended when Italy entered the war. Agreement has since been reached on practically all the remaining privately held bonds. [...] I believe that due regard has been paid to the prospects that Italy would be in a position to meet her obligations under the proposed loan and that in making it, the Bank would be acting prudently in the interests of Italy and of the members of the Bank as a whole[109].

A confidential note, issued in 1951[110], featured Resolution no. 199; through such a resolution, the Bank's executive directors approved the

[109] International Bank for Reconstruction and Development, *Report and Recommendations of the President to the Executive Directors on the Proposed Loan for the Development of Southern Italy*, cit., pp. 7-8.

[110] See International Bank for Reconstruction and Development, *Minutes of the Twenty-ninth Special Meeting of the Executive Directors*, SM-29/Confidential,

proposal by the President concerning the $ 10 million loan to the Cassa per il Mezzogiorno, using a formula by means of which:

> the President or the Vice President or the Assistant to the President or the Loan Director or the Treasurer of the Bank be, and each of them hereby is, authorized in the name and on behalf of the Bank (a) to execute with the Borrower [Cassa per il Mezzogiorno] and to deliver a loan agreement substantially in the form [...] of Loan Agreement presented to the Executive Directors [...]; (b) to execute with the Republic of Italy and to deliver a guarantee agreement substantially in the form [...] of Guarantee Agreement presented to the Executive Directors [...]; and (c) to take any and all such other action and execute and deliver any and all such other documents as they or any of them shall deem necessary or proper in the premises and in order to carry fully into effect the purposes of this Resolution[111].

The formal conclusion of the procedure concerning the first loan to the Cassa was thus sanctioned and the following path, related to the effective use of the financing tools, was open. Its aim was to contribute to the economic development of Southern Italy in a non-episodic way.

1.4 The first steps undertaken by the Cassa per il Mezzogiorno

The International Bank for Reconstruction and Development tackled the issue of the first steps in the extraordinary intervention by means of two reports, issued on September 28, 1953, whose content was for internal use only. Their public disclosure was authorized on April 16 and June 24, 2010 respectively[112]. The first document, issued on September 28, 1953, and

October 10, 1951, <https://documents.worldbank.org/en/publication/documents-reports/documentdetail/542801468253453361/minutes-of-twenty-ninth-special-meeting-of-the-executive-directors-held-on-october-10-1951>.

[111] *Ivi*, pp. 2-3.

[112] See International Bank for Reconstruction and Development, Technical Operations Department, Public Utilities Division, *Italy. Cassa per il Mezzogiorno. Summary and Appraisal of Activities until June 1953*, T.O.–38a/Restricted, September 28, 1953, <https://documents.worldbank.org/en/publication/documents-reports/documentdetail/396891468285875106/italy-second-southern-italy-development-project>; International Bank for Reconstruction and Development, *Report and Recommendations of the President to the Executive Directors on the Cassa per il Mezzogiorno Loan Application guaranteed by the Republic of Italy*, P–57/Restricted, Archives/Records Center, Room HB1–001, Box 935–01, Nus Location 099–1–2, September 28, 1953,

titled *Italy. Cassa per il Mezzogiorno. Summary and Appraisal of Activities until June 1953*, carried out an examination of the activities by the Cassa and evaluated the progress of the extraordinary intervention. Generally speaking, the IBRD pointed out the following about this "Second Southern Italy Development Project"[113]:

> In August 1950 the Italian Parliament adopted a "Ten Year Plan for the Economic and Social Development of Southern Italy" providing for the execution of a vast program of public works, mostly in the agricultural field. It was the first comprehensive large scale attempt by an Italian Government to cope with under employment and the resulting low standards of living from which Southern Italy had suffered for decades[114].

The original program, whose management was entrusted to an Entity with legal personality[115], such as the Cassa per il Mezzogiorno was, envisaged

---

<https://documents.worldbank.org/en/publication/documents-reports/documentdetail/704161468044126559/italy-second-southern-italy-development-project>.

[113] As explained in the presentation abstract of this report, which can be found in the relevant page of the World Bank website (https://documents.worldbank.org/en/publication/documents-reports/documentdetail/396891468285875106/italy-second-southern-italy-development-project):

> The Second Southern Italy Development Project is being created due to a major problem which was not fully recognized in the original plan. The plan did not provide the financial and educational programs necessary to assure full utilization and maintenance for all of the public works and land improvements. This problem is now fully recognized and steps are being taken to solve it. [...] Relief of unemployment in Southern Italy is one of the goals of this project. Presently most of the ground work is being done to collect statistical data on how to increase agricultural production. Most of the land reclamation and agricultural projects are still in their initial stages, and it will take another year or two before the other projects begin.

[114] International Bank for Reconstruction and Development, Technical Operations Department, Public Utilities Division, *Italy. Cassa per il Mezzogiorno. Summary and Appraisal of Activities until June 1953*, cit., p. 2. In the very same page, the following was added: «The social aspects of the Plan are the justification for including some projects which are high-cost in relation to their expected benefits».

[115] Actually, defining the Cassa per il Mezzogiorno juridically is no easy task, especially after it overcame the original indication by Donato Menichella, who had in mind to configure it as a "public law Entity": «now the Cassa is not simply an organization, but neither does it possess legal personality in the traditional sense, as it has no own goals to pursue, its goal simply being the one to implement the plan coming from an external authority (the Committee of Ministers for the Mezzogiorno).

the implementation of projects for the overall amount of 1,000 billion Italian lire within a decade (such a term would then be modified by the Italian law no. 949, of July 25, 1952, to twelve years, with an expenditure provision amounting to 1,280 billion Italian lire). This plan was divided into several fundamental sectors of intervention, as it appears from the initial subdivision of resources indicated in Table 1.3.

Therefore, the jurisprudential doctrine spoke more and more insistently of an organism-juridical person, giving the Cassa such a figure, somewhat anomalous and apparently in contradiction. Truth be told, the dispute concerning the juridical nature of the Cassa loses much of its importance if one admits [...] the existence of the so-called instrumental public legal persons, whose autonomy in pursuing their goals is almost non-extant, while it is indeed wide in the technical- functional field. On the other hand, some organizations exist having also budgetary autonomy, therefore the classical boundary between organization and public legal person is disappearing. It then goes without saying that the classification of the Cassa within one or the other category has no great relevance concerning its operational position within the context of public administration» (G. Marongiu, *Aspetti giuridico-organizzativi*, in A. Parisi, G. Zappa (eds.), *Mezzogiorno e politica di piano*, Bari, Laterza, 1964, p. 320). Gabriele Pescatore give further contributions to comprehend the modification of the juridical meaning of the Cassa, compared with intentions of its original planners, noticing that the legislator had a single alternative: «One could have entrusted to the new entity an absolute autonomy, both in programming and in the executive phase, like it had been done in the U.S.A. for the Tennessee Valley Authority; or imposing to such entity a with the ordinary public administration of the State, both in programming and in implementing its actions. The solution chosen was the second one; this way, while satisfying some needs connected with the more classical juridical schemes, deeply new elements were integrated in the Italian institutional system. It has been said that the Cassa, while partly realizing the British model of the public corporation, itself juxtaposing the authority usually connected with public entities and the freedom election of private enterprises, at the end of the day is a unique legal entity since it submits to the control of the executive power» (G. Pescatore, *L'intervento straordinario nel Mezzogiorno d'Italia*, Milan, Giuffrè, 1962, p. 131).

Table 1.3 *Subdivision by intervention sector of the expenditures envisaged by the Ten-Year Plan for the Economic and Social Development of Southern Italy (Italian law no. 646 of August 10, 1950)*

	Billions of lire
Land reclamation, Irrigation, Flood and Erosion Control	490
Land Transformation and Settlement	280
Aqueducts and Sewers	110
Roads	90
Promotion of Tourism	30
Total	1,000

Source: International Bank for Reconstruction and Development, Technical Operations Department, Public Utilities Division, *Italy. Cassa per il Mezzogiorno. Summary and Appraisal of Activities until June 1953*, T.O.–38a/Restricted, September 28, 1953, p. 2, <https://documents.worldbank.org/en/publication/documents-reports/documentdetail/396891468285875106/italy-second-southern-italy-development-project>.

The tasks of this entity were specified as follows in the IBRD document:

> As a matter of policy, the Cassa does not directly administer any of its projects, but appoints existing agencies, called "concessionaires" for the detailed planning and execution of each project. [...] The Cassa intervention is therefore limited to general guidance of the concessionaires, examination of the projects, review of the award of contracts and general supervision[116].

Furthermore, an initial judgment was expressed on the first experiences of the Cassa, concerning the implementation of its plan. Such a judgment was passed even considering the excessive optimism which biased the forecasts of expenditure timing, but also showing the substantial confidence in the activities carried out by this Entity:

> The original Ten Year Plan envisaged expenditures during the first years at the rate of 100 billion lire a year. The actual progress of work and rate of expenditures have so far fallen considerably short of this goal. The most important reason for this is the original over-optimism about the time required to get the Cassa operation underway. It was unrealistic to expect

[116] International Bank for Reconstruction and Development, Technical Operations Department, Public Utilities Division, *Italy. Cassa per il Mezzogiorno. Summary and Appraisal of Activities until June 1953*, cit., p. 3.

> that a new agency could properly spend 100 billion lire in each of the first few years on the type of projects included in the Plan. Many of these projects were not nearly as advanced as the planners had assumed [...]. It says much in favor of the Cassa, that it has in most cases put careful preparation before rapid spending, even in the fact of heavy political pressure. By the end of June 1953 the Cassa had examined projects estimated to cost 460 billion lire, and had approved projects which committed some 330 billion lire of its funds. With the contribution from other sources, these projects represent a total expenditure of some 370 billion lire. [...] By the end of June 1953, contracts for Cassa projects had been awarded for a total of about 300 billion, and the ascertained expenditures of Cassa funds by the end of August were about 107 billion lire[117].

Anyway, at the end of the report the aforementioned evaluations were accompanied by an overall extremely positive acknowledgment of the activity of the Cassa up to June 1953. This entity stood out for his capacity to manage its plan and for its high-quality staff, although the report expressed concern for the future, should political pressure prevail:

> The Cassa has, in view of all of the difficulties encountered, demonstrated its ability to cope with a Plan of this magnitude. The Staff of the Cassa seems well qualified to deal with the technical and administrative problems which have developed to date. It is difficult to forecast the progress which can be expected in the future. There will probably be many modifications in the Plan and the possibility always exists that political pressure might influence both the future program and its implementation. [...] In view of the progress made to date and the current level of operations, it is believed that the Cassa will be able to handle the future problems which arise[118].

---

[117] *Ivi*, p. 4. Within another excerpt of the document (p. 1), also the evaluations of the works and the activities underway was more favorable to the Cassa when compared with that of the aforementioned excerpt:

> The works which have been started or completed to date have been generally in accordance with the original Plan. However, progress has been much slower than anticipated, and instead of expenditures running at the rate of 100 billion lire per year, total expenditure to September 1953 amounted to only this amount. Delays have been due primarily to over-optimism in the original scheduling of the projects rather than due to any faults in the administration of the Plan. Work on the Plan is now well underway and in the past few months, Cassa expenditures have approximated an annual rate of 100 billion lire as originally contemplated.

[118] International Bank for Reconstruction and Development, Technical Operations Department, Public Utilities Division, *Italy. Cassa per il Mezzogiorno. Summary and Appraisal of Activities until June 1953*, cit., p. 1.

Furthermore, the Bank put some emphasis on the procedures concerning the loans and their payment, by accurately describing the proceedings and the initial amounts of such operations. It put particular emphasis on the so-called "Supplementary Projects", making the importance of industrialization entirely evident from the very beginning. Even though the Cassa did not entail the financing of this economic sector yet, according to the common suggestion of the two entities (both the Bank and the Cassa) this might have represented, «the only long-term solution to the unemployment and low standard of living of Southern Italy»[119]:

> The Loan Agreement provides that withdrawals from the Loan Account, to be made from time to time, should bear the same ratio to US$ 10 million as the Borrower's expenditures in carrying out the plan bear to 100 billion lire. The Cassa submits to the Bank monthly summary accounting statements, showing the amounts expended on the carrying out of the Plan. Advance payments by the Cassa to its agencies do not constitute amounts expended on the carrying out of the Plan for the purpose of computing withdrawals. Shortly after the Loan became effective the Cassa submitted the first application, based on the ascertained expenditures as of October 31, 1952, for a withdrawal of US$ 4.6 million [...]. Since that date, withdrawal applications have been submitted every month, varying from US$ 400,000 to 900,000, and the final disbursement was made in September 1953 [...]. Advance payments by the Cassa to its concessionaires amount to some 35 billion. Part of these advances are undoubtedly spent on the projects several months before they are documented to the Cassa, but their inclusion as a basis for disbursements under the Loan would involve several disadvantages: 1) The documentation for the disbursements would become extremely complicated, in order to avoid double accounting, and our control and checking would become correspondingly more difficult; 2) It would remove one of the incentives of the Cassa and its agencies to process payments in a rapid and business-like manner; this efficiency in processing payments has up to now represented one of the greatest improvements over the traditional bureaucratic methods of administering government projects which the Cassa has made; and 3) It might open the way to the Cassa's increasing the amount of advance payments much beyond the present scale. For these reasons it would seem highly advisable to continue the disbursements of any possible second loan to the Cassa on the present basis. [...] The Loan Agreement provides that upon each withdrawal of dollars from the Loan Account, the Banca d'Italia shall transfer an equivalent amount in lire to a Project Account, to be used for assisting in the financing of Supplementary Projects in Southern Italy which will contribute to the development of that region. The Cassa and the Bank agreed at the time of the Loan negotiations that the type of project which would most effectively achieve this purpose

[119] *Ivi*, p. 7.

> would be industrial, since the Cassa program devotes no funds to this section of the economy, and since at least a moderate industrialization will be the only long-term solution to the unemployment and low standard of living of Southern Italy[120].

As a conclusion, one of the final considerations contained in the document is worth reporting, as it may be useful to understand the very positive judgment the Bank passed on the structure and the skills of the Cassa per il Mezzogiorno:

> The Cassa staff, especially the chiefs of the four principal technical services, have a high professional standing. In general the impression has been that the Italian engineers and technicians fully measure up to the technical problems involved in carrying out the Plan[121].

In the second document issued on September 28, 1953, titled *Report and Recommendations of the President to the Executive Directors on the Cassa per il Mezzogiorno Loan Application guaranteed by the Republic of Italy*, both an evaluation of the first steps of the extraordinary intervention and an analysis of the Italian economic situation, were present. They were linked to the request of a new loan to be implemented towards development in Southern Italy, amounting to $ 10 million. The President of the International Bank for Reconstruction and Development, Eugene Robert Black, noted the following when presenting these interventions within their historical framework:

> The depressed condition of Southern Italy was a national problem which had endured for generations, and only an attack of major proportions could

---

[120] *Ibidem*. In the following page, further information on "Supplementary Projects" may be found:

> The selection of these projects was based primarily on the following criteria:
> (a) The projects should be related to the agricultural program of the Cassa.
> (b) The industries selected should use labor intensively.
> (c) A substantial portion of the capital required for such projects should come from private sources, so that loans from the Project Account would be in accordance with sound lending practices.
> At the date of signing the Loan a list of ten projects was agreed upon, estimated to cost a total of Lit. 15 billion, of which the Cassa was to finance a maximum of Lit. 7,5 billion or 50%. The majority of these projects were to use agricultural products directly or indirectly, or to produce materials usable in carrying out the Plan, such as cement.

[121] International Bank for Reconstruction and Development, Technical Operations Department, Public Utilities Division, *Italy. Cassa per il Mezzogiorno. Summary and Appraisal of Activities until June 1953*, cit., p. 10.

be expected to make any real improvement. Possible Bank participation in a proposed 10-year development plan for Southern Italy had been discussed since the spring of 1949. The law providing for the plan was passed on August 10, 1950. At that time, the Bank indicated its interest in the plan, and its willingness to assist, probably on a continuing basis, the massive investment program established by that law. [...] Although it was clear that the investment of Lit. 100 billion per year would have some direct impact on Italy's dollar balance of payments, it was realized that the major impact would be indirect, resulting from the rising demand for imports of consumption goods stimulated by the additional investment expenditures of the Cassa. The Bank agreed, therefore, to lend $ 10 million to assist in meeting the dollar impact of the plan in its initial stages. No list of goods could be drawn up, and the Bank and the Borrower therefore agreed that disbursement in dollars would be made to the Banca d'Italia, based on lire expenditures of the Cassa on its over-all program [...]. The lire equivalent of the withdrawals would be transferred to the credit of the Borrower, thus adding to the Cassa's resources[122].

Furthermore, a positive evaluation, expressed by an IBRD delegation on a mission to Italy in order to discuss its further interventions of the activity of the Cassa emerged from this document as well. It did clearly indicate that:

a mission visited Italy during October and November 1952. The mission made a general survey of the operations of the Cassa and reached the conclusion that after two years its accomplishments had been considerable; that it had proceeded with care and efficiency in launching its program; and that its staff was competent. The mission also worked with the Cassa in establishing an amended list of supplementary projects, four of which are now well begun and the fifth of which is being commenced[123].

---

[122] International Bank for Reconstruction and Development, *Report and Recommendations of the President to the Executive Directors on the Cassa per il Mezzogiorno Loan Application guaranteed by the Republic of Italy*, cit., p. 1.

[123] *Ivi*, pp. 1-2. In this very same document (p. 2), it was reminded that:

When the report of the mission had been considered, the Bank wrote to the Government of Italy on March 16, 1953, stating it was prepared to enter into negotiations for a second loan in an amount of $ 10 million and that it would be willing to send a representative of the Bank to Italy to pave the way for negotiations and to discuss with the Italian Government the use of the counterpart funds which would be created by the loan.

In the documents sent by Eugene Robert Black to the Bank's executive directors[124], the terms of the new $ 10 million loan were also described – at an interest of 5%, including a 1% commission – with the "Republic of Italy" as a guarantor:

> The purpose of the loan is further to assist the Borrower and the Republic of Italy in promoting the economic and social development of Southern Italy by supplying part of the foreign exchange requirements resulting directly and indirectly from the carrying out of the plan of the Borrower and Guarantor for the development of Southern Italy. The loan would also result in making available the lire equivalent of $ 10 million to be used for a supplementary project or supplementary projects which would contribute to the development of the South[125].

The part dedicated to the analysis of the "Supplementary Projects" – that promoted a series of industrial initiatives within the Mezzogiorno – is very interesting, especially in consideration of the developments in the following years, concerning the shift in the orientation of the Cassa towards industrialization, something that would begin in 1957:

> In the first Cassa loan the counterpart is being used by the Cassa for relending for an agreed list of supplementary industrial projects. Since the first loan was signed, certain changes have taken place in Italy with respect to the availability of industrial credits. A law of April 11, 1953, reorganized Isveimer and two similar institutes operating in Sardinia and Sicily, the credit institutions through which the Cassa operates in extending loans to private industry. These institutes have been allocated Cassa funds amounting to Lit. 15 billion (approximately $ 25 million) for the continuation of this program. In addition, the Cassa will have at its disposal funds accruing from repayments of loans made from ECA-MSA counterpart funds to private enterprises, the amount of which cannot yet be determined but is likely to

---

124 The permission for the second loan of 10 million dollars to the Cassa was given, as in the previous case, during special meeting of the executive directors of the Bank, who adopted resolution no. 264, therefore concluding the financing procedure (See International Bank for Reconstruction and Development, *Minutes of the Sixty-second Special Meeting of the Executive Directors*, SM-62/Confidential, October 6, 1953, <https://documents.worldbank.org/en/publication/documents-reports/documentdetail/264231468253453698/minutes-of-the-sixty-second-special-meeting-of-the-executive-directors-held-in-the-board-room-of-the-bank-on-october-6-1953>).

125 International Bank for Reconstruction and Development, *Report and Recommendations of the President to the Executive Directors on the Cassa per il Mezzogiorno Loan Application guaranteed by the Republic of Italy*, cit., p. 2.

be more than Lit. 5 billion. Moreover, the resources of the credit institutes have recently been substantially extended by authorization to issue their own bonds and by the creation of the "Istituto Centrale per il Credito a Medio Termine a Favore delle Medie e Piccole Industrie (Medio Credito)" which can rediscount the early maturities of Isveimer loans to small industries, presently defined as industries whose capital does not exceed \$ 2½ million. Medio Credito disposes of funds of more than Lit. 60 billion (about \$ 95 million) for use throughout Italy[126].

Nevertheless, the most relevant part of the reflections by the President of the IBRD concerned the evaluation of the economic conditions in Italy, which may be useful to report entirely, given their effectiveness and precision:

The national income of Italy has recovered from the low levels to which it fell during and immediately after World War II. The income per head is now slightly higher than prewar in spite of a 10% increase in population. This growth in national income and in income per head has resulted from an increase in agricultural output of about 7%, an increase in industrial production of approximately one-third and from the generally prosperous conditions in the construction and service fields. Italy continues, of course, to be dependent upon imports of basic foodstuffs and raw materials and minerals. However, the recent discovery and exploitation of natural gas has already led to savings of imports of coal, and according to present plans for its development, should provide Italy with the equivalent of about 9 million tons of coal annually by 1956. [...] With the reconstruction phase completed, Italian investment policy is now being directed toward the development of underdeveloped areas and the creation of additional employment opportunities. The economic development prospects of Italy are relatively limited, but under the stimulus of favorable foreign and domestic demand, considerable increases in output appear possible both in agriculture and in

---

[126] *Ivi*, p. 4. In this very same page, it was also noted that:

In view of the availability to the credit institutions of these new and relatively large credit resources for the financing of supplementary industrial projects in the South, the lack of credit facilities which the Bank helped meet by the use of the counterpart of the first loan to the Cassa now appears to have been met. Therefore, the Cassa has proposed for financing from the counterpart of the proposed second loan the hydroelectric portion of a multi-purpose project in the South of Italy, and the Bank is considering its technical, economic and financial aspects. Since agreement on the use of the lira counterpart is independent from the financing of the dollar effects of the over-all Cassa program and can be determined subsequently, it is proposed that the loan be concluded immediately with the counterpart utilization to be agreed later.

industry. However, because of the rapid growth in population, even an intensive investment program and reasonably favorable emigration prospects are not likely to reduce significantly the present level of structural unemployment of 1.3 million. Unemployment and underemployment remain the most unfavorable feature of the Italian economic and social situation. [...] Italy has enjoyed relative price stability ever since the monetary stabilization of 1947 and even the inflationary pressures which arose after the outbreak of hostilities in Korea have been held in check very satisfactorily. The condition of public finances remains difficult and will be further aggravated by the reduction of counterpart availabilities as U.S. aid declines. However, public revenues should continue increasing as national income rises and a more determined effort is made to collect the newly enacted direct taxes. Moreover, the recently rising level of savings should permit the continuation of projected public investment activity without further encroachment on financing availabilities for the private sector. [...] The Italian balance of payments is affected by two basic weaknesses: (a) while her imports consist of essential foodstuffs and raw materials, her exports largely fall in the "soft" categories, such as textiles and luxury foods; and (b) she generally earns a surplus in inconvertible or partially convertible currencies, while she is in deficit with the dollar area. After achieving a small surplus in her balance of payments in 1950, Italy's external accounts deteriorated seriously during 1951 and 1952. This deterioration largely resulted from a decline in Italian exports to the United Kingdom and other sterling area countries and to France, which had to deliberalize, and from an increase in Italian imports because of a stepped up rate of domestic investment. There is, however, no reason to expect a continuation of an Italian deficit with E.P.U. If her major trading partners pursue liberal commercial policies, Italy should be able to balance her accounts with E.P.U. without any great difficulties. It will probably be more difficult to eliminate the dollar deficit, but increasing availabilities of non-dollar wheat, cotton and fuel (including domestic methane) should make possible a redirection of many basic dollar imports once U.S. aid ends. Moreover, some further increases of Italian exports to the U.S. and increased dollar earnings from tourism and emigrants' remittances is possible provided that the U.S. national income continues to grow and her commercial policies do not become more restrictive. [...] Thus while the balancing of Italian external accounts in general and with the dollar area in particular still remains a serious problem, it does not appear to be insoluble provided that high levels of production, income and trade are maintained by Italy's major trading partners and their commercial policies are further liberalized. Service on the Italian external public debt is relatively light, amounting to between 2 and 3% of Italy's foreign exchange earnings. Its chief burden arises from the fact that most of the Italian debt is in dollars and service payments on this portion account for roughly 10% of her dollar earnings. Because the Italian debt service record has been very satisfactory and in view of the previously mentioned prospects for improving somewhat

> her dollar earnings and diverting elsewhere some of her basic dollar imports, Italy should be able to manage her present, or an even slightly higher dollar indebtedness. In these circumstances, Italy may be regarded as a reasonably good risk for another $ 10 million loan at this time[127].

Within such a context, whereby Italy began the most significant phase of economic growth after completing the postwar reconstruction, the role of the International Bank for Reconstruction and Development resulted particularly meaningful. The Bank was pivotal for the effective grant of loans, which contributed to the creation of new development conditions for Southern Italy. But the Bank also played a fundamental role by punctually analyzing the country's internal situation, and in providing directions towards the productive modernization of the most disadvantaged areas in the country. As it has been noted on the role of the American authorities regarding the Italian situation of the time: «the Americans were confident, after the good results achieved in 1951, which triggered the examination of the projects presented for a total amount of 189 billion lire [...]. Thanks to its independence and shorter red tape [the Cassa] succeeded in concluding contracts and in paying commissions much more rapidly than any other government office. [...] In conclusion, the Americans maintained that everyone had great hopes in the Cassa, in part supported by its initial achievements, and partly by the fact that a few years had to be waited to adequately judge its success and results»[128]. During this specific phase of the extraordinary intervention, the combination of the Cassa's activities – as it became more and more effective after the setup phase – and of the IBRD's presence – which was able to complete, support and enhance the overall project to overcome the backwardness plaguing the Mezzogiorno – gave solid expectations for this huge catching-up action, and formed a prelude to a coherent evolution in the growth strategies of the country as a whole.

---

[127] International Bank for Reconstruction and Development, *Report and Recommendations of the President to the Executive Directors on the Cassa per il Mezzogiorno Loan Application guaranteed by the Republic of Italy*, cit., pp. 5-6.
[128] M. Gesummaria, *Piano Marshall e Mezzogiorno*, cit., pp. 171-172.

CHAPTER TWO

THE EVOLUTION OF THE FINANCING BY THE WORLD BANK TOWARDS THE ECONOMIC AND SOCIAL DEVELOPMENT IN SOUTHERN ITALY

2.1 The new loans provided by the World Bank to Italy and the Cassa's continued activities

As we have seen, the initial financing phase carried out by the International Bank for Reconstruction and Development in favor of the Italian state resulted pivotal not only for the credit resources it granted, but also because it gave a continuity with the interventions carried out during the reconstruction, and because it played a role in spurring and supporting the development strategies which were planned and implemented by the international institutions together with the Italian government, the SVIMEZ and those personalities and researchers that found in the Bank a solid reference point. Therefore, the role played by the IBRD was not limited to the opening of a credit line to support economic growth in Southern Italy. It rather stood up, since its first steps, as a fundamental piece of the complex and financially sophisticated structure that supported and sustained the extraordinary intervention. During the 1950s, such a cooperative process was strengthened and enhanced, offering new elements to evaluate the effectiveness of the authorities on both sides of the Atlantic and new opportunities to finance the activities of the Cassa per il Mezzogiorno, whose results began then to be seen with greater clarity.

The document issued on May 24, 1955, the first of several other similar reports, was dedicated to the "Third Southern Italy Development Project", and featured a very articulate account of the new twelve-year development plan for Southern Italy. This report, titled *Appraisal of Italian Industrial, Irrigation and Power Projects*[129] (whose public disclosure was authorized

[129] See International Bank for Reconstruction and Development, Department of Technical Operations, *Appraisal of Italian Industrial, Irrigation and Power Projects*, T.O.–84a/Restricted, May 24, 1955, <https://documents.worldbank.org/

on April 16, 2010) presented in full detail the projects regarding the development of the areas of Southern Italy, as may be inferred by their relevant abstracts:

> The Third Development Project for Southern Italy will further support the 12-year plan for economic development. The project consists of seven industrial projects, one irrigation project, and three power projects. The goal is to increase agricultural and industrial production in this region by developing the following seven plants: one plant will produce cement to build new plants in the future. Two plants to make complex fertilizers in Sicily. Two plants will process agricultural and forest products; such as Sicilian citrus fruit for the export market, and paper mill to help reduce foreign exchange expenditures. The final two plants will be for light industrial products, one is for the control of pests and diseases to assist the agricultural program by increasing production and land cultivation, and the other plant to produce wool which is a competitive export in Italy[130].

The paper began with an introduction that detailed a mission to Italy by the International Bank for Reconstruction and Development. The mission had been carried out during the months of May and June, 1954, after Italy requested a new loan, amounting to $ 70 million. The new loan would support the twelve-year program in favor of economic development in its Southern areas. The introduction of the document featured a favorable judgment by the Bank on that request, with a call for a list of projects to be used as a base for financing[131]. A new mission, lasting about a month, was then carried out by two members of the IBRD staff in November of that same year. This new mission gathered preliminary data for this project, and it analyzed its impact on the local economy, considering also the program managed by the Cassa per il Mezzogiorno[132]. The establishment phase followed a very complex procedure, which brought to the examination in Washington, in January 1955, of five irrigation projects (the total cost of which amounted to about $ 300 million); of twenty-three energy-related projects (with a total cost of $ 153 million); and of 28 industrial projects (with a total cost of $ 112 million)[133]. After this procedure ended in February and the Italian interlocutors filled the questionnaires set up to evaluate what interventions most deserved to be financed, the Bank carried out the final

---

en/publication/documents-reports/documentdetail/821031468042537885/italy-third-southern-italy-development-project>.

130 *Ibidem*.

131 See *Ivi*, p. 1.

132 See *Ibidem*.

133 See *Ibidem*.

selection of the projects presented. As detailed elsewhere in this book, the Bank chose to finance seven of the industrial projects, three of those that focused on power and one about irrigation[134].

In the following parts of the document, a general illustration of the projects and their features was carried out for each of the considered sectors, followed by a detailed evaluation of their characteristics. Concerning the industrial sector, the general value of the goals to be reached was underlined, and the criteria and methods adopted in selecting the projects were specified:

> The most important factors taken into account in making the selection were the expected benefit to the Italian economy, the financial soundness of the project, and its state of preparation. [...] Some projects under construction and some proposed plant sites were visited. Discussions were held with the promoting groups in order to obtain information and to form a judgment of their capabilities[135].

Furthermore, the document explained the mechanism through which the financial resources were committed. It pointed out the terms of the agreements with the interested subjects, the conditions of the loans by the Cassa per il Mezzogiorno, and the role of the IBRD. The Bank had the final

---

[134] See *Ibidem*. In this part of the documents the seven industrial projects were also indicated, and they concerned Cementerie Siciliane (cement), SICULAZOTO (fertilizers), SINCAT (fertilizers), S.F.A.S. (processing of citrus fruits), S.I.L. (paper), FARMEDI (pharmaceutical), MANITEX (woolen yarn); the irrigation project concerning "the Catania scheme in Sicily"; the three energy projects, concerning the Società Meridionale di Elettricità (SME), the Società Generale Pugliese di Elettricità (Pugliese) and the Unione Esercizi Elettrici (UNES) respectively.

[135] International Bank for Reconstruction and Development, Department of Technical Operations, *Appraisal of Italian Industrial, Irrigation and Power Projects*, May 24, 1955, cit., p. 2. In this very same page, it was noted that, upon closure of the aforementioned proceedings:

> Seven projects with a total cost of $ 43 million equivalent were finally selected which could serve as a basis for loans totalling $ 18.41 million equivalent. The amount proposed for the industrial sector is $ 20 million equivalent. The unallocated balance of $ 1.59 million equivalent could serve as a contingency fund or be available for the inclusion of one or more further projects at a later date. [...] The plants will have competent and experienced management and, with their modern equipment, will be relatively low-cost producers. The total annual sales are estimated at L. 16 billion (U.S. $ 25.4 million) when full production is reached by all. Of this amount, it is estimated that L. 7.0 billion (U.S. $ 11.0 million) will represent foreign exchange earnings and/or savings. When in normal operation, the plants will employ about 2,000 persons.

say on the approval of the agreements, and showed a particular penchant for prudent and sound management strategies:

> The establishment and maintenance of a sound financial position has been discussed with the management of each of the companies. Agreements have been reached on the amount of share capital, the treatment of shareholders' advances, the ratio of long-term debt to equity, the limitation of dividend payments, the maintenance of adequate working capital, etc. [...] In most cases, an equity-debt ratio of 1:1 has been required. Some of the projects have a more favorable ratio. [...] In general, the required ratios are conservative, and more favorable than is usual in Italian practice. [...] In those projects where the share capital is supplemented by shareholders' advances, these advances have been subordinated to the proposed loans from Bank funds, and are in effect to be treated as share capital; they cannot be withdrawn during the life of the loan. [...] For purposes of calculation an interest rate of 6% has been assumed on the proposed loans from Bank funds. The various terms suggested for these loans are based on the probable economic life of the equipment and on the expected generation of funds. The grace periods suggested correspond approximately with the construction periods. The terms on which these loans will be made by the Cassa may differ in some cases from those suggested, but will in all cases be subject to Bank approval. [...] No allowance has been made in the cash flow estimates for the payment of dividends. Funds will be available for dividends in each case, but it will be a matter of management policy how far these funds are paid out in dividends and how far they are used to accumulate reserves, to increase working capital, to retire debt, to make additional capital investments, etc. The funds available have been shown as accumulated surplus, with a corresponding entry shown as "additional assets"[136].

The detailed description of the single activities followed the examination of the main features of the projects, in order to achieve a full evaluation of the terms and the quality of each financing to be granted with the Bank's funds[137]. Rather than recounting the specifics of each project, it may be useful, given the aims of this analysis, to remind the entity of the total sum of the loan to support industrial activities, i.e., $ 20 million[138], and to give an effective overall vision of these interventions within the Mezzogiorno. The following picture (Figure 2.1), taken from the report's attachments,

---

[136] International Bank for Reconstruction and Development, Department of Technical Operations, *Appraisal of Italian Industrial, Irrigation and Power Projects*, May 24, 1955, cit., pp. 3-4.
[137] See *Ivi*, pp. 4-24.
[138] See *Ivi*, p. 3.

shows the localization of industrial projects within Southern Italy, indicating all the single beneficiary firms and the economic sectors they belonged to.

Regarding the only irrigation project approved – out of the five presented by the Cassa per il Mezzogiorno, which concerned the areas of Campidano, Catania, Metaponto, the Tavoliere plain and the Volturno river –, the report explained, first and foremost, the reasons for choosing the Sicilian territory[139]. Then, it carried out an evaluation of the status of agriculture in the area, followed by a precise description of the project itself and a forecast of the agricultural transformations connected with its implementation. It also included a report about management and organizational issues, directly involving the support, management, and supervision roles of the Cassa[140]. Finally, a table of the estimated costs, of the financing lines to be implemented, and of the project's expected benefits was set up[141]. Concerning the IBRD loan, it indicated that an amount of «$ 20,000,000 would be appropriate, and could be drawn before the end of 1957»[142].

Concerning the sector of electric power, the report pointed out that the Cassa per il Mezzogiorno had not envisaged such projects within the programs financed by its own funds: however, since an adequate diffusion of power plants in the regions of Southern Italy was deemed vital in order

---

[139] As it has been pointed out, with a series of very interesting motivations:

> Of these five projects, the Catania project has been chosen as having highest priority, because: a) it is the most productive of the irrigation projects in the long run; b) it concentrates primarily on citrus fruits and provides Italy with an important export crop, and thus strengthens her balance of payments outlook; c) Sicily is one of the most over-populated regions of Italy and suffers from serious under-employment. Irrigated citrus production is the most labor-intensive form of land transformation; d) its execution and successful operation ties in harmoniously with the industrial projects in the island which are recommended for Bank financing: a citrus processing plant, a cement plant, two fertilizer plants and a pharmaceutical plant producing insecticides

(International Bank for Reconstruction and Development, Department of Technical Operations, *Appraisal of Italian Industrial, Irrigation and Power Projects*, May 24, 1955, cit., p. 25).

[140] See *Ivi*, pp. 25-29.

[141] See *Ivi*, pp. 30-32.

[142] *Ivi*, p. 33.

Figure 2.1 *Location of industrial projects in Southern Italy (1955)*

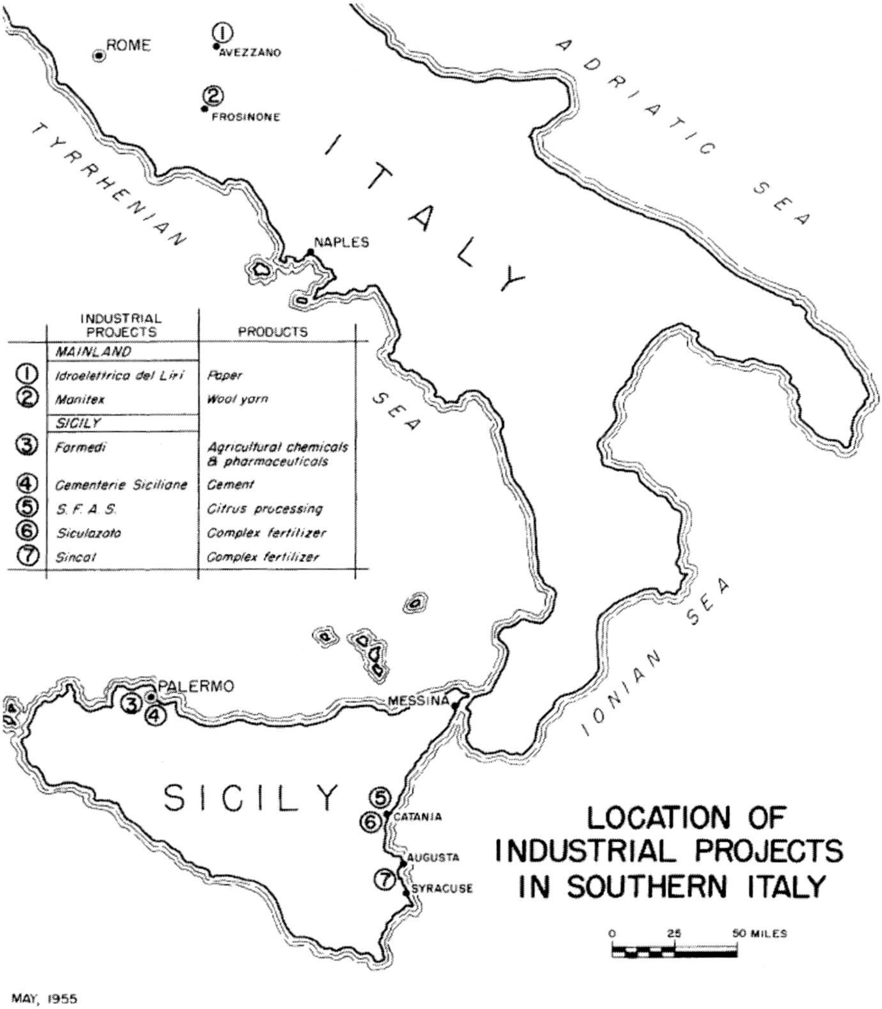

Source: International Bank for Reconstruction and Development, Department of Technical Operations, *Appraisal of Italian Industrial, Irrigation and Power Projects*, T.O.–84a/Restricted, May 24, 1955, Annex 1, <https://documents.worldbank.org/en/publication/documents-reports/documentdetail/821031468042537885/italy-third-southern-italy-development-project>.

to promote economic development, the Bank included this sector as well as a meaningful field within the activity of financial support started in Italy[143]. Thus, as the 1955 document pointed out:

> The programs of nine companies operating in the Cassa area were submitted for Bank consideration. Out of this group, three companies, namely Società Meridionale di Elettricità (SME), Società Generale Pugliese di Elettricità (Pugliese) (a subsidiary of SME) and Unione Esercizi Elettrici (UNES) were selected, since the expansion of their facilities has high priority in the Cassa area[144].

This part of the report also stated that the projects included in the program on the three power companies had been identified as the reference for the greater part of the loan requested by Italy, amounting to $ 30 million out of the overall $ 70 million. This financing would have to be subdivided, granting an amount of $ 9 million to SME, $ 12 million to the Società Generale Pugliese di Elettricità and $ 9 million to the UNES[145]. The following parts of the document explained in detail the evolution, the status and the initiatives of those power companies in Southern Italy that would receive the loan, further discussing the features of the companies involved, of their relevant markets, of their investment programs and of the projects they submitted to the IBRD[146]. The final part of the report concerned themes such as electric power production costs, energy tariffs and the security of financial agreements, reaching the conclusion that the projects proposed for a loan in this sector were sound[147]. The Figure 2.2 shows the localization of power development projects, with an emphasis on the Mezzogiorno areas.

---

143 See *Ivi*, p. 34.
144 *Ibidem*.
145 See *Ibidem*.
146 See *Ivi*, pp. 34-59.
147 See *Ivi*, pp. 60-63.

Figure 2.2 *The location of power projects in Italy (1955)*

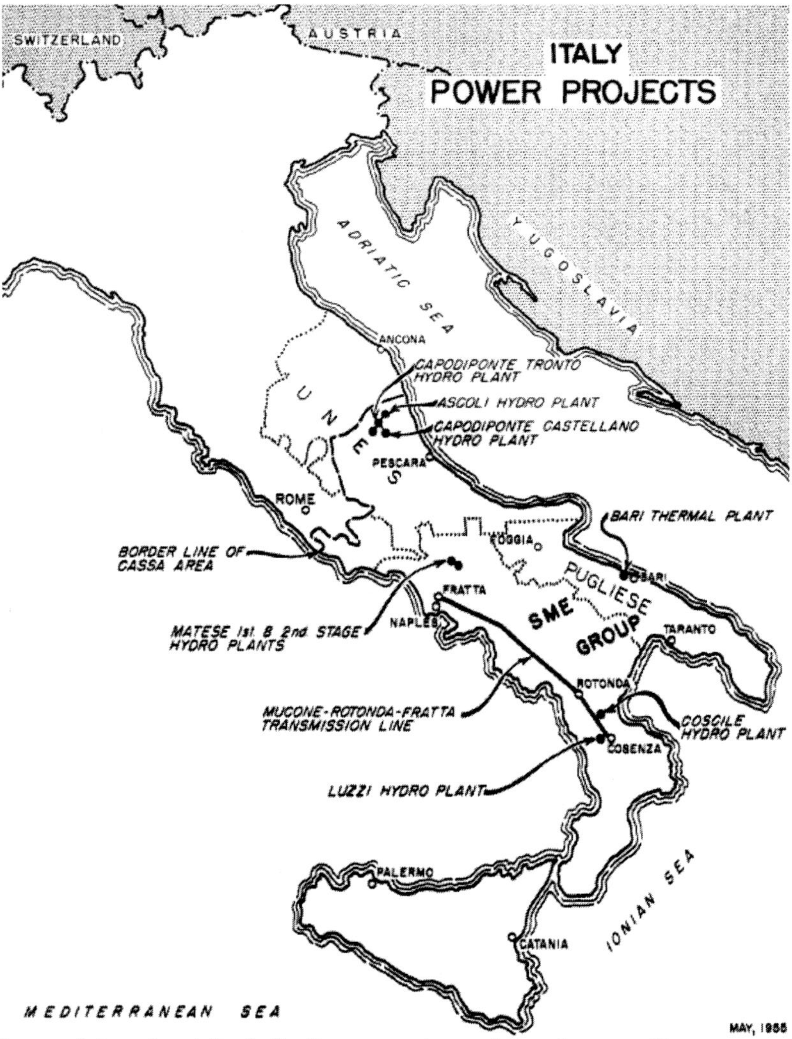

Source: International Bank for Reconstruction and Development, Department of Technical Operations, *Appraisal of Italian Industrial, Irrigation and Power Projects*, T.O.–84a/Restricted, May 24, 1955, Annex 17, <https://documents.worldbank.org/en/publication/documents-reports/documentdetail/821031468042537885/italy-third-southern-italy-development-project>.

In the second document, issued on May 24, 1955, titled *Report and Recommendations of the President to the Executive Directors on the Loan Application of the Cassa per Opere Straordinarie di Pubblico Interesse nell'Italia Meridionale (Cassa per il Mezzogiorno) guaranteed by the Republic of Italy*, whose disclosure was authorized on June 24, 2010, the President of the International Bank for Reconstruction and Development, Eugene Robert Black, carried out a reconnaissance on the hypothesis of a $ 70 million loan to be granted to Italy – as explained above – in order to finance 11 projects involving electric power, industry and irrigation, both in the peninsular areas of Southern Italy and in Sicily[148]. After a recapitulation of the previous phases[149], the report made a reference to the new loan,

[148] See International Bank for Reconstruction and Development, *Report and Recommendations of the President to the Executive Directors on the Loan Application of the Cassa per Opere Straordinarie di Pubblico Interesse nell'Italia Meridionale (Cassa per il Mezzogiorno) guaranteed by the Republic of Italy*, P–85/Restricted, Archives/Records Center, Room HB1–001, Box 935–01, Nus Location 099–1–2, May 24, 1955,
<https://documents.worldbank.org/en/publication/documents-reports/documentdetail/167661468039062077/italy-third-southern-italy-development-project>.

[149] In the initial parts of the relation, the following was in fact reminded:

> In August 1950, a 10-year Development Plan (since enlarged to a 12-year Plan) for the development of Southern Italy was enacted by the Italian Parliament. Thereby for the first time, the Italian nation commenced a massive and integrated attack on the centuries-old problem of the relative underdevelopment of Southern Italy and the Islands of Sicily, Sardinia, and Elba. The law establishing the Plan also created a new agency, the Cassa per il Mezzogiorno, charged with carrying out the Plan. The Cassa was set up independently of existing ministries, with a freedom of action going considerably beyond existing departmental procedures. [...] The Bank has already made two loans of $ 10 million each to the Cassa. The first loan (50 IT) was made on October 10, 1951, and was for 25 years at 4½%; the second (88 IT) was made on October 6, 1953, and was for 25 years at 5%. [...] These two loans to the Cassa were designed to assist Italy in carrying forward the 12-year Plan by covering a part of the impact on Italy's balance of payments in dollars and other convertible currencies, arising from the execution of the Cassa investment effort. Disbursements were made in dollars, based on lire expenditures of the Cassa on its over-all program in the proportion of $ 10 million to lire 100 billion

(International Bank for Reconstruction and Development, *Report and Recommendations of the President to the Executive Directors on the Loan Application of the Cassa per Opere Straordinarie di Pubblico Interesse nell'Italia Meridionale (Cassa per il Mezzogiorno) guaranteed by the Republic of Italy*, May 24, 1955, cit., p. 1).

illustrating its fundamental motivations and explaining the request of a significant increase of its financial endowment, taking the whole situation into account:

> Last year [1954] the Italian Government proposed that the rate of Bank lending to Italy should be substantially increased in view of Italy's increased needs and Italy's ability to service larger loans, and requested consideration of a loan of $ 70 million for the next year. The Government also indicated it would wish to present similar loan proposals during the following few years, if Italy's creditworthiness should continue to improve, and if the Bank agreed that Italy's financial needs would justify assistance of this magnitude[150].

In the same historical recap, the document went on detailing the process of presentation, verification, and approval of the Italian projects, whose preliminary examination had been carried out both by the mission led by Sidney P. Wheelock in Rome and by the Bank's staff in Washington at the same time. Following such examination and evaluation, the decision of allocating the loan to the three aforementioned sectors was taken, and the selection of the single projects started[151].

---

[150] *Ibidem*. The following page of the document, Eugene Robert Black noted that:

> After considering the review of the creditworthiness of Italy [...], I discussed the Italian loan proposal with Budget Minister Vanoni and Governor Menichella in Washington at the time of the Bank's Ninth Annual Meeting. I told them that I would be prepared to recommend to the Board a loan of this magnitude to finance specific projects in the program of the Cassa per il Mezzogiorno or related to the program, providing that projects of this magnitude suitable for Bank financing could be found. The Italian representatives were also informed that, although no commitment could be taken with respect to possible further loans, I expected the Bank's relationship with Italy to be a continuing one and future loan requests would be studied in the light of the then existing situation.

[151] See International Bank for Reconstruction and Development, *Report and Recommendations of the President to the Executive Directors on the Loan Application of the Cassa per Opere Straordinarie di Pubblico Interesse nell'Italia Meridionale (Cassa per il Mezzogiorno) guaranteed by the Republic of Italy*, May 24, 1955, cit., p. 2. In this regard, on the same page, Black specified that:

> Agreement in principle on the broad aspects of the setup of the proposed loan was reached during April and I visited Rome on May 2 and 3 to discuss other general matters affecting future relations between the Bank and the Government of Italy. Meanwhile it had become apparent that because of the complexity of the operation and of the number of negotiations and interests involved, the Bank's usual practice of negotiating loans in Washington would not be appropriate in this case. Therefore, Mr. Martin M. Rosen,

The section of the report focusing on the description of the loan proposal pointed out the following: the beneficiary of the loan was the "Cassa per Opere Straordinarie di Pubblico Interesse nell'Italia Meridionale" and the guarantor was the Italian Republic; the loan amounted to $ 70 million, provided in various currencies; the aim of the loan was to promote the economic and social development of the Mezzogiorno and of Sicily, besides achieving the complementary goal of improving the Italian position concerning its balance of payments and to increase the availability of resources for investments, without inflationary effects. The terms of the loan involved biannual payments for amortization, with a due date of July 15, 1975 and the acknowledgment of interests at a 4.75% rate, including a 1% commission.

Furthermore, the legal documents involved a loan contract, a guarantee agreement and three project agreements[152]. The part of the report that focused on evaluating the financing proposal put emphasis on the shift from rock-solid confidence in the activities of the Cassa, based on expectations, to an initial judgment based on the effective outcomes of its activities, maintaining that:

> The Cassa Plan as originally drawn up proposed a solution to a problem which had proved intractable for centuries. Our study and appraisal of this Plan convinced us that it would be a justified risk to give it some initial encouragement on a modest scale. In October 1951, at the time of the first loan, only the most preliminary work of organization and study had been carried out by the Cassa, and the loan was necessarily based more on the expectation of what the Cassa would be able to do than on any record of accomplishment. Even at the time of the second loan, in October 1953, it was still too early to make a critical evaluation of the results of the Cassa Program although by that time many of its operations were well under way. It was, however, at least clear at that time that the Cassa was beginning to live up to the responsibilities for which it had been created and the Bank

Assistant Director of the Department of Operations Europe, Africa and Australasia, arrived in Rome on May 1 to carry the negotiations to the final stage. Negotiations proceeded smoothly and agreement was reached on the draft documents by May 18, 1955.

152 See International Bank for Reconstruction and Development, *Report and Recommendations of the President to the Executive Directors on the Loan Application of the Cassa per Opere Straordinarie di Pubblico Interesse nell'Italia Meridionale (Cassa per il Mezzogiorno) guaranteed by the Republic of Italy*, May 24, 1955, cit., pp. 2-5.

> believed that a continuation of its support would be appropriate until a more definitive judgment could be made[153].

This document went on considering the economic effects of the Cassa's program, which proved to be very significant, «not only on the South but on all Italy»[154]. Starting with this analysis, Eugene Robert Black recalled that: «I believe that continued support by the Bank of the Program for the development of the South undertaken by the Cassa per il Mezzogiorno is

---

[153] *Ivi*, p. 5. Both on the same and on the following page, Eugene Robert Black, expressing a positive evaluation on the first phase of the Cassa's activity, briefly stated that:

> In view of the magnitude of the loan requested by the Italian authorities, the fact that the Cassa had been in operation for over four years, and that the Plan had been modified and expanded to a 1,280 billion lire program over 12 years, rather than the original 1,000 billion lire for 10 years, I thought it necessary that a fresh review of the Cassa Program and its contribution to the economic development of Southern Italy be undertaken. The results of this study are contained in the report on "The Cassa per il Mezzogiorno and the Economic Development of Southern Italy", EA-51a, circulated to the Board on May 20, 1955 (R-879). This report concludes that the Cassa Program is an appropriate means for the economic development of Southern Italy and a stimulating influence on the rest of the country. Some of the initial problems which retarded the progress of the Plan during the first two years have been overcome and progress has been considerable. In the agricultural sector, which is most important both from the standpoint of money allocated to it and from its contribution to the over-all goals of the Cassa, works have been completed for the drainage of about 18,000 hectares and the irrigation of about 30,000 hectares. Nearly 1,500 kilometers of rural roads have been built and more than 20,000 hectares reforested in mountainous areas. [...] Most of the works are still in progress, however, and the rate of completion should increase rapidly during the next few years.

[154] International Bank for Reconstruction and Development, *Report and Recommendations of the President to the Executive Directors on the Loan Application of the Cassa per Opere Straordinarie di Pubblico Interesse nell'Italia Meridionale (Cassa per il Mezzogiorno) guaranteed by the Republic of Italy*, May 24, 1955, cit., p. 6. The passage continued, highlighting that:

> The execution of the Program has resulted in increased employment equivalent to about 200,000 full-time jobs and the income created by this additional employment is approximately 2% of total Italian national income. The stimulation to industry resulting from the Program has caused an investment of approximately 200 billion lire ($ 320 million equivalent) in about 1,750 private industrial undertakings in the South, which should employ about 90,000 additional workers upon completion.

well justified»[155]. Furthermore, the new financing proposal appeared similar to the two previous loans, particularly on the allocation of sums in foreign currencies to Italy, in order to fund the initiatives carried out by the Cassa in Italian lire. Nevertheless, it featured an interesting elucidation which, amongst other things, clarified that the special feature of this intervention was that it was not connected with the overall expenses needed to implement the investment:

> The normal type of Bank loan, which is limited to the financing of the imported equipment requirements for specific projects, is not appropriate to Italy's requirements because Italy, although underdeveloped in the South, is highly industrialized in the North and produces almost all the equipment needed for the execution of the projects being financed. A local expenditure loan of the type proposed is the only effective way in which the Bank can make a significant contribution to meeting Italy's needs for foreign assistance in carrying out the investment program in Southern Italy. Unlike the earlier loans, the proceeds of this loan will be disbursed for the direct financing of specific projects in accordance with their needs rather than in relation to the total expenditures by the Cassa on the overall Plan[156].

This document ended with a remark concerning Italy's economic conditions – which had substantially improved since 1950, when the postwar reconstruction had been completed – that confirmed the possibility of warranting the compliance with the loan's obligations:

> Italy has made substantial progress since 1950 when the reconstruction phase of the postwar period was completed. There has been an increase in real national income at the rate of about 5% per annum since then which has made possible an increase both in consumption and in investment. Agricultural production has been increasing, and during the next few years Italy should be able to achieve a balanced position in its exports and imports of agricultural products, thus eliminating the burden of the drain on its balance of payments arising from the need to import foodstuffs. […] Recent discoveries of methane and petroleum indicate that Italy is richer in natural resources, especially in the field of energy resources, than had previously been known. The output of Italy's manufacturing industry has expanded considerably and has become more competitive. Italy's membership in the European Iron and Steel Community has resulted in its manufacturing

---

[155] International Bank for Reconstruction and Development, *Report and Recommendations of the President to the Executive Directors on the Loan Application of the Cassa per Opere Straordinarie di Pubblico Interesse nell'Italia Meridionale (Cassa per il Mezzogiorno) guaranteed by the Republic of Italy*, May 24, 1955, cit., p. 6.

[156] *Ibidem*.

> industry having access to these important raw materials on terms equal to those of other European countries. [...] The expansion of activity which has occurred has resulted in an approach to the solution of the problem of chronic and growing unemployment in Italy. During the past two years, new employment opportunities were greater than the increase in the labor force so that there was not only no increase in unemployment but a reduction of about 100,000 in the number of unemployed. [...] The expansion has occurred without impairing monetary and financial stability. During recent years Italy has consistently followed sound monetary policies and the country is aware that a departure from these policies would have serious effects on the balance of payments. The deficit in the balance of payments was reduced from $ 429 million in 1953 to $ 274 million in 1954 and the analysis indicates there are good prospects that Italy can eliminate this deficit by the continued sound expansion of the economy[157].

Furthermore, the final part of the report contained a positive remark on the observance of the articles contained in the agreement. It also included a recommendation by the President of the IBRD, who expressed himself favorably on the loan to the Cassa per il Mezzogiorno, in «an amount in various currencies equivalent to $ 70 million for a term of 20 years»[158], and invited the executive directors of the Bank to approve a solution along those lines[159]. So, the path was open for the approval of a loan which, compared with the precedent credit lines, significantly increased the amount granted by the Bank for the development of Southern Italy, and that envisioned effective growth possibilities for the country as a whole.

2.2 The Cassa per il Mezzogiorno and the economic development of Southern Italy

Another document by the International Bank for Reconstruction and Development, also issued in 1955, titled *Cassa per il Mezzogiorno and the Economic Development of Southern Italy* – whose public disclosure was

---

[157] *Ivi*, p. 7.

[158] *Ibidem*.

[159] See *Ibidem*. The approval of the $ 70 million loan to the Cassa, following the already known procedure, came to be by adopting resolution no. 319, during a meeting of the executive directors of the Bank (See International Bank for Reconstruction and Development, *Minutes of the Ninety-third Special Meeting of the Executive Directors*, SM-93/Confidential, May 31, 1955, <https://documents.worldbank.org/en/publication/documents-reports/documentdetail/446521468253252071/minutes-of-ninety-third-special-meeting-of-the-executive-directors-held-on-may-31-1955>).

authorized on June 12, 2010 – examined the prologue to the extraordinary intervention, the program of the Cassa, its progress and economic effects, and the overall productivity of this initiative and its financial features[160]. The report evaluated the activities of the Cassa, its suitability as a tool to develop the Mezzogiorno, and the consequences of such a program on the whole of the Italian economy, checking out both the results of the first four years of activity and the primary objectives envisioned for all the twelve years of activity[161]. The part of the document dedicated to the premises of the extraordinary intervention highlighted precisely the Italian economic dualism, both in the context of its historical dimension and its different sectors:

> Italy is a country of sharp contrasts. The North, where 30 million persons live, is relatively well developed economically with flourishing industries and a generally prosperous agriculture. On the other hand, the territory lying south of Rome [...], with a population of 18 million, has remained badly underdeveloped. Many reasons account for this basic difference including those of geography, climate and history. Northern Italy, and especially the north-west part, lies adjacent to some of the most prosperous countries of Western Europe, while the South has found itself geographically isolated from the main centers of economic development. Similarly, the North enjoys a central European type of climate, while the very dry climate of the South has resulted in low per capita agricultural output in an area where the population is mainly dependent on agriculture. An equally important factor in the differential rates of growth of the two parts has been the difference in their political and social heritages. The growth of a commercial and industrial civilization in the North, with its emphasis on enterprise and innovations, contrasted sharply with the feudal structure which evolved in the South under the kingdom of Naples and Sicily and which existed from the time of the Middle Ages until Italian unification less than a century ago[162].

---

[160] See International Bank for Reconstruction and Development, Department of Operations Europe, Africa and Australasia, *Cassa per il Mezzogiorno and the Economic Development of Southern Italy*, E.A.–51a/Restricted, May 20, 1955, <https://documents.worldbank.org/en/publication/documents-reports/documentdetail/780051468253817105/italy-cassa-per-il-mezzogiorno-and-the-economic-development-of-southern-italy>.

[161] See International Bank for Reconstruction and Development, Department of Operations Europe, Africa and Australasia, *Cassa per il Mezzogiorno and the Economic Development of Southern Italy*, cit., p. 1.

[162] *Ibidem*. The document went on, in the very same page, giving some quantity of data on the North and the South of Italy:

The section of the report concerned with the program contained a reference to the history of the Cassa and recognized the role of the SVIMEZ within a framework of cooperation between the institutions involved in defining the choices to allocate funds[163]. The section also featured a

---

The great disparities between the North and the South may be readily seen from a comparison of some major economic indicators for the two areas. In the industrialized North, 39% of the labor force is employed in industry and transport, while 37% is in agriculture; in the underdeveloped South the respective percentages are 27 and 54, with much of the farm labor falling in the category of a surplus agrarian population. Furthermore, the average yield per hectare of such a staple commodity as wheat is 20 quintals in the North and only 10 quintals in the South, largely because of the persistence of primitive farm techniques. This situation has resulted in the average real income per head in the South being less than half of that of the North, and while only 3% of the population in the North is estimated to live below the "poverty line", fully 27% is in this category in the South. The low level of income in the South has naturally limited demand for the products of Italian industries, thereby aggravating the problem of industrial unemployment throughout Italy.

[163] As it was written in the document:

The Cassa operates under the direction of a Committee of Ministers for the South, under the chairmanship of Minister Campilli, who has occupied this position continuously since 1950. This Committee laid down the broad outlines of the Cassa ten-year program and allocated funds among the several economic sectors. By and large the allocation of funds was made on the basis of studies prepared by SVIMEZ, an independent and competent research organization, on the degrees of economic and social depression in the several Southern regions and the best means of alleviating these conditions. These allocations were intended to indicate the general magnitudes of the works which would be carried out by the Cassa in the different sectors of the economy and were not in any sense firm commitments. Even the size of the total program may be changed subject to the state of public finances and other considerations. One such change has already taken place in an amendment to the Cassa law of July 1952, which extended the extraordinary public works program from ten to twelve years and increased its funds from Lit. 1,000 billion to Lit. 1,280 billion. In allocating the additional funds the Committee of Ministers increased allocations to most of the sectors, particularly to reforestation and soil erosion control and included railroad construction works as a new sector in the program

(International Bank for Reconstruction and Development, Department of Operations Europe, Africa and Australasia, *Cassa per il Mezzogiorno and the Economic Development of Southern Italy*, cit., pp. 2-3).

synoptic table of the interventions envisioned by the ten-year plan and its extension into twelve years. On this, it was pointed out that while the initial emphasis on the program was put on the topic of public works – with a particular focus on those initiatives being able to directly contribute towards improving the environment for agriculture in Southern Italy – even since 1952 the field of action concerning the policies for the development of the Mezzogiorno had been significantly widened. This was mostly due to the conviction that a significant change for the better in the economic structure of Southern Italy would have required, more than a simple public works plan, the strengthening of the capacity of the Cassa in the field of industrial enterprise financing[164]. Actually, according to the indications and suggestions contained in the report, «the solution of the problem of the South requires the creation of a favorable climate for industrial growth»[165]. Table 2.1 highlights the allocation of funds within the different sectors of intervention, during the two different development plans carried out by the Cassa per il Mezzogiorno.

---

[164] See *Ivi*, p. 4. In the same report page, the following was pointed out:

> For this purpose the Cassa was empowered to lend Lit. 50 billion of its own funds plus any amounts it managed to borrow in the domestic market as well as from abroad. It was in line with this new approach that the Cassa contracted the two IBRD loans of $ 10 million each and reloaned the proceeds of the first loan to expand private industry and of the second loan to increase the hydro power generating capacity in the South.

[165] International Bank for Reconstruction and Development, Department of Operations Europe, Africa and Australasia, *Cassa per il Mezzogiorno and the Economic Development of Southern Italy*, cit., p. 4. On the same page, the IBRD, added also the following:

> Consequent upon this realization, not only were credit facilities for industry and power augmented, but a variety of inducements were offered to Italian and foreign businesses to make investments in the South. Foremost among these inducements are tax and tariff concessions.

Table 2.1 *The Ten-Year and the Twelve-Year Cassa Plans (Allocation of funds by sector, in billions of lire)*

Sectors	Original Ten-Year Plan		Revised Twelve-Year plan		Increase	
	Amount	%	Amount	%	Amount	%
Land reclamation, irrigation and improvement, (including reforestation and soil erosion control within reclamation areas)	440.0	44.0	466.5	36.4	26.5	6.0
Reforestation and soil erosion control (outside of reclamation areas)	50.0	5.0	163.5	12.8	113.5	127.0
Land improvement on farms assigned under the Agrarian Reform	280.0	28.0	280.0	21.9	0	0
Roads	90.0	9.0	115.0	9.0	25.0	27.8
Aqueducts and sewers	110.0	11.0	150.0	11.7	40.0	36.4
Tourism	30.0	3.0	30.0	2.3	0	0
Railways	-	-	75.0	5.9	75.0	-
Total	1,000.0	100.0	1,280.0	100.0	280.0	28.0

Source: International Bank for Reconstruction and Development, Department of Operations Europe, Africa and Australasia, *Cassa per il Mezzogiorno and the Economic Development of Southern Italy*, E.A.–51a/Restricted, May 20, 1955, p. 3, <https://documents.worldbank.org/en/publication/documents-reports/documentdetail/780051468253817105/italy-cassa-per-il-mezzogiorno-and-the-economic-development-of-southern-italy>.

The report went on to evaluate the progress achieved by the program of the Cassa per il Mezzogiorno[166], which – despite having begun its operations very slowly – had been able to recover and achieve, since its very beginning years, encouraging results, considering both the initiatives it

[166] See International Bank for Reconstruction and Development, Department of Operations Europe, Africa and Australasia, *Cassa per il Mezzogiorno and the Economic Development of Southern Italy*, cit., pp. 5-7.

started[167] and in the works it completed[168]. The following part of the document was dedicated to the economic effects of the program. It argued

[167] Within one of the two tables featured in in this part of the document, such early outcomes were considered and also, in particular, the number of the works for which procurements were secured upon the end of the fourth program year, and of the amounts for each sector.

Contracts awarded (June 30, 1954)

Sectors of intervention	Number	Amounts (millions of lire)	% of allocations in Original Plan	Revised Plan
1. Land reclamation	1,449	140,756	36.4	34.3
2. Reforestation	850	28,462	57.1	17.5
3. Aqueducts and sewers	473	57,121	51.9	38.1
4. Roads	1,175	82,172	91.3	71.5
5. Tourism	120	8,020	26.7	26.7
6. Railroads	82	21,516	-	28.7
Total (1-6)	4,149	338,047		
7. Private land improvements	28,637	64,935		
8. Mountain pastures	68	228		
Total (1-8)	32,854	403,210		

Source: International Bank for Reconstruction and Development, Department of Operations Europe, Africa and Australasia, *Cassa per il Mezzogiorno and the Economic Development of Southern Italy*, E.A.–51a/Restricted, May 20, 1955, p. 6, <https://documents.worldbank.org/en/publication/documents-reports/documentdetail/780051468253817105/italy-cassa-per-il-mezzogiorno-and-the-economic-development-of-southern-italy>.

[168] The works completed upon the end of the fourth program year have been included in the following table.

Works completed (June 30, 1954)

Sectors of intervention	Millions of lire	% of allocations in Original Plan	Revised Plan
1. Land reclamation	32,308	8.9	8.3
2. Reforestation	5,514	11.0	3.4
3. Aqueducts and sewers	9,990	9.1	6.7

that the impulse given by the Cassa to the economy of Southern Italy went beyond its material realizations, getting to represent a fundamental contribution towards positive change in economic conditions of Southern Italy[169]. The investments envisioned during this starting phase of the extraordinary intervention had as a matter of fact the twofold goal of rapidly increasing employment by means of various public works and of expanding the agricultural production in Southern Italy, the latter being a more reliable base for a constant growth in employment opportunities[170].

Table 2.2 *Estimate of Real Investment During the First Four Fiscal Years in Connection with the Cassa Program, including the privately financed share under the Cassa program of roughly 10% (in millions of lire)*

Sectors	Investments			
	1950/51	1951/52	1952/53	1953/54
1. Agriculture:				
Land reclamation	1,465	12,085	30,270	36,736
Reforestation	614	1,968	6,345	7,204
Private land improvements	5	4,690	16,657	22,686
Land improvement on farms assigned under the Agrarian Reform	700	6,500	19,300	33,700

4. Roads	37,437	41.6	32.6
5. Tourism	1,812	6.0	6.0
Total (1-5)	87,061		
6. Private land improvements	20,834		
Total (1-6)	107,895		

Source: International Bank for Reconstruction and Development, Department of Operations Europe, Africa and Australasia, *Cassa per il Mezzogiorno and the Economic Development of Southern Italy*, E.A.–51a/Restricted, May 20, 1955, p. 7, <https://documents.worldbank.org/en/publication/documents-reports/documentdetail/780051468253817105/italy-cassa-per-il-mezzogiorno-and-the-economic-development-of-southern-italy>.

169 See International Bank for Reconstruction and Development, Department of Operations Europe, Africa and Australasia, *Cassa per il Mezzogiorno and the Economic Development of Southern Italy*, cit., p. 8.

170 See *Ibidem*.

2. Roads	104	14,199	23,580	20,434
3. Aqueducts and sewers	122	2,874	8,619	12,234
4. Tourism	7	567	1,465	1,993
5. Railways	-	-	76	3,334
Total	3,017	42,883	106,312	138,321
6. Industrial initiatives	-	800	4,000	12,150
Grand total	3,017	43,683	110,312	150,471

Source: International Bank for Reconstruction and Development, Department of Operations Europe, Africa and Australasia, *Cassa per il Mezzogiorno and the Economic Development of Southern Italy*, E.A.–51a/Restricted, May 20, 1955, p. 8, <https://documents.worldbank.org/en/publication/documents-reports/documentdetail/780051468253817105/italy-cassa-per-il-mezzogiorno-and-the-economic-development-of-southern-italy>.

However, such investments were essentially expected to offer «the necessary push to send the economy of the South on the road to development»[171]. Table 2.2 presents an evaluation of the use and the outcomes of the investments realized during the first four years of the program. They have been estimated to amount to over a third of all the investments in the Mezzogiorno and to almost half of the public interventions in the area during that period[172].

According to the report of the IBRD, the effects of the activities of the Cassa per il Mezzogiorno were very significant for the Italian economy, and in particular for the economy of Southern Italy, especially concerning employment[173]. Furthermore, it was noted that the implementation of public works and, in particular, the beginning of supporting interventions realized

---

[171] *Ibidem*.

[172] See *Ibidem*.

[173] See *Ivi*, p. 9. In this very same page, the following has been noted concerning employment:

> The carrying out of the Cassa works has recently directly provided about 140,000 full-time jobs. In addition, the need to produce and transport various construction materials, machinery and equipment for the Cassa works and to satisfy the increased demand of the newly employed workers for a variety of consumers goods, has been responsible for the employment of an additional 50,000 persons throughout the country. If consideration is also given to lands already transformed from extensive to intensive agriculture or from dry to irrigated farming with the resultant increase in manpower requirements, the total rise in employment opportunities is in the neighborhood of 200,000 or roughly 15% of the unemployed in Italy [...]. The income created as a result of this additional employment is in the order of magnitude of approximately 2% of the Italian national income.

by private companies had already generated positive outcomes for the industrialization of Southern Italy[174]. Finally, another visible result of the initiatives of the Cassa was the significant increase for the life standards of the population in Southern Italy, that was proved by the trends in the consumption of several goods and services between 1950 and 1953. As reported in Table 2.3, many categories showed a greater percentage increase in the Mezzogiorno compared with the rest of Italy.

Table 2.3 *Percentage increase in consumption, 1950-1953*

Good or service	North	South
Electricity (subject to tax)	34.7	42.5
Subscription to telephones	52.0	59.9
Licences for radios	49.2	68.4
Animals slaughtered	15.4	22.6
Attendance at movies	45.8	61.3
Motor vehicle registration	52.6	68.3
Motor scooter registration	206.4	378.0
Tobacco	9.8	5.6

Source: International Bank for Reconstruction and Development, Department of Operations Europe, Africa and Australasia, *Cassa per il Mezzogiorno and the Economic Development of Southern Italy*, E.A.–51a/Restricted, May 20, 1955, p. 10, <https://documents.worldbank.org/en/publication/documents-reports/documentdetail/780051468253817105/italy-cassa-per-il-mezzogiorno-and-the-economic-development-of-southern-italy>.

---

174 See International Bank for Reconstruction and Development, Department of Operations Europe, Africa and Australasia, *Cassa per il Mezzogiorno and the Economic Development of Southern Italy*, cit., p. 9. In fact, always on this page, it was stated that:

> It is estimated that during the past four years a minimum of Lit. 200 billion have been invested by some 1,750 firms in either expanding existing industrial plants or launching new ones in the South. The estimated annual normal operating manpower requirements of these firms are in excess of 90,000 workers. The range of industries covered by this expansion is very broad, with primary emphasis, however, being placed either on investment materials required to carry out the development program in the South, such as cement, or on the processing of the increased output of raw materials in the area, for example paper, oil pressing and sugar refineries. Many other industries, including plastics, bricks and tiles, prefabricated building materials, woolen mills and chemicals, have been launched in the South.

In the final parts of the document, concerning the overall productivity of the program and its financial aspects[175], a checkout of the interventions promoted by the Cassa in several sectors was carried out, beginning with infrastructure and agriculture in Southern Italy[176], and the report concluded that:

> In the final analysis, the productivity of the entire Cassa program, just as its economic effects during the first four years of operation, must be measured not only by its productivity within the several sectors but mainly also in terms of its contribution to the over-all economic development of the South and of the rest of the country. During the past four years only a small fraction of the Cassa physical goals were attained; nevertheless, the contribution of the Cassa to the changing economic climate of the South and to the growth

---

[175] See International Bank for Reconstruction and Development, Department of Operations Europe, Africa and Australasia, *Cassa per il Mezzogiorno and the Economic Development of Southern Italy*, cit., pp.10-15. In the first of these pages, it was stressed the following:

> The Cassa program is primarily one of public works whose aim is to improve the productivity of Southern agriculture, help create an economic climate favorable to the general development and industrialization of the South, and lead to the improvement of the living standards of its population. As a consequence, the character of the Cassa's investments has been dictated by their long-run contributions to the output, employment, and living standards of the region. The Cassa program represents the use of public funds for the purpose of "opening-up" a region and making it possible for the people to make better use of its resources as well as of their own labor.

[176] Concerning infrastructure, the IBRD estimated the following: «The combined expansion in the road and railway networks should enable them to cope with the traffic requirements of the South during its early stages of industrialization. The aqueducts will supply a population of about 15 million with adequate supplies of clean drinking water and thereby improve health and sanitation conditions» (International Bank for Reconstruction and Development, Department of Operations Europe, Africa and Australasia, *Cassa per il Mezzogiorno and the Economic Development of Southern Italy*, cit., p. 11). Within another excerpt of this document (p. 13), the following was stated on agriculture: «Since the dominant objective of the Cassa intervention in agriculture is to increase employment and national output, its productivity must be assessed on the basis of these criteria. It is very roughly estimated that a total of public and private investments [...] in agriculture during the life of the Cassa of about Lit. 1,175 billion will increase net agricultural output [...] annually by approximately Lit. 135 billion. This would represent a net return to the economy on capital invested of about 12%. This is a favorable return on capital in agriculture and it reflects the real economic benefits of the Cassa program which lie in the utilization of unemployed and underemployed labor for increased agricultural production».

> in the national income of Italy has been very considerable. [...] There is little doubt now that the Cassa program is an appropriate vehicle for the economic development of Southern Italy and a healthy influence on the rest of the country. This view is now fully shared not only by Italian public authorities, but also by some of the most prominent Italian industrialists, financiers and economists.

Furthermore, the document recalled some elements of the financial situation in the area, referring to both the resources given to the Cassa[177] and to the status of public finance, as well as to the use of capital markets by the Italian Treasury[178]. In its final parts, this document features some comforting remarks on the activities of and the path followed by the Cassa per il Mezzogiorno:

> While in the present Italian situation the Cassa is a definite burden on public finances, it is not without potential rewards. Detailed calculations indicate that the additional revenues which should accrue annually just from the increased gross output of the agricultural program of the Cassa would be

---

[177] Within the report, amongst other things, the following was underlined:

> The Cassa is permitted to carry over unspent appropriations from year to year. It is also empowered to make forward commitments up to the full amount of its program and in advance of the actual appropriations

(International Bank for Reconstruction and Development, Department of Operations Europe, Africa and Australasia, *Cassa per il Mezzogiorno and the Economic Development of Southern Italy*, cit., p. 14).

[178] Concerning this issue, the IBRD carried out a punctual analysis, observing, amongst other things, that:

> Because of the heavy public investment program undertaken by the Italian authorities, public expenditures may be expected to exceed public revenues for some time to come. While the financial resources necessary for the carrying out of the Cassa program are provided for in law, the ability of the Treasury to finance these added investments in an essentially non-inflationary manner depends in large measure on the course of Treasury receipts and on its ability to float loans in the domestic and foreign markets. On the whole, the outlook appears reasonably favorable. Tax revenues have been rising both as a result of the continued growth in national income and of better enforcement procedures. Domestic savings are continuing to increase and while the demands on them are numerous, the Treasury may be expected to secure its share. Lastly, Italy has been able to secure some capital from abroad and the increasing strength of the Italian economy should serve to bolster this tendency

(International Bank for Reconstruction and Development, Department of Operations Europe, Africa and Australasia, *Cassa per il Mezzogiorno and the Economic Development of Southern Italy*, cit., pp. 14-15).

> sufficient to pay an interest of about 6% on the public investment in agriculture by the Cassa. Because of the prevalence of very high gasoline taxes, government revenues from increased motor vehicle traffic will probably yield at least as high a return on the Cassa investments in roads. Moreover, if adequate cognizance is taken of the stimulus the Cassa provides to other parts of the economy and of its contribution to the recent increases in national income, the immediate as well as the long-run costs of the Cassa program should not be too burdensome on the public finances of the country. Provided that the Treasury can borrow the necessary capital at home and abroad for financing the Cassa program from non-inflationary sources, it should be in a position to service the loans from increased tax revenues, at the same time financing a development program which increases considerably the national income and national wealth of the country[179].

In the final part of the report, there was a reference to the benefits of the extraordinary intervention for the rest of the country, and especially for the industrialists and financiers from the Centre-North areas of Italy. This was due to the fact that the extraordinary intervention did not stop its positive effects with providing beneficial support to the economy of Southern Italy, but extended them to the remaining parts of Italy, especially through an increased demand for investment and the consumption of goods:

> Although the South has been the chief beneficiary of the Cassa program, as was originally intended, the rest of the country has also felt its beneficial effects in the form of increased demand for investment and consumption goods. As a result of this, many of the leading northern industrialists and financiers who were somewhat skeptical about the Cassa prior to its inception are now enthusiastic about the outcome and are actively cooperating in the economic development of the South by establishing branch plants there[180].

---

[179] *Ivi*, p. 15.

[180] *Ivi*, p. II. Further down in the document (p. 10), the following was added:

> It is estimated that more than a third of the expenditures in the South have found their way North in the demand for either investment or consumption goods. The demand for 1,300,000 tons of cement, for 250,000 tons of cement pipes and for 60,000 tons of iron and steel tubes was satisfied to a good extent by northern industries, especially prior to the expansion of cement production in the South. Practically all the earth moving machinery and other construction equipment as well as many of the industrial and power installations were manufactured in the North. Lastly, the increases [...] of tractors, motor vehicles, motor scooters, and of a variety of consumers goods, served as a stimulus to industrial production and employment in the

This document was significantly different from the others that have been examined up to now, as it contained a wide framework of analyses and judgments concerning the progress of the program run by the Cassa per il Mezzogiorno and the economic development of Southern Italy; it is effective in giving clear indications on the main phenomena which began about five years after the start of the extraordinary intervention. The other reports by the International Bank for Reconstruction and Development, albeit keeping a constant focus on the general context in which the initiatives of the Cassa were carried out, were just periodical evaluations. Hence, they featured a smaller area of action, as they had the goal of evaluating the progress of some specific development program and its results, in order to renew the financing lines to Italy for its development policies.

2.3 A new turn in the strategies of the Cassa per il Mezzogiorno

The document issued on October 3, 1956 and dedicated to the "Fourth Southern Italy Development Project", whose public disclosure was authorized on April 16, 2010, had the same title of the analogous report issued in the previous year, i.e., *Appraisal of Italian Industrial, Irrigation and Power Project*[181]. It accurately detailed the development projects, as may also be inferred by the abstract thereof, which started with the usual reference to the twelve-year plan for the development of the Mezzogiorno and then described the main features of the projects:

> The Fourth Development Project for Southern Italy will further support the 12-year plan for economic development. The Bank already made three loans towards this program. The Government of Italy submitted a number of projects in three categories: industry, irrigation, and electric power. They are all designed to meet the established needs of the Southern Italy economy. A final selection was made consisting of 10 industrial projects, one irrigation project and three power projects. The Flumendosa irrigation

---

rest of the country as well as in the South. Thus [...], development of the southern economy, has not only benefited the South, but also the North.

181 See International Bank for Reconstruction and Development, Department of Technical Operations, *Appraisal of Italian Industrial, Irrigation and Power Projects*, T.O.–121a/Restricted, Archives/Records Center, Room HB1–001, Box 263–23, Nus Location 066–2–5, October 3, 1956, <https://documents.worldbank.org/en/publication/documents-reports/documentdetail/323931468049198829/italy-fourth-southern-italy-development-project>.

> project is one integral part of the Cassa program in Sardinia and is the only large single opportunity to increase agricultural production on the island. The three power projects, two on the mainland and one in Sicily, will all be needed to meet the growing demand for electricity which is evidence of the success of the Cassa program to foster the economic development of southern Italy. The various industrial plants, of which seven are on the mainland, two in Sicily and one in Sardinia, will complement the projects of the Cassa program. The impact of the project on the economy of the region will be very significant. The increase in farm production will provide additional business to traders, processors, transporters of agricultural commodities, as well as to those who supply the farmers with goods and services. The project will also have a favorable influence on employment, the number of man-days in agriculture alone will increase dramatically[182].

In the introduction to the document it was reported that in September 1955 the Italian government had asked the Bank for further financing, after the loans it had granted in 1951, 1953 and 1955 (the first two amounted to $ 10 million each and the third one amounted to $ 70 million, respectively)[183]. The International Bank for Reconstruction and Development showed its willingness to accept this further request, based on a list of works proposed by Italy, whose preliminary elements – concerning an irrigation project costing $ 85 million; five energy-related projects with a worth of $ 83 million; nineteen industrial projects for a total cost of $ 74 million – were presented during January and February 1956[184]. The examination of these intervention proposals ended with the selection of ten industrial projects, an irrigation project, three energy-related projects, and a final prospect, in order to obtain the availability of technical services supporting the initiatives of the Cassa by the Bank[185]. These fifteen projects – themselves a vital part of the development program for Southern Italy, since they had to be implemented by the Cassa or were directly connected with the goals

---

[182] *Ibidem*.

[183] See *Ivi*, p. 4.

[184] See *Ibidem*.

[185] See *Ivi*, pp. 4-5. In this part of the document the industrial projects were indicated, and they concerned Forino (cannery), Novilegno (hardboard), Chimica del Tirreno (fertilizers), Vetreria di Latina (pressed glass), Saint Gobain (plate and pressed glass), Viberti (truck and bus bodies), Fiat (automobile assembly), A.B.C.D. (polyethylene), Cementerie di Augusta (cement) Cementerie di Sardegna (cement); irrigation project, concerning the Sardinian Flumendosa river; the energy- related projects involving the Società Romana di Elettricità (SRE), the Società Generale Elettrica della Sicilia (SGES) and the Società Meridionale di Elettricità (SME), all power companies.

of the extraordinary intervention – were the prerequisites for a new loan, amounting to about $ 75 million, to be granted by the IBRD[186].

The other parts of the document described the general features and guidelines of the projects for each of the sectors involved, and a detailed examination of each specific proposal was then carried out. The industrial projects were financed for an amount of about $ 24 million, as it was the case with the previous, similar report – it showed even the same wording – the criteria used in choosing the interventions were meticulous, as the proposed projects were submitted to the Bank by the Cassa per il Mezzogiorno and then examined by the special credit institutions in the area (ISVEIMER, IRFIS and CIS), following the procedures set up for the loan[187]:

> In most cases involving expansion and modernization, Bank representatives visited the existing plant; visits were made also to the sites of a number of proposed plants. Meetings were held to discuss the projects with the promoting groups together with representatives of the Cassa and of the appropriate regional institutes. These meetings enabled the Bank to obtain additional information where necessary and also to form a judgment as to the capabilities of the promoting group. The most important factors taken into account in deciding whether to recommend a project for financing were

---

[186] See International Bank for Reconstruction and Development, Department of Technical Operations, *Appraisal of Italian Industrial, Irrigation and Power Projects*, October 3, 1956, cit., p. 1. In this very same page, the selected projects were listed, as well as the amount of the loan proposed for each of them, with indication of their amount for the industrial sector (23.963 million dollars), for irrigation (25 million dollars), for electricity (25.2 million dollars) and for the technical services related to the program of the Cassa (0.465 million dollars), for a sum total amounting to 74.628 million dollars.

[187] See International Bank for Reconstruction and Development, Department of Technical Operations, *Appraisal of Italian Industrial, Irrigation and Power Projects*, October 3, 1956, cit., p. 6. In the very same page the following was noted:

> the regional institutes [...] are to be directly responsible for making the loans. The funds required for the loans will be made available to the institutes by the Cassa out of the loan from the Bank. The Cassa takes the foreign exchange risk but the institutes take the normal commercial risks and administer the funds for the Cassa. [...] Before the submission of the loan applications, the institutes had examined both the projects and the credit standing of their promoters. The submission of an application to the Bank was, in fact, an indication that the appropriate institute had found the project sound according to its standards.

the benefits that might be expected to accrue to the Italian economy, the financial soundness, and the state of preparation[188].

The document highlighted the fact that the number of industrial projects chosen for financing had increased, despite the decrease in the number of the proposals submitted (more precisely, they went down from twenty-eight in 1955, to nineteen in 1956). According to the International Bank for Reconstruction and Development, this outcome depended on the economic expansion registered during this short period in the Mezzogiorno and it was a proof of the good progress of the first phase of the development program promoted by the Cassa[189]. This section reported again the description of the procedure to activate the credit lines, highlighting the contents of the agreements with the management of each firm involved, the terms of the loans granted by ISVEIMER, IRFIS and CIS, as well as the role of the IBRD, which kept the power to approve them. The new document differed from the previous one as it mentioned the regional credit institutions, and it recorded a reduction in the interest rate from 6% to 5½%[190].

---

[188] International Bank for Reconstruction and Development, Department of Technical Operations, *Appraisal of Italian Industrial, Irrigation and Power Projects*, October 3, 1956, cit., p. 6. It is also being clarified that, concerning loan procedures:

> Of the 13 projects examined in detail, 10 were selected for Bank financing, in the amount of about $ 24 million equivalent. Their total estimated cost is about $ 51 million equivalent. [...] The plants will have competent and experienced managements [...]. When operating at a normal rate, they are expected to have total annual sales estimated at Lit. 48.4 billion ($ 77.5 million equivalent). Their potential foreign exchange earnings and/or savings are estimated at Lit. 6.0 billion ($ 9.6 million equivalent). They will also make possible an increase in domestic consumption of certain items (e.g. cement, fertilizer, polyethylene) the sales of which would probably not increase if the items had to be imported. [...] When in normal operation, the projects will provide employment for about 3,100 persons in the plants and another 1,000 persons in directly connected employment

(International Bank for Reconstruction and Development, Department of Technical Operations, *Appraisal of Italian Industrial, Irrigation and Power Projects*, October 3, 1956, cit., pp. 6-7).

[189] See *Ibidem*.

[190] As the document itself indicates:

> For purposes of calculation, an interest rate of 5½% has been assumed on the proposed loans from Bank funds. [...] The terms on which the loans will be made by the several regional institutes (ISVEIMER, IRFIS or CIS) may differ in some cases from those suggested, but will in all cases be subject to Bank approval. [...] The financial forecasts make no allowance for the

The document then examined the projects in their overall features; this part came before each specific initiative was detailed; it was done in order to judge the terms and the amount of every loan by the Bank fairly[191]. Finally, the following graph (Figure 2.3) from the original attachments to the document, proved useful to pinpoint the localization of industrial projects within the Mezzogiorno, indicating the firms involved and their products.

After precise explanation of each industrial project, the report detailed the only irrigation project approved, i.e., the one concerning the Campidano area in Cagliari (Flumendosa), the bigger and more expensive intervention in the sector, which was financed for an amount of about $ 25 million, compared with an overall cost of about $ 85 million[192]. The document by the IBRD contained an account of the agricultural situation in the area where the initiative was to be implemented, a detailed description of the project, a clarification concerning management and organizational issues – directly involving the supervisory role carried out by the Cassa per il Mezzogiorno –, a verification on the progress of work, an evaluation of the costs of the relevant public works, an indication of the total investments envisioned and of the total financing sources, a forecast of the agricultural transformations

---

> payment of dividends. Funds are expected to be available for dividend payments in every case and, subject to a provision in every agreement binding the borrower to maintain current ratios ranging from 1.5:1 to 2:1, dividends are expected to be paid out

(International Bank for Reconstruction and Development, Department of Technical Operations, *Appraisal of Italian Industrial, Irrigation and Power Projects*, October 3, 1956, cit., p. 9).

[191] See *Ivi*, pp. 9-48.

[192] See *Ivi*, p. 49.

Figure 2.3 *The location of industrial projects in Southern Italy (1956)*

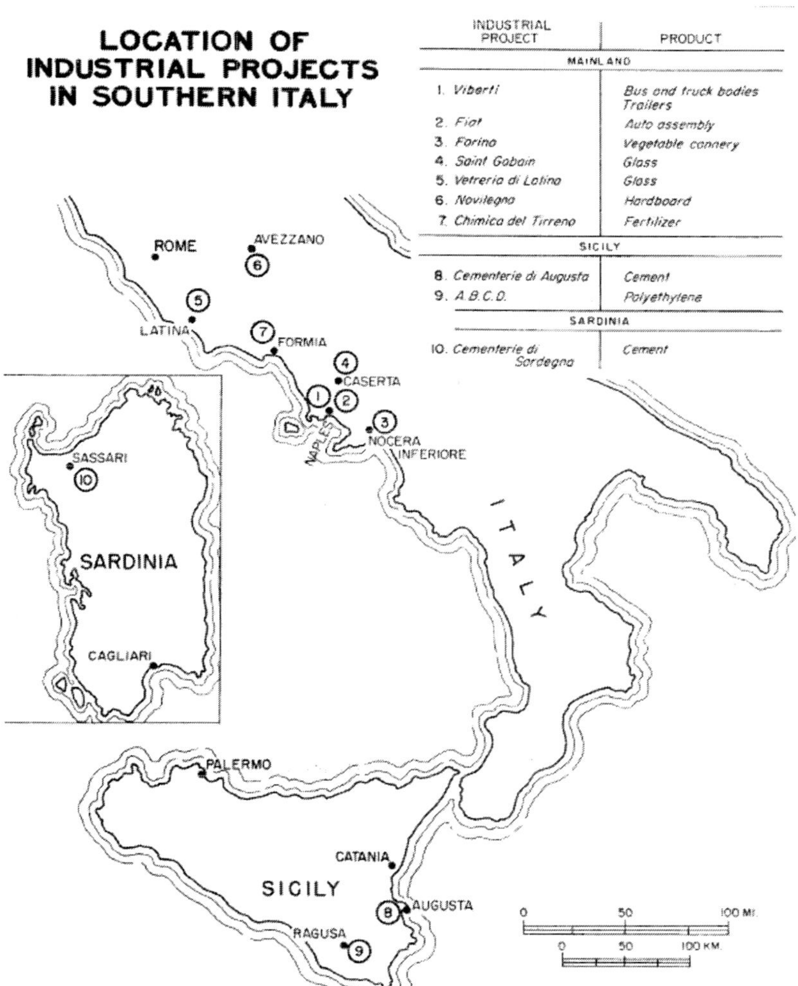

Source: International Bank for Reconstruction and Development, Department of Technical Operations, *Appraisal of Italian Industrial, Irrigation and Power Projects*, T.O.–121a/Restricted, Archives/Records Center, Room HB1–001, Box 263–23, Nus Location 066–2–5, October 3, 1956, Annex 1, <https://documents.worldbank.org/en/publication/documents-reports/documentdetail/323931468049198829/italy-fourth-southern-italy-development-project>.

that the project would have brought, and its benefits[193].

The report issued in 1956 also highlighted the absence of initiatives concerning the sector of electric power financed by the Cassa per il Mezzogiorno with its own funds[194]. However, in this case – as before – the Bank showed its willingness to tackle it as one of the main issues for the development in the Mezzogiorno:

> Six expansion programs to be carried out by companies operating in the Cassa area have been submitted for Bank consideration. Out of this group, three projects were selected, since they had priority in the Cassa area. They are to be carried out by three power companies: Società Idroelettrica Alto Tiri (Romana group), the Tifeo Company (a subsidiary of the Società Generale Elettrica della Sicilia), and the Società Meridionale di Elettricità, (SME)[195] .

In this part of the document, the main features of the three electric power companies were analyzed (first and foremost, their organization and

---

[193] See *Ivi*, pp. 49-66. Within the conclusion of this section of the report the lights in the shadows of this project were examined, expressing a favorable judgment to a loan by the Bank:

> The Flumendosa irrigation project is well-designed to bring into full production an area of 50,000 ha. A comparison between total investments and increase in farm production shows however that the project is expensive. The sum of public and private investments is estimated at Lit. 81.6 billion. Agricultural production is expected to increase annually by Lit. 12.7 billion. [...] Revenue on total money investments has been estimated at 4.5% which is low but still satisfactory. [...] In judging the project, one should, moreover, keep in mind that this irrigation scheme is the only large single opportunity to strengthen the agricultural economy of the island of Sardinia. The Cassa and the Ente Flumendosa are responsible for the execution of the project. The Ente Flumendosa is well-organized and competent, mainly, in the field of civil engineering works. The construction cost estimates are reasonable. [...] The arrangements for financing the public investment and the credit facilities available for the private investment are satisfactory until 1962. An undertaking has been obtained from the Government for the completion of the project in the unlikely event that the Cassa should cease to exist after 1962 as is presently provided by law. [...] The project is suitable for Bank financing. An amount of $ 25 million, to be drawn during the three years 1956-1958, would be appropriate

(International Bank for Reconstruction and Development, Department of Technical Operations, *Appraisal of Italian Industrial, Irrigation and Power Projects*, October 3, 1956, cit., p. 67).

[194] See *Ivi*, p. 68.

[195] *Ibidem*.

management, their structures, as relevant markets and investment programs) and the single projects submitted for an IBRD loan were then examined in minute detail (especially concerning the status and progress of the works, the estimated costs and expenditures deadlines). The financing methods and the credit lines were then verified[196]. The specific financing for the project, amounting to 25.2 million dollars, was to be divided by granting an amount of 8.2 billion dollars to the Società Idroelettrica Alto Tiri (SIAL), an amount of 10.5 million dollars to the Tifeo company (of the SGES group) and 6.5 million dollars to the Società Meridionale di Elettricità (SME)[197]. Furthermore, an evaluation concerning electric power projects reached the conclusion that the proposals appeared sound and that a duration of twenty years was justified for such loans[198]. Finally, in the following picture (Figure 2.4), the localization for the energetic development projects in the Center and Southern areas of Italy was shown.

Within the second document, issued on October 3, 1956 bearing the usual title of *Report and Recommendations of the President to the Executive Directors on the Loan Application of the Cassa per Opere Straordinarie di Pubblico Interesse nell'Italia Meridionale (Cassa per il Mezzogiorno) guaranteed by the Republic of Italy*, whose public disclosure was authorized on June 25, 2010, the President of the International Bank for Reconstruction and Development examined the hypothesis of a loan amounting to almost 75 million dollars to be granted to Italy, as highlighted above, in order to finance 15 projects to develop Southern Italy[199]. After a quick summary of

[196] See *Ivi*, pp. 68-98.
[197] See *Ivi*, p. 99.
[198] See *Ivi*, pp. 98-99.
[199] See International Bank for Reconstruction and Development, *Report and Recommendations of the President to the Executive Directors on the Loan Application of the Cassa per Opere Straordinarie di Pubblico Interesse nell'Italia Meridionale (Cassa per il Mezzogiorno) guaranteed by the Republic of Italy*, P–117/Restricted, Archives/Records Center, Room HB1–001, Box 935–01, Nus Location 099–1–2, October 3, 1956, <https://documents.worldbank.org/en/publication/documents-reports/documentdetail/412051468285875685/italy-fourth-southern-italy-development-project>.

Figure 2.4 *The location of the Italian power projects (1956)*

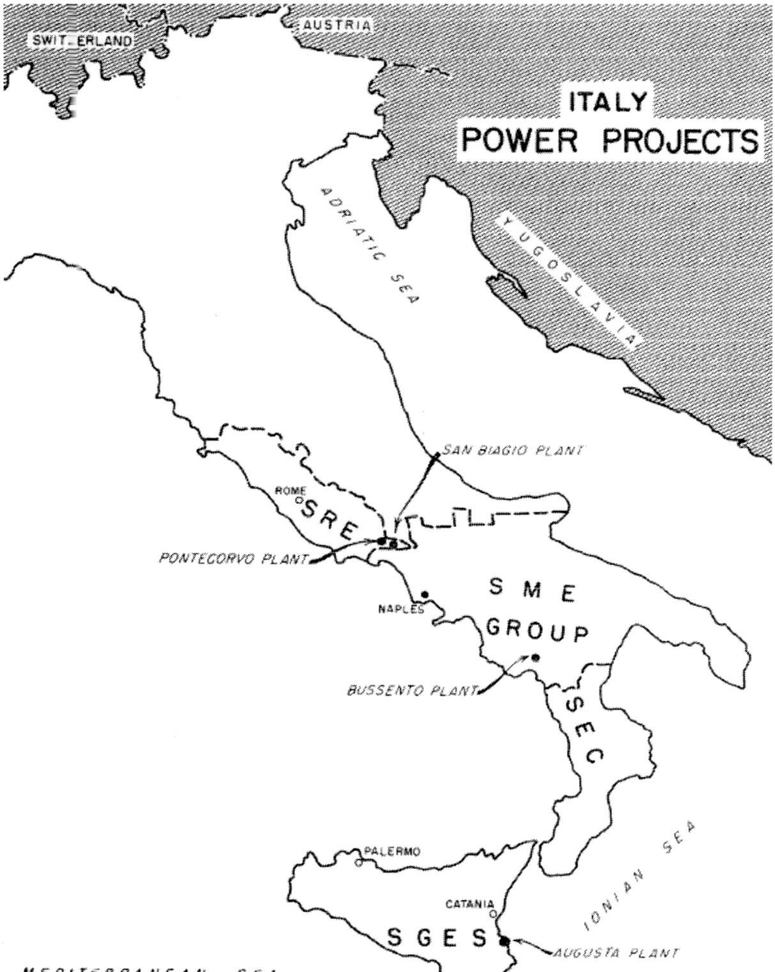

Source: International Bank for Reconstruction and Development, Department of Technical Operations, *Appraisal of Italian Industrial, Irrigation and Power Projects*, T.O.–121a/Restricted, Archives/Records Center, Room HB1–001, Box 263–23, Nus Location 066–2–5, October 3, 1956, Annex 30, <https://documents.worldbank.org/en/publication/documents-reports/documentdetail/323931468049198829/italy-fourth-southern-italy-development-project>.

the previous main points[200], Eugene Robert Black gave information about his trip to Italy, during which he had had the opportunity to appreciate the size and the status of the activities carried out by the Cassa per il Mezzogiorno:

> In September 1955, I spent ten days travelling in Southern Italy and made visits to Sicily and Sardinia. I was impressed by the scale of the Cassa's activity, by the evidence of the work already accomplished, by the size and difficulty of the work still ahead, and by the energy and ability of those charged with carrying it forward. [...] Following my tour of the Cassa area, I had meetings in Rome with the Prime Minister and with other members of the Italian Government, who expressed the wish that the Bank make a loan in 1956 similar in size and composition to the one made in 1955. I therefore arranged for members of the Bank staff to visit Italy to bring our assessment of the economic position up to date and to examine projects which could serve as the basis for a loan[201].

The document then went on to consider the new financing proposal, describing its main features, as it had been done within the previous report: in particular, this loan amounted to 74.628 million dollars, supplied in several currencies. Its goal was to support development in Southern Italy by

---

[200] The first part of the report stated in fact that:

> The Italian Twelve-Year Development Program for the development of Southern Italy has been in existence since 1950. The Program was designed to raise the standard of living in the relatively less developed part of Italy [...], by the investment of a sum equivalent to about two billion dollars. The Cassa per il Mezzogiorno [...] was created as the agency for executing the Program. [...] The Bank has made three loans totaling $ 90,000,000 to the Cassa. The first loan (50 IT) of $ 10,000,000 was made on October 10, 1951, and was for 25 years at 4-½%; the second, also for $ 10,000,000 (88 IT), was made on October 6, 1953, and was for 25 years at 5%. The third Cassa loan (117 IT) was of $ 70,000,000 and was made on June 1, 1955. It was for 20 years at 4-3/4%. [...] Disbursement, all in dollars, on the first two loans was completed in September 1954. As of October 1, 1956, $ 27,200,000 in various currencies had been disbursed on the third loan: $ 15,500,000 in U.S. dollars; $ 8,200,000 in Netherlands guilders; $ 2,000,000 in French francs and $1,500,000 in Swiss francs. One industrial project had been cancelled at the borrower's request, reducing the loan to $ 68,400,000

(International Bank for Reconstruction and Development, *Report and Recommendations of the President to the Executive Directors on the Loan Application of the Cassa per Opere Straordinarie di Pubblico Interesse nell'Italia Meridionale (Cassa per il Mezzogiorno) guaranteed by the Republic of Italy*, October 3, 1956, cit., p. 1).

[201] *Ibidem*.

financing power plants, irrigation works and private industrial projects[202]. After a summary concerning the features of the projects, involving also some of the technical services requested by the Cassa[203], the President explained the terms of the loan – which, like in the previous case, involved biannual payments for amortization, with the due date of September 1, 1976 and interest rates of 5% –, besides indicating some of the implementing procedures for interventions and the necessary legal tools[204]. Within the section of the report dedicated to the evaluation of the financing, Eugene Robert Black observed, by means of a wide line of reasoning, that:

> The Bank's interest in the Cassa program has been continuous since its inception. In my previous Reports and Recommendations I have given an account of its slow and careful beginnings and its more recently accelerating activities and have attempted to measure its achievements. Its record to date has been such that the Italian Government is giving serious consideration to prolonging the life of the Cassa for a further three years, i.e., until 1965. Consideration is also being given to placing more emphasis in Cassa activities on industrial development, the progress of which so far has been encouraging. [...] What account can the Cassa give of itself at the half-way mark? It has approved projects amounting to 51% of its planned resources and awarded more than 55,000 contracts. It has paid out against work in progress or completed work the equivalent of $ 760,000,000 on work to be completed by itself, and disbursed an additional $ 75,000,000 on loans to third parties. Induced private investments have added another 20% to the total of its own activities. In physical terms, it has completed 1,600 km of canals and improved river beds; 1,200 km of main and secondary irrigation canals; irrigated 46,000 ha. of land; constructed 2,100 km of new roads and

---

202 See *Ivi*, p. 2.

203 As indicated in the report by Mr. Eugene Robert Black:

> The Cassa has signed a two-year contract with the Development and Resources Corporation of New York, effective October 1, 1956, which provides for advisory and consulting services to the Cassa. The Corporation, whose members and personnel have had wide experience with regional development problems and practices in other parts of the world, will be available to assist the Cassa in the coordination of its over-all programming, and for consultation on specific problems as they arise. The Bank will contribute $ 35,000 to the cost of these services, the remaining cost over a two-year period, viz., $ 465,000, being included in the loan now proposed

(International Bank for Reconstruction and Development, *Report and Recommendations of the President to the Executive Directors on the Loan Application of the Cassa per Opere Straordinarie di Pubblico Interesse nell'Italia Meridionale (Cassa per il Mezzogiorno) guaranteed by the Republic of Italy*, October 3, 1956, cit., p. 3).

204 See *Ivi*, pp. 3-5.

> improved 9,300 km of old ones; planted 67 million trees; and brought potable water to 245 villages with 1,350,000 inhabitants. It is estimated that farm improvement works already financed by the Cassa would provide the equivalent of 47,500 permanent farm jobs, and that more than 100,000 new permanent industrial jobs have been created by investments in the Cassa area. [...] The Cassa program is an appropriate means for the economic development of Southern Italy, and is going forward at a satisfactory pace. However, much work is still to be done and the capital available is still limited. I believe that the Bank is justified in continuing its support for the Cassa program through the proposed loan[205].

The report ended, like the previous one, with a mention of Italy's economic position and perspectives, in order to check the compliance of the country to its obligations, with a reference to the conformity of this loan to the agreement criteria. It also contained a recommendation by the President of the IBRD that approved this financing on behalf of the Cassa per il Mezzogiorno, and invited the Bank's executive directors to adopt a solution among those lines[206].

As the first half of the chronological path set up for the duration of the Cassa per il Mezzogiorno expired, some fundamental features of the initiative to develop the more backwards part of Italy, corresponding to the Southern part of the country, began to emerge. These traits were strictly linked to international credit lines and the interaction with the Bank. This institution punctually followed and checked on the progress of the Italian economy, year after year, as well as on the effectiveness of those measures and proceedings adopted to implement the approved projects. The IBRD also followed the evolution of Southern Italy in those sectors interested by the interventions of the Cassa. The most interesting aspect of the IBRD reports (besides the significant amount of economic data and information) lies in the evaluations of the financing Italy requested and, most of all, revolves around the judgments passed by the IBRD on the advancement status of the development program for Southern Italy. After a slow start on the use of financial resources, the activities of the Cassa and its penetration within the economic and social fabric of Southern Italy became more and more deep and intense, offering an effective demonstration of a useful set of tools and of a crucial strategy towards the development and progress of Southern Italy, but also of the country as a whole.

---

[205] *Ivi*, p. 5.

[206] See *Ivi*, pp. 6-7.

CHAPTER THREE

THE MOST MATURE PERIOD IN THE INTERVENTIONS BY THE WORLD BANK AND THE ECONOMIC DYNAMISM IN SOUTHERN ITALY

3.1 The second phase of the loans by the World Bank and the penchant of the Cassa for productive investments

The second phase of the relationship between the International Bank for Reconstruction and Development and the Cassa per il Mezzogiorno was characterized by a smaller quantity of information produced internally at the Bank. This was partly due to the fact that interaction between Italy and the IBRD had become routinary, procedures had been standardized and the extraordinary intervention was deemed successful (and the majority of its functioning mechanisms had been already tried and tested), but it was also due to the attenuation in loan frequency. Nonetheless, this phase appeared similar to the previous period, especially concerning the regulation of credit provision and the supervision over its use.

The document issued on February 19, 1958, and dedicated to the "Sixth Southern Italy Development Project", whose public disclosure was authorized on April 16, 2010, had a similar title to the reports issued in the previous years, i.e., *Appraisal of Italian Industrial, Power and Irrigation Projects*[207]. It examined also other projects focused on the economic development of the Mezzogiorno, submitted by the Italian government in

[207] See International Bank for Reconstruction and Development, Department of Technical Operations, *Appraisal of Italian Industrial, Power and Irrigation Projects*, T.O.–162a/Restricted, February 19, 1958, <https://documents.worldbank.org/en/publication/documents-reports/documentdetail/827521468262473118/italy-fifth-southern-italy-development-project>. Despite its reference to the "Sixth Southern Italy Development Project", this document concerned the fifth loan made by the Bank to the Cassa per il Mezzogiorno.

order to obtain a loan from the Bank, as it was also indicated in the relevant abstract:

> In connection with the loan under consideration, the Government of Italy submitted a number of projects in three categories: industry, irrigation, and electric power. All these projects were either an integral part of the development program for the south of Italy being carried out by the Cassa per il Mezzogiorno or directly related to the objectives of that program. Ten projects have been selected as the basis for a Bank loan. The projects selected include two power projects, one on the mainland and one in Sicily, which are needed to meet the growing demand for power stemming from the industrial growth of southern Italy. There are two irrigation projects, which are an integral part of the Cassa program on the Italian mainland. The six industrial plants, of which three are on the mainland and three in Sicily, will complement the projects in the Cassa program proper, which is primarily concerned with large public works in the fields of agriculture, transport, and public health[208].

Within this report's introduction, it was observed that in March 1957, after the loans that had been granted in 1951, 1953, 1955 and in 1956 (the first two amounted to $ 20 million, the third amounted to $ 70 million, and the fourth amounted to 74.628 million dollars, respectively), the Italian government had asked the Bank to keep supporting the program carried out by the Cassa per il Mezzogiorno[209]. The International Bank for Reconstruction and Development stated its willingness to consent to a new financing request, provided that it was supported by a list of projects by the Italian authorities. The first materials in response to such indications concerned four irrigation projects costing about 54 million dollars, five energy projects worth 69.2 million dollars, as well as eleven industrial projects with a cost of 96 million dollars. The documentation was submitted to Washington during the summer of 1957[210]. After examining these intervention hypotheses, the IBRD concluded to choose six industrial projects, two energy projects, and two irrigation projects[211]. The ten projects that were

---

208 *Ibidem*.

209 See *Ivi*, p. 3. The loans granted in 1955 and 1956, for a sum total of 144.628 million dollars, were given after a single submission by Italy, requesting 200 million dollars and presented in 1954.

210 See International Bank for Reconstruction and Development, Department of Technical Operations, *Appraisal of Italian Industrial, Power and Irrigation Projects*, cit., p. 3.

211 See *Ibidem*. In this very same page, the industrial projects were listed, concerning CONE (electric appliances), C.M.I. (electrolytic tinplate), Marzotto (clothing), SINCAT (fertilizers and chemicals), Montecatini (potash fertilizers), Trinacria (potash

chosen were considered as a prerequisite, an essential part of the development program for Southern Italy, leading to the grant of a $ 75 million loan by the Bank[212].

In the respective sections of the documentation, one for each chosen sector, general features and guidelines of the projects were detailed, with a precise analysis of the single proposals. Concerning the industrial projects, which were financed for an amount of 29.36 million dollars, the criteria influencing the choice were highlighted, as it had been the case with previous reports. The projects were presented to the Bank by the Cassa per il Mezzogiorno and evaluated by the local special credit institutions (ISVEIMER, IRFIS and CIS)[213], according to the procedures set up for the loan[214]. Furthermore, in this section of the report, the regulations for the loan

---

fertilizers); the energy projects, concerning the Società Meridionale di Elettricità (SME) and the Società Generale Elettrica della Sicilia (SGES), two power companies; the irrigation projects, concerning the Volturno (in the province of Caserta) and Fortore (near Foggia) rivers.

[212] In the first part of the document, the projects were described and the amount proposed for each of them was indicated, with a sum total for the industrial sector (29.36 million dollars), electric power (29.2 million dollars) and for irrigation (16.44 million dollars), for a sum total of 75 million dollars (See International Bank for Reconstruction and Development, Department of Technical Operations, *Appraisal of Italian Industrial, Power and Irrigation Projects*, cit., p. 1).

[213] See *Ivi*, pp. 4-5. In the first of the two pages, it was noted that:

> Before the submission of the loan applications, the institutes had examined both the projects and the credit standings of their promoters. The submission of an application to the Bank was, in fact, an indication that the appropriate institute had found the project sound according to its standards.

[214] In this document, it has also be noted that, at the end of the loan procedures:

> Of the 8 projects examined in detail, 6 were selected for Bank financing, in the amount of $ 29.36 million equivalent. Their total estimated cost is about $ 68.16 million equivalent. [...] All the plants will have competent and experienced managements [...]. When operating at a normal rate, they are expected to have total annual sales estimated at Lit. 32.3 billion ($ 51.7 million equivalent). Their potential direct annual foreign exchange earnings and/or savings are estimated at about Lit. 9.0 billion ($ 14.4 million equivalent). The projects also make possible an increase in domestic consumption of certain items (e.g. read-to-wear clothing, electric appliances), the sales of which would probably not increase if the items were not readily available or had to be imported. [...] In normal operation the projects will provide employment for about 4,000 persons in the plants

(International Bank for Reconstruction and Development, Department of Technical Operations, *Appraisal of Italian Industrial, Power and Irrigation Projects*, cit., p. 5).

were repeated, effectively stating again the features of the agreements with company boards, the loan conditions, as well as the role of the IBRD. The main difference with the previous document was the interest rate, which had risen to 7%[215].

After an examination of the overall features of the projects, a detailed explanation of the single activities followed, to allow a full evaluation of the terms and the amount of financing by the IBRD[216]. Finally, the picture below (Figure 3.1), which was included in the attachments to the report, highlighted the localization of the industrial projects in Southern Italy, showing the involved firms and their sectors.

The document issued in 1958 regarding the power and energy sector stressed the fact that the Cassa did not include such projects in its program for the Mezzogiorno, which meant that they would not be financed with government funds. However, since an adequate presence of such plants was instrumental to promote economic development, some of the proposals by companies operating in Southern Italy were submitted to the Bank, which selected two of them in turn for the loan[217]. Therefore, by means of IBRD financing, it was possible to keep giving a significant impulse to such a productive sector in Southern Italy:

> Five companies operating in the Cassa area submitted projects for Bank consideration in connection with the proposed new loan. Of these, the projects to be carried out by Società Meridionale di Elettricità (SME) and Società Generale Elettrica della Sicilia (SGES) were selected as they were found to have a higher economic priority and were suitable to form the basis for a Bank loan. The two companies, which serve respectively most of the southern part of the Italian peninsula and Sicily, have at present a total effective generating capacity of 848 MW and serve a population of about 16 million[218].

---

[215] On this specific topic, it has been indicated that:

> For the purposes of calculation, an interest rate of 7% has been assumed for the proposed loans from Bank funds

(International Bank for Reconstruction and Development, Department of Technical Operations, *Appraisal of Italian Industrial, Power and Irrigation Projects*, cit., p. 7).

[216] See *Ivi*, pp. 7-33.

[217] See *Ivi*, p. 34.

[218] *Ibidem*.

Figure 3.1 *The location of industrial projects in Southern Italy (1957)*

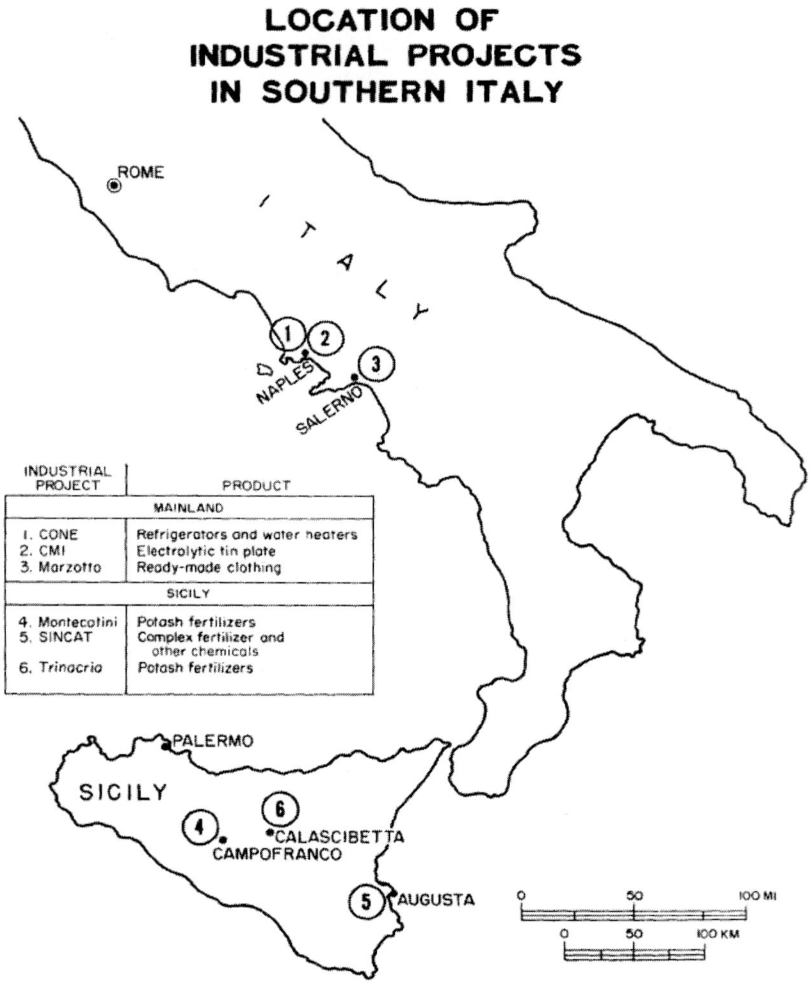

Source: International Bank for Reconstruction and Development, Department of Technical Operations, *Appraisal of Italian Industrial, Power and Irrigation Projects*, T.O.–162a/Restricted, February 19, 1958, Annex A-1, <https://documents.worldbank.org/en/publication/documents-reports/documentdetail/827521468262473118/italy-fifth-southern-italy-development-project>.

In this part of the document, the initiatives of the two power companies in Southern Italy were examined, with a particular focus on checking their essential features (i.e., organization and management, plants, relevant markets and investment programs), on financing sources, production costs and energy tariffs, as well as financial estimations[219]. The last part of the report concerned issues such as the economic soundness of the interventions and safety of the investments. The document concluded that the projects were sound and that the loan would be subdivided, bestowing a sum amounting to 22 million dollars to the SME and to 7.2 million dollars to the SGES[220]. In the following picture (Figure 3.2), taken from the attachments to that document, the localization of energy development projects in Southern Italy was described in detail.

Concerning the financing of irrigation projects, the document recalled the reasons for choosing two (namely those within the areas around Caserta and Foggia) out of the four submitted by the Cassa per il Mezzogiorno (including the areas of the Volturno, Fortore and Ofanto rivers and of Metaponto)[221]. Furthermore, a reconnaissance was carried out concerning agriculture in those two territories in which the interventions were to be implemented. The document also reported organizational and management features, a careful examination of the two projects and an evaluation of their costs, a planning of expenditures, a feedback on the progress of work, the total calculation of investment and their financing sources, as well as some forecasts on the transformations those projects would bring to agriculture, and their benefits[222]. Finally, the following statement was given on the IBRD loan, encompassing both for the project in the Volturno and the one in the Fortore area:

> The project is suitable for Bank financing in the allocated amount of $ 6.44 million [Volturno] [...] of $ 10 million [Fortore]. A term of 20 years including a 3-year grace period would be appropriate[223].

---

[219] See *Ivi*, pp. 35-53.
[220] See *Ivi*, pp. 54-55.
[221] See *Ivi*, p. 56.
[222] See *Ivi*, pp. 57-85.
[223] *Ivi*, p. 71 and p. 85.

Figure 3.2 *The location of the Italian power projects (1957)*

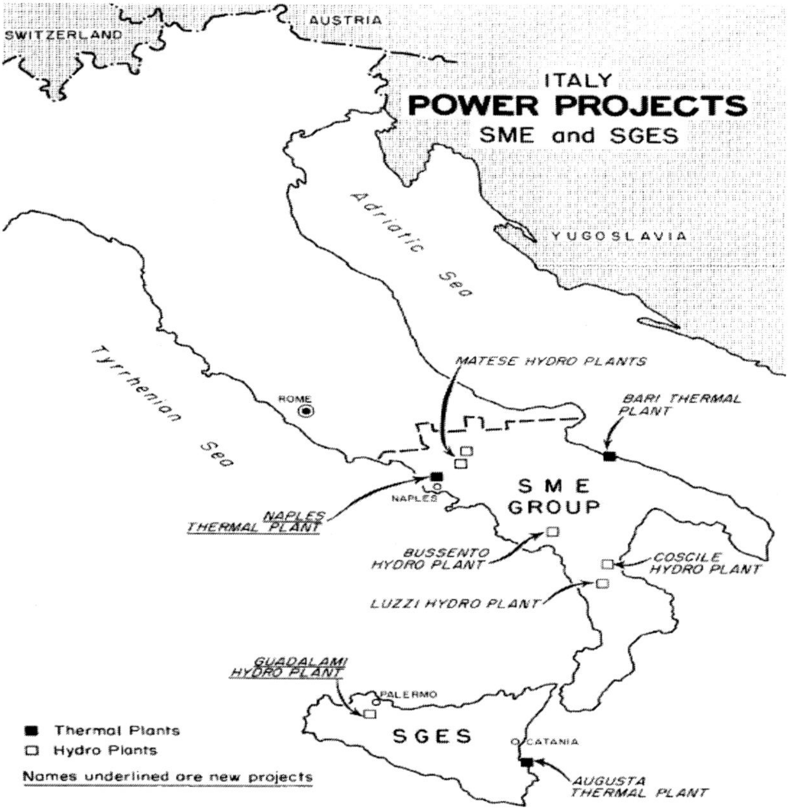

Source: International Bank for Reconstruction and Development, Department of Technical Operations, *Appraisal of Italian Industrial, Power and Irrigation Projects*, T.O.–162a/Restricted, February 19, 1958, Annex B-1, <https://documents.worldbank.org/en/publication/documents-reports/documentdetail/827521468262473118/italy-fifth-southern-italy-development-project>.

In the document issued on February 18, 1958, titled *Report and Recommendations of the President to the Executive Directors Concerning a Proposed Loan for Southern Italy Development Projects*, whose public disclosure was authorized on June 24, 2010, the President of the International Bank for Reconstruction and Development – Eugene Robert Black – analyzed the opportunity for a $ 75 million loan to be granted to

Italy, with the goal of financing and implementing ten projects to develop Southern Italy[224]. After a brief reconstruction of the previous phases[225], the note by the President described the financing hypothesis submitted to the Bank, and its more meaningful aspects, as was the case for the reports issued in previous years, beginning with the goals of the loan itself:

---

[224] See International Bank for Reconstruction and Development, *Report and Recommendations of the President to the Executive Directors Concerning a Proposed Loan for Southern Italy Development Projects*, P–152/Restricted, Archives/Records Center, Room HB1–001, Box 935–01, Nus Location 099–1–2, February 18, 1958, <https://documents.worldbank.org/en/publication/documents-reports/documentdetail/621201468253816639/italy-fifth-southern-italy-development-project>.

[225] Concerning these specific issues, Eugene Robert Black reminded that:

> The program for the development of Southern Italy was drawn up in 1950. Originally a 10-year program, it has been extended, first to 12 years and more recently to 15 years, i.e., to 1965. Over the 15 years about $ 3.2 billion will be invested in the effort to raise the standard of living in that part of Italy lying south of Rome and including the islands of Sicily, Sardinia and Elba. The governmental agency charged with carrying out this program is the Cassa per il Mezzogiorno. [...] The Bank has already made loans aggregating $ 164.6 million to the Cassa per il Mezzogiorno. Their status on January 31, 1958, is given below (in millions of dollars):

			Outstanding	
Year	*Amount*	*Repayments*	*Held by the Bank*	*Held by others*
1951	10.00	.46	9.44	.10
1953	10.00	-	10.00	-
1955	68.40*	-	62.40	6.00
1956	76.63**	-	73.63	1.00
	163.03*	.46	155.47	7.10

* Allowing for the $ 1.60 million cancelled. ** Including $ 900,000, but not yet effective.

> Members of the staff visited Italy in the fall of 1957 to bring the Bank's evaluation of the economic position up to date, to assess the impact of the Cassa program on the economy of the South, and to study on the spot projects which could serve as the basis for a loan. Negotiations were completed in Washington in February 1958. The proposed loan would complete the series of loans to the Cassa inaugurated in 1955 as a result of the request of the Italian Government for a loan of about $ 200 million

(International Bank for Reconstruction and Development, *Report and Recommendations of the President to the Executive Directors Concerning a Proposed Loan for Southern Italy Development Projects*, cit., p. 1).

> The purpose of the loan would be to aid the development of Southern Italy by providing financing for a selected group of industrial, power and irrigation projects. All the industrial projects are privately sponsored. One power project will be carried out by a publicly controlled and the other by a privately owned power company, and the irrigation projects will be carried out directly by the Cassa[226].

It was furthermore explained that: the beneficiary was the "Cassa per Opere Straordinarie di Pubblico Interesse nell'Italia Meridionale" and the Italian Republic was its guarantor; the loan amounted to \$ 75 million, provided in several currencies; the terms of the loan envisaged 35 bimonthly installments for amortization, ending on 15 February 1978, and it featured a 5½% interest rate, including a 1% commission; its legal documents were a loan contract, a warranty agreement and two project agreements[227]. After evaluating the projects' content and summarizing the main elements of the *Appraisal of Italian Industrial, Power and Irrigation Projects*, the President pointed out the main procedures for industrial supply and loan distribution, as well as his reasons for approval, based on the analysis of the Italian situation[228]. On this point, Eugene Robert Black reaffirmed his positive views concerning the interventions of the Cassa per il Mezzogiorno, which were deemed to have made the economic context of Southern Italy, and that of the country as a whole, more dynamic:

> By Italian legislation in 1957, new resources have been provided for the Cassa, its life has been extended to 1965, and by a shift in emphasis toward industrialization new goals have been set for it. Its impact on the economic life of Southern Italy, and indeed that of all Italy, has been remarkable. [...] Already 57,000 hectares have been provided with irrigation facilities out of a total program of 352,000 hectares, although the large irrigation projects for which the Bank has lent money are still under construction. Two thousand eight hundred km of rural roads have been built and 10,600 km of

---

[226] *Ibidem.*

[227] See *Ivi*, p. 2.

[228] See *Ivi*, pp. 3-4. In the second of these two pages, in particular, concerning loan distribution, the following was underlined:

> As in loans 117 IT and 150 IT, the proposed loan will be disbursed against evidence of expenditure in lire on individual projects. This expenditure will be mainly for locally produced goods and services and it was therefore not possible to tie disbursement to specific imports. The loan will thus provide foreign exchange to meet the cost of imports arising indirectly out of the Cassa program. The Bank will decide the particular currencies to be disbursed in the light of the currencies available to the Bank at the time of disbursement.

> provincial roads improved. Twenty three thousand farm homes have been built and 621 new agricultural processing plants have been established. New aqueducts bring potable water to 2.7 million people in 572 villages. These and related investments have cost $ 1 billion. An additional $ 350 million of Cassa funds has directly or indirectly supported new industrial investment, increasing industrial employment in the Cassa area by 12% and value added by manufacturing by about 26%. In human terms, these figures mean the creation of 20,000 full time jobs in industry and 35,000 in agriculture. [...] Since 1950, a general improvement in the economy has taken place throughout Italy. In the North the existence of an established industrial complex with idle capacity, a pool of skilled labor and markets near at hand all favored economic expansion. That a comparable improvement has taken place in the South is attributable to the investments made directly and indirectly through the Cassa. In fact, the growth of agricultural production in the South has exceeded the national average and industrial growth has kept pace with it, and the results from current investment have still to appear. Cement production, with help from the Bank, has grown at double the national rate. Housing construction, power consumption, use of fertilizers and tractors, all indices directly related to the Cassa's program, have grown faster than in the North. During the life of the Cassa, income in the South grew by 71% as compared with 64% for the North, and this is reflected in higher consumption and savings[229].

The report ended, like the previous one, with the outlook on Italy's honoring its commitments[230], with an appreciation for the compliance of the

---

[229] International Bank for Reconstruction and Development, *Report and Recommendations of the President to the Executive Directors Concerning a Proposed Loan for Southern Italy Development Projects*, cit., pp. 4-5.

[230] These opportunities were based on the good trends in its own economy, as observed by Eugene Robert Black, who, amongst other things pointed out the passing, in 1957, of the number of workers employed in manufacture, compared with those active in the agricultural sector:

> The report on "Current Economic Position and Prospects of Italy" (EA 81) (No. 8) shows that real national income has continued its post 1950 rise of 5% per annum through the past two years. This growth has permitted simultaneous increases in consumption, savings and investment with a concomitant fall in unemployment. Agriculture suffered from the effects of bad weather during the past two years, but manufacturing, construction and service industries have all expanded rapidly. In 1957, for the first time, more people were employed in manufacturing than in agriculture. Public finances are sound and price stability has been maintained. [...] Exports have increased and so have earnings from invisibles. But imports have increased faster, in large part due to heavy imports of capital goods, and increased needs of industry for imported fuel and raw materials. United States aid and capital inflow have more than offset current account deficits and foreign

loan with the articles of the agreement[231], as well as with the recommendations by the President of the Bank, who expressed his favorable views on financing the loan[232].

3.2 The World Bank and the first seven years of the Cassa per il Mezzogiorno

In a document issued by the IBRD in 1958, titled *Cassa per il Mezzogiorno and the Economic Development of Southern Italy* (whose public disclosure was authorized on June 12, 2010), the premises of the extraordinary intervention, the program of the Cassa and its financial features, its progress, as well as the economic consequences of the interventions and their perspectives, were examined[233]. In the introduction to the document, the Bank recalled the four loans that had been granted up to that moment, and it offered an evaluation of the progress achieved by the Cassa per il Mezzogiorno during its first seven years of activity. Here, the

---

> exchange reserves have therefore increased. They now stand at $ 1300 million, higher than ever before. [...] Italy's debt record is good. Service charges on her external debt are relatively small. Annual debt service in 1956 was less than 4% of global foreign exchange earnings and this percentage will diminish rapidly after 1963. Italy is a good risk for the proposed loan of $ 75 million

(International Bank for Reconstruction and Development, *Report and Recommendations of the President to the Executive Directors Concerning a Proposed Loan for Southern Italy Development Projects*, cit., p. 5).

231 See *Ibidem*.

232 This document in fact ended with this indication:

> I recommend that the Bank at this time lend to the Cassa per Opere Straordinarie di Pubblico Interesse nell'Italia Meridionale an amount in various currencies equivalent to $ 75,000,000 for a term of 20 years with interest, commission and commitment charges and on such other terms as are specified in the [...] draft Loan and Guarantee Agreements, and that the Executive Directors adopt a resolution to that effect

(International Bank for Reconstruction and Development, *Report and Recommendations of the President to the Executive Directors Concerning a Proposed Loan for Southern Italy Development Projects*, cit., p. 6).

233 See International Bank for Reconstruction and Development, Department of Operations Europe, Africa and Australasia, *Cassa per il Mezzogiorno and the Economic Development of Southern Italy*, E.A.–80a/Restricted, February 18, 1958, <https://documents.worldbank.org/en/publication/documents-reports/documentdetail/752391468049200134/italy-cassa-per-il-mezzogiorno-and-the-economic-development-of-southern-italy>.

IBRD considered the initiatives already completed and the direction to point towards during the second half of its experience[234]. The first part of the document, right after the table of contents and the introduction, retraced the contents of the 1955 report of the same title. The new document recounted once again the differences between the economies of Northern and Southern Italy and the explanation of the reasons behind the creation of the Cassa[235]. However, the viewpoint of this report was by no means the same, as it highlighted the birth of the strategies to foster development in the Mezzogiorno, after the postwar reconstruction:

> Once postwar reconstruction was substantially completed, the major social and economic problem facing Italian authorities was that of persistent and heavy unemployment throughout the country and the continuing underdevelopment of the South with its concomitants of underemployment and poverty. [...] Several alternative approaches to the solution of the southern problem were considered in 1950. Increasing investments in the already developed North with a view to encouraging internal migration from the South was rejected on the grounds that considerable overcapacity characterized much of northern industry and that a substantial expansion in output could take place by the better utilization of manpower already available there. Similarly, any substantial increase in public works in the North was not expected to bring any benefits to the South through the

---

[234] See *Ivi*, p. 1. In this very same page, the following was pointed out:

> By way of providing the essential background, this report starts with a brief description of the differences between the economies of Northern and Southern Italy and an explanation of the reasons for the creation of the Cassa. It then proceeds to explain the steps taken by the Cassa to formulate a development plan for the South and to evaluate the Cassa's performance in carrying it out. This evaluation is largely based on the Cassa's record of examining and preparing public works projects as exemplified by "Contracts awarded". The Cassa's performance is shown in terms of expenditure on "works completed" and the physical progress achieved in carrying out public works within its program. The over-all economic effects of the Cassa, however, far transcend its own activities. In part this is due to the very nature of the Cassa program, which has sought from the start to associate private investment with its own public works, and in part to the general stimulation which the Cassa has provided to the economic development of the South. For these reasons, an attempt is made to assess the changes in the economy of the South during the Cassa's seven-year life. The report concludes with a brief analysis of the problems now facing the Cassa and of the economic prospects of Southern Italy.

[235] See International Bank for Reconstruction and Development, Department of Operations Europe, Africa and Australasia, *Cassa per il Mezzogiorno and the Economic Development of Southern Italy*, cit., pp. 1-3.

> movement of manpower or the purchase of goods and services there. On the other hand, immediate industrialization of the South appeared out of the question because of the overcapacity in northern industry and the limitations set by the local market. Confronted with this situation, the best approach appeared to be to launch a "pre-industrialization" program in the South, and the Italian Government undertook to increase the level of public investment under a ten-year development program for the South. [...] The major objective of this program was to raise the productivity of land and labor and to eliminate the economic waste involved in unemployment and underemployment. It was felt that an increase in the productivity of land and labor in the South would not only raise living standards within the region, and subsequently lead to its industrialization, but would also reduce unemployment in the North by stimulating demand for its industrial products and services. The Italian authorities placed primary emphasis on the development of a healthy and prosperous agriculture as a prerequisite for the entire region, an emphasis similar to that contained in various general survey mission reports sponsored by the Bank for underdeveloped countries. With a view to providing a degree of coordination and continuity which could not be [...] achieved by the regular ministries, the Government entrusted the execution of the program to a new agency, the Cassa per il Mezzogiorno[236].

In the sections dedicated to the Cassa program, the document offered a recapitulation of the Cassa's history, up to the moment when its mandate was extended to fifteen years[237]. The document gave particular relevance to the role of the Committee of Ministers for Southern Italy, as it set up the strategic guidelines for the extraordinary intervention and made a preliminary assignment of funds, based on the existing population and on the level of economic and social depression in various areas of the Mezzogiorno[238]. Furthermore, this part of the report included a summary, similar to the one featured in a previous text from 1955, concerning the allocation of financing between the main sectors of interventions of the

---

[236] *Ivi*, pp. 2-3.

[237] This report does indeed underline that:

> In July 1952 the life of the Cassa was extended from ten to twelve years and its funds were increased from a total of Lit. 1,000 billion ($ 1.6 billion) to Lit. 1,280 billion ($ 2 billion). In July 1957, a new law further extended the life of the Cassa to a total of fifteen years ending in 1965 and raised its appropriations by an additional Lit. 760 billion ($ 1.216 billion). The Cassa therefore will dispose of $ 3.2 billion over the fifteen-year period

(International Bank for Reconstruction and Development, Department of Operations Europe, Africa and Australasia, *Cassa per il Mezzogiorno and the Economic Development of Southern Italy*, cit., p. 3).

[238] See *Ivi*, p. 3.

Cassa, both in the 10-year and in the 12-year development programs[239]. After an examination of the initiatives envisioned for agriculture and the sectors connected to it[240], the document highlighted the evolution – since

---

[239] See *Ivi*, p. 4. In this very same page, reference was made to the summary table, indicating the main features and leanings of the programs carried out by the Cassa:

> Its "pre-industrialization" character is clearly revealed by the concentration on agriculture and on the linking of the various parts of the area by a network of roads. Although the relative proportion of agriculture declined somewhat in the twelve-year plan, it still claimed nearly 70% of the financial resources. On the other hand, transportation increased both absolutely and relatively through the addition of funds for the railroads. The health and welfare aspects of the plans are reflected in the substantial sums allocated to aqueducts and sewers. "Tourism" claimed a small proportion from the start and was further reduced, although many of the improvements in transportation and sanitation will also make the South more attractive for tourists.

[240] See International Bank for Reconstruction and Development, Department of Operations Europe, Africa and Australasia, *Cassa per il Mezzogiorno and the Economic Development of Southern Italy*, cit., pp. 4-5. In these pages, in particular, the following was clarified:

> A great deal of effort went into the formulation of an agricultural development program, which was finally adopted by the Committee of Ministers for the South in April 1955. According to this program Cassa intervention in one form, or another would affect 9,548,000 hectares or about 73% of the total farm land and forests in the South. This comprehensive coverage resulted largely from social and political pressures to alleviate on as broad a scale as possible the conditions of Southern agriculture. It was intended to create the impression that no significant part of Southern agriculture was to be neglected and that something was going to be done for nearly everyone. Actually, the extent of Cassa intervention was to vary greatly from one area to another. The most intensive effort in agriculture was to be limited to irrigating some 440,000 hectares. At the opposite extreme are some 3.4 million hectares among which some scattered reforestation was to be carried out. Within the remainder of the area, accounting for about three-fifths of the total, a transformation from extensive to intensive dry land cultivation was to be promoted. Specifically, the Cassa's land reclamation program contemplated that by 1962 it will have
>
> a) provided irrigation for 440,000 hectares, 352,000 hectares of the total being irrigated annually including 40,000 hectares coming under citrus cultivation;
>
> b) intensively transformed 550,000 hectares with tree-crops on small landed properties under rain-fed cultivation;
>
> c) developed 560,000 hectares of dry-farmed land at different levels of intensity; and

the beginning of the 1950s – of a critical aspect, that of industrial development. This sector was now concerned by a new law provision, approved in July 1957, which extended the duration of the Cassa to fifteen years, delegating it to carry out a significant effort in the direction of industrial development. The industrialization program was to be based on the original potential of Southern Italy, and was geared towards helping this area overcome its historical backwardness:

> Although the Cassa program started out as essentially a "pre-industrialization" effort for the South with primary emphasis on improving the output and incomes of the farm population, it was soon realized that the long-run manpower requirements of the more intensive agriculture resulting from the Cassa efforts would eliminate only a part of the existing agricultural underemployment and that employment outside of agriculture would have to be found for the rest. Furthermore, given the heavy population density in the South in relation to the land available, the opportunities for raising incomes through agricultural development alone were severely limited. Since the South has certain natural advantages that have not been fully exploited – her position vis-a-vis the Mediterranean and North Africa, mineral resources, (systematic exploration has only recently begun and oil and potash have already been found in commercial quantities); good ports with unused capacity; cheap and willing labor; and a growing local market, the need to eventually industrialize the South was recognized and efforts in this direction began to take shape at an early stage

---

d) undertaken initial development of an area of 62,000 hectares in particularly difficult and backward regions.

[...] The program in agriculture, among other things, called for the construction of 16,400 km. of irrigation canals, 2,900 krm. of drainage canals, 4,700 km. of diversion channels with necessary embankments and regulators, 6,370 km. of access roads in reclamation districts, and the reforestation of 163,000 hectares of woodlands. The program called for the building of more than 60,000 farm houses, for barns for 277,000 head of cattle, for 1,510 processing plants and for other farm structures such as wells, silos and warehouses. The road program envisaged the improvement of some 11,600 km. of provincial roads and the construction of 2,800 km. of new roads to increase the highway network of the South by about 7%. The aqueduct program is intended to bring an adequate supply of potable water to 1,650 localities with a population of about 13 million out of a total of 18 million inhabiting the South. The railroad program will increase capacity by building longer sidings and electrifying a number of main southern railways. Lastly, the investments to encourage tourists will provide better roads and improved water supplies (in addition to the programs mentioned above) in recognized tourist centers and expand the variety of archeological excavations and other attractions.

> although a large-scale program has materialized only recently. [...] As a result of this recognition and the growing demand in the South for some industrial products, the scope of the Cassa's activities in furthering the economic development of Southern Italy was greatly extended by a special law of March 22, 1952. This law recognized that the solution of the problem of the South required as a first step the creation of a favorable climate for industrial growth and it empowered the Cassa to start financing industrial enterprises. A variety of inducements were offered to Italian and foreign businesses to make investments in the South. Foremost among these inducements were tax and tariff concessions, freight rebates, as well as long-term credit on favorable terms. The Cassa was authorized to allocate Lit. 50 billion of its own funds plus any amounts it could borrow in the domestic market as well as abroad. Under this new authority the Cassa was able to relend the bulk of the proceeds of IBRD loans of $ 164.4 million to expand private industry and to increase the electric power generating capacity in the South. These early beginnings were greatly strengthened by means of a new law of July 1957 which extended the life of the Cassa to fifteen years and empowered it to launch a major effort for the industrialization of the South[241].

In the section of the report concerning the progress of the development program for Southern Italy, an evaluation of the first seven years of the extraordinary intervention was carried out. The report analyzed the context in which the activity had begun. The Cassa went through a slow start, which was due to unforeseen difficulties, often due to organisational complexity, problems in recruiting personnel, inappropriateness of land consortia to the task bestowed, and a lack of firms based in Southern Italy which were able to provide soundly-priced offers and be equipped with adequate tools[242].

---

[241] International Bank for Reconstruction and Development, Department of Operations Europe, Africa and Australasia, *Cassa per il Mezzogiorno and the Economic Development of Southern Italy*, cit., pp. 5-6.

[242] As it has been noted:

> A proper evaluation of the Cassa program during the first seven years of its life must consider its achievements, its shortcomings and its mistakes in the light of the background against which it has had to operate. The immense size and diversity of the Cassa program rendered a quick take-off very difficult and operations got off to a rather slow start. As so often happens, it encountered a number of difficulties which were not fully foreseen in the preparation of plans. Organizing and staffing took longer than expected. Cassa personnel soon discovered that in many of the projects put forward for financing (by local and regional associations of landowners called "consorzi" which initiate the bulk of the projects), much detailed technical preparation remained to be done. [...] A good deal of time was thus spent in the administrative and technical review of projects before contracts could be awarded. Even at this stage,

However, the IBRD deemed that the Cassa «handled each problem as it arose and, in general, has done a satisfactory job in overcoming these difficulties»[243]. During this first period, which ended on June 30, 1957, investment demands were examined for a total sum of 884 billion lire, i.e., 1.4 billion dollars. Projects were approved for a total amount of 799 billion lire, equivalent to 1.3 billion dollars. Contracts were drawn up for a total of 508 billion lire, i.e., 813 million dollars. Furthermore, the Cassa financed expenditures for the activities connected with the Agrarian Reform, for an amount of 226 billion lire, and it also contributed to improve privately-owned lands, for an amount of 48 billion lire.[244] At the end of the last year

---

> however, difficulties were encountered, primarily because bidding was originally limited to Southern contractors, whose prices were on the whole high. The contractors experienced difficulties in obtaining the equipment and machinery necessary for such a rapidly stepped up public works program [...] and an unexpected dearth of skilled and semi-skilled workers impeded the implementation of the works. To meet these problems, the Cassa encouraged bidding by qualified Italian contractors even though they are not located in Southern Italy and appears to have succeeded in overcoming the original reluctance on the part of many established construction firms to bid. In this manner it has not only saved money but has also assured itself of high grade performance

(International Bank for Reconstruction and Development, Department of Operations Europe, Africa and Australasia, *Cassa per il Mezzogiorno and the Economic Development of Southern Italy*, cit., pp. 6-7).

243 *Ivi*, p. 7.

244 See *Ibidem*. In this part of the document, a table allowed to summarize the worth of the procurements subcontracted to the Cassa per il Mezzogiorno, together with the expenses for the agrarian reform program and for the subsidies aimed to improve privately-owned land.

Contracts awarded for Cassa Works (June 30, 1957)

Economic Sectors	Amounts (in billions of lire)	% of Allocations in Revised Twelve-Year Plan
Agriculture	529	60
Land reclamation	(218)	62
Reforestation	(37)	30
Land reform	(226)	81
Private land improvement	(48)	37
Transport	144	77
Roads	(92)	80
Railways	(52)	69

of activity, the Cassa had completed interventions for an amount of 262 billion lire, while an equal volume of works was under construction or close to start[245]. Finally, the document presented, in a very short summary, the

---

Aqueducts and sewers	93	52
Tourism	16	64
Total	782	61

Source: International Bank for Reconstruction and Development, Department of Operations Europe, Africa and Australasia, *Cassa per il Mezzogiorno and the Economic Development of Southern Italy*, E.A.–80a/Restricted, February 18, 1958, p. 7, <https://documents.worldbank.org/en/publication/documents-reports/documentdetail/752391468049200134/italy-cassa-per-il-mezzogiorno-and-the-economic-development-of-southern-italy>.

[245] See International Bank for Reconstruction and Development, Department of Operations Europe, Africa and Australasia, *Cassa per il Mezzogiorno and the Economic Development of Southern Italy*, cit., p. 8. Within another table, always connected to such topics, the works already completed, or in construction, were highlighted, including their average completion percentage.

Works Completed or Under Construction and Estimated Average Percentage of Completion (June 30, 1957)

Economic Sectors	Works completed		Works in progress or about to be started		
	Amounts (Billions of Lit.)	% of Allocations	Amounts (Billions of Lit.)	% of Allocations	Average % of Completion
Agriculture	316	36	228	26	80
Land reclamation	(104)	29	(130)	37	80
Reforestation	(19)	15	(17)	14	88
Land reform	(158)	56	(68)	24	80
Private land improvement	(35)	27	(13)	10	80
Transport	94	49	50	26	88
Roads	(73)	63	(19)	16	93
Railways	(21)	28	(31)	41	85
Aqueducts and sewers	38	21	56	32	77
Tourism	7	28	9	36	82
Total	455	36	343	27	81

Source: International Bank for Reconstruction and Development, Department of Operations Europe, Africa and Australasia, *Cassa per il Mezzogiorno and the*

material results achieved after the first seven years of the extraordinary intervention:

> In agriculture, which is most important both from the standpoint of money allocated to it and from its contribution to the goals of the Cassa, 1,219 km. of drainage canals and 1,030 km. of diversion channels with necessary embankments and regulators, out of the programmed 2,900 km. and 4,700 km. respectively, have been completed and a land area of about 369,000 hectares has already been drained by these works. In irrigation, a network of 1,425 km. of canals, out of a programmed total of 16,400 km. has been built, as a result of which 57,400 hectares were irrigated in the summer of 1957, as against a total goal of 352,000 hectares. A total of 2,800 km. of rural roads was built, as against a goal of 6,370 km. In the mountains, some 50,000 hectares, out of the programmed 163,000 hectares, have been reforested. At the farm level, an estimated 23,000 houses of the planned 60,000, barns for 107,000 head of cattle of the planned 277,000, and other farm structures, including wells, silos and warehouses have been built. Likewise, 621 new agricultural processing plants of the 1,510 planned were established. [...] Physical progress in road improvement and construction has also been considerable. About 10,600 km. of provincial roads out of a goal of 11,600 km. have been improved and this part of the program is virtually complete. New roads have also been built to the extent of 970 km. out of the planned total of 2,800 km. The aqueduct works completed supply potable water to 572 localities with a population of 2.7 million, roughly one-third of the 1,650 localities with a population of 13 million for which aqueduct works were planned. To attract tourists, archeological excavations have been carried out at Pompeii and elsewhere, several historic structures have been restored and 100 km. of sightseeing roads have been improved or newly built. Thus physical progress under the Cassa program has been considerable[246].

Within the section of the document concerning the financial aspects of the program, the Figure 3.3 was featured. By examining the expenses of the

---

Economic Development of Southern Italy, E.A.–80a/Restricted, February 18, 1958, p. 8,
<https://documents.worldbank.org/en/publication/documents-reports/documentdetail/752391468049200134/italy-cassa-per-il-mezzogiorno-and-the-economic-development-of-southern-italy>.

[246] International Bank for Reconstruction and Development, Department of Operations Europe, Africa and Australasia, *Cassa per il Mezzogiorno and the Economic Development of Southern Italy*, cit., *infra* pp. 9-10.

Figure 3.3 *Receipts and expenditures of the Cassa per il Mezzogiorno – Annual and cumulative differences between receipts and expenditures – 1950/51-1956/57 (in billions of lire)*

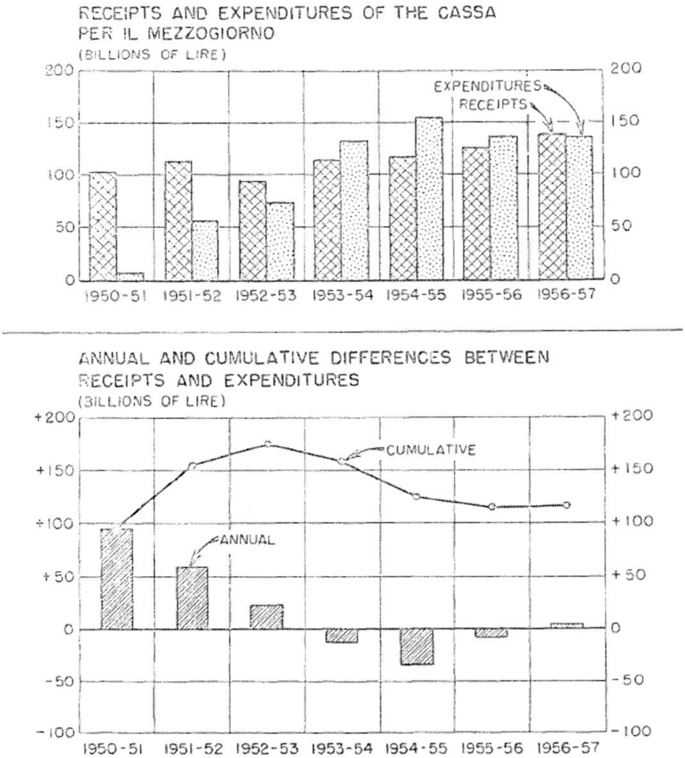

Source: International Bank for Reconstruction and Development, Department of Operations Europe, Africa and Australasia, *Cassa per il Mezzogiorno and the Economic Development of Southern Italy*, E.A.–80a/Restricted, February 18, 1958, p. 10, <https://documents.worldbank.org/en/publication/documents-reports/documentdetail/752391468049200134/italy-cassa-per-il-mezzogiorno-and-the-economic-development-of-southern-italy>.

Cassa per il Mezzogiorno, it allowed to understand the slow start and the following acceleration of its activities. Furthermore, the trends in yearly assignments and the expenses incurred by the Cassa, in the period between

1950/51 and 1956/57, where also shown within a simple and effective summary table[247].

The report also clarified the main additional financing sources for the Cassa, indicating a subdivision of expenses by broad categories:

> The source of most of the Cassa funds is the government budget. It furnished Lit. 640 billion. An additional Lit. 74 billion was provided by the Italian government from the repayments of Marshall Plan loans, raising the total to Lit. 714 billion. The remaining Lit. 94 billion includes Lit. 26 billion in interest on Cassa deposits, Lit. 49 billion in loans from IBRD as well as a number of other smaller items. Of the Lit. 689 billion spent by the Cassa, approximately Lit. 426 billion was on the Cassa program proper, Lit. 193 billion on behalf of the land reform administered by the Ministry of Agriculture, and Lit. 70 billion on credits to industrial and electric power concerns[248].

The section of the document dedicated to the economic effects of the program of the Cassa found two types of consequences of the extraordinary

---

[247] The table below provides some summary data, in billions of lire, which are of remarkable interest.

1. Fiscal Year	*2. Appropriations*	*3. Expenditures*	*4. Annual difference (between 2 and 3)*	*Cumulative difference (between 2 and 3)*
1950/51	101.6	7.9	+ 93.7	-
1951/52	114.2	54.9	+ 59.2	93.7
1952/53	93.7	72.8	+ 20.9	152.9
1953/54	115.5	130.6	- 15.1	173.8
1954/55	118.0	153.7	- 35.6	158.7
1955/56	125.7	135.6	- 9.9	123.1
1956/57	139.1	137.5	+ 1.6	113.2
Total	807.8	693.0	114.8	114.8

Source: International Bank for Reconstruction and Development, Department of Operations Europe, Africa and Australasia, Cassa per il Mezzogiorno and the Economic Development of Southern Italy, E.A.–80a/Restricted, February 18, 1958, p. 10,
<https://documents.worldbank.org/en/publication/documents-reports/documentdetail/752391468049200134/italy-cassa-per-il-mezzogiorno-and-the-economic-development-of-southern-italy>.

[248] International Bank for Reconstruction and Development, Department of Operations Europe, Africa and Australasia, *Cassa per il Mezzogiorno and the Economic Development of Southern Italy*, cit., p. 10.

intervention on the development of Southern Italy. On one hand, investments for public works and those directly induced by policies supporting the private sector (including land improvements, the diffusion of food processing plants and the construction of hotels). On the other hand, large-scale investments to enhance electric power and others focusing on the growth of private industrial plants and residential constructions[249]. The combined outcomes of these two different lines of interventions despite the fact that «they have not yet basically changed the economic structure of the South»[250], was very deep and significant for the economy in Southern Italy. This effect, combined with the loan strategy carried out by the World Bank, foreshadowed the existence of a model for the Italian economic development. During the first seven years of initiatives by the Cassa per il Mezzogiorno, as it is stated in Table 3.1, the investments carried out by the Cassa itself and by private actors amounted to a total of about 843 billion lire[251].

Another section of the report, featuring a reflection on the prevalence of the investments by the Cassa per il Mezzogiorno in the agricultural sector, highlighted the results achieved during this period of the intervention[252].

---

[249] See *Ibidem*.

[250] *Ibidem*.

[251] On this topic, the following has been noted:

> Of the Cassa total of Lit. 699 billion only Lit. 648 billion represents a charge against the allocations to the Cassa of Lit. 1,280 billion since the remaining investments are based on Cassa borrowings. Investments by private interests in connection with the Cassa program in land improvement, warehouses, hotels and private industrial plants amounted to Lit. 195 billion, of which loans from the Cassa covered Lit. 51 billion. It is estimated that these combined Cassa and private investments required a total of 163.5 million man-days of work with a total wage bill of Lit. 236 billion ($ 378 million)

(International Bank for Reconstruction and Development, Department of Operations Europe, Africa and Australasia, *Cassa per il Mezzogiorno and the Economic Development of Southern Italy*, cit., p. 11).

[252] In particular, the document highlighted that:

> The Cassa's largest investments have been in agriculture and although the greatest benefits to be realized must wait the completion of the irrigation works, achievements are already substantial. Private interests have already invested in the neighborhood of Lit. 78 billion ($ 125 million) in land improvement in conjunction with Cassa operations and these investments have increased the annual manpower requirements in agriculture by some 7 million man-days, thereby providing the equivalent of approximately 35,000 full-time jobs, of the 275,000 to 300,000 expected to result from the carrying out of the full agricultural program. A sample study covering 408,000 hectares (about 7.3% of all farming land in the Cassa jurisdiction) reveals

Table 3.1 *Amounts of "real investments" by the Cassa at the end of 1957 (in billions of lire)*

Economic sectors	Total investments	Investments by the Cassa
Agriculture	536.2	448.3
Land reclamation	(174.6)	(164.2)
Reforestation	(31.9)	(31.9)
Agrarian Reform	(204.3)	(204.3)
Private land improvement	(125.4)	(47.9)
Transports	122.3	120.9
Roads	(84.6)	(84.6)
Railways	(37.7)	(36.3)
Aqueducts and sewers	66.9	66.6
Tourism	12.0	12.0
Industry, power and hotels	105.2	50.9
Total	842.6	698.7

Source: International Bank for Reconstruction and Development, Department of Operations Europe, Africa and Australasia, *Cassa per il Mezzogiorno and the Economic Development of Southern Italy*, E.A.–80a/Restricted, February 18, 1958, p. 11, <https://documents.worldbank.org/en/publication/documents-reports/documentdetail/752391468049200134/italy-cassa-per-il-mezzogiorno-and-the-economic-development-of-southern-italy>.

Remarkable emphasis was put on the shift brought about by the progressive growth towards the industrialization of the Southern areas of Italy:

> that the investments have already produced a fundamental change in the productive pattern of 46% of the farms transformed by the end of 1955. Most of these have passed from extensive to intensive farming following the availability of irrigation water, or have introduced mixed farming with tree crops and livestock, or changed to a more remunerative cropping pattern. Gross saleable production on these farms increased on an average by about 40%, with the increase being concentrated mainly on the irrigated farms growing citrus fruit and vegetables. Although these figures are based on a small sample and cover only a limited period, they indicate the direction Southern agriculture is taking under the priming of the Cassa. Moreover, they suggest that the goal of raising agricultural output in the South by some 25 to 30 percent is reasonable

(International Bank for Reconstruction and Development, Department of Operations Europe, Africa and Australasia, *Cassa per il Mezzogiorno and the Economic Development of Southern Italy*, cit., pp. 11-12).

> Although [...] the Cassa program was originally envisaged as a public works program, it was also intended that the Cassa stimulate private initiative in both agriculture and industry. [...] the Cassa's most noteworthy accomplishment has been to create the basis for private and public industrial investment in the South by improving transportation and sanitation, increasing the supply of electric power and extending credits on attractive terms to industrialists. [...] The monumental task of industrializing the South has begun in earnest as is evidenced by the recent diversification of industrial investments[253].

In particular, according to the IBRD report, the Banco di Napoli had financed 2,500 industrial plants in the Southern peninsular, paying an amount of 58 billion lire in advance. Only about a fifth (452) of such establishments could be considered new, as in the majority of the cases, those were expansions or renewals of existing structures[254]. In the years between 1953 and 1957, further investments amounting to 57 billion lire concerned 537 industrial plants, 337 of which were new and just about two hundred were an expansion of pre-existing ones[255]. During the first phase, only 33% of the whole sum invested was assigned to new plants, while, during the second phase, a significant 80% was allocated for this purpose[256]. Furthermore, between the two periods, the characters of industrial investments had changed as well, shifting from giving preeminent impulse to the traditional food processing plants, to decidedly focusing on mechanical and chemical industries, totaling 112 new plants[257]. Sicily was in step with the rest of the Mezzogiorno, with investments amounting to 191 billion lire in 789 new installations, out of a total of over three thousand industrial enterprises financed[258]. Finally, it was noted that the average size of financed plants grew from 100 million to 300 million lire, something that «Although this is still a modest figure for an industrial enterprise, it is a significant indicator of direction»[259].

However, the interventions for the industrialization of the Mezzogiorno had also followed a different route, relying on direct financial support, amounting to 225 billion, assigned by the Cassa and by the special credit institutions (namely ISVEIMER, IRFIS and CIS)[260], out of the total 350

---

[253] *Ivi*, p. 12.
[254] See *Ibidem*.
[255] See *Ibidem*.
[256] See *Ibidem*.
[257] See *Ibidem*.
[258] See *Ibidem*.
[259] *Ibidem*.
[260] See *Ibidem*. In the very same page, the following was clarified:

billion lire directed to industrial investments in Southern Italy between 1951 and 1957[261]. At this point in the document, a picture (featured in Figure 3.4) showed the industrial projects financed by the International Bank for Reconstruction and Development in the whole of Southern up to that date. It was thus possible, by means of a simple and effective representation, to also localize such productive initiatives.

Within the analysis of the program of the Cassa during its first seven years of activity, a reference was made to a study concerning industrial plants. The study had been promoted in 1956 by the Cassa and by the special credit institutions. The study provided additional significant data, pointing out the existence of 284 new plants, with a relevant investment of 78 billion lire. In addition, the study noted that 51 new factories were under construction, with investments amounting to 40 billion lire. Finally, the study recalled that 11 additional complexes had yet to be implemented, for a total investment of 13 billion lire[262]. Said initiatives were supposed to create 20,000 new jobs. Moreover, while their contribution to the growth in industrial employment would have amounted to 11-12%, their contribution to added value would have reached 26%[263]. Furthermore, the report highlighted that some relevant changes had occurred in the sources of industrial financing as well: up to 1952, only a third of the total for private investment came from Northern Italy and from abroad; during the following years, this element grew up to two thirds[264]. On this specific issue, an important observation was made on all those endowments of capitals, modern technologies, management skills, entrepreneurial spirit and research-

---

These institutes were established in 1952, their capital being subscribed by the government, the Cassa and such regional banks as the Bank of Sicily, the Bank of Naples and the Bank of Sardinia. Their directors and managements are in effect appointed by the government. Thus both in ownership and administrative structure, but not in operation, they bear a strong resemblance to the rest of the Italian banking system. They raise funds by sales of bonds to the public at an effective cost of 7.05% and make loans primarily to private industrialists at 5 to 6 percent. A government subsidy covers the operating losses of the institutes and no dividend is paid on the equity capital.

261 See International Bank for Reconstruction and Development, Department of Operations Europe, Africa and Australasia, *Cassa per il Mezzogiorno and the Economic Development of Southern Italy*, cit., p. 12.

262 See *Ivi*, p. 13.

263 See *Ibidem*.

264 See *Ibidem*.

Figure 3.4 *Industrial projects on the Southern mainland and in Sardinia financed by the IBRD (1958)*

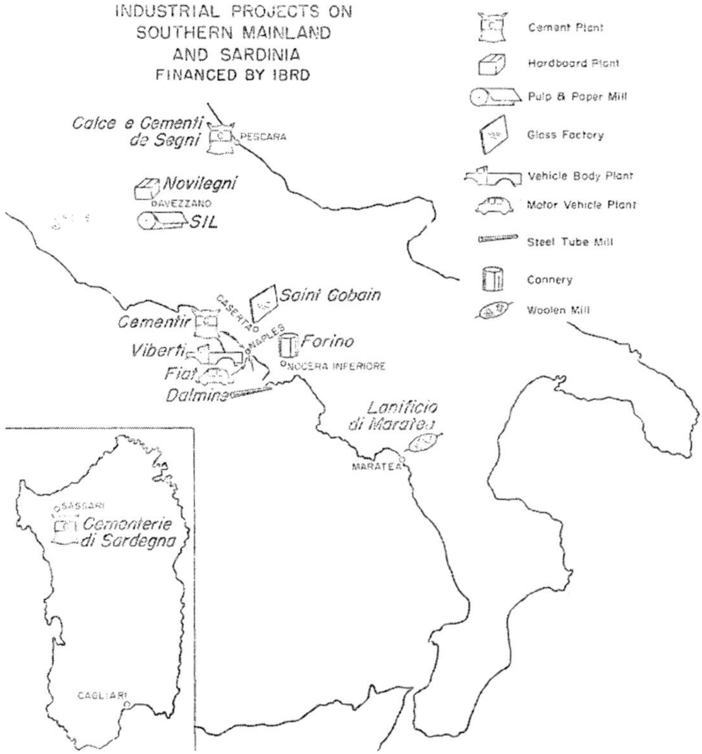

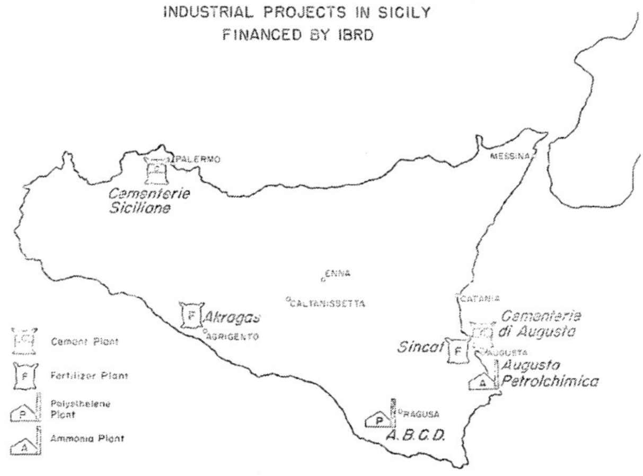

Source: International Bank for Reconstruction and Development, Department of Operations Europe, Africa and Australasia, *Cassa per il Mezzogiorno and the Economic Development of Southern Italy*, E.A.–80a/Restricted, February 18, 1958, *infra* pp. 12-13, <https://documents.worldbank.org/en/publication/documents-reports/documentdetail/752391468049200134/italy-cassa-per-il-mezzogiorno-and-the-economic-development-of-southern-italy>.

oriented mindset, able to be transferred in southern Italy from the most advanced regions of Italy, also thanks to the IBRD loans:

> This shift is most important not only because it brings to the South the necessary capital but also modern technology, the managerial ability, the spirit of enterprise, the research mentality, and the whole complex of forces which have industrialized the North and made it prosperous and which in the South could at best have developed spontaneously only very slowly. In this connection, the role of IBRD loans to the special industrial credit institutes through the Cassa, has been vital[265].

---

[265] *Ibidem*. Such an evaluation went on, in the same page, with a reference to the role of the special credit institutions and to the effects of their loans:

> These institutes were endowed with limited funds and have had to spread their resources as widely as possible (special approval by the Committee of Ministers for the South is required for loans over Lit. 300 million and because of regional and political pressures this is difficult to secure) with the result that most of their loans are under Lit. 300 million each. They have thus relied heavily on IBRD funds to finance the large chemical, fertilizer,

The document then sketched a profile of the progress achieved during seven years by the economy of Southern Italy, «some of which may be attributed to Cassa operations and others to the general growth of the Italian economy»[266]. And it was exactly in highlighting this demarcation line between the contribution to the development of Southern Italy given by the general growth of the Italian economy and the one specifically linked with the extraordinary intervention, that the evaluation by the International Bank for Reconstruction and Development was carried out. Up to 1957, overall production went up by about 42%, with respect to the average of the years between 1949 and 1952, that is to say about 5% yearly. This was a better achievement, compared with the national growth rate during the same timeframe[267]. Industrial production grew by about 50%. In particular, the growth rate in the sugar, cement and paper industries in Southern Italy were higher than the national average, with figures doubling in the first two industries[268]. Concerning residential construction, electric power consumption, and the use of fertilizers and tractors, Southern Italy had also achieved a proportionally higher increase when compared with the Northern regions[269]. The overall income in Southern Italy grew by 71%, compared with the 64% recorded in Northern Italy, therefore achieving a higher consumption rate[270]. This improvement of the conditions in the Mezzogiorno came thanks to a growth of 138% in private investments and of 106% in public ones, while in the Northern regions they grew by 83% and 36% respectively[271].

> mechanical and building materials plants which have been sponsored in the South as branch plants by northern industrialists. [...] While there were other inducements and pressures to locate in the South and some private industrialists may have responded to them, there is no reason to doubt that the money provided by IBRD both fortified and accelerated the movement.

[266] International Bank for Reconstruction and Development, Department of Operations Europe, Africa and Australasia, *Cassa per il Mezzogiorno and the Economic Development of Southern Italy*, cit., p. 13.

[267] See *Ibidem*.

[268] See *Ibidem*.

[269] See *Ibidem*.

[270] See *Ibidem*.

[271] See *Ivi*, p. 14. In this page, the following was added:

> These improvements have contributed toward a reduction of unemployment which constitutes Italy's outstanding economic problem. Because of the increased public and private investments as well as the general expansion in economic activity employment has risen faster than the labor force has grown and combined with a high emigration rate have reduced registered unemployment to its lowest postwar level of 1.6 million. In the South the labor situation has profited greatly from these developments as well as from

This section of the report ended with an overall evaluation of the outcomes connected with the current phase of the development program. The document recalled some of the issues still unresolved in Southern Italy and the measures adopted to effectively face them, starting with implementing a deeper and more intense industrialization, based on a new investment strategy:

> In spite of Cassa operations, the per capita investment in the North has continued to be about 25% higher than in the South every year since 1950 and a larger proportion of this investment was channeled into the more directly productive pursuits than in the South where a good deal of investment went into public works. Moreover, the natural resources of the South are on the whole poorer than those of the North with less favorable capital to output ratio. Because of these factors as well as the stimulation to the economy of the North provided by the additional demand for investment and consumers goods as a result of the accelerated development in the South, the gap in income per head between the North and the South has probably not diminished. Thus, while the Cassa's objective of raising living standards in the South is plainly succeeding, the objective of the Vanoni Plan to close the gap between the North and the South is not being fulfilled. This situation has produced a clamor for stepping up investment in the South and resulted in the adoption of a new policy measure in 1957 which requires that public industrial enterprises devote a minimum of 40% of their total new investment to projects in Southern Italy[272].

In the outlook section of this document, it was also noted that the context in which the Cassa per il Mezzogiorno acted had widened considerably, shifting from a 12-years development program – of which the first seven had passed –, with an overall resources assignment of more than 2 billion dollars, to a 15-years one (lasting up to the first half of 1965). This widening of horizons meant a consequential increase of the Cassa's assignments up to 1.216 billion dollars, as established by the Italian law no. 634, passed on July 29, 1957[273]. The issuing of this provision mirrored the Italian commitment to

---

> the continuing emigration and internal migration. The latter, particularly, has become important as job opportunities in the North have expanded and it is estimated that in recent years approximately 1.2 million persons have moved there from the South. This combination of more jobs in the South, emigration and internal migration have not only already ameliorated the unemployment and underemployment problem of the South, but also hold out hopes of its eventual solution.

[272] International Bank for Reconstruction and Development, Department of Operations Europe, Africa and Australasia, *Cassa per il Mezzogiorno and the Economic Development of Southern Italy*, cit., p. 14.

[273] See *Ibidem*. In a note within the same page, the following was noted on the matter:

> The Cassa will now receive Lit. 100 billion in 1958/59; Lit. 150 billion in

keep on pursuing the goal of developing Southern Italy and the widespread conviction in the Cassa's capacity to make it a reality. Despite having been «popularly referred to as the second stage of the Cassa's operations»[274], this law mostly represented the enhancement of the previous activities of this Entity, with a sharp upturn in the industrialization of the territories of Southern Italy[275]. Table 3.2 intended to offer a summary of the advantages which could be gained in this new phase, through an examination of the preliminary funds allocated by the Committee of Ministers for Southern Italy.

Table 3.2 *The Twelve-Year Cassa Program and Allocations Under the Law of July 31, 1957 (in billions of lire)*

	Twelve-Year Plan		New Appropriations		Total		
Economic sectors	Amount	%	Amount	%	Amount	Amount*	%
Agriculture	887	69	250	33	1,137	1,819	55
Land reclamation	(353)	(27)	(111)	(15)	(464)	(742)	(23)
Reforestation	(124)	(10)	(19)	(2)	(143)	(229)	(7)
Land Reform	(280)	(22)	-	-	(280)	(448)	(13)
Private land improvement	(130)	(10)	(120)	(16)	(250)	(400)	(12)
Transport	190	15	45	6	235	376	12
Roads	(115)	(9)	(45)	(6)	(160)	(256)	(8)
Railways	(75)	(6)	-	-	(75)	(120)	(4)
Aqueducts and sewers	178	14	140	18	318	509	16
Tourism	25	2	-	-	25	40	1
Industrialization	-	-	300	40	300	480	15
Training**	-	-	25	3	25	40	1
Total	1,280	100	760	100	2,040	3,264	100

Source: International Bank for Reconstruction and Development, Department of Operations Europe, Africa and Australasia, *Cassa per il Mezzogiorno and the Economic Development of Southern Italy*, E.A.–80a/Restricted, February 18, 1958, p. 15, <https://documents.worldbank.org/en/publication/documents-reports/documentdetail/752391468049200134/italy-cassa-per-il-mezzogiorno-and-the-economic-development-of-southern-italy>.

*Millions of dollars. **Training of technicians, vocational schools and training of specialized personnel.

1959/60; and Lit. 180 billion each year in the period 1960/61 - 1964/65.

[274] International Bank for Reconstruction and Development, Department of Operations Europe, Africa and Australasia, *Cassa per il Mezzogiorno and the Economic Development of Southern Italy*, cit., p. 15.

[275] See *Ibidem*.

The IBRD report contained, in those very same pages, the following picture (Figure 3.5), highlighting the receipts and the expenditures of the Cassa per il Mezzogiorno from 1950 to 1965 and dividing them between effective and estimated entries.

Furthermore, the document stated that, unlike the previous program, the resources allocated to agriculture amounted to just a third of the total, but this sector still held fundamental relevance. A total of 89 billion lire was assigned for irrigation, which was considered a very productive investment. The funds assigned to favor land improvements (Table 3.2) «may also be expected to give a satisfactory account of themselves since the real test of the value of the agricultural program will be in the extent and degree to which it manages to induce large-scale private land improvements with resulting increases in productivity and output»[276]. The economic resources given to reforestation (Table 3.2), a sector with relatively low productivity, were more limited and answered to a political agenda, focused on supporting mountain areas[277]. The roadways sector held a good relevance within the new program, considering also its financing (Table 3.2). Several interventions in this sector were planned, mainly focusing on improving existing roads and on building regional and interregional highways, as well as road links between agricultural production centers and their markets, and the enhancement of municipal and provincial road networks[278]. Other sizable funds (Table 3.2) were reserved to waterworks-related infrastructure, in order to complete the water supply systems in Southern Italy[279]. The new assignments, granted for the training of technicians and the establishment

---

276 *Ivi*, pp. 15-16.

277 See *Ibidem*. Within the second of the two aforementioned pages, it was affirmed that:

> By and large, the allocations reveal a high degree of economic sophistication in the commitment of public funds for the agriculture of the South and if effectively implemented, they should produce sound results. No doubt the general improvement in the overall economic conditions of the South made possible this type of concentration of efforts, but it also reflects a determination to support long-range productive objectives as against immediate benefits from work-relief.

278 See International Bank for Reconstruction and Development, Department of Operations Europe, Africa and Australasia, *Cassa per il Mezzogiorno and the Economic Development of Southern Italy*, cit., p. 16.

279 See *Ibidem*. On this topic, within the aforementioned page, a very interesting remark was expressed, according to which:

> Although these public works will reduce the price of water to the consumers, the entire undertaking must be judged primarily in terms of public health and social benefits, rather than economic criteria.

Figure 3.5 *Receipts and expenditures of the Cassa per il Mezzogiorno, 1950/51-1964/65 (in billions of lire)*

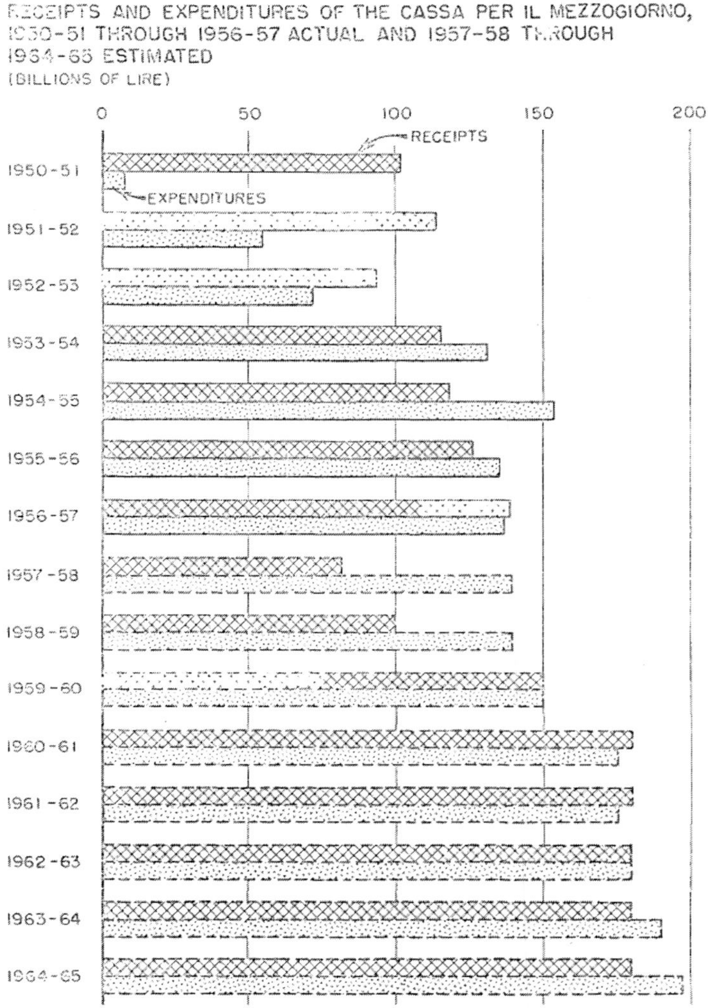

Source: International Bank for Reconstruction and Development, Department of Operations Europe, Africa and Australasia, *Cassa per il Mezzogiorno and the Economic Development of Southern Italy*, E.A.–80a/Restricted, February 18, 1958, *infra* pp. 14-15, <https://documents.worldbank.org/en/publication/documents-reports/documentdetail/752391468049200134/italy-cassa-per-il-mezzogiorno-and-the-economic-development-of-southern-italy>.

of vocational schools (Table 3.2) had a huge importance, given the lack of specific skills and qualified jobs in the whole of the Mezzogiorno[280].

However, considering a long-term perspective, the most meaningful feature of the Italian law no. 634 of 1957 was the provision assigning funds for industrialization. This feature allowed the Cassa per il Mezzogiorno to strongly support industrial production. This could be achieved in three ways: by means of an assignment amounting to 19 billion lire (i.e., 144 million dollars), to be used «to pay a subsidy of 2½% per annum towards the interest on the bonds to be issued by the special financial institutes»[281], in order to obtain funds to grant loans; with another assignment amounting to 170 billion lire (that is to say, 272 million dollars), «for subsidies for buildings and machinery for projects to be located in towns with a population of 70,000 or under»[282]; by means of another assignment, amounting to 40 billion lire (i.e., 64 million dollars), in order to create other industrial areas, as it had been done in Naples and Catania: «These funds are expected to meet up to 50% of such costs as the purchase of sites, installation of water supplies and sewers, construction of roads, sidings, transmission lines, and the like»[283].

---

[280] See International Bank for Reconstruction and Development, Department of Operations Europe, Africa and Australasia, *Cassa per il Mezzogiorno and the Economic Development of Southern Italy*, cit., p. 16.

[281] *Ibidem*.

[282] *Ivi*, pp. 16-17. Within the second of those two pages, the following was clarified:

> These subsidies are limited to 20% of the cost of buildings and 10% of the cost of machinery and installations.

[283] International Bank for Reconstruction and Development, Department of Operations Europe, Africa and Australasia, *Cassa per il Mezzogiorno and the Economic Development of Southern Italy*, cit., p. 17. The excerpt went on, in the same page, with some critical evaluations and further clarifying the relevant issues:

> Funds available in this way are quite substantial since the bond interest subsidy alone, if used fully, could support a total industrial investment of approximately $ 750 million, which is about three times the current annual rate of industrial investment in the South. Since, however, these subsidies are expected to last until 1965, they seem to be quite realistic. No crash industrialization program is likely to be undertaken in the immediate future for a number of considerations. To begin with, any greatly increased resort to the Italian capital market would cause a severe strain on it and it is reasonable to expect that the Capital Issues Committee would preclude such a development. Even more limiting, however, is the social and technical absorptive capacity for industry in the South. The shortage of technically trained and skilled labor, the absence of properly prepared projects and the limited entrepreneurial talents, will all militate against an unrestrained application of the industrialization policy. [...] Since the establishment of the

Therefore, after having examined the growth condition of agriculture, infrastructure, services and especially of the new industrial sector in the Mezzogiorno, the report contained an evaluation on the sense of opportunity and challenge – both represented in the situation at the time – for the Cassa. The Cassa had indeed been able to receive and implement the previous opportunities, but extreme caution and wisdom were recommended in its choices for industrial investments:

> The current situation presents both an opportunity and a challenge to the Cassa. While there are now in existence only limited facilities for carrying out on a private basis an industrial program of such magnitude, the pressures to proceed with it will be very great. The Cassa has once before demonstrated its ability to cope with such pressures but in a country like Italy where the line of demarcation is much fainter than elsewhere between private, semi-public and public industry, there is always a danger that industrialization in the South will become much more of a state affair than it is in the North. A sign in this direction is the [...] measure adopted last year which requires that a minimum of 40% of all new investments in state industrial enterprises take place in Southern Italy. This was a political and social decision and its underlying economic soundness is open to serious questioning. While the industrialization of the South makes much more sense today than it did in 1950 when widespread overcapacity characterized much of northern industry, an indiscriminate forced industrialization of the South may prove costly to the Italian economy. To the extent that raw materials, actual and prospective markets, a favorable manpower situation and other such inducements exist, the location of industrial plants in the South is fully justified, but there are still numerous instances where further industrial expansion of the North would be more economical. At this stage it can only be hoped that in the zeal to industrialize the South, the costs of

---

> three special regional institutions for the financing of industry – ISVEIMER for the southern mainland, IRFIS for Sicily and CIS for Sardinia in 1952 – the Cassa's role in programming and financing industry in the South has been subordinated to that of the institutes. The new law seems to maintain the policy of leaving the active promotional functions to the institutes, except that it gives the Cassa a new task of subsidizing the creation of industrial zones in the larger centers and of granting direct subsidies to industrial plants in small towns. The successful discharge of the additional functions will require a substantial strengthening of the industrial section of the Cassa and of the institutes. The formation in 1957 of ISAP to promote the industrialization of the South by encouraging Italian and foreign private investors was a promising step, but thus far it has very little to show in the way of practical results.

The ISAP was made up by the IMI, the Banca Nazionale del Lavoro, the Banco di Napoli, by Mediobanca and by the Banco di Sicilia.

> alternative plant location will be adequately weighed and serious errors will be minimized[284].

The document ended with a very positive judgment on the overall activity carried out by the Cassa per il Mezzogiorno. During the seven starting years of its experience the Cassa had given a good account of itself, setting up a credible and feasible development program, despite the regional and political pressure it had to constantly sustain[285]. From this evaluation, the IBRD gave an opinion which assigned paradigmatic value and cornerstone importance to the extraordinary intervention. Through such an evaluation, the Bank not only expressed its standpoint, but it also showed a wider appreciation for the Cassa's overall activities: «In the context of Italian public works history, the Cassa is an extraordinary agency in more than one sense»[286].

Finally, in the last part of this report, new challenges for the Cassa were described as it extended the duration of its interventions to fifteen years and moved its focus from agriculture to industry. As a matter of fact, after the modifications in its mission, the Cassa was relieved from a more immediate burden, i.e., the realization of public works, and would give a greater drive towards other actors, in order to carry out the investments needed in Southern Italy[287]. To effectively summarize, a vision was proposed for

---

[284] International Bank for Reconstruction and Development, Department of Operations Europe, Africa and Australasia, *Cassa per il Mezzogiorno and the Economic Development of Southern Italy*, cit., pp. 17-18.

[285] See *Ivi*, p. 18. In this very same page, the following was noted:

> The Cassa has also been implementing the program reasonably well. The projects have been on the whole scrutinized carefully and the diligence exercised in awarding contracts has resulted in large savings of public funds. Work progress during the past seven years has been satisfactory and the goals of the Twelve-Year Plan are likely to be achieved on time or with only relatively slight delays.

[286] International Bank for Reconstruction and Development, Department of Operations Europe, Africa and Australasia, *Cassa per il Mezzogiorno and the Economic Development of Southern Italy*, cit., p. 18.

[287] See *Ibidem*. On this topic, and the aforementioned document page, it was underlined that:

> In the past, as is exemplified both by private land transformations and by industrial enterprises, this has been by far the more complex task. However, the Cassa has already acquired some useful experience in this field which it may be expected to utilize to full advantage. The task now confronting the Cassa is by no means simple and the manner in which it is handled will determine for many years to come the success and character of the industrialization of the South.

economic development of Southern Italy, remarking the existence of a previously absent dynamism and having the effect to clearly increase investments in both production and income, at the same (or at a quicker) pace than in the country as a whole, besides bringing about an improvement in the living standard of the people of Southern Italy, therefore triggering a self-propelling growth mechanism of no short duration:

> On the whole the Cassa's mandate to accelerate the economic development of Southern Italy is being diligently discharged. Both as the result of the Cassa's direct intervention, as well as by the stimulus which it has provided to private and public initiatives, the economic situation of the South has improved and the economic climate has acquired a degree of dynamism previously absent. Private and public investment have doubled, output and income have risen in agriculture and industry at rates equal or greater than for the country as a whole, and the standard of living has been improving. Most significant of all the Cassa has stirred up the economy of the South and generated a self-sustaining process of growth which may be expected to continue long after its own objectives are achieved[288].

The appendix of this document featured also some very interesting tables. These tables allow to understand the overall progress the Mezzogiorno experienced during the first seven years it operated within the extraordinary intervention. Amongst these elaborations and tables, three at least seemed particularly meaningful, so much that they deserve to be presented here. The first of them (Table 3.3) concerns the economic development of Northern and Southern Italy in the years between 1954 and 1956.

Table 3.3 *The economic development of Northern and Southern Italy 1954-1956 (1950 =100)*

Economic indicator	Area	1954	1955	1956
1) *Per capita* gross income*	North	136.5	149.2	159.3
	South	143.1	150.6	163.6
2) *Per capita* investment	North	149.8	166.2	182.5
	South	189.6	209.8	222.1
3) *Per capita* food consumed	North	115.1	118.3	130.2
(in kgs. of meat)	South	122.6	122.6	138.7

[288] International Bank for Reconstruction and Development, Department of Operations Europe, Africa and Australasia, *Cassa per il Mezzogiorno and the Economic Development of Southern Italy*, cit., pp. 18-19.

4) *Per capita* consumption other than food	North	149.2	156.2	-
	South	159.9	177.7	-
5) *Per capita* gross agricultural production	North	*	114.1	-
	South	*	120.8	-
6) *Per capita* consumption of electricity for industrial use	North	142.8	153.5	-
	South	150.7	156.6	-
7) *Per capita* rooms built	North	245.7	294.5	312.6
	South	300.0	358.5	400.0
8) Shipments of merchandise (in tons per 1,000 inhabitants)	North	131.5	148.1	-
	South	136.4	142.4	-
9) Automobile registration (number per 1,000 inhabitants)	North	144.3	154.1	162.3
	South	154.5	168.2	181.8
10) *Per capita* monetary savings	North	191.8	216.3	-
	South	183.2	201.1	-
Average of indices 2 to 10 above**	North	158.8	175.9	
	South	174.6	192.1	

Source: International Bank for Reconstruction and Development, Department of Operations Europe, Africa and Australasia, *Cassa per il Mezzogiorno and the Economic Development of Southern Italy*, E.A.–80a/Restricted, February 18, 1958, p. 26, <https://documents.worldbank.org/en/publication/documents-reports/documentdetail/752391468049200134/italy-cassa-per-il-mezzogiorno-and-the-economic-development-of-southern-italy>.

*To reduce the effects of yearly variation in crops, the 1950/52 average is compared with that of 1953/55 and reported under 1955. **This mean excludes point 5, which, if included, would modify the 1955 index, giving it a value of 169.0 for Northern Italy and of 184.2 for Southern Italy.

The second of them (Table 3.4) described the yearly variations of the main economic indicators in Northern and Southern Italy, between the beginning and the first half of the 1950s.

Table 3.4 *Yearly variations of the main economic indicators in Northern and Southern Italy, 1950/51-1955/56*

Economic indicator	Area	Yearly percentage variations 1950/51	1954/55	1955/56
1) *Per capita* gross income	North South	15.4 16.2	9.2 5.3	6.8 8.6
2) *Per capita* investment	North South	19.5 25.5	11.0 10.6	9.8 5.9
3) *Per capita* food consumed (in kgs. of meat)	North South	- 2.4 - 6.5	2.8 0.0	10.1 13.2
4) *Per capita* consumption other than food	North South	12.9 7.8	4.7 11.1	- -
5) *Per capita* gross agricultural production	North South	- -	- -	- -
6) *Per capita* consumption of electricity for industrial use	North South	24.1 19.3	7.5 3.9	- -
7) *Per capita* rooms built	North South	31.5 29.3	19.9 19.5	6.1 11.6
8) Shipments of merchandise (in tons per 1,000 inhabitants)	North South	16.3 23.4	12.6 4.4	- -
9) Automobile registration (number per 1,000 inhabitants)	North South	9.8 9.1	6.8 8.8	5.3 8.1
10) *Per capita* monetary savings	North South	16.2 15.5	12.8 9.8	- -
Algebraic average of changes in items from 2 to 10 (excluding 5)	North South	16.0 15.4	9.8 8.5	- -

Source: International Bank for Reconstruction and Development, Department of Operations Europe, Africa and Australasia, *Cassa per il Mezzogiorno and the Economic Development of Southern Italy*, E.A.–80a/Restricted, February 18, 1958, p. 27, <https://documents.worldbank.org/en/publication/documents-reports/documentdetail/752391468049200134/italy-cassa-per-il-mezzogiorno-and-the-economic-development-of-southern-italy>.

The third of them (Table 3.5) presented the data on the relative economic distance between Northern and Southern Italy, between 1950 and 1956.

Table 3.5 *Relative economic distance between Northern and Southern Italy, 1950-1956*

	South as percentage of North				Decrease (-) or increase (+) with respect to 1950		
Economic indicator	1950	1954	1955	1956	1954	1955	1956
1) *Per capita* gross income	42.7	44.7	43.1	43.8	- 2.0	- 0.4	- 1.1
2) *Per capita* investment	43.2	54.7	54.5	52.6	- 11.5	- 11.3	- 9.4
3) *Per capita* food consumed (in kgs. of meat)	49.2	52.4	51.0	52.4	- 3.2	- 1.8	- 3.2
4) *Per capita* consumption other than food	31.5	33.8	35.9	-	- 2.3	- 4.4	-
5) *Per capita* gross agricultural production	79.2*	-	83.9**	-	-	- 4.7	-
6) Power for industrial use *per capita* consumption	19.4	20.5	19.8	-	- 1.1	- 0.4	-
7) *Per capita* rooms built	32.3	39.4	39.3	41.3	- 7.1	- 7.0	- 9.0
8) Shipments of merchandise (in tons per 1,000 inhabitants)***	64.9	67.3	62.4	-	- 2.4	+ 2.5	-
9) Automobile registration (number per 1,000 inhabitants)	36.1	38.6	39.4	40.4	- 2.5	- 3.3	- 4.3

10) *Per capita* monetary savings	44.5	42.5	41.4	-	+ 2.0	+ 3.1	-
Average of indices 2 to 10 above****	44.5 ***** 40.1 ******	43.7	47.5 *****	-	- 3.6	- 3.0	-

Source: International Bank for Reconstruction and Development, Department of Operations Europe, Africa and Australasia, *Cassa per il Mezzogiorno and the Economic Development of Southern Italy*, E.A.–80a/Restricted, February 18, 1958, p. 28, <https://documents.worldbank.org/en/publication/documents-reports/documentdetail/752391468049200134/italy-cassa-per-il-mezzogiorno-and-the-economic-development-of-southern-italy>.

*Calculations based on the 1950/52 average. ***Calculations based on the 1953/55 average. ***Goods shipped by railway and by sea. ****Excluding point 5, in 1950 and in 1954. *****Data involving all the points from 2 to 10. ****** Excluding point 5, to make it comparable with 1954.

The report issued in 1958 by the International Bank for Reconstruction and Development did indeed represent the most meaningful document to understand the benefits of the intervention carried out by the Cassa per il Mezzogiorno towards the development of Southern Italian economy, besides showing the scope and importance of the initiatives carried out by the Bank itself on behalf of Italy and its more backwards area. As it was noted in the report, many of the advancements experienced in Southern Italy during the years between 1950 and 1957 could be credited to the extraordinary intervention and to the actions carried out by the Cassa, as well as to the combination of the reform-oriented provisions enacted in favor of southern Italy. Other improvements were instead justified by the general growth process of both the national and international economies. Such a distinction allowed appreciating the specific contribution made by the Cassa to the Southern situation. The results highlighted the importance of a policy instrument without which the Mezzogiorno would have been stuck in its undeveloped condition, doomed to an irreparable dualism with respect to the national economic system. The economy of Southern Italy had significantly improved within a few years after the beginning of the extraordinary intervention, achieving the unexpected result of an increase in growth rates proportionally greater than in the rest of the country. This was achieved in the most disparate sectors: from agriculture to several industries, from residential construction to electricity. Infrastructures were considerably advanced and significantly useful services had spread widely in the whole of Southern Italy. Additionally, income and consumption had grown more intensely in Southern Italy, as did private and, most of all, public investments.

Hence, even at the very beginning of the industrialization process, which would introduce the essential strategic variable for the economic development of the Mezzogiorno, the Bank had already acknowledged a significant, albeit partial, outcome – which originated from the first seven years of the Cassa's activity. After all, the tables contained in the final part of the IBRD paper, particularly those displayed above (Table 3.3, Table 3.4 and Table 3.5), showed clearly that some of the fundamental indicators (*per capita* gross income, *per capita* investments, *per capita* consumption of food and of other goods, gross agricultural production *per capita*, *per capita* industrial electric power consumption, *per capita* housing, shipping of goods, registrations of cars, and monetary savings) were in favor of Southern Italy, bearing witness to the fact that, after a situation of stasis, economic dynamism had finally begun in Southern Italy. Hence, there was hope that those areas would be able to bridge the gap they had with the rest of the country during a growing part of the economic cycle. As a matter of fact, from the elaborations presented by the IBRD report, it was clear that a remarkable and increasingly steady capability on Southern Italy's part to bridge the gap with the North was buying built. This was the first time since the Italian unification that such an event happened, and it was also the first time ever that the project of an economic unification between the two parts of the country began to take concrete shape.

3.3 The main commitments by the World Bank and the European Investment Bank towards the development of Southern Italy

The year 1959 was truly meaningful with respect to the several ways the IBRD could support the Southern Italian economy. The Bank's role evolved from the usual evaluation of projects for industry and energy to the then brand-new hypothesis to build a nuclear power plant in Southern Italy. The document issued on March 26, 1959 and dedicated to the "Seventh Southern Italy Development Project", whose public disclosure was authorized on April 16, 2010, had a similar denomination to that of the report issued in the previous year, *Appraisal of Italian Industrial and Power Projects*[289]. The

[289] See International Bank for Reconstruction and Development, Department of Technical Operations, *Appraisal of Italian Industrial and Power Projects*, T.O.–202a/Restricted, March 26, 1959,

document examined new projects for the economic development of Southern Italy. The projects had been proposed by the Italian government in order to obtain a loan from the Bank. As detailed in the abstract:

> The Seventh Southern Italy Development Project for Italy will assist in financing a program for the economic development of southern Italy. It will entail three specific projects: two industrial (SINCAT and CELENE) and one power (MERCURE). The first project is SINCAT. It will develop an integrated chemical manufacturing complex at Priolo, Sicily, based on the local availability of raw materials. Some of the SINCAT project components are: 1) installation of an integrated complex fertilizer plant; 2) opening of a mine for mineral extraction; and 3) installing a steam cracking plant. The second project is CELENE. It will construct a plant at Priolo also for the production and processing of polyethylene and ethylene oxide and derivatives. The third and final project is MERCURE. It will construct a thermal power plant to meet the increasing demands for power. Some of its components are procurement of turbo generator units, boilers, and a cooling system and construction of an outdoor substation with phase three transformers. These three projects will help to foster the economic development of southern Italy by increasing industry growth and power production[290].

The introduction to this report reminded that, in the summer of 1958, the Italian government had asked to the International Bank for Reconstruction and Development to keep on supporting the 12-year development plan on behalf of the Mezzogiorno, under the aegis of the Cassa, to whom the Bank had already granted five loans. As the document reported: «It was proposed that a Bank loan be made in conjunction with the Cassa's entry into the New York capital market»[291]. Furthermore, it was added that also the European Investment Bank (EIB) had shown some interest in financing projects in Italy[292]. It must be said that the IBRD, after a debate involving the European Investment Bank, the Italian government and the Cassa, informed the

<https://documents.worldbank.org/en/publication/documents-reports/documentdetail/977591468253454017/italy-sixth-Southern-italy-development-project>.

[290] *Ibidem*.

[291] *Ivi*, p. 1.

[292] See *Ibidem*. On this topic, it may be made reference to a recent publication, in order to further study the main intervention lines chosen by the European Investment Bank towards economic development policies, in particular concerning Italy and in the specific features of its areas (See D. Strangio, *La rinascita economica dell'Europa. Dall'European Recovery program all'integrazione economica europea e alla Banca europea per gli investimenti*, Soveria Mannelli, Rubbettino, 2011).

relevant Italian authorities that it would take into consideration a loan request based on three conditions: the EIB would equally share the financing of the projects with the IBRD; the sum total of the joint loans granted by the EIB and the IBRD could not reach beyond $ 40 million (in installments amounting to $ 20 million coming from each Bank); the relevant market operations had to proceed together with the loans granted by the EIB and the IBRD, but the latter would evaluate only the projects to be financed with the aforementioned $ 40 million[293]. On this basis, the IBRD had requested a list of proposals to be examined for a loan, whose preliminary elements, concerning six power and energy-related projects and eight industrial projects, where submitted to Washington in the winter of 1958[294]. The examination of such projects, which could not be financed overall, was carried out following the criteria, agreed with the Cassa, of maximum priority and completeness of the relevant programs. Through such procedures, three projects were approved (the SINCAT and CELENE industrial ones and the "Mercure" power-related one), involving reviewed sums compared with the initial forecasts[295].

In the section of the IBRD document focused on industrial projects, the previous interventions were recapped. They had brought forth the granting of loans amounting to about $ 80 million, concerning 22 productive initiatives, with an estimated overall cost of $ 187 million. Nine of these projects had already been completed, while the others were well under way.

---

[293] See International Bank for Reconstruction and Development, Department of Technical Operations, *Appraisal of Italian Industrial and Power Projects*, cit., p. 1.

[294] See *Ibidem*.

[295] See *Ibidem*. In the following table, both the amounts requested and the recommended allocations were included.

	Amount requested ($ million)	Recommended allocation ($ million)
SINCAT	16	14
CELENE	8	8
Mercure	22	18
Total	46	40

Source: International Bank for Reconstruction and Development, Department of Technical Operations, *Appraisal of Italian Industrial and Power Projects*, T.O.–202a/Restricted, March 26, 1959, p. 2, <https://documents.worldbank.org/en/publication/documents-reports/documentdetail/977591468253454017/italy-sixth-Southern-italy-development-project>.

Their completion was foreseen by the end of 1961[296]. Furthermore, the projects presented were examined[297], with an indication of the general evaluation procedures. The projects were to be financed for an amount of $ 22 million, each. Half of the sum was to be provided by the Bank for Reconstruction and Development and the other half by the European Investment Bank. Along with the description of the other features of the loan, it was made clear that the interest rate was 6.25%, lower than in the case of the previous credit line (see note 9). Additionally, in any case the IBRD had the task of the final approval of the proposal terms[298]. A detailed evaluation of the single activities then followed the overall analysis of the industrial initiatives[299].

In the section of the report concerning the energy sector, it was stressed that the funds assigned to the development program for the Mezzogiorno could not be used for this purpose. Therefore, the total sum, amounting to little more than $ 84 million and pertaining to the tree loans previously made by the IBRD on behalf of the Cassa (in 1955, 1956 and 1958), had been

---

[296] See International Bank for Reconstruction and Development, Department of Technical Operations, *Appraisal of Italian Industrial and Power Projects*, cit., p. 3.

[297] See *Ivi*, pp. 3-4. On this topic the following was noted in the first of the two pages:

> The two projects presented for consideration under the proposed loan are estimated to have a total cost of $ 51 million equivalent. The applications had been screened by the Sicilian regional institute (IRFIS) which would be directly responsible for the loans. The funds required would be made available to IRFIS by the Cassa out of the loans from the IBRD and EIB. The Cassa would take the foreign exchange risk but IRFIS would bear the normal commercial risks and administer the funds for the Cassa.

[298] See International Bank for Reconstruction and Development, Department of Technical Operations, *Appraisal of Italian Industrial and Power Projects*, cit., p. 5. In the very same page, the following was clarified:

> For purposes of calculation, an interest rate of 6.25% has been assumed for the proposed loans by IRFIS from IBRD and EIB funds. The repayment of the proposed loans has been assumed on the basis of level service payments, including interest and amortization. The term suggested for each loan is based on estimates of the probable economic life of equipment, taking into account the high obsolescence rate in the chemical industry, and on the expected generation of funds. The grace periods suggested for the loans correspond approximately to the length of the construction period plus a reasonable time to run in the facilities. The terms on which the loans would be made by IRFIS may differ slightly from those suggested, but in each case would be subject to IBRD approval.

[299] See International Bank for Reconstruction and Development, Department of Technical Operations, *Appraisal of Italian Industrial and Power Projects*, cit., pp. 6-16.

allocated for eight interventions concerning the energy sector in several areas of Southern Italy[300]. Furthermore, it was noted that the project regarding the Società Meridionale di Elettricità called "Mercure", and described both in its general and its particular features, could rely on a grant of $ 18 million, jointly provided in equal parts by the International Bank for Reconstruction and Development and by the European Investment Bank[301]. Finally, the following picture (Figure 3.6) was attached to this document, showing the location of the industrial and energy-related interventions in Southern Italy, the companies involved in them, and their production.

Another very interesting graph (Figure 3.7) was included within the appendix of the IBRD report. It concerned the role of the Società Meridionale di Elettricità group within the development policies on behalf of the Mezzogiorno and, in particular, its effective power capacity, which was able to bestow further resources and a significant reserve capacity on the system[302], by means of the interventions, be they completed or underway.

[300] See *Ivi*, p. 17.
[301] See *Ivi*, pp. 17-28.
[302] See *Ivi*, p. 19.

Figure 3.6 *Locations of the industrial and power projects in Southern Italy (1959)*

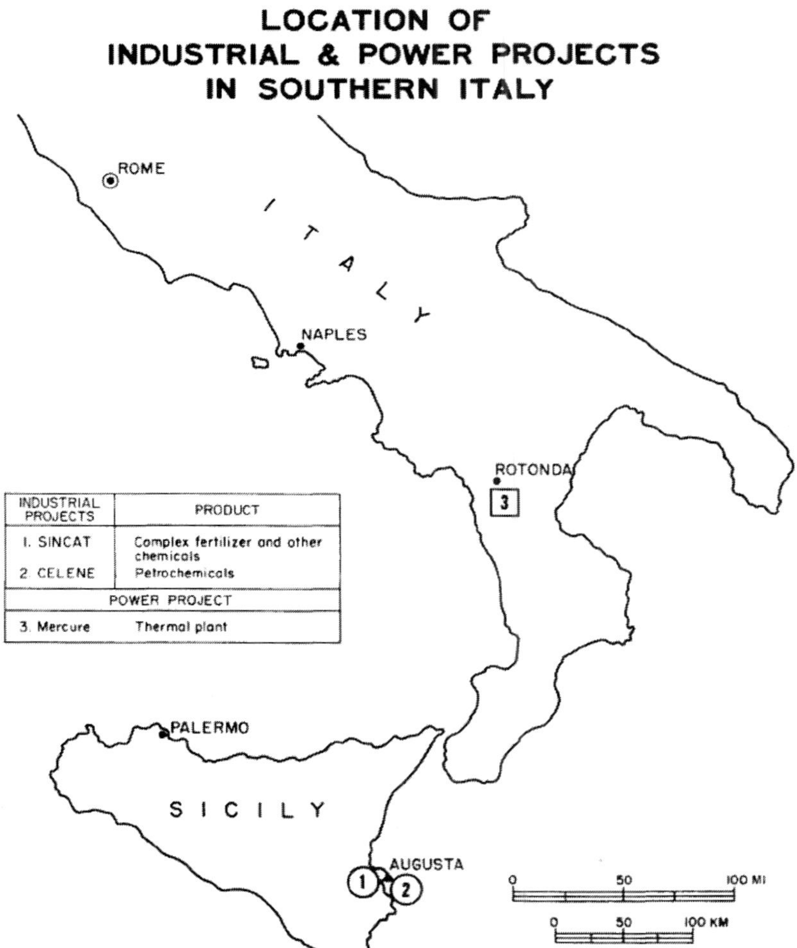

Source: International Bank for Reconstruction and Development, Department of Technical Operations, *Appraisal of Italian Industrial and Power Projects*, T.O.–202a/Restricted, March 26, 1959, *Map showing Location of Projects*, <https://documents.worldbank.org/en/publication/documents-reports/documentdetail/977591468253454017/italy-sixth-southern-italy-development-project>.

Figure 3.7 *Italy: SME group effective energy-generating capacity and peak load (1957-1965)*

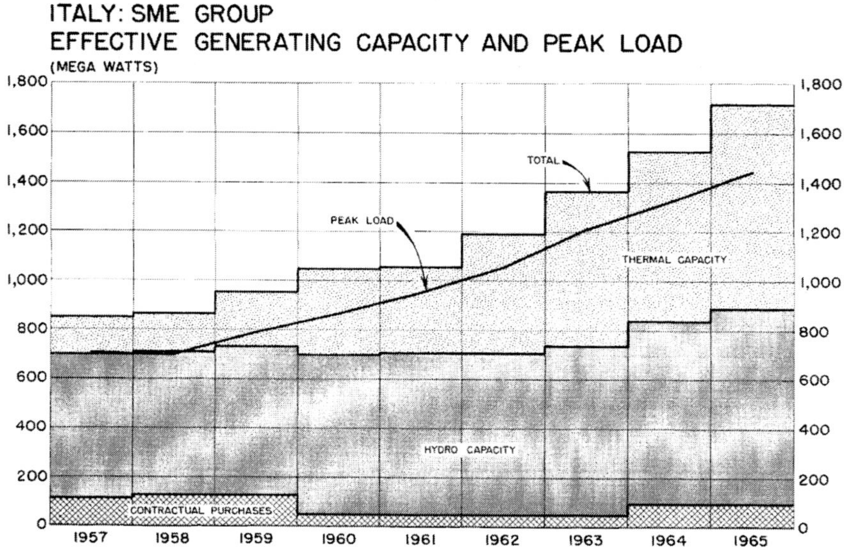

Source: International Bank for Reconstruction and Development, Department of Technical Operations, *Appraisal of Italian Industrial and Power Projects*, T.O.–202a/Restricted, March 26, 1959, Annex B-4, <https://documents.worldbank.org/en/publication/documents-reports/documentdetail/977591468253454017/italy-sixth-southern-italy-development-project>.

In the document issued on March 25, 1959, titled *Preliminary Report of the President to the Executive Directors on a Proposed Loan for Southern Italy Development Projects*, whose public disclosure was authorized on June 25, 2010, the President of the International Bank for Reconstruction and Development, Eugene Robert Black, examined the hypothesis of $ 20 million loan to the Cassa per il Mezzogiorno, in order to finance the three aforementioned projects, thus advancing the power-generating capacity of Southern Italy[303]. First and foremost, he drew up an historical synopsis of

[303] See International Bank for Reconstruction and Development, *Preliminary Report of the President to the Executive Directors on a Proposed Loan for Southern Italy Development Projects*, P–190/Restricted, Archives/Records Center, Room HB1–001, Box 935–01, Nus Location 099–1–2, March 25, 1959,

the loans the Bank had granted to Italy, which amounted to about $ 240 million by then[304]. Afterwards, he recapped the further financial commitments to be undertaken in order to develop the Mezzogiorno, following the evaluations carried out by the IBRD, the EIB and Morgan Stanley:

> Following discussions early in 1958, the Bank agreed to consider a further loan to the Cassa which would be made in conjunction with an issue in the New York market. Shortly thereafter it developed that the European Investment Bank (EIB) would be interested in participating in the proposed joint lending. It was agreed in principle that the EIB and the Bank would cooperate in the selection and appraisal of projects and that each institution would provide half the external finance being provided for each project. Both loans would be made simultaneously with a public issue to be arranged by Morgan Stanley and Co. [...] A Bank mission visited Italy in February and March of this year to discuss the general lines of the operation and to appraise the projects. Representatives of the EIB and of Morgan Stanley were in Italy at the same time. Three projects were selected as being most suitable as a basis for lending by both the Bank and the EIB. The proceeds of the public issue would be used for the general development program of the Cassa. [...] In addition to the loan described in this report, discussions are now in progress for a loan of $ 40 million equivalent to the Cassa for the SENN nuclear power project[305].

Afterwards, the report considered the most important features of this credit line, beginning with its total amount, for a sum of $ 70 million, $ 30 million of which concerned a public issue, $ 20 million came from the IBRD and $ 20 million from the EIB[306]. The overall financing commitment had the following features: its beneficiary was the Cassa per il Mezzogiorno; its guarantor was the Italian Republic; the common goal of the IBRD and the EIB was to finance two industrial projects and an energy-related one in the areas of Southern Italy, while the public issue was directly linked to the development program for Southern Italy. The loan conditions envisioned a series of biannual installments for amortization, starting in 1963 and ending in 1978, while the public issue was half divided in a 15-year amortization bonds fund (the so-called *fifteen year sinking fund bonds*) and the other half

---

<https://documents.worldbank.org/en/publication/documents-reports/documentdetail/490151468253455122/italy-sixth--italy-development-project>.

304 See *Ivi*, p. 1.

305 *Ivi*, p. 2.

306 See *Ibidem*.

into 3- 4- and 5- year bonds[307]. After a summary evaluation of the projects, which made specific reference to the essential content presented in the *Appraisal of Italian Industrial and Power Projects*, the President of the International Bank for Reconstruction and Development tackled the issues concerning industrial supply, loan granting and amortization, as well as the perspectives of Italy complying towards its obligations. These perspectives were based on the examination of the projects and on the analysis of Italy's economic situation[308]. On this specific issue, Eugene Robert Black proposed a supplement to the preliminary report[309], in order to further define loan

---

[307] See *Ivi*, pp. 2-3. Within the second of these two pages, the following was highlighted:

> The Bank loan would be similar in form to previous loans to the Cassa for the development of Southern Italy. The Bank loan and the EIB loan would together provide financing for three projects; \$ 18 million for the Mercure power project, \$ 14 million for the Sincat petrochemical project and \$ 8 million for the Celene polyethylene project. Half of these amounts would be provided by the Bank and half by the EIB.

[308] See International Bank for Reconstruction and Development, *Preliminary Report of the President to the Executive Directors on a Proposed Loan for Southern Italy Development Projects*, cit., pp. 3-6. Within the part of the document concerning "disbursement" (p. 5), it was possible to notice that:

> As expenditures are made on the projects, requests for disbursements will be made to the Cassa. The Cassa will thereupon request disbursement in equal amounts from the Bank and the EIB. The funds so obtained by the Cassa will be lent in lire to SME in respect of the Mercure project and to IRFIS [...] in respect of the Sincat and Celene projects. This procedure is essentially the same as under previous Bank loans to the Cassa, with the modification necessitated by the participation of the EIB.

[309] The President of the IBRD summarized in some final data and numbers the sense of a suggestion which was preparatory to the next document:

> Recent developments in Italy's external accounts have been favorable. A decline in the volume of imports simultaneously with continued high exports, the fall in import prices and rapidly rising receipts from invisibles have resulted in a sharp rise in reserves. Net official reserves increased by \$ 286 million in 1957 and \$ 850 million in 1958, and at the end of the year were more than \$ 2.2 billion. [...] There can be no doubt of Italy's ability to service the additional external debt now contemplated. On December 31, 1958 the external public debt of Italy was estimated at \$ 849 million. Service payments constitute at present less than 4% of Italy's global foreign exchange earnings at the 1958 rate. The financing described in this report would increase the Bank's investment in Italy to \$ 233.5 million, and Italy's total external debt to \$ 919 million

terms, to focus the judgment on the Italian economy and to offer some recommendations when granting the loan was concerned[310].

In the document of April 13, 1959, signed by the Vice-President of the International Bank for Reconstruction and Development, William A.B. Iliff, titled *Report and Recommendations of the President to the Executive Directors on a Proposed Loan of $ 20 million to the Cassa for Development Projects in Southern Italy* (whose public disclosure was authorized on June 24, 2010), further elements were given about the loan in favor of the "Cassa per Opere Straordinarie di Pubblico Interesse nell'Italia Meridionale", bound to support two industrial projects and a power-related one[311]. Concerning the public bonds issue, it was clarified that:

> Following the meeting of the Executive Directors on April 2, I advised the underwriters, Morgan Stanley & Co. that in the absence of some major adverse development there seemed no reason to believe that the proposed loan would not be approved by the Executive Directors in time for the proposed public issue. Arrangements to make the public offering on April 22 have been practically concluded except for the determination of price and interest. The underwriters have filed a Registration Statement with the Securities and Exchange Commission for an issue of $ 30 million, Southern Italy Development Fund (Cassa per il Mezzogiorno) guaranteed external loan bonds as follows:
>
> $ 5 million 4 year bonds due May 1, 1963

(International Bank for Reconstruction and Development, *Preliminary Report of the President to the Executive Directors on a Proposed Loan for Southern Italy Development Projects*, cit., p. 6).

[310] As it was proposed to the executive directors, in the final section of the report:

> In this event, I propose to submit to you at a meeting before the public issue (which at present is planned for April 22, 1959) a supplement to this report setting forth the proposed final terms of the borrowing, attaching the loan documents, a report on the economy of Italy, and containing my recommendations regarding the loan

(International Bank for Reconstruction and Development, *Preliminary Report of the President to the Executive Directors on a Proposed Loan for Southern Italy Development Projects*, cit., p. 7).

[311] See International Bank for Reconstruction and Development, *Report and Recommendations of the President to the Executive Directors on a Proposed Loan of $ 20 million to the Cassa for Development Projects in Southern Italy*, P–192/Restricted, Archives/Records Center, Room HB1–001, Box 935–01, Nus Location 099–1–2, April 13, 1959, <https://documents.worldbank.org/en/publication/documents-reports/documentdetail/537241468262474317/italy-sixth-southern-italy-development-project>.

> $ 5 million 5 year bonds due May 1, 1964
> $ 20 million 15 year sinking fund bonds due May 1, 1974
> The 4 and 5 year bonds will not be redeemable. The 15 year bonds will be redeemable on or after May 1, 1969 at the option of the Cassa per il Mezzogiorno and also by operation of a sinking fund starting November 1, 1964 and designed to retire the entire issue by maturity. Principal and interest on the bonds will be payable in U. S. dollars. [...] The proceeds of the issue will be applied toward the Cassa per il Mezzogiorno's general program of economic development and rehabilitation in Southern Italy but no allocation has been made to any specific project[312].

The report then made a reference to the financing, proposed in several currencies, assigned to the Cassa per il Mezzogiorno by the European Investment Bank, which had raised an amount of 12.5 billion lire (that is to say 20 million dollars) and featured loan terms and conditions substantially equal to those of the IBRD[313]. Furthermore, the loan granted by the International Bank for Reconstruction and Development had an interest rate of 5 and 3/4%, including commission. The legal documents requested for the financing were a loan contract, a guarantee agreement and a project agreement[314]. The loan credit lines followed the regulations that had been set up for the three previous financial interventions in favor of the Cassa. However, in this case, this initiative was coordinated with the analogous one undertaken by the EIB, connecting the two different financial agreements with each other[315].

---

[312] *Ivi*, p. 1.
[313] See *Ibidem*.
[314] See *Ivi*, p. 2.
[315] See *Ibidem*. Within the aforementioned report page, it was also clarified that:
> Thus the Bank may cancel or require repayment in advance of maturity of a portion of its loan corresponding to any portion of the EIB loan cancelled or repaid in advance of maturity [...]. The Bank will also have the right to require immediate repayment of the principal of its loan if the EIB requires immediate repayment under its Loan Agreement with the Cassa [...]. As in our previous loans to the Cassa, the Loan and Guarantee Agreements may become effective and be suspended separately with respect to each project and the amount of the loan allocated thereto. There will be the usual Project Agreement, this time with the Società Meridionale di Elettricità (SME). Società Finanziaria Elettrica Nazionale per Azioni ("Finelettrica") and Società Italiana per le Strade Ferrate Meridionali ("Bastogi") will be additional parties to the Project Agreement, guaranteeing performance of the Agreement and agreeing to become sureties for the performance of all obligations (including financial) of SME to the Cassa. [...] A new feature of this loan is that the Cassa will repay the Bank as it receives repayment from

The analysis of the Italian economic situation at the time, which was attached to the report, showed that the proposed loan was compatible with Italy's creditworthiness and, due to the necessity of tackling the problem of unemployment and of speeding up development in Southern Italy, it was deemed suitable to continue importing long-term capitals. However, the IBRD pointed out the fact that, if the long-term savings offer coming from internal sources would have kept its growing trajectory, and the capitals markets would have consolidated their progressive enlargement, Italy would have had to limit more and more the use of such foreign capitals[316]. The document ended with a recommendation to the Bank's Board of Directors, which held a positive orientation towards financing the loan[317].

Concerning the intervention by the European Investment Bank – an institution that preeminently dedicated its activities to regional development initiatives – it is worth noting that the EIB kept a constant focus on regions that perceived as chronically late in development, such as it was the case with the Italian Mezzogiorno[318], while its commitment for other territories,

---

> the beneficiary enterprises and this is reflected in the amortization schedule. Due to the fact that the two industrial projects will be repaid by the beneficiary enterprises in 12 years, the average amount outstanding over the life of the loan is substantially reduced. Another new feature is that the Cassa is required to repay both Banks in advance of maturity an amount equivalent to any repayment made by the beneficiary enterprises in advance of maturity [...].

[316] See International Bank for Reconstruction and Development, *Report and Recommendations of the President to the Executive Directors on a Proposed Loan of $ 20 million to the Cassa for Development Projects in Southern Italy*, cit., p. 3.

[317] The report did in fact feature the presidential formula supporting the loan, which stated:

> I recommend that the Bank at this time make a loan to the Cassa per Opere Straordinarie di Pubblico Interesse nell'Italia Meridionale in an amount in various currencies equivalent to $ 20 million to be guaranteed by the Republic of Italy for a term of 20 years with interest, commission and commitment charges and on such other terms as are specified in the attached draft Loan and Guarantee Agreements and that the Executive Directors adopt a resolution to that effect in the form attached

(International Bank for Reconstruction and Development, *Report and Recommendations of the President to the Executive Directors on a Proposed Loan of $ 20 million to the Cassa for Development Projects in Southern Italy*, cit., p. 3).

[318] As it has been noted: «already in the Treaty of Rome the mission of this entity was sanctioned by a special protocol [...] concerning Italy; it compels the institution to adequately employ its resources in favor of the Italian context, in particular on behalf of Southern Italy. [...] In Italy, we note that [...] the public hand mostly used the EIB, through the Cassa per il Mezzogiorno, the Iri, the Ferrovie dello Stato, the

such as those of the Centre-Northern Italy, was less constant and depended on the economic situation. The concentration of financing tools within the regions of Southern Italy was so intense that it absorbed more than 400 million accounting units, amounting to more than half of the loans granted to its member States, considering the first decade of activity by the EIB[319]. Through such resources, various projects were completed, including infrastructure, projects aimed at increasing the power capacity, improving railway transport, roads and telecommunication networks, enhancing irrigation structures, and deeply improving agricultural techniques. In the industrial sector, the aim was to augment production tools, most of all in the areas of Campania, Apulia, Sicily and Sardinia[320]. As confirmation of the soundness of the interventions carried by the European Investment Bank in the Mezzogiorno, the document reported that: «Through its constant and coherent action, the Bank undoubtedly contributed to significant progress in the regional development in Italy. Important infrastructure has been completed and enhanced in several areas, dynamic and useful industrial complexes were built in others and in other areas still a network of medium-sized enterprises have been helped in establishing themselves»[321]. Of course, such evaluations must be compared with the overall dimension of this part of the initiatives in favor of Southern Italy, which only accounted for about 10% of the overall financing granted by the special credit institutions during the years between 1959 and 1966[322].

Therefore, by the end of the 1950s, the framework of the extraordinary intervention was completed and found new lifeblood in the joint strategies carried out by the World Bank and the European Investment Bank, who joined their efforts in order to provide a more effective credit line. Indeed, the complex economic and financial model started with the Cassa per il

---

Italian Railway Company and, to some degree, also the Eni and the Efim. Wisely authorized, since the inception of its activities, to contract loans abroad, the Cassa was without a doubt the entity which most used EIB interventions, with a double task as an intermediary to provide funds to Southern Italy credit institutions (such as Isveimer, Irfis and Cis) and of direct beneficiary for the works to implement in its own, such as the Special Projects» (D. Strangio, *La rinascita economica dell'Europa. Dall'European Recovery program all'integrazione economica europea e alla Banca europea per gli investimenti*, cit., pp. 61-63).

319 See ASBI, *Raccolte diverse*, *Relazioni e Bilanci*, Folder, no. 699 (See D. Strangio, *La rinascita economica dell'Europa. Dall'European Recovery program all'integrazione economica europea e alla Banca europea per gli investimenti*, cit., p. 68).

320 See *Ivi*, p. 69.

321 *Ibidem*.

322 See *Ivi*, p. 73.

Mezzogiorno, thanks to the contribution of the two aforementioned international Banks was, on one hand, the pinnacle of the evolution of the policies for Southern Italy. These policies were as a matter of fact spurred by "new meridionalism" and where consolidated by a tight network of relations and a combination of initiatives between the Italian government and one of the Bretton Woods institutions, such as the IBRD. On the other hand, these interventions manifested a general drive for "systemic" growth, which had created strong connections and correspondences between the interests of Southern Italy, those in the rest of the country and the political, economic and financial interests on the other side of the Atlantic. In such a context, first and foremost thanks to the beginning of the industrialization process in the Mezzogiorno, a significant space was given to an effective commitment in modernizing the Italian production and to the process of bridging the gap between the South and the North of Italy. These different ingredients, mixed with great wisdom following the postwar reconstruction phase, gave life to the Italian "economic miracle" and to the Italian "golden age", two achievements in which the role of the Cassa far exceeded pro-cyclical measures, as it created the capacity for the economy of Southern Italy to develop more quickly than the most advanced areas of Italy.

CHAPTER FOUR

THE LATTER PERIOD OF WORLD BANK FINANCING AND THE RESULTS OF "SYSTEMIC" INTERVENTION

4.1 The World Bank and the Cassa per il Mezzogiorno tackling the "nuclear issue"

The document the International Bank for Reconstruction and Development issued on September 4, 1959 and titled *Appraisal of the Senn Nuclear Power Plant – Italy*[323], whose public disclosure was authorized on June 18, 2010, examined the financing tools covering 60% of the estimated building costs of the Garigliano nuclear power plant. The abstract of the document provided a brief summary of the project's main features:

> The project consists of 1) a nuclear power plant located on the southern bank of the Garigliano River, about 7 kilometers inland from the point of its outflow into the Gulf of Gaeta; 2) a primary step-up substation; and 3) two single circuit 220 kv transmission lines – one 44 kilometers long, extending northward, connecting the plant with the Ceprano substation of the Società Romana di Elettricità system, and the other 56 kilometers long, extending southward, connecting the plant with the Fratta Maggiore substation of the SME system. The site of the plant, between Rome and Naples, was selected because of its favorable characteristics for the safe release of waste gases and for disposal of solid radioactive wastes, good supply of cooling water, its satisfactory geological and meteorological conditions and the low population density. The generating station would incorporate a dual-cycle forced circulation boiling water nuclear reactor supplying steam to a dual

[323] See International Bank for Reconstruction and Development, Department of Technical Operations, *Appraisal of the Senn Nuclear Power Plant – Italy*, T.O.–200/Restricted, September 4, 1959, <https://documents.worldbank.org/en/publication/documents-reports/documentdetail/377991468262473745/italy-senn-nuclear-power-plant-project>.

admission, tandem compound turbine, directly connected to a single generator[324].

Indeed, the Italian government requested a $ 40 million loan to the Bank to build a plant able to warrant a power output of 160 MW, whose total construction costs had been estimated to amount to 66.4 million dollars. The beneficiary, as in previous cases, was to be the Cassa per il Mezzogiorno, which would then transfer the loan to the Società Elettronucleare Nazionale (SENN)[325]. This company had been established in 1957 within the IRI-Finelettrica group. By the very next year, the company was able to provide up to 36% of the whole Italian electrical power demand[326]. The IBRD document appraising the project was based on the results of a study concerning the opportunity to establish a nuclear power plant in Southern Italy. Such a study was promoted by the Italian government and the Bank, which collected information from staff members of the aforementioned institution during their visits in Italy between the second half of 1958 and the spring of 1959[327].

Already in June 1956, the IBRD had drawn up a general report that identified good opportunities for nuclear power to be produced in a conventional plant at competitive costs[328], provided the following conditions

---

[324] *Ibidem*.

[325] On this topic, it has been noted that:

> The proceeds of the proposed loan would be relent by Cassa to SENN. The subsidiary loan agreement, between Cassa and SENN would be subject to Bank approval and would protect the interests and rights of the Cassa and provide for security and guarantees appropriate to the circumstances. Furthermore, SENN would undertake various obligations in regard to the construction and operation of the project in a project agreement with the Bank

(International Bank for Reconstruction and Development, Department of Technical Operations, *Appraisal of the Senn Nuclear Power Plant – Italy*, cit., p. 5).

[326] See *Ivi*, p. 1. On the same page it was noted that:

> This company, which would build, own and operate the project, is largely owned by a group of public utility companies. In 1958 these companies accounted for about 36% of total electric energy requirements in Italy.

[327] See International Bank for Reconstruction and Development, Department of Technical Operations, *Appraisal of the Senn Nuclear Power Plant – Italy*, cit., p. 1.

[328] As it has been noted: «In 1955 the World Bank, encouraged by the favorable results of the first Geneva Conference, took upon itself to carry out a series of studies concerning the use of nuclear energy for peaceful purposes. Mr. Eugene Black deemed necessary to know the times and conditions in which nuclear energy could become economically competitive, considering the high financing percentage granted by the World Bank in the energy sector, given also the expectations of more

were met: the plant had to be integrated through a vast power generating and distributing system; it had to be based on a 100 MW or greater base unit; the plant had to be established in a country featuring relatively high fuel costs and a relatively low inclination towards hydroelectric power; at the same time the country to be chosen had to provide an adequate availability of capital, in order to guarantee a low cost of money. Such a country had also to ensure intergovernmental agreements towards a continuous supply of fuel and all the necessary technologies and materials. Furthermore, the power level of the distributing system connected to the plant had to be flexible, in order to absorb the possible excesses in costs or difference in working compared with the original project. Finally, the nuclear power plant had not to represent, until an advanced state of operations was achieved, the main source of power in the area[329].

Following the evaluation that «the conditions in Southern Italy appeared to be favorable for the construction of a nuclear plant»[330], an analysis started in July 1957 and was carried out to consider several locations. This study, which was promoted by the Italian government and the IBRD, was known as ENSI (Energia Nucleare Sud-Italia, i.e., *Nuclear Energy in Southern Italy*). The study tackled the following issues: the choice of a location to build the plant; the setting up of tenders to selected international operators

---

significant loans. Therefore, the report by Mr. Corbin Allardice, titled "Economic nuclear power today: where and under what circumstances" and issued on June 4, 1956 was born. This study, after comparing the costs of a conventional plant with those of a nuclear one, concluded that this new type of energy was a competitive investment with respect to traditional energy sources and was able to give a series of prerequisites for future plant building» (A.R. Rigano, *La Banca d'Italia e il progetto ENSI. Fonti per la storia dello sviluppo energetico italiano degli anni cinquanta nelle carte dell'Archivio della Banca d'Italia*, in "Quaderni dell'Ufficio Ricerche Storiche", Banca d'Italia, no. 4, June 2002, pp. 21-22, <https://www.bancaditalia.it/pubblicazioni/quaderni-storia/2002-0001/index.html>).

[329] See International Bank for Reconstruction and Development, Department of Technical Operations, *Appraisal of the Senn Nuclear Power Plant – Italy*, cit., pp. 1-2.

[330] *Ivi*, p. 2. The following was clarified within the very same page:

> This study was to serve three purposes: a) By obtaining tenders on an international competitive basis, it would provide firm data on the relative costs of competing types of nuclear plants. b) It would ascertain the relative capital and operating costs of a nuclear power plant of a given output compared with a conventional power plant of the same capacity and output. c) By providing these facts and the judgment on them of qualified nuclear specialists, the study would assist the Italians in selecting for construction the plant which seemed to have most merit taking all factors into consideration.

who would be capable of bidding for its construction; the review of the offers received and the preparation of their examination, with particular attention to the technical feasibility, the comparative costs and the performances; the general verification of the information on the costs of such a structure[331]. Executive responsibility for the Italian participation to the ENSI Project was entrusted to the Comitato Nazionale per le Ricerche Nucleari (CNRN, i.e., the Italian National Committee for Nuclear Research), while the overall management was assigned to Felice Ippolito, the General secretary of the Committee, and the IBRD Councilor for Nuclear Energy, Corbin Allardice[332]. Furthermore, the Bank set up a group of experts in the field of nuclear energy, with the task to ensure a common view in the study, to follow and evaluate the tenders and to report on costs and performances concerning the building of the power plant[333].

The Italian government had, in turn, given ownership and management of this plant to the aforementioned Società Elettronucleare Nazionale (SENN), which had been established on March 22, 1957 with registered address in Naples and offices in Rome[334]. Closely following the building phases of the power plant, the company's equity was to reach about 8 billion

---

[331] See International Bank for Reconstruction and Development, Department of Technical Operations, *Appraisal of the Senn Nuclear Power Plant – Italy*, cit., p. 2.

[332] See *Ibidem*.

[333] See *Ivi*, pp. 2-3.

[334] See *Ivi*, p. 3 and p. 5. The beginning phase of the choice to locate a nuclear power plant in the Mezzogiorno was summarized in a publication available in the "Archivio Storico dell'Enel", the historical archive of the main Italian power company:

> In April 1956 the public company part of Finelettrica (IRI) was spun off from SELNI, establishing the Società Elettro Nucleare Nazionale (SENN), in order to build a nuclear power plant in Southern Italy. Shortly after, ENI as well had publicly shown its willingness to build a nuclear power plant in Southern Italy by establishing the Società italiana meridionale per l'energia atomica (SIMEA). In July 1957, the International Bank for Reconstruction and Development (IBRD) signed an agreement with the Italian government to build a nuclear power station. The Cassa del Mezzogiorno had to provide resources coming from a loan by the IBRD itself. Therefore, the Bank and the Italian government set up a series of procedures in order to warrant the best choice between several procurement providers. The executive responsibility thereof was given to a Direction Commitee involving Mr. Corbin Allardice, a nuclear power expert representing the IBRD, and Mr. Ippolito, representing the top government. The implementation of this project (called *Progetto ENSI, Energia Nucleare Sud Italia*) was entrusted to the SENN

(Archivio Storico Enel, *Il Nucleare in Italia*, a text by G. Paoloni, Rome, Eccigraphica, 2009, pp. 71-72, <https://issuu.com/enelsharing/docs/01_nucleare_enel>).

lire. The majority of its equity shares (90%) was held by twelve companies – indirectly controlled by the Istituto per la Ricostruzione Industriale (IRI) – and the remaining shares by two private power companies[335]. Shareholders split their shares as follows: 25% to the Società Meridionale di Elettricità (SME), 10% to the Unione Esercizi Elettrici (UNES), 20% to the Società Idroelettrica Piemonte (SIP), 10% to the Terni – Società per l'Industria e l'Elettricità, 0.625% to the Società Finanziaria Elettrica Nazionale (Finelettrica), 4.375% to the Società Trentina di Elettricità (STE) and 5% to the Società Lombarda per la Distribuzione di Energia Elettrica (Vizzola) – part of the Finelettrica group, reaching a total of 75% – 3% to Ansaldo S.p.A. and 2% to Ansaldo San Giorgio S.p.A. – of the Finmeccanica group, reaching a total of 5% – then 4% to Dalmine S.p.A., 4% to Ilva Alti Forni e Acciaierie d'Italia and 2% to the Società Italiana Acciaierie di Cornigliano – of the Finsider group, reaching a total of 10%; specifically 7.5% belonged to the Società Romana di Elettricità (SRE) and 2.5% to Società Generale Elettrica della Sicilia (SGES) – themselves independent and privately-owned, for a total of 10%[336]. The Società Elettronucleare Nazionale was managed by a Board of 15 members, the majority of which were presidents and managers of companies belonging to the IRI group; furthermore, it had a general director and 68 employees, half of which had management and professional duties[337].

---

[335] See International Bank for Reconstruction and Development, Department of Technical Operations, *Appraisal of the Senn Nuclear Power Plant – Italy*, cit., p. 5.

[336] See *Ivi*, Annex 1. In the very same document (p. 6), the following was noted:

> The two largest shareholders of SENN, Società Meridionale di Elettricità (SME) and Società Idroelettrica Piemonte (SIP) as well as the holding company of Finelettrica, which is also a direct shareholder of SENN, would be parties to the Project Agreement between the Bank and SENN, guaranteeing its performance [...]. SME was a beneficiary of the four previous loans made by the Bank to Cassa with a total amount of $ 58.5 million. The share capital of SME, as of December 31, 1958, amounted to Lit. 75 billion of which 36% was owned by IRI and Finelettrica and the balance by private interests. Net fixed assets amounted to Lit. 116 billion. The long-term debt was Lit. 33 billion, resulting in a debt/equity ratio of 24/76. SME's investments, mainly in subsidiary and associated utility companies, amounted to Lit. 24.6 billion. The company's earnings record is good. Net profit before distribution of dividends for the financial year ended March 31, 1958, was Lit. 5.6 billion. The net income represented a return of 7.5% on net fixed assets in operation. A dividend of 7.5% has been paid in recent years.

[337] See International Bank for Reconstruction and Development, Department of Technical Operations, *Appraisal of the Senn Nuclear Power Plant – Italy*, cit., p. 7. On this very page, it was noted that SENN itself requested the needed government

In the month of October 1957, the call for bids towards building a nuclear power plant in Southern Italy having a power between 130 and 150 MW, was sent to 17 companies (eight of them were American, five British, two French, one was Canadian and the other one was Belgian-American) as they had shown interest in the project. The aim was to complete the construction within four years from the procurement[338]. Together with the start of such a selection, SENN set up a detailed report on the chosen building site and sent it to the competing companies. Nine of them (namely four American, four British and one French one) made their final bids to build the power plant in April 1958[339]. After this procedure and an accurate examination of the proposals, the Società Elettronucleare Nazionale accepted the offer of the International General Electric Company, an American subsidiary of General Electric[340]. On this, the following has been noted:

> In September 1958 the builder was chosen: it was the US General Electric Company (its reactor would employ enriched and moderated uranium and cooled with boiling water). The power plant envisioned a power of up to 160 MW, and was to be built in Punta Fiume, to the estuary of the Garigliano River. To the choice in favor of General Electric had surely contributed a decision by ENI to adopt the British setup (natural uranium graphite-moderated and gas-cooled reactor) for its own power plant, in November 1957[341].

permission to build a nuclear power plant having a power of 160 MW and the permission to reroute and use the water of the Garigliano river towards this goal.

[338] See International Bank for Reconstruction and Development, Department of Technical Operations, *Appraisal of the Senn Nuclear Power Plant – Italy*, cit., p. 3.

[339] See *Ibidem*.

[340] See *Ivi*, pp. 4-5.

[341] Archivio Storico Enel, *Il Nucleare in Italia*, cit., p. 72.

Figure 4.1 *Front of a Finelettrica brochure – SENN (1957). Explanation table of the ENSI projects (1958)*

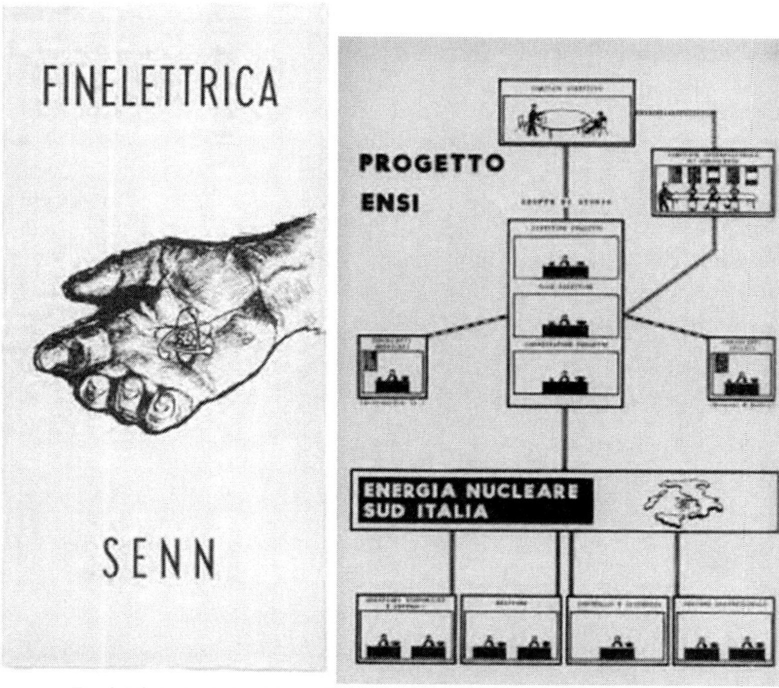

Source: Enel Historical Archive, *Il Nucleare in Italia*, text by G. Paoloni, Rome, Eccigraphica, 2009, p. 69 and p. 72, <https://issuu.com/enelsharing/docs/01_nucleare_enel>.

The document by the International Bank for Reconstruction and Development, after an analysis of the conditions of the Italian energy market[342], described the ENSI project in detail, focusing on its economic and financial features (Figure 4.1)[343].

The project description began with the indication of the power plant site and the reasons for its choice[344]. The description then recorded the technical features of the plant, how it was to be built, and the role of each subject

---

342 On this topic, the IBRD considered the following:

> At the end of 1958 the total installed capacity of the interconnected Italian power system amounted to 13,500 MW, consisting of 10,400 MW hydro and 3,100 MW thermal capacity. Total generation amounted to about 45 billion kwh. [...] Utility companies, which are shareholders of SENN would purchase the power to be generated by the nuclear plant. The detailed arrangements including the proportion to be taken by each of these Companies have not yet been worked out. In considering the potential market for the SENN plant, the future demand of the interconnected system of all the utility shareholders of SENN has been studied. The area supplied by these companies and their affiliates is about 158,000 square kilometers or 50% of the total area of Italy. It covers the southern, central and north western parts of the country. [...] The population in this area is 26.5 million, representing 55% of the country's total population. [...] The power demand has in recent years increased at an average annual rate of 7% in the north of Italy, 8% in the central and south and 15% in Sicily. The higher rate in the southern part of the country is a result of the activities of Cassa

(International Bank for Reconstruction and Development, Department of Technical Operations, *Appraisal of the Senn Nuclear Power Plant – Italy*, cit., p. 8).

343 See *Ivi*, pp. 10-21.

344 On this topic, the following has been reminded: «The government representatives expressed only their preference for Southern Italy; such a choice answer the need to establish a synergy between infrastructure policies and industrialization. The issues concerning the placement of the power plant had to respond to other, more stringent criteria. The main issue was that the plant had to be placed near highly power-using facilities, both to allow industries the use of such power and to integrate such energy within existing electric lines. Therefore, such a plant had to be built not too far from the Centre-Southern areas of Italy, that is to say the Rome-Naples axis, considering also the relative proximity of the Terni conventional power plant, where the connection could be achieved by means of the national networks and with a few small modifications. On the other hand, an adequate distance had to be kept from cities, both for psychological reasons and to avoid that possible accident affect the population. Furthermore, some experts preferred to use sweet water compared to seawater, as the former proved to be less aggressive on condensation machinery» (A.R. Rigano, *La Banca d'Italia e il progetto ENSI. Fonti per la storia dello sviluppo energetico italiano degli anni cinquanta nelle carte dell'Archivio della Banca d'Italia*, cit., pp. 36-37).

involved and interested in this initiative. In particular, it was envisioned that the program could be complete and the plant be ready for the summer of 1963. The overall cost of such an intervention, estimated in excess of $ 66 million, was computed on prices taken from the bid by General Electric and was subdivided into single points specifying the expenditures for the reactor, the turbo generator, the spare parts, the electrical substations and other supporting facilities, the transmission cables, the uranium core, as well as the funds to cover unforeseen contingencies and the other building commitments[345]. Financially speaking, the $ 40 million loan by the IBRD to the Cassa per il Mezzogiorno and a contribution by the fourteen shareholders for the remaining 26.4 million dollars could cover the estimated costs for the project[346].

The document went on indicating the annual expenditure and income forecasts considering the first 16 years of activity of the nuclear power plant, that is to say, for the whole period of loan reimbursement to the Bank. Furthermore, the document contained an estimate of the cash flow, and the foreseen budgets to cover the debt for the whole period[347]. Finally, the analysis by the Bank involved an articulate comparison between the costs of the nuclear power plant and those of a conventional one, checking, from, the feasibility of the plant and of this new kind of energy production from that angle as well[348]. As a matter of fact, between the conclusions of the IBRD report, there was an optimistic evaluation of the choice that had been made. This positive evaluation was not limited to the single plant for which

---

[345] See International Bank for Reconstruction and Development, Department of Technical Operations, *Appraisal of the Senn Nuclear Power Plant – Italy*, cit., pp. 10-12.

[346] See *Ivi*, p. 13. In the very same page, the following was clarified:

> The Bank loan is assumed to be for a period of 20 years of which about 4 years is the estimated period of construction, leaving 16 years for amortization. An interest rate of 6% and level debt service payments have been assumed for the Bank loan to Cassa and it has been assumed that Cassa would relend the proceeds of the proposed Bank loan on the same terms to SENN, except for an additional charge of 1/4% making the cost of the money to the latter 6–1/4%. [...] It is also assumed that no dividends or interest would be paid, either on the shares or on shareholders' advances, during the construction period. Thereafter, dividends and interest on the advances have been assumed at 7% per annum.

[347] See International Bank for Reconstruction and Development, Department of Technical Operations, *Appraisal of the Senn Nuclear Power Plant – Italy*, cit., pp. 13-16, Annex 6, Annex 7, Annex 8, Annex 9.

[348] See *Ivi*, pp. 16-19, Annex 12, Annex 13, Annex 14.

financing was agreed on by the Bank, but it also envisioned the start of a nuclear energy program:

> The project is technically sound. Satisfactory arrangements have been made for the detailed design and construction of the project. The cost estimate is realistic and the proposed financing plan is sound. The estimated demand for power in the area to be served by the plant would permit it to be operated at a high plant factor. [...] The organization and management of SENN are satisfactory. On the assumptions made in this report, the financial forecasts show that the future financial position of SENN would be sound. [...] A comparison of nuclear and conventional thermal generation costs shows that the energy costs to SENN would be about the same with either alternative if an average annual plant factor of 80% was achieved. Excluding taxes on oil from the comparison, the cost to the Italian economy of nuclear generation would be about 15% higher than the cost of conventional thermal generation at this plant factor. [...] There are reasonable prospects of achieving an 80% plant factor, but even if only 75% were realized, in which case the costs to the Italian economy of nuclear generation would exceed those of conventional generation by about 18%, or $ 1,450,000 per annum, it would still seem advisable that the SENN nuclear project should be carried out. In arriving at this conclusion, it is taken into account that future increases in base load requirements in Italy's power system will have to be met by new thermal plants. In due course, as nuclear generation becomes cheaper Italy will no doubt have to embark on a substantial nuclear power program and in the meantime needs to obtain the necessary experience in the construction and operation of nuclear power plants. [...] The figures quoted above do not take account of the possibility that the output of the nuclear reactor may be increased. If this possibility were realized the costs to the Italian economy of nuclear generation and of conventional thermal generation may be about the same at 75% plant factor. [...] The project is suitable for a Bank loan of $ 40 million equivalent. A term of 20 years, including a grace period of 4-1/2 years would be appropriate[349].

Another document of the International Bank for Reconstruction and Development, also issued on September 4, 1959 by its Vice-President, William A.B. Iliff, and titled *Report and Recommendations of the President to the Executive Directors on a Proposed Loan of $ 40 million to the Cassa for the Construction of a Nuclear Power Plant in Southern Italy*[350] (whose

---

[349] *Ivi*, p. 21.

[350] See International Bank for Reconstruction and Development, *Report and Recommendations of the President to the Executive Directors on a Proposed Loan of $ 40 million to the Cassa for the Construction of a Nuclear Power Plant in Southern Italy*, P–204/Restricted, Archives/Records Center, Room HB1–001, Box 935–02, Nus Location 099–1–2, September 4, 1959,

public disclosure was authorized on June 24, 2010), summarized the main issues connected with the loan to build the nuclear power plant and provided a summary of the loans awarded to the Cassa per il Mezzogiorno up to that point (Table 4.1).

Table 4.1 *Loans granted by the IBRD to Italy (1959)*

Number	Borrower	Purpose	Amount (in million $, net of cancellations)
50 IT	Cassa per il Mezzogiorno	Development of Southern Italy	10.0
88 IT	Cassa per il Mezzogiorno	Development of Southern Italy	10.0
117 IT	Cassa per il Mezzogiorno	Development of Southern Italy	68.4
150 IT	Cassa per il Mezzogiorno	Development of Southern Italy	74.6
189 IT	Cassa per il Mezzogiorno	Development of Southern Italy	75.0
224 IT	Cassa per il Mezzogiorno	Development of Southern Italy	20.0
	Total, net of cancellations		258.0
	… of which has been repaid		4.2
	Total now outstanding		253.8
	Amount sold	24.3	
	… of which has been repaid	3.8	20.5
	Net amount now held by Bank		233.3

Source: International Bank for Reconstruction and Development, *Report and Recommendations of the President to the Executive Directors on a Proposed Loan of $ 40 million to the Cassa for the Construction of a Nuclear Power Plant in Southern Italy*, P–204/Restricted, Archives/Records Center, Room HB1–001, Box 935–02, Nus Location 099–1–2, September 4, 1959, p. 2, <https://documents.worldbank.org/en/publication/documents-reports/documentdetail/698201468285875405/italy-senn-nuclear-power-plant-project>.

<https://documents.worldbank.org/en/publication/documents-reports/documentdetail/698201468285875405/italy-senn-nuclear-power-plant-project>.

The report began with a summary of the origins, the aims and a description of the various phases of this initiative, i.e. the financing a nuclear power plant near the estuary of the Garigliano River, to be built and managed by the Società Elettronucleare Nazionale:

> The Bank has been actively considering the application of nuclear power on a commercial scale since 1955. It appeared that Italy was a country where nuclear power should have early commercial application, and it was accordingly agreed between the Bank and the Italian Government, in 1957 that a joint study would be undertaken for the examination of a large nuclear power station to be established by SENN in Southern Italy. The cost of the study was to be shared by the Bank, the Italian Government, and SENN. Work on the study, which was assisted by an International Panel of nuclear scientists established by the Bank, continued until late 1958. The first phase of the work was the preparation of an invitation for tenders for the construction of a nuclear power plant at a given site. The second phase was to assist SENN to review the tenders received. Nine tenders were eventually submitted. Aided by a report of the International Panel and by a study of SENN's consultants and technical staff, SENN selected the tender put forward by the International General Electric Company, a division of General Electric Company[351].

The report went on describing the proposed loan, indicating that its beneficiary was the Cassa per il Mezzogiorno, its guarantor was the Italian Republic, and the loan amounted to $ 40 million. The goal of the loan was to give the necessary support to finance the construction of a nuclear power plant in Southern Italy by SENN; the specific conditions of the loan involved biannual installments for amortization, starting on February 15, 1964 and ending on August 15, 1979 and featured an interest rate of 6%, including a 1% commission. Finally, legal documents included a loan contract, a guarantee agreement, and a project agreement[352]. After the

---

[351] *Ivi*, p. 1. In this very same page, the mission of the IBRD in Italy was recalled, as well as the following negotiations and implementation of the agreement, clarifying the following:

> In September and October of 1958 a Bank mission visited Rome and discussed the financial and technical aspects of the SENN project. Negotiations then took place in Washington in April, and were completed in Rome in July.

[352] See International Bank for Reconstruction and Development, *Report and Recommendations of the President to the Executive Directors on a Proposed Loan of $ 40 million to the Cassa for the Construction of a Nuclear Power Plant in Southern Italy*, cit., pp. 2-3.

evaluation of the contents of this project[353], which recalled the main elements of the *Appraisal of the Senn Nuclear Power Plant – Italy*, the Vice-President of the IBRD summarized the main contractual elements of this procurement and, before the usual recommendation formula to the executive directors of the Bank to approve the loan[354], he explicitly referred to an

---

[353] See *Ivi*, p. 4. This part of the document, the following was underlined:

The total cost of the plant is estimated to be $ 66.4 million. SENN plans to raise the equivalent of about $ 26.4 million in about equal proportions by the issue of shares and by shareholders' advances, subordinated to its loan from the Cassa per il Mezzogiorno; the balance, $ 40 million, would be covered by the loan from the Cassa per il Mezzogiorno. [...] Nine of the fourteen shareholders of SENN are public utility companies, the other five are industrial companies. Twelve of the fourteen are directly or indirectly controlled by the Istituto Ricostruzione Industriale (IRI). The utility shareholders form part of the Italian electric power network into which SENN's output will be fed. Three of the strongest of these utility companies will guarantee performance of the Project Agreement and become sureties for the performance of all obligations of SENN to the Cassa per il Mezzogiorno. SENN will give written assurances to the Bank that it will conduct its operations in accordance with sound business principles to ensure a sound financial position. [...] International General Electric Operations, S.A., a wholly owned Swiss subsidiary of the General Electric Company, with Ebasco Services, would erect the plant on a "turn-key" basis, including the detailed design, supply of equipment, erection and operation of the plant during an initial test period. The plant design includes reliable safeguards to prevent hazardous incidents and to minimize hazard to plant personnel and the surrounding area. [...] The site for SENN was chosen not only because of a good water supply and favorable conditions for the release of waste gases and disposal of radioactive waste, but also because from it the plant could be easily linked with the extensive generation and distribution system of the utility shareholders of SENN, covering about half of Italy and serving over half of the population. [...] Power demand is growing at a fast rate in the area served by this system. Studies indicate that it will be necessary to increase capacity from the 4,140 MW existing at the end of 1958 to 7,250 MW by 1965. SENN will form part of this increase. [...] Nuclear power plants, to be economic, must use their generating capacity as fully as possible because of their high capital cost. Studies indicate that the base load requirements of the system are such that SENN could be operated at a high plant factor, i.e., at a high proportion of the number of hours in each year.

[354] See International Bank for Reconstruction and Development, *Report and Recommendations of the President to the Executive Directors on a Proposed Loan of $ 40 million to the Cassa for the Construction of a Nuclear Power Plant in Southern Italy*, cit., p. 6.

analysis of the Italian economic situation[355]. On this topic, William A. B. Iliff referred to data contained in a report titled *Current Economic Position and Prospects of Italy*[356]. According to this publication, Italy was deeply affected by the international recession of 1958, slowing down the significant growth which had been achieved up to that point mostly thanks to consistent improvement of its balance of payments, a decrease in imports and an increase in the invisible balance. Nonetheless, growth trends remained significantly positive and the economic outlook did not seem to have been compromised[357].

The IBRD report evaluated also the «committed effort» that Italy was keeping up with, since the beginning of the 1950s, in order to solve the two structural problems of its economy: the presence of a great number of unemployed and underemployed people as well as the significant gap between a highly industrialized North and a mostly agricultural South[358]. According to the Bank, these two phenomena were strictly linked and the conditions to tackle them effectively were present. In particular, by establishing a «special development fund for Southern Italy» (i.e., the Cassa per il Mezzogiorno) and following the setup of a 10-year plan in order to support and foster the growth of both employment and income (i.e., the Vanoni Plan, a plan set up by the then Italian Minister for Economy), new growth perspectives opened up[359]. However, despite acknowledging the «remarkable progress» of Southern Italy compared to the past, the International Bank for Reconstruction and Development emphasized the uneven results that had been achieved up to that moment, as they did not effectively show a substantial bridging of the regional gap. More importantly, the IBRD proposed a remarkably interesting reflection on the

---

[355] See *Ivi*, pp. 5-6.

[356] See International Bank for Reconstruction and Development, Department of Operations Europe, Africa and Australasia, *Current Economic Position and Prospects of Italy*, EA–94a/Restricted, April 13, 1959, <https://documents.worldbank.org/en/publication/documents-reports/documentdetail/502081468049199883/italy-current-economic-position-and-prospects>.

[357] See International Bank for Reconstruction and Development, *Report and Recommendations of the President to the Executive Directors on a Proposed Loan of $ 40 million to the Cassa for the Construction of a Nuclear Power Plant in Southern Italy*, cit., p. 5.

[358] See International Bank for Reconstruction and Development, Department of Operations Europe, Africa and Australasia, *Current Economic Position and Prospects of Italy*, cit., p. 1.

[359] See *Ivi*, pp. 1-2.

situation in the Mezzogiorno and the need to fully understand the scope of the problems affecting (as they still do) this part of Italy:

> Progress in the development of the South has been impressive compared to the past but, so far, the improvement in living standards, income levels and employment has been mostly confined to a few areas. Moreover, since development in the North has continued, the efforts in the South have merely enabled it to keep pace with the North, but they have not succeeded in significantly reducing the gap between the two regions. In 1957 the income per capita in the South amounted to 44% of the income per capita in the North, compared to 42% in the years 1950 to 1952. Per capita public and private investment remained higher in the North than in the South in spite of the extraordinary investment by the Cassa per il Mezzogiorno. [...] Remedying the backwardness of the South is not only a question of additional investments and of providing special economic incentives. It is as much a question of sociological changes and of adopting new educational and cultural standards[360].

In the part of the report dedicated to the outlook of the Italian economy, the Bank remarked the transitional and unfinished status of the interventions in the Mezzogiorno during the shift from pre-industrialization to the industrialization program, pointing out its main reasons, showing the main features of the new provisions, but at the same time expressing some justified concerns about the possible loss of drive for the development programs in Southern Italy:

> While public investment in the South has been transforming agriculture and improving and expanding the basic services and facilities, private industry and agriculture have not taken full advantage of the new facilities available. Whereas public investment in the South on a per capita basis has been about equal to the North, private investment is still under a third of the North. Private industry has, so far, not responded as rapidly and as effectively as it was hoped to the additional incentives introduced in 1957. These came in when the development program for the South shifted its emphasis from a pre-industrialization to an industrialization program. [...] The already existing inducements for the industrial development of the South (tax and tariff concessions, freight rebates and long-term credits mainly through the Cassa per il Mezzogiorno and its regional industrial credit institutes) are now supplemented by new provisions. They empower the Cassa to pay a subsidy of 2½% per annum towards the interest on the bonds to be issued by the industrial credit institutes, to allocate funds for the subsidy of projects to be located in towns with a population of 70,000 or under, and to create additional industrial zones on the mainland such as now exist in Catania and

[360] *Ivi*, p. 2.

> Naples. In Sicily, further aid to new industries is provided by the regional government. Also adopted was a measure which requires that a minimum of 40% of all new investments in state enterprises take place in Southern Italy. [...] The slowing down of investment activity in Italy may be partly responsible for the small progress, which industrialization of the South has made in the recent past. Northern enterprises on whose initiatives the industrialization of the South largely depends, prefer to expand their existing facilities in the North, because of closeness to markets and better supply of skilled labor, rather than to move South. The advent of the European Common Market may further enhance the advantages of the North in this respect. The South has relatively few natural advantages to offer industry and the existence of raw materials for a chemical industry in Sicily is a notable exception. There is therefore some fear that the long-range development program of the South may lose momentum and the pressure on the government to embark on a program of forced industrialization has increased. At this stage it can only be hoped that in the zeal to industrialize the South, the costs of alternative plant location will be adequately weighed and serious errors will be avoided[361].

Thus, the Bank flagged the necessity for a more focused industrialization process. This had to be based on careful examination and planning, with consideration to the localization costs for alternative plants, to avoid any error in estimates. The Bank's analysis was influenced by complications connected to the unfavorable economic conjuncture, by the outcomes of the first phase of the extraordinary intervention – whose effects were largely limited to investments in infrastructure and agriculture – and by the opening of the Single European Market, whose economic consequences and repercussions on the North-South gap remained yet unclear. However, the period between the 1950s and the 1960s would eventually be the main watershed in dispelling such fears and definitely confirming the results of the economic reforms and the propelling role of the Cassa per il Mezzogiorno.

The financing and building of the Garigliano nuclear power plant were almost parallel to another two similar initiatives to build nuclear plants in Trino Vercellese (in Piedmont) and Torre Astura (near Latina), whose reactors reached the required critical mass in June 1963 and began producing electricity on January 23, 1964[362]. However, due to the «scarce

---

[361] *Ivi*, pp. 11-12. The final part of this report was almost identical to the one of another, previously quoted, document confirming the sound evaluations by the IBRD (see footnote no.78 of Chapter III).

[362] See Archivio Storico Enel, *Il Nucleare in Italia*, cit., pp. 94-95; A.R. Rigano, *La Banca d'Italia e il progetto ENSI. Fonti per la storia dello sviluppo energetico italiano degli anni cinquanta nelle carte dell'Archivio della Banca d'Italia*, cit., p.

technological maturity of the plants», two significant outages affected the Piedmont-based reactor, while the plant on the Campania border had to be closed ahead of the planned date in 1981 — six years before the Italian referendum on nuclear power[363]. Therefore, despite the fact that Italy fully respected the requirements the IBRD indicated for the building of a nuclear power plant[364], the project by the ENSI did not experience a good outcome.

---

53. Within this publication of the "Archivio Storico dell'Enel" (pp. 95-96, p. 97 and p. 99), the following was reminded about the completion of the Garigliano power plant compared with the other two:

> Construction began in November 1959, exactly one year after the beginning of the SIMEA construction activity in Latina, nevertheless rector criticality was reached in a shorter time, i.e. six months after the other power plant. The Garigliano power plant had a lower nominal power (160 MW), itself reached in May 1964, commercial energy production began immediately after. The first link between the plant and the power network happened in January 1964. If in the case of Latina five years since amounts passed between starting the building and commercial energy production, the Garigliano plant took four years and six months. A similar time span was needed for the building of the SELNI plant of Trino Vercellese, in July 1961, and commercial power production, in December 1965 [...]. The three plants had also other interesting features: in all the three cases the Italian customers ordered still experimental plants, without a working prototype and built at the same time in the United States of America and the United Kingdom [...] The prototype for the Garigliano SENN plant was [...] the Dresden, IL, near Chicago, itself active since the 1960s [...]. As their building works had begun before the nationalization, the plants had to be given to Enel. The relevant decrees were issued in October 1963 (Latina), December 1964 (Garigliano) and in January 1965 (Trino), even if the actual transfer to Enel required more than a year and took place in December 1964 for Latina and January and February 1966 for the Garigliano and Trino respectively; they concerned an overall power of more than 600 MW, the production reaching in 1965 3,5 billion kWh, i.e. 4.2% of the total Italian electricity production. When in September 1964 the new Geneva Conference opened, Italy was able to present itself as the third Western country by actual electronuclear power, after United States and Great Britain.

363 See Archivio Storico Enel, *Il Nucleare in Italia*, cit., p. 98. In particular, concerning the Garigliano power plant, it has been noted that: «in 1978 an accident happened to the steam generator and energy production was stopped. This plant effectively ceased its functioning in 1981 as, also because of the Three Mile Island accident in 1979, it was decided not to reactivate it» (AR. Rigano, *La Banca d'Italia e il progetto ENSI. Fonti per la storia dello sviluppo energetico italiano degli anni cinquanta nelle carte dell'Archivio della Banca d'Italia*, cit., p. 53).

364 In fact, as it has been noticed, the favorable conditions where more than one: «For the IBRD, the construction of the nuclear plant rather than a conventional plant was

Nevertheless, the history of this ambitious project «may be read in several ways» and should be seen as an element of the relationship between the International Bank for Reconstruction and Development and Italy, «whose main coordinates were the beginning of the Italian "economic miracle" and a further phase of the international economic and military policies carried out by the USA»[365]. In particular, the following has been noted: «concerning the Italian side, the Ensi project, whose buildup was again due to the meridionalist technocracy responsible for the Cassa per il Mezzogiorno, was conceived as the beginning of a long-term program to modernize energy infrastructures in the Mezzogiorno [...]. Based on a strategic definition of the Italian national economic development, this project was to be again a winner at the international level, as it was the case with the Cassa a few years prior. However, during the following years, this was to remain a more and more unique case, both concerning the Italian meridionalist policies and the energy-related ones»[366].

4.2 The loans provided to Italy by the World Bank and the industrialization process in its Southern half

The last information concerning IBRD financing towards the development of the Mezzogiorno is contained in some documents dating to 1965, when attention finally focused on fully mobilizing the force of the industrialization process in Southern Italy. A report issued by the International Bank for Reconstruction and Development, in cooperation with the International Development Association (IDA)[367], on June 10, 1965,

justified by the lack of energetic resources and the consequential need to import them at high costs with an evident fallout on the balance of payments. Italy unquestionably met the requisites but another peculiar feature was present in our country, taken into account by the World Bank personnel: the territorial imbalance between Southern Italy and the rest of the country, coupled with the need for interventions able to bridge the economic gap» (A.R. Rigano, *La Banca d'Italia e il progetto ENSI. Fonti per la storia dello sviluppo energetico italiano degli anni cinquanta nelle carte dell'Archivio della Banca d'Italia*, cit., p. 23).

[365] B. Curli, *Energia nucleare per il Mezzogiorno. L'Italia e la Banca mondiale (1955-1959)*, in *Italia, Europa, America. L'integrazione internazionale dell'economia italiana (1945-1963)*, in "Studi Storici", year 37, no. 1, 1996, p. 322.

[366] *Ibidem*.

[367] The International Development Association was established in 1960, within the World Bank, in order to help the 81 poorest countries in the world, reducing poverty, by granting credits without interest and by financing programs able to promote economic growth, fight inequality and improving living standards for the concerned populations. Therefore the IDA integrated the action by the IBRD, the other

titled *The Development of Southern Italy. The Cassa per il Mezzogiorno and the Three Special Credit Institutes, Isveimer, Irfis and Cis. Italy*[368] (whose public disclosure was authorized on April 16, 2010) examined the proposal for a $ 100 million loan, to be granted in different currencies, on behalf of the "Cassa per Opere Straordinarie di Pubblico Interesse nell'Italia Meridionale", in order to finance industrial projects in Southern Italy[369]. This text was an effective summary of the economic situation of the Mezzogiorno and the public interventions implemented until that moment. The document, which also featured an ample supply of tables, graphs and statistical data, stated the following:

> Since 1950, the Italian Government has been carrying on an intensive development program in Southern Italy, aimed at narrowing the wide gap that has long existed between income levels in that region and in the North and increasing local employment opportunities for its fast growing population. For most of the first decade, the program was concentrated on public works which were expected to improve conditions for productive activity, especially in agriculture, and, by raising consumer incomes, to expand the local market [...]. Although employment in the region increased and per capita income at constant prices rose by nearly 25% between 1951 and 1957, the development of industry, which had been counted on to provide a basis for self-sustaining growth, was slow. Beginning in 1957, therefore, the government increased the incentives offered to investors in industry in the South to offset the disadvantages of the region as compared with the industrially advanced North. The tax concessions granted since the late 1940's were increased, and interest subsidies on medium and long-term loans and capital grants to cover part of investment costs were added [...]. The policy of incentives began to show results in the late 1950's. Since 1959, there has been a sharp upturn in industrial investment and the rate of regional economic growth. In the three years 1960-63, the South for the first time showed a greater increase in per capita income at constant prices than the North [...]. Continued promotion of industry in the South through the

---

operating entity concerned with the World Bank loans used within average income countries, in order to carry out capital investments and provide development consulting services (See International Development Association, *What is IDA?*, <http://ida.worldbank.org/about/what-is-ida>).

368 See International Bank for Reconstruction and Development, Projects Department, *The Development of Southern Italy. The Cassa per il Mezzogiorno and the Three Special Credit Institutes, Isveimer, Irfis and Cis. Italy*, T.O.–467a/Restricted, June 10, 1965, <https://documents.worldbank.org/en/publication/documents-reports/documentdetail/904741468044126033/italy-southern-italy-industrial-financing-project>.

369 See *Ibidem*.

various forms of assistance now offered seems justifiable. The incentives serve mainly to reduce initial capital costs and do not provide shelter indefinitely for uneconomic enterprises. Part of their cost is offset by the savings resulting from increased local employment and a resulting lessening of the pressure to migrate with its accompanying losses of the most energetic elements of the population and increased strains in the North. Greater local purchasing power, improved access to outside markets and sources of industrial raw materials, education and training, and the industrial base that has already been created should facilitate a fairly rapid development of industry, if assistance to investors can be continued until industry is more solidly established [...]. Major responsibility for the program for Southern Italy rests with the Cassa per il Mezzogiorno which was established in 1950, and is now being extended to December 31, 1980. In its 15 years of operation, the Cassa has received close to Lit. 2,400 billion (US$ 3.9 billion). The Bank made seven loans to the Cassa between 1951 and 1959, totaling US$ 298 million [...]. In its first ten years of operation, the bulk of the Cassa's funds were used for agriculture; the balance went almost entirely for transportation and water and sewage disposal projects. In the last few years, steadily increasing amounts have been made available for industry, and the Cassa has also branched into tourism, education, etc. [...]. Cassa expenditures supplement and do not replace the regular expenditures of the Ministries and the local governments, and except in agriculture, have accounted for only a small part of total government expenditures in the several sectors. However, as the center of the government's developmental efforts in the South, the Cassa's importance for the region cannot be measured by its financial contribution alone [...]. Judged by the improvement in economic conditions since the early 1950's these efforts must be regarded as successful [...][370].

Therefore, the first part of the document summary provided a very effective evaluation of the interventions and their initial outcomes. Without hesitation, it went on observing that the horizons of the Cassa were extended up to 1980 and its financial endowment for the 1965-1969 was to amount to 1,640 billion lire (that is to say 2.6 billion dollars), thus featuring a 35% growth in funding availability compared with the last twelve years and a half. However, while some sectors like agriculture and transports would have suffered a reduction in public interventions, other sectors like water utilities and, most of all, industry were to experience a significant increase in the resources allocated to them[371]. The second part of the summary

---

370 *Ivi*, pp. I-II.

371 See *Ivi*, p. II. As it has been noted in this very same page:

[...] annual availabilities for water supply projects would be increased by one-third, and availabilities for industry would be increased three and one-quarter times. The increase in the amounts available for industry would be

underlined the fact that the Italian government asked the Bank for support, not for the direct Cassa expenditures – which were covered by national funds – but for medium- and long-term loans to industrial projects in Southern Italy instead. On that specific issue, the proposal for a $ 100 million financing had been submitted[372]. As the following excerpt shows, the Cassa would then lend the same amount of funds to three special credit institutions, which would loan them for the industrial development of Southern Italy:

> The Cassa would relend the local currency counterpart of the proposed loan to three Special Credit Institutes, ISVEIMER, IRFIS and CIS which were set up in 1953 to make loans to industry in the South [...]. The Institutes have an impressive investment record. To the end of 1963 they had made over 4,500 loans, mainly medium and long-term, for about US$ 1.2 billion equivalent. About 80% were made in the four years 1960-63 [...]. In 1963, they accounted for 47% of all lending for industry in Southern Italy by credit institutions operating in the region [...]. The Institutes were channels for four of the earlier Bank loans made to Italy [...]. In the case of these earlier loans, the Bank was mainly responsible for project appraisal, and the Institutes, the Cassa and the Bank shared responsibility for project supervision. Under the proposed loan, the Institutes would be fully responsible for the selection, appraisal and follow-up of the projects for which the loan proceeds would be used. However, the Bank has agreed with the Cassa on certain criteria to be applied in the selection of these projects, the most important of which is their size. Normally, loans would be made only for projects with an investment cost between US$ 100,000 and $ 8 million equivalent, but projects with a slightly higher cost would not be excluded if they seemed justified. The Institutes and the Cassa have presented to the Bank a list of projects to which the Bank has agreed. The list contains 185 projects with total loan requirements of US$ 132 million. Other projects could be added as required for the full utilization of the loan. The Bank's role in supervising the proposed loan would be limited to ensuring that the standard provisions of the subsidiary loan agreements between the Institutes and their borrowers are satisfactory and that the Institutes continue to follow sound investment practices[373].

---

the most important change, and that sector would replace agriculture as the major object of Cassa expenditures [...].

[372] See International Bank for Reconstruction and Development, Projects Department, *The Development of Southern Italy. The Cassa per il Mezzogiorno and the Three Special Credit Institutes, Isveimer, Irfis and Cis. Italy*, cit., p. II.

[373] *Ivi*, pp. II-III. However, within the last part of the summary (pp. III-IV), some significant issues were highlighted. Such problems were liable to slow down the process of industrial investment. On the other hand, the conclusion of this part of the

4.2.1 The economic development in Southern Italy and the Cassa per il Mezzogiorno

The introduction to the aforementioned report described two missions carried out in 1964 by the International Bank for Reconstruction and

---

document recapped the actual terms and conditions of the loan, including the implementation and use thereof:

> The Institutes obtain only a small part of their loan funds from the government. Nearly half of their loan capital consists of funds raised through the sale of bonds on the domestic market, 34% comes from Cassa borrowings abroad which are reloaned to them and only 17% from the Treasury and other sources [...]. As a result of the congestion of domestic and foreign markets they are at present unable to maintain anything approaching their recent rate of lending [...]. This shortage cannot be made up from existing sources. As at the end of November 1964 the institutes had approve loans for a total of over US$ 220 million for which they could not sign contracts for lack of funds. In addition, they had loan applications totalling about US$ 750 million under active consideration. Based on these known requirements, it was estimated at the end of November that in the period to September 30, 1966, their loan requirements, assuming a rate of lending somewhat lower than that of the last few years, would fall short of the funds they could reasonably count on (apart from the proposed Bank loan) by US$ 180 million equivalent. The position has not changed materially since that time. The proposed Bank loan would partially fill this gap. Unless the Institutes can maintain a fairly high rate of lending, the development of industry in the South is bound to be slowed up [...]. The loan to the Cassa would be for 15 years, including a grace period of four years. As provided by law, the Treasury would bear the exchange risk. The Cassa would relend the lire equivalent to the Institutes in the following proportions: ISVEIMER, 55; IRFIS, 25; CIS, 20. The duration and grace periods of the Cassa's loans to the Institutes would be the same as those for the Bank loan to the Cassa. The interest rate on the Cassa loans to the Institutes would not exceed 3.55%. The Treasury would reimburse the Cassa for the difference between this rate and the rate the Cassa would pay. The Institutes would relend the loan proceeds at 4% and would be free to reinvest repayments by sub-borrowers. The 0.45% spread, which is the spread the Institutes have been receiving on loans made from foreign borrowings in recent years, together with their earnings from other sources, would be adequate to enable them to administer the loan proceeds satisfactorily [...]. It is expected that the loan can be utilized rapidly and that not more than 10-15% would be spent outside Italy [...]. The proposed Bank loan of US$ 100 million would make a substantial contribution to the lending resources of the Institutes, fill an urgent need for additional funds for industrial lending in the South, and thus support the government's program for the development of that region which has so far been effective in improving economic conditions in the region [...].

Development in Italy under the direction of Leonard B. Rist. The first of such missions had the task to verify the feasibility of the loan request submitted by the Italian government in order to support the investment program in Southern Italy. Such a task was carried out by examining the Italian economy, the level of development of its Southern regions and the special features of the Cassa initiatives. The second mission was tasked with analyzing the activity and the operations of the special credit institutions[374]. The results of these two missions were recorded in the first part of a paper by the Bank, titled *Economic Development of Southern Italy and the Cassa per il Mezzogiorno*[375]. The paragraph dedicated to the "Southern Question" started from the observation that Southern Italy presented very different conditions compared with the rest of the country, both for its economic structure and income level. While the Centre-Northern regions of Italy featured a significant mechanized industrial sector and an income which could be compared with the most advanced areas of Europe, the South mostly still depended on an inefficient agricultural sector, it lacked industries, and its *per capita* income was significantly lower than the one achieved in the Centre North. However, in order to clear any doubt on the origin of the "Italian dualism", the following was specified:

> A wide disparity between the two sections existed when Italy was unified politically in 1861, and its magnitude and the importance of the South (the southern mainland and the islands include about 40% of the area and population of the country) have combined to make the "Southern Question" a major social and political issue during most of Italy's existence as a political unit[376].

The document went on to describe the efforts carried out by the Italian government, ever since the end of the 19th century, in order to improve the economic situation of the Mezzogiorno, especially in the following three

---

[374] See International Bank for Reconstruction and Development, Projects Department, *The Development of Southern Italy. The Cassa per il Mezzogiorno and the Three Special Credit Institutes, Isveimer, Irfis and Cis. Italy*, cit., p. 1. In this very page, the following was noted concerning the first mission:

> The mission concluded that the Cassa would be an appropriate vehicle for a Bank loan of US$ 100 million equivalent and that Southern industry in particular would be a desirable recipient of the proceeds of the loan. The mission also suggested that the three Special Credit Institutes, ISVEIMER, IRFIS and CIS [...] would be a suitable channel for the Bank's loans.

[375] See International Bank for Reconstruction and Development, Projects Department, *The Development of Southern Italy. The Cassa per il Mezzogiorno and the Three Special Credit Institutes, Isveimer, Irfis and Cis. Italy*, cit., pp. 2-17.

[376] *Ivi*, p. 2.

directions: improving the physical and institutional conditions for agriculture, enhancing infrastructure, and promoting industrialization. However, up to WWII, the programs had restricted themselves to short-term action and to a limited geographic area, thus not succeeding in reducing the economic gap between the Northern and Southern areas of Italy. On the contrary, since the 1947-1948 period, the postwar situation allowed to pass economic measures useful to provide incentives in favor of industrial investments, by means of fiscal facilitations and medium and long-term credits at reduced interest rates. From 1950 onwards, the extraordinary intervention began, aiming to accelerate the economic development of Southern Italian regions[377].

Such a meridionalist initiative, which involved the cooperation of several institutions tasked with developing this area, revolved around the Cassa per il Mezzogiorno. The Cassa's official name was "Cassa per Opere Straordinarie di Pubblico Interesse nell'Italia Meridionale", indicating its prevailing task, which was «to supplement rather than replace those of the *regular government departments*»[378]. As a matter of fact, the extraordinary intervention by the Italian State went to ensure investments being proportional to the percentage of population present in Southern Italy

---

[377] On such a topic, the following was underlined:

> Initially, the Cassa concentrated mainly on agriculture (irrigation, land improvement and the execution of the postwar land reform program) and infrastructure (water supply, sewerage and transportation). However, the expectation was that Cassa expenditures would not only increase agricultural output and bring the standards of the public services in the South to levels considered necessary in a modern society but also, by raising incomes, would expand the local market and stimulate investment in industry, thus providing a base for self-sustaining economic growth. [...] Southern Italian per capita income did rise substantially in the early 1950's. But despite the rise, the tax concessions offered to industrial investors and the expansion, with government help, of industrial credit facilities, the growth of industry was slow. In 1957, therefore, the Act which extended the Cassa's life to 1965 and virtually doubled its funds for the activities which it was already carrying on also increased the incentives for industrial investment in the South. The Act provided for additional tax concessions and empowered the Cassa to make available interest subsidies and capital grants to industrial investors and financial assistance to local entities constructing infrastructure in industrial development concentrations. Further increases in the incentives were authorized in a 1959 Act (the Colombo Law)

(International Bank for Reconstruction and Development, Projects Department, *The Development of Southern Italy. The Cassa per il Mezzogiorno and the Three Special Credit Institutes, Isveimer, Irfis and Cis. Italy*, cit., pp. 2-3).

[378] *Ivi*, p. 3.

(amounting to the 40% of the total), as the Cassa had to provide further interventions to bridge the gap between the two areas. The overall coordination of governmental activities and of the development policies for Southern Italy was entrusted to the Committee of Ministers for Southern Italy, an entity including several Ministries and Departments (Treasury, Public Works, Agriculture and Forestry, Industry and Trade, Transports and Civil Aviation, Education, Labor and Welfare, State Enterprises and Tourism) and led by a «full-time Chairman»[379].

The management of the initiatives envisioned that, as it was written in the report, «local bodies as well as agencies of the national government share in the responsibility for public investment in the South»[380], while local policymakers had the responsibility to control, manage and maintain public works, including those realized through the extraordinary intervention. In some cases, they took charge of building these works, relying on financial support by the Cassa. Usually, the design and implementation of public works or investment programs was entrusted to special entities (agencies or consortia). The Cassa, in turn, shared its tasks of promoting industrial development with other organizations. Medium and long-term subsidized credit was offered, at reduced rates, to industrial investors in the Mezzogiorno, by several credit institutions through dedicated sections. This was, for example, the case with the industrial credit sections of three big

---

[379] *Ibidem*. This part of the text (pp. 3-4), the following was added:

> The new Cassa law would add to the Committee the Ministers of the Budget and Health, and would give the Minister for Extraordinary Intervention in the South, who is the Chairman of the Committee, and the Committee as a whole, powers they do not now possess. [...] The policies for the development of Southern Italy formulated by the Committee for the South have been fairly general in character. And in spite of the broad range of its membership, the Committee has had only limited success in coordinating the activities of government agencies in the region because, of all the member agencies, only the Cassa has given the Committee full information in advance about its annual investment plans. To achieve better coordination of public investment in the South as well as between Southern investment programs and the national economic plans, the new Cassa law provides for the Committee for the South to prepare plans for the coordination of public intervention in the South covering periods of several years which are to be in conformity with the national economic plans to be formulated in the future by the Interministerial Committee for Reconstruction. The Committee for the South is itself to operate within the Interministerial Committee for Reconstruction.

[380] International Bank for Reconstruction and Development, Projects Department, *The Development of Southern Italy. The Cassa per il Mezzogiorno and the Three Special Credit Institutes, Isveimer, Irfis and Cis. Italy*, cit., p. 4.

commercial banks (Banco di Napoli, Banco di Sicilia and Banca Nazionale del Lavoro), since the end of the 1940s; the Istituto Mobiliare Italiano (IMI), the bigger industrial medium and long-term financing source, active in Southern Italy from 1950 onwards; the three special credit institutions (ISVEIMER, IRFIS and CIS), established in 1953 (of which the Cassa had a 40% participation in each); four non-local institutions, established between 1953 and 1955, such as Mediobanca, Efibanca, Mediocredito del Lazio and Centrobanca[381].

The grants for industrial investors were subject to an evaluation of the requests by the special credit institutions and to further examination by the Cassa. The latter assigned the financial support for productive infrastructure to the consortia[382], with the aim of concentrating industrial enterprises within two types of areas to maximize external economies: These places were either industrial "nuclei" (made of single municipalities or parts thereof), and industrial "areas" (bigger geographical units which could include more than one municipality and featured a population larger than 100,000). Furthermore, four wider regional units were present, called industrial "poles", which included both "nuclei" and "areas". Such subdivisions, which meant to concentrate industrial development in Southern Italy, were represented in the following picture (Figure 4.2).

---

[381] As it has been noted:

> The three Special Credit Institutes together have been the largest source of such credit. They provided about 45% of the total amount loaned for industry in the South between 1947 and 1963; 40% was provided by IMI; and the remaining 15% by the other credit institutions

(International Bank for Reconstruction and Development, Projects Department, *The Development of Southern Italy. The Cassa per il Mezzogiorno and the Three Special Credit Institutes, Isveimer, Irfis and Cis. Italy*, cit., p. 6).

[382] Within the report, the meaning of this term was also explained:

> The "consorzi" are local bodies, including representatives of all local interests (official and non-official), which are responsible for making plans to develop the concentrations and, after approval by the Prime Minister acting on the recommendations of both the Minister of Public Works and the Committee of Ministers for the South, for carrying these plans out

(International Bank for Reconstruction and Development, Projects Department, *The Development of Southern Italy. The Cassa per il Mezzogiorno and the Three Special Credit Institutes, Isveimer, Irfis and Cis. Italy*, cit., p. 6).

Figure 4.2 *Italy. Industrial development concentration (1965)*

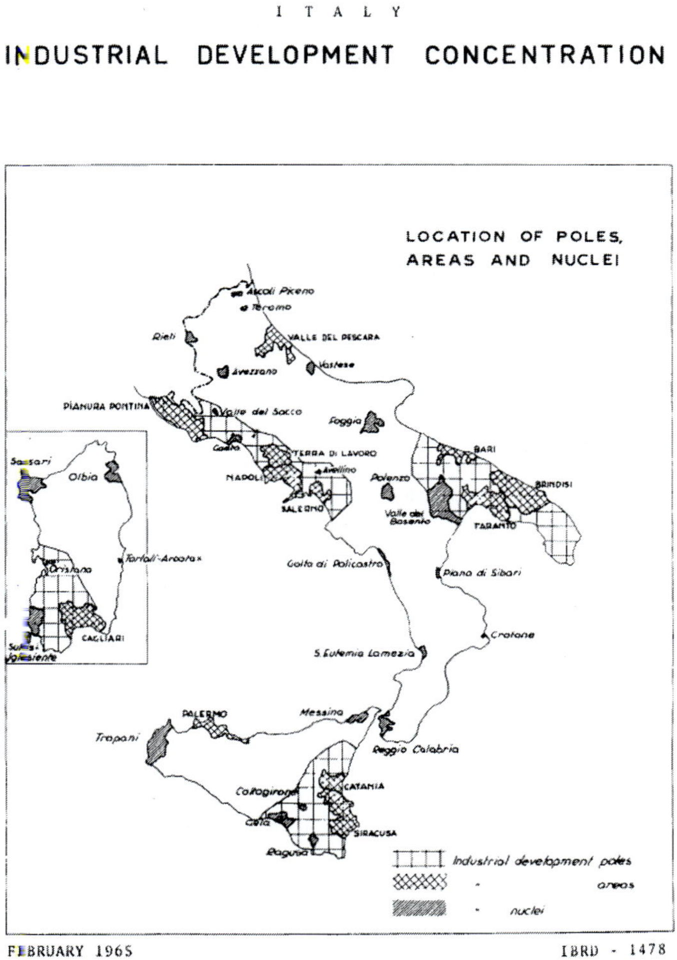

Source: International Bank for Reconstruction and Development, Projects Department, *The Development of Southern Italy. The Cassa per il Mezzogiorno and the Three Special Credit Institutes, Isveimer, Irfis and Cis. Italy*, T.O.–467a/Restricted, June 10, 1965, MAP 2, <https://documents.worldbank.org/en/publication/documents-reports/documentdetail/904741468044126033/italy-southern-italy-industrial-financing-project>.

Besides loans and subsidies, investors could obtain equity capital from some investment companies established with the help of the Italian government (INSUD, ISAP, SOFIS and FINSARDA). These companies had very defined roles, such as acquiring shares in industrial enterprises, especially in Southern Italy[383]. The Italian State surely had a much more challenging commitment in mind for the Mezzogiorno:

> In addition to the incentives to private investors, the government has promoted the industrialization of the South since 1957 by requiring the State Participations to place in the region 60% of their investment in new plant and 40% of their total investment. The aim was not so much to increase State industrial activity in the Mezzogiorno as to provide it with a heavy industry as a basis for further industrial growth. By 1962, the State-owned companies had brought their investments in the South to the specified level and in 1964, they placed over 45% of their total investments there. Their total investment in Southern Italy over the period 1957-64 has amounted to Lit. 1,400 billion (US$ 2.2 billion), of which about 60% was in industry and the remaining 40% in power, radio and telecommunications and express highways[384].

One paragraph of the IBRD document, addressing the role of the Cassa per il Mezzogiorno (aptly titled *The Role of the Cassa*), described the various aspects of this commitment in detail: how the Cassa was managed, its financial resources and their allocation, the past programs (especially

---

[383] As noted by Gisèle Podbielski: «Always concerning investment financing, several special financing institutions were created in the examined timeframe (ISAP, INSUD, SOFIS and FINSARDA) with the opportunity to gather funds on internal and foreign financial markets as well as providing risk capital for new initiatives, especially industrial ones. On the other side, technical assistance and support to enterprises and similar activities was very present. However, such institutions were to have a really limited political importance» (G. Podbielski, *Venticinque anni di intervento straordinario nel Mezzogiorno*, Milan, Giuffré, 1978, p. 49).

[384] International Bank for Reconstruction and Development, Projects Department, *The Development of Southern Italy. The Cassa per il Mezzogiorno and the Three Special Credit Institutes, Isveimer, Irfis and Cis. Italy*, cit., p. 6. In a note of the same page the meaning of the Participations by the State was explained in detail:

> The State Participations [...] are government organizations holding participations in companies engaged in a wide variety of activities – steel production, shipbuilding, oil production, refining and distribution, petrochemicals, heavy engineering, cement production, road building, banking, etc. The most important State Participations are IRI (Institute for Industrial Reconstruction) and ENI (National Hydrocarbons Board). ENEL (National Electric Power Board) also falls under the regulation with respect to investment in the South.

concerning the use of its resources and its main sectors of activity), the current situation in the status of the funds as well as the future programs, activities and perspectives, including the policies of incentive to industrial investments. Concerning its organization, the Cassa had twelve operating departments, employing about two thousand people overall. Six departments were active in specific sectors (agriculture; waterworks and sewers; transports; industry; tourism, crafts and fisheries; education and training); two departments had general functions (planning and programming; credit and finance); four of them had general administrative tasks. The Board of Directors included a President, two Vice-Presidents and ten members, appointed for four years on the basis of their specific professional qualifications. There was also the possibility for them to be appointed indefinitely. The approval by the Board was necessary for every project the Cassa started. Furthermore, a generally favorable evaluation of the structure and functions of the Cassa emerged from this report as well:

> The complexity and scope of the Cassa's activities make it difficult to evaluate its performance in detail. However, the staff gives a definite impression of competence and the criteria which have been developed for assigning priority for assistance seem sound. Responsibility for the overall development of Southern Italy has enabled the organization to see the broad implications of its activities in individual fields and to fit them into a coherent program which can be modified to meet changing circumstances[385].

Concerning its financial resources, the majority of the funds of the Cassa per il Mezzogiorno came from governmental allocations, which allowed for long-term planning, warranting continuity of action. The Italian treasury allocated this financing year by year, granting on time what was due[386]. Furthermore, the Bank's report recalled some data proving very interesting in understanding the width and the origin of the resources made available to the Cassa until 1965 (Table 4.2). Besides the grants allocated by the Treasury, the Cassa received other funds coming from internal sources,

---

[385] International Bank for Reconstruction and Development, Projects Department, *The Development of Southern Italy. The Cassa per il Mezzogiorno and the Three Special Credit Institutes, Isveimer, Irfis and Cis. Italy*, cit., p. 7.

[386] On this, the following was clarified:

> The organization is empowered to anticipate future government allocations by discounting them at a number of national banks and to issue bonds on the domestic market but has not used either facility

(International Bank for Reconstruction and Development, Projects Department, *The Development of Southern Italy. The Cassa per il Mezzogiorno and the Three Special Credit Institutes, Isveimer, Irfis and Cis. Italy*, cit., p. 7).

namely repayments of principal and interest on loans granted by the IMI for postwar reconstruction, in relation to the counterparties in lire obtained from the sale of goods supplied to Italy under the European Recovery Program (ERP) and transferred by the Italian Treasury to the Cassa. Furthermore, the interest on Treasury financing was deposited in banks before its use in order to cover the working expenses of the Cassa, together with capital reimbursements and the interest on credit operations. The Cassa was then authorized to take out loans abroad with the Italian government as a guarantor. At the beginning of 1965, the Cassa obtained 381.6 billion lire (that is to say 610.5 million dollars) from international sources. About two thirds of these funds were employed for industrial projects while many of the remaining resources went into electric power plants, whereas a lesser amount supported technical assistance.

Table 4.2 *Financial resources of the Cassa per il Mezzogiorno, position as at February 28, 1965 (in millions of lire)*

	Domestic sources						Foreign borrowings				Total
	Endowment fund		Revenues and other funds								
Years* (July 1 - June 30)	**Treasury allocations**	**IMI-ERP (Principal)**	**IMI-ERP (interest)**	**Interest on bank deposits ****	**Credit operations (Principal and interests)**	**Total**	**IBRD loans**	**EIB loans**	**Bond emissions**	**Total**	**Aggregate cumulative total**
1950-51	100,000	-	-	1,046	-	101,046	-	-	-	-	101,046
1951-52	100,000	-	-	3,535	-	103,535	6,250	-	-	6,250	210,831
1952-53	80,000	2,996	5,623	4,654	-	93,273	-	-	-	-	304,104
1953-54	90,000	5,905	4,532	6,471	4	106,912	6,250	-	-	6,250	417,266
1954-55	90,000	8,778	4,718	4,573	161	108,230	42,750	-	-	42,750	568,246
1955-56	90,000	16,132	7,595	4,940	476	119,143	-	-	-	-	687,389
1956-57	90,000	12,253	5,420	3,367	629	111,669	46,643	-	-	46,643	845,701
1957-58	90,000	13,343	4,097	4,031	724	112,195	46,875	-	-	46,875	1,004,771
1958-59	100,000	12,722	4,868	4,016	1,084	122,690	12,500	12,500	18,750	43,750	1,171,211
1959-60	179,000	12,433	3,309	6,058	1,919	202,719	25,000	-	-	25,000	1,398,930
1960-61	190,000	11,372	3,503	8,326	3,276	216,477	-	25,625	7,146	32,771	1,648,178
1961-62	191,350	10,731	2,800	7,378	4,233	216,492	-	2,350	-	2,350	1,867,020
1962-63	186,940	11,540	2,371	10,650	3,715	215,216	-	45,325	-	45,325	2,127,561
1963-64	186,850	9,004	1,773	14,293	6,338	218,258	-	29,762	11,250	41,012	2,386,831
after June 1964	267,700***	32,791	-	-	90,338****	390,829	-	30,100	12,500	42,600	2,820,260**
Total	2,031,840	160,000	50,609	83,338**	112,897	2,438,684**	186,268	145,662	49,646	381,576	
	Total net of 54.0 billion lire operating expenses					2,384,700					2,766,300

*Years 1950-51 to 1951-52 relate to the Ten-Year Program; years 1952-53 to 1956-57 relate to the Twelve-Year Program; years 1957-58 and following relate to the Fifteen-Year Program. **Including Lit. 54.0 billion covering Cassa's operating expenses. ***Formed by: Lit. 186,000 million for 1964-65 from Law no. 634 of July 29, 1957 (and its amendment); Lit. 850 million for 1964-65 and Lit. 850 million for 1965-66 from Law no. 28 of January 30, 1962 (Palermo); Lit. 80,000 million from Law no. 608 of July 6, 1964, to be spread over four years. ****Including Lit. 25 billion lent by the sector "Contribution to interest on bonds and loans" to the sector "Hotels and Tourism credits".

Source: International Bank for Reconstruction and Development, Projects Department, *The Development of Southern Italy. The Cassa per il Mezzogiorno and the Three Special Credit Institutes, Isveimer, Irfis and Cis. Italy*, T.O.–467a/Restricted, June 10, 1965, Annex 3, <https://documents.worldbank.org/en/publication/documents-reports/documentdetail/904741468044126033/italy-southern-italy-industrial-financing-project>.

The document also recalled that, between 1951 and 1959, the World Bank had granted seven loans to the Cassa per il Mezzogiorno, each amounting to between 10 and 75 million dollars, for a grand total of 186.3 billion lire (that is to say 298 million dollars). Between 1959 and 1965, the European Investment Bank granted fifty loans to the Cassa, each amounting between 0.4 and 24 million dollars, for a total of 145.7 billion lire (that is to say 233.1 million dollars). Finally, to complete the credit lines framework, four bonds were issued in the United States, Switzerland, Belgium and Luxembourg, for a total of 49.7 billion lire (that is to say 79.4 million dollars).

Concerning the allocation of resources for Southern Italy, the analysis indicated that the majority of these funds were focused on public works. In some interventions, such as the ones concerning aqueducts, the Cassa kept direct responsibility for the work, fully covering the projects' costs. In other cases, the responsibility for implementing the interventions was taken by local authorities, entities, or consortia, while the Cassa provided, completely or in part, the funds for the projects. Furthermore, the Cassa itself provided subsidies to private and enterprises: besides the contributions given to industrial investors, credit lines were opened for farmers, covering up to 30-40% of the costs for improvements. Modest amounts were provided as loans – mostly concerning agriculture and tourism, with interest rates between 2 and 3½% –, directly by the Cassa or by banks, following the criteria set up by the former. Concerning the use of financial resources within the different programs run by the Cassa per il Mezzogiorno, a reference may be made to the interventions by sector and to the evolution of their importance, according to the prospect within Table 4.3.

Table 4.3 *Comparison of the three Cassa programs, position as at February 28, 1965 (in billions of lire)*

	Ten-year program (1950)		Twelve-year program (1952)		Fifteen-year program (1957)	
Sector	Amount	% of total	Amount	% of total	Amount	% of total
I. DIRECT ACTION	870.0	87.0	1,150.0	89.8	1,745.8	73.2
Agriculture	640.0	64.0	757.0	59.1	946.9	39.7
Public works (including reforestation)	360.0	36.0	477.0	37.2	666.9	28.0
Land reform	280.0	28.0	280.0	21.9	280.0	11.7
Aqueducts	90.0	9.0	178.0	13.9	307.0	12.9
Transportation	110.0	11.0	190.0	14.8	339.6	14.2
Roads	110.0	11.0	115.0	9.0	214.5	9.0
Railways, Ferries and Ports	-	-	75.0	5.8	125.1	5.2
Other	30.0	3.0	25.0	2.0	152.3	6.4
Tourism	30.0	3.0	25.0	2.0	54.2	2.3
Industrial Areas and Nuclei	-	-	-	-	23.0	1.0
School buildings, Social institutions, Vocational Training, Hospitals	-	-	-	-	70.8	2.9
City of Palermo (a special slum clearance project)	-	-	-	-	4.3	0.2

II. INCENTIVES TO PRIVATE INVESTMENTS	130.0	13.0	130.0	10.2	625.8	26.3
Contribution to private land improvement (Agriculture)	130.0	13.0	130.0	10.2	228.7	9.6
Fishing, Handcraft	-	-	-	-	44.3	1.9
Industry	-	-	-	-	230.5	9.7
Capital grants	-	-	-	-	49.4	2.1
Contributions to financing institutes, and participations	-	-	-	-	42.1	1.8
Interest subsidization	-	-	-	-	139.0	5.8
Credits	-	-	-	-	122.3	5.1
Agriculture	-	-	-	-	68.2	2.9
Hotels and tourism	-	-	-	-	54.1	2.2
I+II TOTAL	1,000.0	100.0	1,280.0	100.0	2,371.6	99.5
Unallocated as to sector	-	-	-	-	13.1	0.5
TOTAL	1,000.0	100.0	1,280.0	100.0	2,384.7	100.0
RECAPITULATION						
Total agriculture	770.0	77.0	887.0	69.3	1,243.8	52.2
Total industry	-	-	-	-	253.5	10.6
Total other	230.0	23.0	393.0	30.7	874.3	36.7

Source: International Bank for Reconstruction and Development, Projects Department, *The Development of Southern Italy. The Cassa per il Mezzogiorno and the Three Special Credit Institutes, Isveimer, Irfis and Cis. Italy*, T.O.–467a/Restricted, June 10, 1965, Annex 4, <https://documents.worldbank.org/en/publication/documents-reports/documentdetail/904741468044126033/italy-southern-italy-industrial-financing-project>.

The main sectors of activity reflected the choices contained in the programs. Concerning the agricultural sector, the Cassa, besides its support for productivity increases, tackled also other economic and social issues. The more significant expenditures concerned agricultural infrastructure but also the implementation of the agrarian reform, in order to break up latifundia and redistribute land to rural households, which required some essential interventions: irrigation works in land reclamation areas, involving an area of over 500,000 hectares; the development of barren land, involving more than 3.3 million hectares; soil and flood control, reforestation and other requalification projects in mountain regions, amounting to about 5 million hectares. Concerning transports, the greater Cassa expenditures were focused on roadways – manly those linking urban areas and the new highways –, railways and ferries, even if a more significant contribution, according to the data, went into the consulting work that the Cassa carried out for transport agencies in order to plan investments and start up the necessary projects, which however were not included in other programs. Considering water supply and waterworks, the Cassa was involved in a 50-year plan with the goal to provide water for the whole population of Southern Italy, with coverage ensured to 1,815 communities up to that moment. Within the industrial sector, the Cassa limited itself to offer incentives for investors, both directly or by means of other institutions: anyway, industry had increasingly grown in importance and was bound to become the main object of the efforts and initiatives by the Cassa[387].

On February 28, 1965, the sum total available for the ordinary activities of the Cassa per il Mezzogiorno amounted to about 2,385 billion lire (that is to say 3.8 billion dollars). Table 4.4 contains a subdivision by sector of this sum total, according to the availability, the commitments and the expenditures of the Cassa.

---

[387] As it was clarified within the IBRD report:

> The incentives offered vary somewhat with size of project (interest subsidies vary inversely with size), location (larger incentives are offered to projects in the less industrialized areas), labor intensiveness, etc. They are varied also to encourage concentration in the industrial development centers where Cassa funds are to be used to help create conditions favorable for industrial growth. The program to build up these centers is still in its early stages. The plan is to establish 26 industrial nuclei and 12 areas; to date plans for eight areas have been prepared and one has been approved

(International Bank for Reconstruction and Development, Projects Department, *The Development of Southern Italy. The Cassa per il Mezzogiorno and the Three Special Credit Institutes, Isveimer, Irfis and Cis. Italy*, cit., p. 11).

Table 4.4 *Availabilities, commitments and expenditures of the Cassa per il Mezzogiorno, as at February 28, 1965 (in billions of lire)**

Sectors	Availabilities	Commitments	Expenditures	Balance to be committed
I. DIRECT ACTION	1,745.8	1,724.0	1,455.1	21.8
Agriculture	946.9	943.0	845.9	3.9
Public works	666.9	663.0	565.9	3.9
Land reform	280.0	280.0	280.0	-
Aqueducts	307.0	305.8	253.8	1.2
External works	282.8	282.1	238.1	0.7
Internal distribution	24.2	23.7	15.7	0.5
Roads	214.5	210.7	167.1	3.8
Railways, Ferries and Ports	125.1	121.2	97.6	3.9
Tourism	54.2	53.9	44.1	0.3
Industrial Areas and Nuclei	23.0	20.9	8.0	2.1
School buildings, Social institutions, Vocational training, Hospitals	70.8	68.5	38.6	2.3
City of Palermo	4.3	-	-	4.3
II. INCENTIVES TO PRIVATE INVESTMENTS	625.8	564.0	347.1	61.8
Agriculture				
Contributions for land improvement	228.7	220.5	166.2	8.2
Fishing and Handicraft	44.3	39.7	29.3	4.6
Industry				
Capital grants	49.4	49.1	31.2	0.3
Contribution to interest on bonds and loans	139.0	112.2	20.2	26.8
Contributions to financing institutes, and participations	42.1	42.1	38.1	-

Credits				
Agriculture	68.2	56.5	41.1	11.7
Hotels and tourism	54.1**	43.9	21.0	10.2
I+II TOTAL	2,371.6	2,288.0	1,802.2	83.6
Unallocated as to sector	13.1	-	-	13.1
TOTAL	2,384.7	2,288.0	1,802.2	96.7
Other elements				
Operating expenses	54.0	54.0	54.0	-
Temporary anticipations	-	-	48.0	-
Grand Total	2,438.7	2,342.0	1,904.2	96.7

Source: International Bank for Reconstruction and Development, Projects Department, *The Development of Southern Italy. The Cassa per il Mezzogiorno and the Three Special Credit Institutes, Isveimer, Irfis and Cis. Italy*, T.O.–467a/Restricted, June 10, 1965, Annex 5, <https://documents.worldbank.org/en/publication/documents-reports/documentdetail/904741468044126033/italy-southern-italy-industrial-financing-project>.

* Internal sources alone. **Including 25 billion lire lent by the "Interest-bearing accounts on bonds and loans".

Within such a framework, drawing conclusions from the first phase of credit facilities for the extraordinary intervention, the IBRD document clarified that:

> In the early years of Cassa operations, projects were prepared and processed relatively slowly, and idle funds accumulated. As a result of the momentum developed by the programs and improved preparation and accelerated processing of projects, funds are now committed very promptly. There is also little delay between commitments and expenditures, except in the case of industry where a lag is unavoidable because interest subsidies are paid to the Credit Institutes over the life of the bonds they issue to raise funds for lending. [...] As at February 28, 1965, only Lit. 97 billion (US$ 155 million) had not been committed, and the Cassa had already made firm decisions as to how these uncommitted funds were to be used. Projects with a total cost estimated at Lit. 183 billion (US$ 293 million) had been found acceptable after examination, but had not been approved for lack of funds to commit. In addition, applications for capital grants for industrial projects which might require expenditures of as much as Lit. 140 billion were being processed by the Cassa and the three Special Credit Institutes and potential requirements for interest subsidies on domestic bond issues of the Institutes (either outstanding or authorized) amounted to about Lit. 110 billion. In the

case of capital grants and interest subsidies for industry, also, lack of funds made impossible further commitments[388].

However, the new law for the extraordinary intervention allocated 1,640 billion lire (that is to say 2.6 billion dollars) for the period from 1965 to 1969. Additionally, it envisioned that 1,350 billion lire (2.16 million dollars) would be used during those very same years, while 290 billion lire (464 million dollars) would be employed in 1970-1971. The Cassa per il Mezzogiorno set up a possible proposal to allocate the new funds, as Table 4.5 explains.

Table 4.5 *Estimated breakdown by sectors of Cassa contributions, under the general program for 1965-1969 (in billions of lire)*

Sector	Total investments		Contributions by the Cassa	
General infrastructure:		320		320
Aqueducts	200		200	
Transportations	120		120	
Agricultural infrastructure:		580		450
Irrigation and related projects	265		250	
Soil conservation and reforestation	60		60	
Other:				
Land improvement works	200		100	
Processing plants	40		25	
Technical assistance and applied research	15		15	
Industry and industrial development areas:		2,660		700
Industrial areas and nuclei	95		80	
Housing	25		10	
Ports	40		40	
Incentives:				
Capital grants	2,500		280	
Interest subsides			290	
Tourism		150		90
Vocational training, social institutions		90		80
Total		3,800		1,640*

Source: International Bank for Reconstruction and Development, Projects Department, *The Development of Southern Italy. The Cassa per il Mezzogiorno and the Three Special Credit Institutes, Isveimer, Irfis and Cis. Italy*, T.O.–467a/Restricted, June 10, 1965, Annex 6,

---

388 *Ivi*, p. 12.

<https://documents.worldbank.org/en/publication/documents-reports/documentdetail/904741468044126033/italy-southern-italy-industrial-financing-project>.

*The indicated sum had to be increased by 60 billion lire, as per the Italian law no. 608 of July 6, 1964. Such an amount was under the 1965-69 programme, but it had already been used as a part of the last biannual allocations, within the first 15-years plan.

Only 70 billion lire (i.e., 42 million dollars) of the new allocations were to be made available in 1965. The annual average, in the period between 1966 and 1969, would have amounted to 320 billion lire, 34% more when compared to the average availability during the six years between 1959 and 1965 (amounting to 238 billion lire). Although sectoral comparisons were difficult, the IBRD estimated that the amounts in favor of industry would have more than tripled, making it the priority sector of intervention among the Cassa activities, as it was to receive 43% of the total funds. The increase in funds for industry would come at the expenses of the agricultural sector, where resources were to be drastically reduced to 27%[389]. The "future programs" of the Cassa per il Mezzogiorno, according to World Bank forecasts, were to be developed in a significant direction:

> *In agriculture*, the main emphasis is to be placed on the extension of the irrigated area through a number of individual projects for which planning is far advanced. In addition, greater efforts are to be made to facilitate the transition from traditional to more modern methods of farming, in particular through on-farm improvements, land consolidation and land transformation. [...] *In transportation*, the major object of expenditures will continue to be roads, especially those going from irrigated areas to markets, those within

---

[389] In the IBRD document, the following was noted:

> Sector comparisons are difficult because the Cassa distribution covers the entire appropriation, not the amount to be made available to 1969, but it can be estimated roughly that the amounts available for industry would be more than trebled and those for aqueducts increased by almost one-third, while amounts for agriculture and for other purposes would be reduced slightly and those for transportation would be reduced by almost one-third. As a result, industry would replace agriculture as the major object of Cassa expenditures and would account for 43% of the total, as against 18% in 1959-65. The share of agriculture would fall sharply (from 40% to 27%) as would that of transportation, while the share of aqueducts would remain unchanged

(International Bank for Reconstruction and Development, Projects Department, *The Development of Southern Italy. The Cassa per il Mezzogiorno and the Three Special Credit Institutes, Isveimer, Irfis and Cis. Italy*, cit., p. 13).

> the industrial development poles and linking these regions to main highways, and those leading to tourist attractions. Expenditures on ports will increase, but expenditures on railways will be largely limited to the completion of projects already under way. [...] *In water and sewerage*, the Cassa expects to continue constructing major works, but plans also to increase assistance to municipalities to help them improve local distribution and collection systems. Its aim is to make possible fuller utilization of works already in existence as well as to increase overall capacity. [...] *In industry*, the objectives are an increase of 8-10% per annum in investment and a total investment (excluding State-owned industries), over the period ending December 31, 1969, of about Lit. 3,000 billion (US$ 4.8 billion). It is expected that there will be a shift from such capital-intensive industries as steel and chemicals, which have accounted for a large part of the investment in recent years, to the more labor-intensive industries processing the semi-finished products now available locally. The mechanical industries in particular are expected to grow rapidly, especially around the new steel plant at Taranto. At the same time, the growth of incomes and the movement to the cities are expected to expand the markets for a wide variety of finished products. Industrial employment is expected to increase by an estimated 275,000. This compares with the expected natural increase of about 900,000 in the total population (male and female) of working age (15 – 65) between 1966 and 1971. The Cassa expects to increase its contributions for the development of tourist facilities. It believes that, in view of the rapid increase in European travel, larger expenditures would be justified. Improvements in accommodation and in the accessibility of the many spots of national beauty and historic interest would bring a much larger number of tourists to Southern Italy. [...] Certain fields in which the Cassa has been active until now, in particular the construction of schools and hospitals, rural electrification, welfare projects, adult education, etc., are to revert to the appropriate ministries[390].

Concerning the results and perspectives of the extraordinary intervention, the International Bank for Reconstruction and Development maintained the following: «Judged by the improvement in the economic position of Southern Italy since the early 1950's, the program for its development must be considered a success»[391]. According to the data in their possession, the Bank estimated that *per capita* income (at constant prices) grew by two thirds (i.e., about 4.5% per annum) between 1951 and 1963. Additionally, unemployment fell to circa 3% (compared with 12% at the beginning of the 1950s), even though such a decrease was mostly due to emigration. Furthermore, between 1959 and 1963, the rate of economic growth in Southern Italy accelerated, featuring an average yearly increase of *per capita* income (at constant prices) by almost 8%. As a consequence,

---

[390] *Ivi*, pp. 13-14.
[391] *Ivi*, p. 14.

during the years between 1960 and 1963, for the first time ever, Southern Italy developed more rapidly than the North. Such a revolutionary change was accompanied by an analogous increase of industrial investments in Southern Italy: since the beginning of the Cassa program, the total investment in Southern Italy had significantly grown. However, it was only after 1958 that industrial investments developed more quickly than the total ones, partly because of the then impending Italian "economic miracle". Industrial investments accelerated also in Northern Italy, but several factors brought a more significant increase to Southern Italy and the gap in growth rates between the two areas widened in favor of the Mezzogiorno: indeed, the Northern regions of Italy registered yearly percentage increases amounting to 3.7% between 1951 and 1958, 9% between 1958 and 1963, and 8.3% between 1960 and 1963. The Mezzogiorno experienced a more significant evolution instead, as the investments in the area grew from 7.6% between 1951 and 1958, to 22% between 1958 and 1963, and to 22.5% between 1960 and 1963[392].

According to the IBRD, about half of the recent increase of industrial investment in Southern regions was due to State-owned companies. However, a significant increase in private investment had occurred as well. This was mostly due to the incentives offered to industrial investors since 1957, which had built up a significant flow of capital and technical know-how from outside[393]. Finally, it was highlighted that investments in more recent years had not been fully implemented yet, because the construction of many plants was still underway, the completed ones needed a long time to break even, and entrepreneurs in Southern Italy had the tendency to build smaller plants than what was considered optimal size. Nevertheless, the Bank expressed optimism concerning productivity growth in the Mezzogiorno, keeping faith in its soon-to-be full development, thanks to the new establishments in heavy industries and to the industrial development poles. Table 4.6, which was included within the appendix of the Bank's report, contained the data on gross investments, subdivided by sector and area.

---

[392] See *Ivi*, p. 15.

[393] On this, the following was also noted:

> The Cassa estimates that the share of total equity capital supplied for industrial projects in the South by North Italians rose from 40% in the years through 1957 to 60% of the much larger total in 1958-63; foreign equity capital rose from a negligible percentage prior to 1957 to 14% in the later period

(International Bank for Reconstruction and Development, Projects Department, *The Development of Southern Italy. The Cassa per il Mezzogiorno and the Three Special Credit Institutes, Isveimer, Irfis and Cis. Italy*, cit., p. 15).

Table 4.6 *Italy – Gross fixed investments by economic branch and region (in billion lire, at 1954 prices)*

	1951	1954	1955	1956	1957	1958	1959	1960	1961	1962	1963
North-Center											
Agriculture	188	186	203	215	211	212	233	292	259	291	287
Industry	609	632	681	756	828	795	832	967	1,136	1,198	1,227
Transports and communications	211	307	303	348	335	346	431	579	702	760	836
Housing	277	478	579	646	734	755	815	805	875	1,016	1,090
Public works*	102	130	133	119	164	188	241	264	284	244	236
Miscellaneous	103	102	110	123	152	167	181	212	244	281	290
Total	1,490	1,835	2,009	2,207	2,424	2,463	2,733	3,119	3,500	3,790	3,966
South											
Agriculture	89	151	158	139	162	167	182	199	214	208	212
Industry	92	118	151	148	159	154	181	235	289	358	435
Transports and communications	53	107	130	151	152	132	146	191	215	248	261
Housing	46	101	122	143	162	163	168	178	197	220	251
Public works*	92	112	106	106	96	117	110	135	135	124	120
Miscellaneous	28	30	30	33	41	45	48	65	84	98	98
Total	400	619	697	720	772	778	835	1,003	1,134	1,256	1,377

Italy											
Agriculture	277	337	361	354	373	379	415	491	473	499	499
Industry	701	750	832	904	987	949	1,013	1,202	1,425	1,556	1,662
Transports and communications	264	414	433	499	487	478	577	770	918	1,008	1,097
Housing	323	579	701	789	896	918	983	983	1,071	1,236	1,341
Public works*	194	242	239	225	260	305	351	399	419	368	355
Miscellaneous	131	132	140	156	193	212	229	277	328	379	388
Total	1,890	2,454	2,706	2,927	3,196	3,241	3,568	4,122	4,634	5,046	5,342

Source: International Bank for Reconstruction and Development, Projects Department, *The Development of Southern Italy. The Cassa per il Mezzogiorno and the Three Special Credit Institutes, Isveimer, Irfis and Cis. Italy*, T.O.–467a/Restricted, June 10, 1965, Annex 7, <https://documents.worldbank.org/en/publication/documents-reports/documentdetail/904741468044126033/italy-southern-italy-industrial-financing-project>.

*Including roads, ports, waterworks, hospitals and sanitation, public buildings and various interventions.

Considering the most suitable choices for the following years, the IBRD maintained that sufficient reasons to continue granting incentives to industrial investments in the Mezzogiorno were present. These reasons were the disadvantages Southern Italy had when compared to the North in terms of market size, distance from complementary and ancillary industries, lack of expertise among the local management and operational staff. Such obstacles to growth were not set off by lower wages, as it was instead the case with developing countries. Actually, wages in Southern Italy were not significantly lower than the ones in northern Italy; on the contrary they were rapidly bridging the gap, as firms had to entice management professionals and specialized workers from Northern areas. However, a considerable improvement in the perspectives concerning industrialization in Southern Italy could be noticed, especially when it came to infrastructure enhancements, the increase of *per capita* income, the expansion of local markets and of external economies connected to industrial growth and to the emerging Mediterranean area as a source of industrial raw materials and as a market:

> Given this improved climate for industry, continued assistance to offset Northern advantages ought to make possible a fairly rapid development of an industrial sector capable of self-sustaining growth, and thus enable Italy to realize a return on its already large investment in a relatively short time[394].

The document also focused one of its sections on the ongoing incentives policy, carrying out a wide evaluation, according to which «its cost should be balanced against the cost of alternatives»[395]. One of the main objectives of industrialization in Southern Italy was as a matter of fact to balance the costs of workforce emigration, a phenomenon draining Southern Italy of an essential resource for its development. Concerning the incentives themselves, the Bank maintained that:

> The commonest form of assistance provided to "infant industries" – tariff protection – cannot, of course, be given to Southern Italian industries as against Northern. But the incentives that are offered as an alternative compare favorably with a tariff in their economic effect. They reduce capital costs and the tax burden in the early years of operation, but do not introduce price distortions which often prove difficult to eliminate. From the time they begin operations, the industrial firms in Southern Italy that receive

[394] *Ivi*, p. 16.
[395] *Ibidem*.

> assistance must be preparing to meet competition without assistance, in their case, not only from the rest of Italy but from the entire Common Market[396].

However, the IBRD report did not shy away from the questions on the topic that were opened since then, wondering whether the level of incentives was greater than the one needed to achieve the desired investment rate for industry in Southern Italy. The Cassa per il Mezzogiorno carried out some analyses on this issue, albeit without reaching precise conclusions: anyway, according to the IBRD, it had been only thanks to a high level of incentives that capital accumulation for production had begun its fast growth in Southern Italy; there was no indication whatsoever that the incentives had helped establish anti-economic enterprises[397].

4.2.2 The three special credit institutions and their role in developing Southern Italy

The second part of the IBRD document, titled *The Institutes*, was entirely dedicated to the special credit institutions (ISVEIMER, IRFIS and CIS) and to their role in the development of southern Italy, in direct relationship with the Cassa per il Mezzogiorno[398]. Those three institutions were tasked to grant medium- and long-term loans to small and medium

---

[396] *Ibidem*.

[397] The document, within such long parts focused to the economic development of the Mezzogiorno, ended noting the following:

> It can be argued that in the case of certain enterprises or somewhat already industrialized areas, the incentives may be too high. The Italian government is aware of this possibility, and as has been indicated, differentiates to a certain extent. It does not seem advisable, however, to make any significant changes in the incentive system at this time because that might shake the confidence of investors in the continuity of government policy and halt the still new investment boom. Although changes are likely to be gradual, the program is susceptible to change. Interest rates on industrial loans, one of the major incentives, can be altered at any time by the Interministerial Committee for Credit and Savings. [...] In the long run, it is unlikely that the incentives will be maintained at a level high enough to support the establishment or continued operation of uneconomic enterprises in the South. The Italian authorities are aware that Italy cannot afford to provide assistance for a substantial segment of industry except on a temporary basis. The policy of incentives can be regarded as self-limiting

(International Bank for Reconstruction and Development, Projects Department, *The Development of Southern Italy. The Cassa per il Mezzogiorno and the Three Special Credit Institutes, Isveimer, Irfis and Cis. Italy*, cit., pp. 16-17).

[398] See *Ivi*, pp. 18-36.

industrial firms in the Mezzogiorno. The primary aim was to increase employment and the use of natural resources in the treated areas. Hence, four of the seven credit lines granted to the Cassa by the IBRD between 1951 and 1959 were routed to these three institutions. This way, the special credit institutions made 90.7 billion dollars available to 21 enterprises operating in Southern Italy, out of a total cost for their project amounting to 222.49 million dollars[399]. The operations made during the first ten years of the new activity of these institutions concerned 4,500 loans and an amount of over 1.2 million dollars overall. These funds came for 58% from ISVEIMER, for 23% from IRFIS, and for 19% from CIS[400]. As may be inferred from the following graph (Figure 4.3), such loans had increased especially during the latter years, when rapid growth affected also credit lines that had previously been approved but not yet granted for lack of funds. In addition to these funds there were also other ones labelled "actively considered", which made the total rise to the significant amount of about 790 million dollars.

From an analysis conducted by each of the three special credit institutions at the end of 1963, it resulted that about 50% of the loans granted by IRFIS and CIS were allocated to projects in capital-intensive chemicals, and that much smaller percentages were allocated towards industrial sectors that required significant technical know-how. These results showed that Sicily and Sardinia were still in the initial phases of the industrialization process. In contrast, the financing granted by ISVEIMER privileged mechanical industries, therefore revealing the more advanced industrialization of the mainland Mezzogiorno[401]. The following picture (Figure 4.4) reports a breakdown of industrial loans by size, showing that, in the case of IRFIS and CIS, almost 70% of the credit lines by number involved amounts below 50 million lire each. However, because of the focus of IRFIS and CIS on capital-intensive industries, almost 60% of the overall amount of their operations involved loans above a billion and a half lire. On the contrary, in the case of ISVEIMER, 40% of the credit lines by number involved less than 50 million lire each, whereas only 30% of the total loans amounted to more than a billion and a half lire each.

---

[399] See *Ivi*, Annex 9.

[400] See *Ivi*, p. 18. In the very same page, the following was clarified:

> A large number of their loans were made to relatively small enterprises and were for amounts of less than Lit. 50 million (US$ 80,000) each, but the Institutes have also made individual loans as large as US$ 10 million equivalent.

[401] See *Ivi*, Annex 11.

Figure 4.3 *Industrial loans made by the special credit institutions (ISVEIMER, IRFIS and CIS), by the IMI and other banks in Southern Italy, during 1954 to 1963/1964*

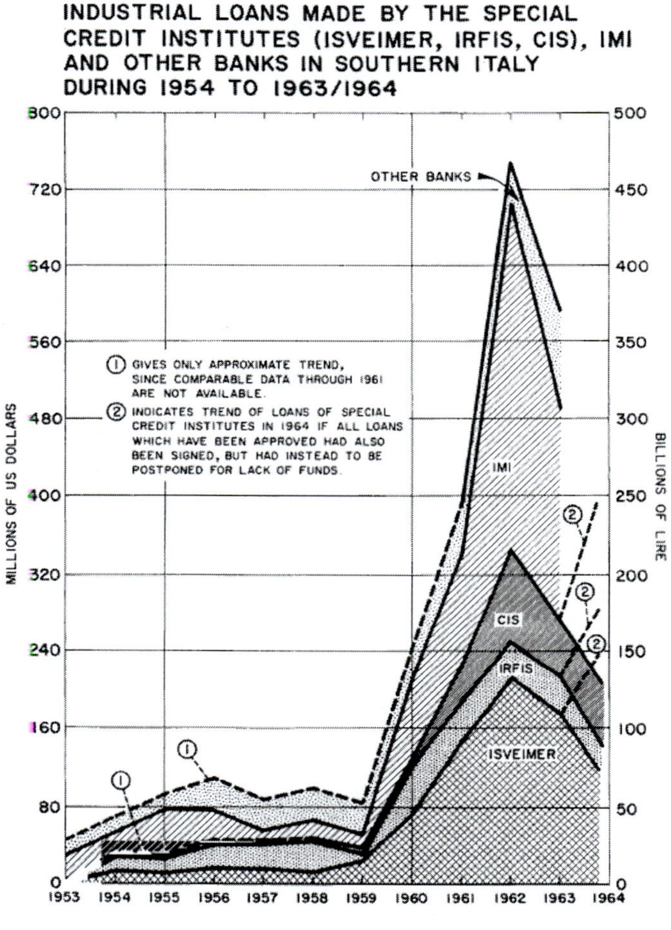

Source: International Bank for Reconstruction and Development, Projects Department, *The Development of Southern Italy. The Cassa per il Mezzogiorno and the Three Special Credit Institutes, Isveimer, Irfis and Cis. Italy*, T.O.–467a/Restricted, June 10, 1965, Annex 10, <https://documents.worldbank.org/en/publication/documents-reports/documentdetail/904741468044126033/italy-southern-italy-industrial-financing-project>.

Figure 4.4 *Breakdown of industrial loans by size from 1954 to 1963*

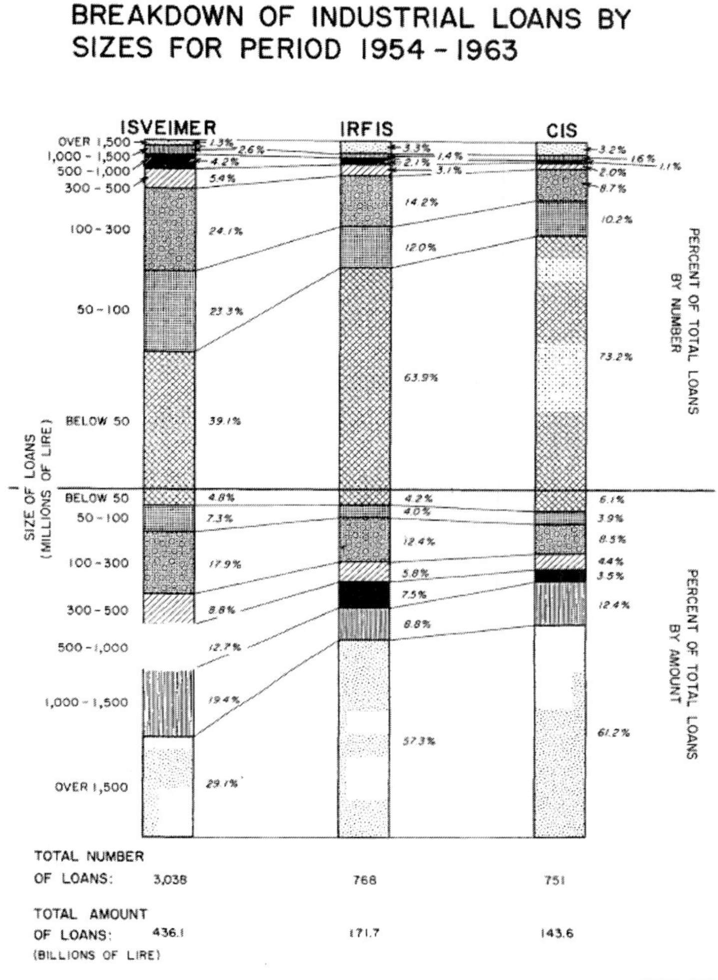

Source: International Bank for Reconstruction and Development, Projects Department, *The Development of Southern Italy. The Cassa per il Mezzogiorno and the Three Special Credit Institutes, Isveimer, Irfis and Cis. Italy*, T.O.–467a/Restricted, June 10, 1965, Annex 12, <https://documents.worldbank.org/en/publication/documents-reports/documentdetail/904741468044126033/italy-southern-italy-industrial-financing-project>.

Furthermore, the document reported that the Cassa per il Mezzogiorno had three ways to directly control the special credit institutes: the Cassa participated to their equity; maintained a presence in their Boards of Directors and Boards of Statutory Auditors; had the power to approve or reject projects, making grants and subsidized loans available; finally, the Cassa provided loans from foreign credit lines. The Cassa had also an indirect influence on the three credit institutes by means of its relationship with the Committee of Ministers for the Mezzogiorno, which held the ultimate responsibility on the policies for the development of Southern Italy. Practically speaking, direct control by the Cassa was more formal than substantial; on the other hand, such a situation was balanced by a significant capacity to influence the three special credit institutes indirectly[402]. Other

---

[402] Within the report, the following was in fact noted:

> The Boards of Directors of the Institutes tend to rely heavily on the recommendations of their managements. Cassa representation on the Board of Auditors may be as important as its representation on the Board of Directors, but its influence on Institute activity through that Board is indirect and difficult to measure. Cassa approval of projects for interest subsidies and capital grants is largely formal; approval is virtually assured if the projects meet the standards set for location, size, branch of industry, etc. The Cassa does not itself make thorough checks of the technical, financial and economic soundness of projects; it relies largely on the recommendations of the Institutes. [...] As an obligor to foreign lenders, the Cassa is responsible for presenting and following up projects. However, the major responsibility for the selection of projects has in the past rested with the lenders, who have applied their own criteria, while the Cassa has shared responsibility for follow-up with both the lenders and the Institutes. In the case of bond issues and loans the purposes of which are not specified, the Cassa has usually distributed the proceeds among the Institutes either in accordance with the formula applied by the Treasury in apportioning its contributions or in accordance with the overall capital requirements of the Institutes. [...] However, the Cassa does exercise a considerable indirect influence on the Institutes. Under the former law, the criteria for eligibility for capital grants were set by the Committee of Ministers for the South, following a recommendation by the Cassa and after consultation with the Ministry of Industry and Commerce. The amount of interest subsidy to be given by the Cassa to industrial lending institutions was determined under the old law by the Interministerial Committee for Credit and Savings, following a recommendation by the Committee of Ministers for the South. The close relations between the Cassa and the Committee of Ministers for the South make it probable that the Cassa exercises an influence on the Committee's recommendations, even where Cassa participation is not formally provided for. In general, the Cassa has exercised more influence on the Institutes

forms of supervision over the credit institutes' activities were those that affected all Italian banks, including the presentation of a quarterly report by ISVEIMER, IRFIS and CIS to the Bank of Italy, which in turn carried out the auditing duties as supervisory authority and provided indications that had to be applied for financing procedures[403]. The Comitato Interministeriale per il Credito e il Risparmio (CICR), an interministerial committee on credit and savings, carried out other significant tasks, such as establishing the structure of interest rates to be employed in the operations of Italian banking and credit institutions, authorizing bonds on the internal markets and approving their deadlines, as well as pointing out those sectors to be considered a priority for financing. Finally, the Italian Ministry for Industry and Trade had representatives in the Boards of Auditors of these three institutes, in the Interministerial Committee for Southern Italy and was also tasked with approving, together with the Ministry of Treasury and the Interministerial Committee for Southern Italy, all interest subsidies and grants and, together with the Cassa, all those loans having a special interest rate (i.e., 3%, rather than the usual 4%)[404].

> indirectly through its recommendations to the Committee of Ministers for the South on development policy in general as well as specific matters than through its direct control over their activities

(International Bank for Reconstruction and Development, Projects Department, *The Development of Southern Italy. The Cassa per il Mezzogiorno and the Three Special Credit Institutes, Isveimer, Irfis and Cis. Italy*, cit., p. 20).

[403] In particular, the following was highlighted:

> The Bank [of Italy] also serves as the executive organ of the *Interministerial Committee for Credit and Savings* and, in that connection, reviews and makes recommendations on proposed Institute loans of Lit. 500 million and over, which must be approved by the Interministerial Committee. It should be noted, however, that the criteria applied by both the Bank of Italy and the Interministerial Committee in passing on such loans is the financial position of the borrower, not the technical, financial or economic soundness of the project to be financed

(International Bank for Reconstruction and Development, Projects Department, *The Development of Southern Italy. The Cassa per il Mezzogiorno and the Three Special Credit Institutes, Isveimer, Irfis and Cis. Italy*, cit., p. 21).

[404] See *Ibidem*. In this page and in the following one, the document by the IBRD underlined that:

> In general, in spite of the formal authority of various government bodies with respect to the Institutes, they enjoy a considerable measure of independence. This is due to the diffusion of government authority and the government's choice of the role of vigilance rather than of intervention; however, the government has a reserve of power which it could exercise to check the Institutes, if it considered it necessary. Moreover, as public interest

The report went on describing the position of ISVEIMER, IRFIS and CIS within the Italian credit system and clarifying that these institutes, despite having been established to promote industrial development in Southern Italy, did not go beyond granting loans and giving firms assistance regarding such credit lines. Nevertheless, the Bank noted that:

> However, the Institutes are more projects oriented than other lending institutions, and are in other ways more responsive to the general economic policies of the government for the development of the Mezzogiorno. As one example, all the Institutes have been very active in promoting investment in the South and have actively attempted to attract North Italian and foreign capital and technology [405].

Special credit institutes, even if they were not the only ones granting loans with favorable credit terms for industrial projects in Southern Italy, were the most important sources for such credit lines, amounting to 45% of the total loans granted between 1947 and 1963. IMI contributed for 40% of the total, and all other credit institutes managed the remaining 15%[406]. In such a framework, it has been observed that these three institutes, besides being more government-dependent financially, were different from other credit institutes under several features. Each of them was active in a limited area, which gave them a detailed knowledge of local conditions and problems; their loan portfolios privileged the food industry, textiles, leather and leatherworking, paper, printing and publishing industries, while the IMI and the other credit institutions mostly supported mining, metalworking and

---

entities, the Institutes' interest rates for borrowing and lending are fixed by the government and their earnings are therefore determined by it.

405 International Bank for Reconstruction and Development, Projects Department, *The Development of Southern Italy. The Cassa per il Mezzogiorno and the Three Special Credit Institutes, Isveimer, Irfis and Cis. Italy*, cit., p. 22.

406 See *Ivi*, Annex 13. The following institutions were mentioned, in particular: Banco di Sicilia (1947), Banco di Napoli (1947), Banca Nazionale del Lavoro (1947), Medio Credito del Lazio (1955), Efibanca (1955), Centrobanca (1955), Mediobanca (1955). The dates between brackets signal the moment when the industrial credit lines within Southern Italy were activated by each institution. According to the IBRD, the three special credit institutes, the IMI and the other aforementioned relevant bodies were the only significant long-term capital sources for the industry in the Mezzogiorno (See International Bank for Reconstruction and Development, Projects Department, *The Development of Southern Italy. The Cassa per il Mezzogiorno and the Three Special Credit Institutes, Isveimer, Irfis and Cis. Italy*, cit., p. 22).

rubber industries; sectors such as chemicals, machinery and construction had the same importance for both groups instead[407].

Furthermore, the IBRD document went on to illustrate the relevant loan strategies and procedures, clarifying project evaluation methods, as well as the financing terms and criteria[408]. The main credit lines provided by ISVEIMER, IRFIS and CIS in Southern Italy, as reported in Table 4.7, included long-term financing to establish new plants or upgrade and rationalize existing ones, as well as for starting equipment, and medium-

---

[407] See *Ivi*, pp. 22-23.

[408] As it was noted:

> The Institutes are authorized to make loans of up to 15 years, divided into three distinct periods: (1) the disbursement period which, except in special cases, is limited to two years; (2) the pre-amortization period which may not exceed three years; and (3) the repayment period which is a maximum of ten years. ISVEIMER permits interest to accrue during the period of disbursement; the two other Institutes require interest to be paid during this period. None of the Institutes provide in their loans for capitalizing interest during construction. [...] In setting the length of the disbursement and pre-amortization periods all the Institutes now give their borrowers as much margin as possible, and in the last few years, the duration of loans has tended to amount to 13 – 15 years. Before 1959, loans could not be made for more than ten years, and repayment had to start almost as soon as construction was completed. These conditions proved unduly onerous and a considerable amount of rescheduling of amortization became necessary. [...] The rates of interest on loans are fixed by the Boards of Directors of the Institutes within the limits established by the Interministerial Committee for Credit and Savings. The minimum rates [...] are 4% per year for small and medium-scale enterprises, which by legal definition are production units in which capital investment does not exceed Lit. 6.0 billion (US$ 9.6 million equivalent), and 5% for large-scale enterprises. The interest rate may be further reduced to 3% for small loans to enterprises in specified industrial sectors meeting certain criteria [...]. Even if it were possible for industrial firms in the South to issue their own bonds – and this is generally not the case – the cost of borrowing would amount to about 8%. Thus, the Institutes provide funds at about 3% to 4% under the market rate, or even more in the case of small loans. [...] Loans are limited to 70% of project costs (which cover land, buildings, machinery, equipment, essential services and initial inventories); the inventory component may not exceed 30% of project costs (40% under the new Cassa bill). [...] There is no upper limit for Institute loans. The lower limit is Lit. 5.0 million (US$ 8,000), but the average size of loans of less than Lit. 50 million has been over three times the minimum

(International Bank for Reconstruction and Development, Projects Department, *The Development of Southern Italy. The Cassa per il Mezzogiorno and the Three Special Credit Institutes, Isveimer, Irfis and Cis. Italy*, cit., p. 25, p. 27 and p. 28).

term financing for machinery and facilities. On this, it was noted that medium and long-term unsubsidized industrial credit was available, at the time, with an interest rate of about 8%[409].

Furthermore, the document by the Bank described the organization and management of the three special credit institutions in detail[410], ending with an overall representation of their peculiar organization chart (Figure 4.5). As the report itself clarified:

> The activities of each Institute are supervised by a Shareholders Assembly, a Board of Directors, a Board of Auditors and a Technical Consultative Committee. *The Shareholders Assembly* convenes annually to receive the Annual Report and to approve the financial statements. Among its more important powers are the power to authorize increases in share capital, to vote dividends, to initiate changes in the statutes and to determine the size of the professional staff of the Institute. *The Board of Directors* meets at least every second month and has the final decision on loan applications. However, since the Board must review a great number of loans at each meeting (sometimes 50 or more) it must necessarily rely heavily on the recommendations of management. In only rare instances, has any one of the Boards gone against management recommendations. Besides passing on loans, the Board has important policy and administrative responsibilities with respect to the borrowing activities of the Institute and the establishment of the terms and criteria for lending within the general guidelines established by the Committee of Ministers for the South. In each Institute, the Chairman of the Board maintains an office and is in daily attendance. His role in the day-to-day activities and lending operations of the Institute varies markedly from one Institute to the other, and depends mainly on the personalities of and the relationship between the Chairman and the General Manager. [...] *The Board of Auditors* attends every Board Meeting. Its main function is to make sure that the Institute acts within the terms of its statutes and the provisions of the laws governing these statutes. [...] Each of the Institutes makes use of a Technical Consultative Committee to pass judgment on the technical and economic aspects of all projects before they are submitted to the Board of Directors. This is an external Committee whose members are appointed for two year terms by the Board of Directors. The Committee is chaired by the General Manager. ISVEIMER's Committee has seven members, IRFIS' and CIS' five each. [...] *The General Manager* is the chief executive officer of the Institute and is responsible for its general administration. In making an investment decision, the Board acts on his recommendation[411].

---

409 See *Ivi*, p. 26.

410 See *Ivi*, Annex 15, pp. 1-4.

411 *Ivi*, Annex 15, pp. 1-2.

Table 4.7 *Summary of most important medium and long-term credit facilities for industrial enterprises in Southern Italy*

	Purpose	*Interest rate*	*Amount of credit*	*Terms of credit*	*Security*
Small and Medium-Size Enterprises. Excluding cottage-type enterprises, production units in which investment does not exceed Lit. 6 billion (US$ 9.6 million).	Financing of new plant (including initial inventories) and expansion/rationalization of existing plant.	4% per annum. A 3% rate may be granted for loans up to Lit. 1.0 billion (in exceptional cases up to Lit. 1.5 billion) for new plant and up to Lit. 0.5 billion for expansion/rationalization projects.	Up to 70% of total project cost including plant and initial inventories. Inventories financed may not exceed 30% of total project costs (under new law, limit on inventories financed is raised to 40%).	Maximum, 15 years, including a maximum of 2 years during which disbursements are made and an additional 3 year period during which interest but no principal is paid.	Mortgage, chattel mortgage and personal guarantees. For loans for new plant not exceeding Lit. 50 million, supplemental government guarantees may be obtained, covering up to 50% of losses.
	Special financing for machinery and equipment.	5.5 – 5.6% per annum.	Up to 75% of expenditures not exceeding Lit. 10 million (Lit. 15 m. in case of IRFIS).	Maximum 5 years.	Chattel mortgage.
	Special financing of inventories for new plant only (raw materials, semi-finished and finished products).	IRFIS – 4% per annum; CIS – 3.5% per annum (for loans of Lit. 25-75 million).	Up to 100% of inventories. Maximum of Lit. 75 million.	Maximum 5 years, of which up to one-third as grace period.	Inventories.

Large-Scale Enterprises. Production units in which investment exceeds Lit. 6 billion.	Financing of new plant and expansion/rationalization of existing plant.	5%.	Up to 50 – 60% of fixed assets.	Normally not exceeding 15 years, but based on life of fixed assets.	Mortgage, chattel mortgage and other guarantees.
Enterprises Exporting Agricultural Products.	Financing of exports.	5.6% per annum.	Up to Lit. 100 million for unincorporated single owner enterprises; may be increased to Lit. 200 million for incorporated enterprises or partnerships.	Maximum 15 years, including two years of grace.	Mortgage, chattel mortgage and other guarantees.

Source: International Bank for Reconstruction and Development, Projects Department, *The Development of Southern Italy. The Cassa per il Mezzogiorno and the Three Special Credit Institutes, Isveimer, Irfis and Cis. Italy*, T.O.–467a/Restricted, June 10, 1965, p. 26, <https://documents.worldbank.org/en/publication/documents-reports/documentdetail/904741468044126033/italy-southern-italy-industrial-financing-project>.

Figure 4.5 *Organization chart of the three special credit institutes: ISVEIMER, IRFIS and CIS*

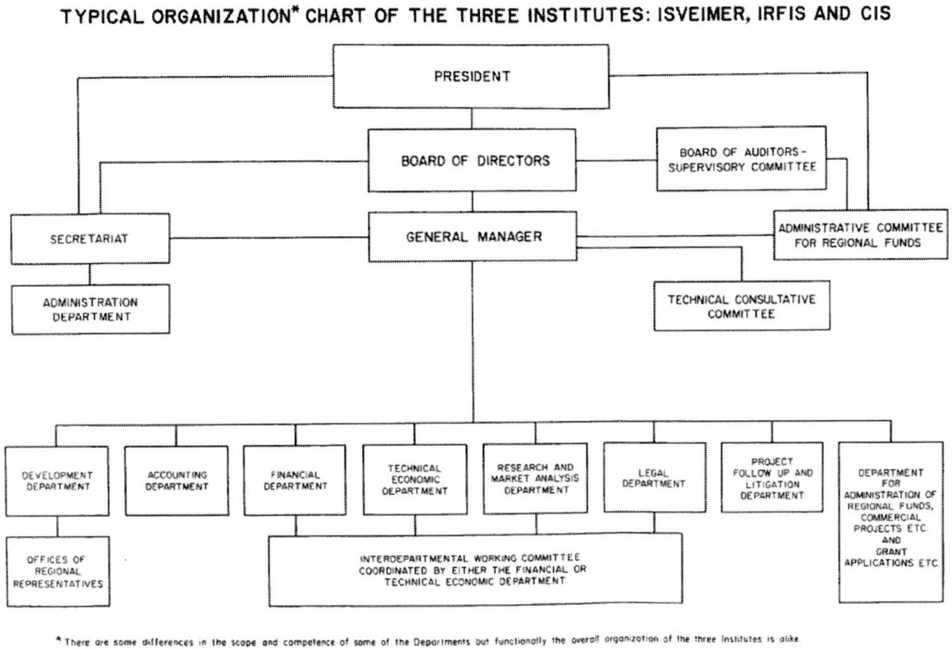

Source: International Bank for Reconstruction and Development, Projects Department, *The Development of Southern Italy. The Cassa per il Mezzogiorno and the Three Special Credit Institutes, Isveimer, Irfis and Cis. Italy*, T.O.–467a/Restricted, June 10, 1965, Annex 15, <https://documents.worldbank.org/en/publication/documents-reports/documentdetail/904741468044126033/italy-southern-italy-industrial-financing-project>.

This organization chart shows that the three institutes were mostly organized in the same way and offered almost the same services, carrying out some other basic functions, such as promoting industrialization by means of the contact with potential investors and special market researches. These institutes did also evaluate the technical and economic feasibility of the projects to be financed, verifying estimates and costs and providing technical assistance, as well as judging the financial and commercial conditions of entrepreneurs, of the assets they offered as collateral, and of the financial soundness of the projects. The three special credit institutes also controlled and evaluated the legal aspects of the project, as well as the paperwork connected with negotiating the loan, supervising the use of the grant and the general administration of the loan itself, and the managing of its organization and relevant accounting. The institutes carried out their task of industrial promotion in a variety of ways, through several offices – be they a development office (or service), a research and statistical office, and representative offices – which set up contacts with potential investors and promoted the services the three institutes provided, as well as the incentives for investment in the Mezzogiorno, also offering support for the loan procedures and to verify project costs: this specific activity was shared with the Istituto per l'Assistenza allo Sviluppo del Mezzogiorno (IASM)[412]. Concerning technical and financial evaluations, each institution had its own department, but the activities were carried out in a climate of full cooperation[413]. The three special credit institutes gave assistance also on

---

[412] On this, the following was underlined:

> Like the development and representative offices, the *research offices* have a function which is partly external, or promotional, and partly internal. Their market studies are used by the Institutes which they serve to help attract potential investors as well as to provide a basis for project evaluation. In addition, they provide the Institute managements with economic data which may be used as a basis for the formulation of lending policies. The statistical data which the Institutes (and particularly ISVEIMER) compile on industry and individual borrowers are impressive; they are clearly presented and kept up to date and could be of great value to management and staff in making investment decisions and appraising projects. The mission gained the impression, however, that the data are not yet being used fully

(International Bank for Reconstruction and Development, Projects Department, *The Development of Southern Italy. The Cassa per il Mezzogiorno and the Three Special Credit Institutes, Isveimer, Irfis and Cis. Italy*, cit., Annex 15, p. 3).

[413] On this, the following was noted:

> The financial department is generally the controlling department and uses the data supplied in a technical report to make up an overall technical and financial report for the General Manager to submit to the Board of Directors

legal aspects, by means of their specific departments and offices which set up letters of commitment and loan contracts. Finally, the responsibility for loan management and project supervision was subdivided between financial, technical, and bookkeeping services. Besides this, the three institutions were also called upon to render services to their shareholders[414].

During the final paragraphs of the chapter dedicated to the special credit institutions, the IBRD focused on their financial resources, economic availability and financial situations. The document noted that, even if these three institutions could tap the same sources of capital, each of them had a different fund attraction capacity. These funds were divided into five main categories: endowment funds (which provided up to 40%, that is to say 4.8 billion lire, by the Cassa per il Mezzogiorno); the funds provided by the Italian ministry of Treasury (including capital grants and long-term loans); the funds provided by the Cassa (including those credit lines from abroad and interests on loans by the IMI with income provided by the aid provided to Italy within the framework of the European Recovery Program); there were also the funds coming from the bonds on internal markets, as well as interests and reimbursements of those loans carried out by the institutes themselves[415]. The document, after having examined those aspects connected

---

(International Bank for Reconstruction and Development, Projects Department, *The Development of Southern Italy. The Cassa per il Mezzogiorno and the Three Special Credit Institutes, Isveimer, Irfis and Cis. Italy*, cit., Annex 15, p. 3).

[414] Indeed:

> All three Institutes work for the Cassa in processing applications for capital grants. In addition, IRFIS and CIS administer loans out of the regional funds of Sicily and Sardinia, in part to provide working capital loans for projects financed by these two Institutes

(International Bank for Reconstruction and Development, Projects Department, *The Development of Southern Italy. The Cassa per il Mezzogiorno and the Three Special Credit Institutes, Isveimer, Irfis and Cis. Italy*, cit., Annex 15, p. 3).

[415] The following was noted on the matter:

> The Institutes' two principal sources of loan capital have been their bonds, which have made up 47% of the total, and the funds supplied to them by the Cassa, mainly from its foreign borrowings, which have constituted 42%. [...] Treasury funds are distributed among the Institutes in proportions which do not correspond with their present relative importance as lenders or their capital needs. ISVEIMER receives 61%, IRFIS 29%, and CIS 10%, while their respective shares in loans made to the end of 1963 were 58%, 23% and 19%. [...] [The Cassa] has remitted to the Institutes the interest payments on loans made by the government from the lire proceeds of funds made available to Italy under the European Recovery Plan. [...] To October 31, 1964, the amounts contributed totaled Lit. 23.3 billion; they were distributed in the customary proportions of 61% for ISVEIMER, 29% for

with capital structure, portfolios' evaluation and cash flow forecasts for those three institutions in detail, gave some information on the relationship with the European Investment Bank as well:

> The Cassa's foreign borrowings, apart from the proposed Bank loan, could include loans from the European Investment Bank [...]. The Institutes have been receiving loans from the EIB through the Cassa at an annual rate of about US$ 38 million equivalent in the past three years, but there is good reason to believe that the flow will slacken. Up till now, Italy has been the principal recipient of EIB loans. To the end of November 1964, it had received US$ 245 million (about 65% of all EIB loans made to that date) of which about US$ 213 million (87%) was used for projects in the Mezzogiorno, including about US$ 128 million (over half the total amount loaned to Italy) reloaned by the Cassa to the Institutes. [...] At present the EIB is extending the scope of its operations beyond the Common Market countries to the Associated States, such as Greece. In addition, it has indicated that it intends to direct a larger share of its lending to Italy to large State-owned enterprises and to agriculture. It did not seem realistic, therefore, to assume that the Institutes would obtain more than US$ 15 – $ 20 million equivalent a year from the EIB in the next few years, and the projections assume EIB lending at an annual rate of US$ 17.5 million, to be drawn down over a two year period[416].

However, such a wide-ranging explanation of the role of the three special credit institutions ended with a worrying note for the near future, as some emerging limitation on their available credit could have slowed loans down: according to the IBRD, should such a perspective become a reality, it would have reverberated in a negative way on Southern Italy, blocking some of the ongoing projects and seriously delaying industrial development in the Mezzogiorno[417].

IRFIS and 10% for CIS. […] When funds have been raised through bond issues, the Cassa has distributed the proceeds either according to the 61-29-10 pattern or its own estimate of the capital requirements of the Institutes (International Bank for Reconstruction and Development, Projects Department, *The Development of Southern Italy. The Cassa per il Mezzogiorno and the Three Special Credit Institutes, Isveimer, Irfis and Cis. Italy*, cit., p. 30 and Annex 16, p. 1, p. 2 and p. 3).

[416] *Ivi*, p. 35.

[417] See *Ivi*, p. 36.

4.2.3 The credit lines, their management and the industrial policies in Southern Italy

The final part of the IBRD document concerned loan management and regulations[418]. With regard to the first point, it was underlined that the loan by the International Bank for Reconstruction and Development was to be granted to the Cassa per il Mezzogiorno, with the Italian Republic as its guarantor. The Cassa would have transferred the receiving amounts in turn to the special credit institutes, in the following proportions: ISVEIMER was to receive 55 million dollars, IRFIS 25 million and CIS 20 million[419]. The IBRD was not to carry out evaluations on the projects to be financed, as had instead been the case with the first loans to the Cassa. The IBRD would rather indicate some management criteria and let the Cassa carry responsibility to select and manage the single projects. The report also pointed out the main goals of the International Bank for Reconstruction and Development, stating that:

> The Bank would not follow up individual projects. Its supervision of the loan would be limited to determining that its funds were on the whole being used efficiently and effectively. To that end, it would follow the Institutes' general performance closely, paying particular attention to their defaults and losses, changes in their lending policies and the impact of their lending activities on the industrial economy of the Mezzogiorno. The Bank would expect to examine the reasons for project successes and failures and compare the results for projects financed out of the proceeds of the loan with those for other projects financed by the Institutes[420].

Considering a few important indications[421], a list of 185 projects had been approved, for a total amount of 132 million dollars[422]: the industrial

---

[418] See *Ivi*, pp. 37-40.
[419] See *Ivi*, p. 37.
[420] *Ivi*, p. 38.
[421] As it was detailed:

> The Bank has, however, agreed with the Cassa that certain criteria will be applied in the selection of projects to be financed under the proposed loan. There will be upper and lower limits for project size; the projects will be confined almost entirely to the field of manufacturing; and finally, selection will be limited to projects of high economic priority which seem likely to be carried out quickly and efficiently

(International Bank for Reconstruction and Development, Projects Department, *The Development of Southern Italy. The Cassa per il Mezzogiorno and the Three Special Credit Institutes, Isveimer, Irfis and Cis. Italy*, cit., p. 37).
[422] See *Ibidem*. In the very same page the following was stated:

sectors most present overall were chemistry, metalworking and general mechanics, as they made up about 45% of the total loan[423]. The borrowing terms foresaw a 15-years duration, including an extension of four years and a reimbursement plan from the three aforementioned institutes to the Cassa, itself corresponding with the amortization of the credit lines requested to the Bank[424]. Furthermore, it was noted that, like the previous IBRD loans,

---

> All projects on the list will be eligible for financing under the loan up to the limit set for each Institute. Since the list includes projects with loan requirements of about US$ 70 million equivalent which had already been approved by the Boards of the Institutes by the end of May 1965 and most of the remaining projects are expected to be approved (to the extent that financing is available) by the end of July, the list would seem to provide enough projects for rapid utilization of the proceeds of the loan.

[423] See International Bank for Reconstruction and Development, Projects Department, *The Development of Southern Italy. The Cassa per il Mezzogiorno and the Three Special Credit Institutes, Isveimer, Irfis and Cis. Italy*, cit., p. 38. In this very same page, it was underlined that:

> Total sales of all projects listed are estimated at about US$ 450 million; the total number of jobs to be provided by them is estimated at about 18,000. The projects are about equally divided between new plants and expansions. The loans to be made for fixed assets and inventories amount on the average to about 55% of total project costs, including initial inventories; the percentages for ISVEIMER, IRFIS and CIS are respectively 59%, 51% and 55%.

[424] This document also provided other information on the matter:

> The Institutes would be free to reinvest repayments by sub-borrowers. As provided by law, the Treasury would bear the exchange risk. The Cassa would relend the lire equivalent of the Bank loan to the Institutes at an interest rate not exceeding 3.55%. The Treasury would reimburse the Cassa for the difference between the rate and the rate it would pay on the Bank loan and for other charges. The Institutes would relend the loan proceeds at 4%. That would give them a spread of at least 0.45%, which is the spread they have received on the relending of foreign loans in recent years. Since the Institutes receive a spread of over 1.00% on loans made from domestic bond issues and the Treasury allocation and, in addition, recover a part of the cost of appraisal from their borrowers, the Bank is satisfied that their overall earnings will give them sufficient margin to administer the loan proceeds properly. The Treasury representative also indicated during negotiations that interest spreads on loans from all major sources of the Institutes would be adjusted so as to provide the Institutes with adequate operating funds

(International Bank for Reconstruction and Development, Projects Department, *The Development of Southern Italy. The Cassa per il Mezzogiorno and the Three Special Credit Institutes, Isveimer, Irfis and Cis. Italy*, cit., p. 38).

their amounts would have been given to the Cassa. The decision to provide the loans was based on the Cassa's statements regarding feasibility of the projects and on information provided by the special credit institutes. Concerning the second point, it was underlined that the loan documents had to contain specific clauses so that the proceeds by the Bank had to be used in an effective and efficient way in favor of industrial enterprises. Additionally, it was stipulated that the financing agreements between the Cassa per il Mezzogiorno and the special credit institutions would have to be agreed on by the IBRD. Furthermore, the general provisions contained in the loan agreements between the three special credit institutions and the beneficiaries of their loans had to satisfy the IBRD as well.

Among the conclusions of the paper[425], it was noted that the demand for industrial credit in Southern Italy was growing steadily and the investments carried out during the previous years in infrastructure and basic industries were a crucial support in developing small and medium-size enterprises. Such enterprises were specialized in transforming semi-finished products coming from the basic industries themselves, in order to make available a wide variety of goods, which were critical for a fast-growing economy. Therefore, the premises for setting up productive self-sufficiency in Southern Italy seemed promising. The loan requested to the International Bank for Reconstruction and Development would have supported the intent of the Italian government of advancing the industrialization program, fulfilling a need unable to be financed by other sources, be they national or foreign. Furthermore, based on the deep analysis contained in the report, an overall evaluation was carried out, according to which:

> The project and the arrangements to channel funds through the Institutes to industry in Southern Italy are sound and would be a suitable basis for a Bank loan of US$ 100 million equivalent to the Cassa per il Mezzogiorno for a term of 15 years including a grace period of four years[426].

Upon the end of the examination of the complex IBRD document, Table 4.8 is worth reporting, itself contained within the first pages of the report and describing the most important measures promoting the process of industrialization in Southern Italy and detailing their main features.

---

[425] See *Ivi*, p. 41.

[426] *Ibidem*.

Table 4.8 *Summary of major measures to encourage industrialization in Southern Italy*
(Benefits available to industrial firms – excluding cottage-type firms)

Interest subsidies	*See Table 4.7*
Capital grants	
Cassa grants (available throughout Southern Italy)	A) For new plant or expansion/rationalization of existing plant. Limited to projects in which investment per production unit does not exceed Lit. 6 billion (for expansions, investment represents sum of depreciated value of existing fixed assets plus new investment). *Present law* 1) Up to 25% of expenditures on industrial buildings and road, railway and utility connections; 2) Up to 10% of expenditures for domestic machinery and equipment (imported machinery is exempt from customs duties, see below), but 3) Up to 20% of expenditures for machinery and equipment produced in Southern Italy. *Proposed new law* Up to 20% of all expenditures, except that the grant may be increased to 30% of expenditures on machinery and equipment produced in Southern Italy. B) For new plant or expansion/rationalization of existing plant, in which investment exceeds Lit. 6 billion per production unit, if project is located in industrial development areas or nuclei (see C) in amounts determined by the Committee of Ministers for the South and related to the first Lit. 6 billion of investment. C) For expenditures by Consortia in industrial development concentrations on investments in industrial infrastructure.

	Present law 1) Up to 85% of expenditures for establishment of industrial estates and compensation for land expropriated for use in infrastructure in these industrial development concentrations. Grant may be made in lump sum or as subsidy to support credit operations of Consortia; 2) Up to 50% of cost of constructing buildings to be leased to industrial enterprises. (Cassa may also make loans for this purpose and to cover the cost of compensation for land expropriated for sites for industrial buildings). *Proposed new law* The Minister for the South, in consultation with the Minister of Industry and Trade may, if the Consortia involved demonstrate that they cannot carry out the projects, authorize the Cassa: 1) To assume full financial responsibility for projects under 1) and 2) above; 2) To delegate responsibility for executing such projects to another public entity or cooperative and assume, directly or indirectly, responsibility for their maintenance and management.
Regional grants (supplementary to Cassa grants) for Sardinia only	For new plant or expansion/rationalization of existing plant; no size limitation but mainly for projects in designated areas. 1) Up to 66% of expenditures for: (a) factory site; (b) road, rail and utility connections; (c) electric power and water consumed (by new enterprises) for a maximum period of 10 years; (d) transportation of raw materials and finished products (for new enterprises only) for a maximum period of 3 years; (e) cost of social security and insurance during initial operating period, if warranted; 2) Up to 40% of total project cost. If project is eligible for other grants, they may be supplemented by regional grants under this provision, provided that the total amount of all grants does not exceed 40% of total project costs.
Equity participations	Various percentages of equity participation are taken by several financial institutes. ISAP, SOFIS and FINSARDA may take only minority participations and INSUD only a majority participation.

Tax exemptions and/or reductions	*Present law* 1) Building materials and machinery for new plant or expansion/rationalization of existing plant are exempt from customs duties and “conguaglia” tax (*ad valorem* tax on imports); 2) Turnover tax (IGE) reduced by 50% on building materials, whether purchased in Italy or imported; 3) Ten-year exemption from income tax (IRM) of income from manufacturing activities of new industrial plant or additional income attributable to expansion/rationalization of plant; 4) Exemption from income tax of up to 50% of income earned in any part of Italy if reinvested in Southern Italy in new plant, expansion/rationalization of existing plant or transformation or improvement of agricultural land. Deduction is limited to 50% of cost of investment, i.e. total investment must be twice the amount of income exempted from tax; 5) Municipalities are empowered to exempt industrial enterprises from municipal tax in whole or in part; 6) Registration and mortgage taxes are reduced in certain cases; 7) Excise duty on electric power used by industrial enterprises is reduced by 50%. *Proposed new law* 1) Exemption from customs duties and “conguaglia” tax eliminated; 3) Ten-year exemption from income tax extended to income from related commercial activities carried on by industrial production units whose manufacturing income is exempt from income tax for ten years; 5) Authority of Municipalities to exempt industrial enterprises from municipal tax eliminated; 8) Ten year exemption of industrial firms from company tax. For firms already in operation, the period of exemption will begin with the enactment of the new law.

Freight rate reductions

Present law

1) The Italian State Railways may reduce by up to 50% the freight rates on items needed for the construction of new industrial plants and the expansion/rationalization of existing plants and up to 20% on goods produced by them;
2) Freight rates on raw materials and equipment shipped by water to industrial enterprises in Sardinia are reduced by 20%.

Proposed new law

1) The Minister of Transport in consultation with the Ministers of the South and the Treasury is authorized within 90 days after the enactment of the law to establish rules for the determination of freight rates on items needed for the construction of industrial plants and goods produced by them.

Expropriation of land

Present law

1) Land required for projects eligible for assistance may be expropriated subject to normal subsequent legal action and determination of compensation;
2) Municipalities are authorized to sell or lease on special terms land and buildings to be used for industrial purposes.

Proposed new law

1) The right of Municipalities to sell or lease on special terms land and buildings to be used for industrial purposes is eliminated.

Award of contracts by Public Administrations

Present law

Public administrations are required to place with South Italian enterprises 20% of their orders for equipment and works each year.

Proposed new law

1) The percentage of orders to be placed in the South is increased from 20% to 30%;
2) The public administrations subject to this provision are to be listed in a decree issued by the Premier in consultation with the Ministers for the South and Industry. They will include, in addition to regular government agencies autonomous government agencies and public entities.

Investments by State-owned enterprises

State-owned enterprises are required to place in the South each year 60% of their investments in new plant and 40% of their total investments.

Bearer shares	In Sicily and Sardinia, bearer shares may be issued by newly established enterprises.
Foreign investments	Foreign capital may be invested in all except a few fields, e.g., hydrocarbons, aviation, credit, insurance. Firms with foreign capital are eligible for all benefits listed above.

Source: International Bank for Reconstruction and Development, Projects Department, *The Development of Southern Italy. The Cassa per il Mezzogiorno and the Three Special Credit Institutes, Isveimer, Irfis and Cis. Italy*, T.O.–467a/Restricted, June 10, 1965, p. 5, <https://documents.worldbank.org/en/publication/documents-reports/documentdetail/904741468044126033/italy-southern-italy-industrial-financing-project>.

Finally, the following picture (Figure 4.6) shows the regions in which the Cassa per il Mezzogiorno operated, fully detailing the wide range of the direct interventions carried out by the Cassa, which were supposed to trigger a virtuous circle involving the whole of Italy and serve as a base for industrial and productive advancement of the Northern regions, setting up and supporting the Italian "economic miracle". Therefore, the extraordinary intervention appeared as an effective tool to relate the interests of economic activities in Northern Italy with the new productive structure in the Mezzogiorno: the process of modernization in southern Italy was thus carried out in a framework of common interest with the rest of Italy.

Figure 4.6 *Italian regions. Areas in which the Cassa per il Mezzogiorno performed its functions (1965)*

Source: International Bank for Reconstruction and Development, Projects Department, *The Development of Southern Italy. The Cassa per il Mezzogiorno and the Three Special Credit Institutes, Isveimer, Irfis and Cis. Italy*, T.O.–467a/Restricted, June 10, 1965, MAP 1, <https://documents.worldbank.org/en/publication/documents-reports/documentdetail/904741468044126033/italy-southern-italy-industrial-financing-project>.

4.3 The last loan by the World Bank to the Cassa per il Mezzogiorno

In 1963, George David Woods took over from Eugene Robert Black as President of the World Bank, and would keep his post until 1968[427]. The final document studied here was dated June 11, 1965 and titled Report *and Recommendations of the President to the Executive Directors on a Proposed Loan to the Cassa per il Mezzogiorno for Industrial Financing in Southern Italy*[428], a title that made clear the industrial priorities of the program. The document's public disclosure was authorized on June 24, 2010. This document, featuring the signature of the new President, analyzed the opportunity for a $ 100 million loan to be granted to the Cassa per il Mezzogiorno, with the objective to finance industrial projects on behalf of Southern Italy regions, as reported in the relevant abstract:

---

[427] In an archive document of the World Bank, the new President was described like that:

> Woods came to the Bank full of vigor and with strong views about the changing role of the Bank. His Bank would not be the same as the Bank of his predecessor Eugene Black; he would transform the Bank by putting his own ideas to work. In the process he became one of the Bank's most innovative presidents, reinforcing the Bank's role as a development institution and preparing it for the global development role it was to play. Woods recognized the evolving state of development, and moved the Bank to meet the new challenges. The horizons of Bank lending expanded, economic analysis took a central role, IFC [International Finance Corporation] was strengthened, and aid coordination (through the rapid expansion of consultative groups) allowed more effective use of donor resources. Woods oversaw the evolution of the Bank from a primarily conservative financial institution to a development institution by redirecting its focus and resources to the analysis of development and the support of more relevant economic activities

(The World Bank, Archives, *George David Woods*, <https://www.worldbank.org/en/about/archives/history/past-presidents/george-david-woods>).

[428] See International Bank for Reconstruction and Development, *Report and Recommendations of the President to the Executive Directors on a Proposed Loan to the Cassa per il Mezzogiorno for Industrial Financing in Southern Italy*, P–437/Restricted, June 11, 1965, <https://documents.worldbank.org/en/publication/documents-reports/documentdetail/416131468262474622/italy-southern-italy-industrial-financing-project>.

> The proposed loan in an amount in various currencies equivalent to $ 100 million to the Cassa per Opere Straordinarie di Pubblico Interesse nell'Italia Meridionale (Cassa per il Mezzogiorno) would assist in the financing of industrial projects in Southern Italy[429].

Its introduction bore important witness to the role and the evaluations carried out by Guido Carli – who discussed the loan firsthand with the President of the International Bank for Reconstruction and Development, during his visit in March 1964 – besides the positive feedback by this international institution following the good results of the missions sent by George David Woods, to Italy. On this issue, the latter wrote the following:

> Dr. Guido Carli, the Governor of the Banca d'Italia, visited the Bank to discuss the possibility of the Bank's resuming lending to Italy, to which the Bank had last made a loan in 1959. In reviewing Italy's economic problems Dr. Carli pointed out that while the measures already taken by the Government were expected to meet the immediate difficulties, an inflow of foreign long-term capital in excess of what could be raised through the private financial markets would be needed for some time to come to make possible investments on a scale required to maintain a satisfactory rate of economic growth. I told Dr. Carli that I could make no commitment at that stage. However, I agreed to send a mission to Italy to study the economy, establish the country's need for external capital, and examine where Bank assistance could be most useful. [...] Missions headed by Mr. Leonard Rist were in Italy from May to July and from November to December of last year. They concluded that, at least in the near future, Italy would require more long-term capital from external sources than could be raised in the private markets and that Bank lending would be most useful if channeled to industry in Southern Italy through the Cassa per il Mezzogiorno. The negotiations for the proposed loan were held in Washington in March 1965. However, the passage of new legislation for extending the life of the Cassa after the expiration of the present law on June 30, 1965 and for amending its constitution required more time than was expected and conclusion of the proposed loan had therefore to be postponed[430].

Furthermore, the IBRD President, recalled, in his *memorandum* titled *Market Eligible Loans* issued on January 25, 1965, that Italy had been included in the "market eligible" category of countries, considering the fact that the flow of long-term private capital, in the form of portfolio and direct investments, amounted between $ 250 and $ 400 million yearly during the most recent phases[431]. With the requested loan, the total amount of financing

---

429 *Ibidem*.

430 *Ivi*, p. 1.

431 See *Ibidem*.

the Bank gave to Italy was to reach 398 million dollars: therefore, the status of the seven loans allocated to the Cassa per il Mezzogiorno had been upgraded as follows (Table 4.9).

Table 4.9 *Loans granted by IBRD to Italy (May 31, 1965)*

Loan year	Loan number	Purpose	Amount (in millions of dollars, net of cancellations)
1951	50 IT	Equipment for development	10.0
1953	88 IT	Equipment for development	10.0
1955	117 IT	Power, agriculture and industry	68.4
1956	150 IT	Power, agriculture and industry	74.6
1958	189 IT	Power, agriculture and industry	75.0
1959	224 IT	Power and industry	20.0
1959	235 IT	Nuclear power	40.0
	Total loans		298.0
	… of which has been repaid		62.5
	Total now outstanding		235.5
	Amount sold	164.0	
	… of which has been repaid	60.1	103.9
	Net amount held by Bank		131.6

Source: International Bank for Reconstruction and Development, *Report and Recommendations of the President to the Executive Directors on a Proposed Loan to the Cassa per il Mezzogiorno for Industrial Financing in Southern Italy*, P–437/Restricted, June 11, 1965, p. 2, <https://documents.worldbank.org/en/publication/documents-reports/documentdetail/416131468262474622/italy-southern-italy-industrial-financing-project>.

Furthermore, the main features of the required loan were described as follows: its beneficiary was the Cassa per il Mezzogiorno; its guarantor was the Italian Republic; its amount was of $ 100 million, in several currencies, to favor credits lines on behalf of industrial development in Southern Italy; amortization was to last for 23 biannual installments, beginning on July 1st,

1969 and ending on July 1st, 1980 (with a very similar capital reimbursement and interests payment); the interest rate amounted to 6.1/4% per annum and its commission to 0.375% yearly; finally, the Cassa would have granted the loan income to the three special credit institutes, who would give them to industrial beneficiaries in turn[432].

The report by the President went on describing the features of industrial development in Southern Italy, following the analysis contained in the wider document titled *The Development of Southern Italy. The Cassa per il Mezzogiorno and the Three Special Credit Institutes, Isveimer, Irfis and Cis*. Actually, it was observed that the growth in incentives to interventions in the industrial sector, beginning in 1957, brought an increase in such investments in Southern Italy: unemployment went down from 6% in 1959 to 3% in 1963 and for the very first time, real *per capita* GDP grew more rapidly than in the North, reaching a rate of almost 8% in later years[433]. Furthermore, the attention was focused on the Cassa per il Mezzogiorno and its relationships with the special credit institutes[434]. This part of the document ended stressing the fact that the financing sources and the credit lines of the institutes were of two kinds: obligations on internal markets and the income from the foreign loans granted to the Cassa up to that moment; during the final phase the latter also included funds granted by the European

---

432 See *Ivi*, p. 3.

433 See *Ivi*, pp. 3-4.

434 On this issue, the following was noted:

> The principal instrument of the Government for developing Southern Italy is the Cassa per il Mezzogiorno which was established in 1950 and whose life is just being extended to the end of 1980. [...] Initially, it concentrated mainly on agriculture, transport, water supply and sewage disposal but, in recent years, it has given increasing support to industry. The primary channels for medium and long-term lending to industry under the Cassa program are three special credit institutes which operate on a regional basis: ISVEIMER on the Italian mainland, IRFIS in Sicily, and CIS in Sardinia. The Cassa holds 40% of the share capital of each Institute, and the remainder is held by regional banks and the Autonomous Regions of Sicily and Sardinia. The Institutes are, together with other institutions lending in the South, the channel through which the Cassa provides important incentives to industrial investors, including interest subsidies. [...] The Institutes were used as channels for industrial lending under four of the Bank loans, and reloaned a total of $ 90.8 million to 21 enterprises

(International Bank for Reconstruction and Development, *Report and Recommendations of the President to the Executive Directors on a Proposed Loan to the Cassa per il Mezzogiorno for Industrial Financing in Southern Italy*, cit., p. 4).

Investment Bank[435]. According to Mr. Woods, these sources would not have been able to ensure adequate credit lines, given the huge number of valid projects presented to the special credit institutes: therefore, the proposed loan would have bridged the gap, making industrial investment possible, and in the significant amount necessary for the economic development of Southern Italy[436].

Furthermore, the specific loan rules were detailed, as it recorded in the previous text (see note number 50). In the part detailing the juridical tools, the following was noted, amongst other things:

> The arrangements between the Cassa and the Institutes will contain obligations on the part of the Institutes to cause these projects to be constructed and operated efficiently and in accordance with sound technical, financial and business standards [...][437].

Finally, the report focused on the situation and on the perspectives Italy sported, following a wider and more detailed document, dated December 23, 1964[438]. Such a document recounted the most important structural changes enacted in Italy from the postwar era to 1963, particularly referring to the quick economic growth experienced during the 1950s and the beginning of the 1960s, the gradual reduction of unemployment and its effects on wages, on income distribution, consumption and savings[439]. A negative consequence of the development process was a gradual worsening of the Italian balance of payments between 1962 and 1964, deepened by growing inflationary pressures and by diminishing confidence in the Italian currency in the last two years, joined with a massive capital flight[440]. To address this situation, the Italian government had adopted rigorous monetary and fiscal provisions that achieved good results, allowing, through

---

435 See *Ibidem*.
436 See *Ibidem*.
437 *Ivi*, p. 5.
438 See International Bank for Reconstruction and Development, Department of Operations Europe, *The Situation and Prospects of the Italian Economy. Report of a Mission to Italy (May-July and November 1964)*, EA–150a/Restricted, December 23, 1964,
<https://documents.worldbank.org/en/publication/documents-reports/documentdetail/814131468285874758/italy-situation-and-prospects-of-the-economy>.
439 See International Bank for Reconstruction and Development, *Report and Recommendations of the President to the Executive Directors on a Proposed Loan to the Cassa per il Mezzogiorno for Industrial Financing in Southern Italy*, cit., p. 6.
440 See *Ibidem*.

a slowdown of internal demand, to get back to previous levels already by the first half of 1964, besides raising exports by 15% and reducing imports by 3%, all the while limiting capital flight and achieving a positive balance of payments by $ 780 million in 1964, compared with a loss of 1,250 million dollars during the previous year[441]. The positive trend continued during 1965, achieving a growth in currency reserves amounting to 3,860 million dollars, compared with the 2,942 million dollars of the previous year[442]. However, as it was noted with an observation of more general validity:

> [...] the price for checking inflation and stabilizing the balance of payments was the interruption of economic growth. For the first time in many years, industrial production stagnated in 1964 and despite good harvests GNP increased by only 2.7%, compared to an average of about 7% in the previous five years. As a result of weakening demand and declining profits, investments in real terms were almost 10% lower in 1964 than in 1963. Employment declined in several industries and underemployment and underutilized capacities became widespread[443].

In the second half of 1964, restricting monetary and fiscal policies were gradually canceled and, in the beginning of 1965, the Italian government approved provisions aiming to give impulse to the economy. On this issue, it appeared particularly important the introduction of guarantees on bonds issued by the special credit institutions in order to finance public works by local entities and the central administration, the implementation of fiscal exemptions for construction industries, as well as the reduction of retirement contributions to be granted by private employers[444]. This analysis ended with an indication that, within older economic sectors, significant investments where necessary and a consistent part thereof was to be focused on the Mezzogiorno in order to ensure its effective long-term growth[445].

Concluding the document, George David Woods, recommended to the executive directors of the IBRD to develop the following resolution, being favorable to the granting of the loan:

> [...] the Bank shall grant a loan to the Cassa per il Mezzogiorno, to be guaranteed by the Republic of Italy, in an amount in various currencies equivalent to one hundred million United States dollars (U.S.$ 100,000,000), to mature on and prior to July 1, 1980, to bear interest at the rate of six and one-quarter per cent (6-1/4%) per annum, and to be upon

441 See *Ibidem*.
442 See *Ibidem*.
443 *Ibidem*.
444 See *Ivi*, pp. 6-7.
445 See *Ivi*, p. 7.

> such other terms and conditions as shall be substantially in accordance with the terms and conditions set forth in the form of Loan Agreement (Southern Italy Industrial Projects – 1965) between the Bank and Cassa per il Mezzogiorno and the form of Guarantee Agreement (Southern Italy Industrial Projects – 1965) between the Republic of Italy and the Bank [...][446].

Therefore, not only did the Bank approve the required loan after a detailed evaluation but, by means of such a final act, a crucial phase of international development strategies ended. By means of the credit lines triggered by the International Bank for Reconstruction and Development, these strategies had allowed to stimulate Italian economy. This marked the beginning of the use of significant financial resources towards objectives of productive growth and the effective start the "economic miracle" in Italy and to experiment, trough the Cassa per il Mezzogiorno, a unique economic and policy model. Such an innovative model proved to be particularly effective during the whole of the "golden age" for the industrialization of Southern Italy and the substantial reduction of the gap between Northern and Southern Italy.

4.4 The commitment of the World Bank to Southern Italy and its model of economic development

The process of economic development after the destruction brought about by the Second World War, the restoration of international economic relations following the Bretton Woods agreements, and the intense phase of reconstruction emerged as some of the most important stimuli for formulating economic theories, as well as providing an effective action field for both public institution and private operators. Internationally speaking, the focus would turn mostly to poorer countries; this was also due to the phenomena of decolonization and political emancipation bringing to bear the experience of an extended, economically underdeveloped area of the world on the scene, under the moniker of "Third World". Indeed, as it was noted shortly after the second half of the 1950s: «In recent years most of the poorer countries of the world have set up development programs in the belief that governmental intervention in the process of resource allocation will speed up the rate of economic growth. This belief is based on the demonstrable imperfections in the competitive system under the conditions typical of the less industrialized countries. The procedures followed in establishing these programs tend to substitute intuitive judgments and rules

---

[446] *Ibidem.*

of thumb for the investment decisions of the market economy, however, and may or may not lead to any improvement over the latter»[447].

The extraordinary intervention in Italy followed this type of "development policies", even if it focused on a backward area within a developed country, rather than an overall undeveloped one. However, the choice to develop the Mezzogiorno was not born only out of a combination of internal factors and a mere national necessity, albeit historically motivated. As a matter of fact, the new meridionalist strategy was based on an often overlooked connection between the goal of economic convergence of the two more important areas in Italy and another, different one: the experimentation of an innovative growth model, which would be able to represent a precedent for the strategies to be applied in underdeveloped regions, as well as being a sure reference to verify and evolve development theories in all their implications. On this, it has as a matter of fact been observed that: «two distinct stories are the base of the activity of the Cassa [...] beginning and developing on their own between Rome and Washington, remaining somewhat parallel even when the Cassa takes shape and begins its activity»[448]. Anyway, these stories found very important moments of conflict and integration, especially during the years featuring a greater action towards Southern Italy, when the "golden age" of the development was in full swing. In particular, between the 1950s and the first half of the 1960s, the relationship between the IBRD and the Cassa was very strong, defining a very meaningful model of interaction, focused on overcoming the Italian dualism and on the economic advancement of the whole country.

The birth and the evolution of the Cassa per il Mezzogiorno were based on the idea of spreading, by means of specific programs, those investments useful to achieve infrastructure and facilities supporting productive initiatives in Southern Italy, using two essential credits lines. On one side, there were national grants, having different weights according to the different laws for Southern Italy and on the other there were the loans granted by international institutions and, in particular, by the World Bank, which played a cornerstone role in defining a framework of interventions and fundamental economic relationships for a long-term growth project. Furthermore, some people included the latter actions between the fundamental factors in building a special structure to promote development in the Mezzogiorno. Gisèle Podbielski stated that: «on the other hand, the idea of a special organism operating in Southern Italy was inspired by the

---

[447] H.B. Chenery, K.S. Kretschmer, *Resource Allocation for Economic Development*, in "Econometrica", vol. 24, no. 4, 1956, p. 365.

[448] L. Paganetto, P.L. Scandizzo, *La Banca mondiale e l'Italia: dalla ricostruzione allo sviluppo*, Bologna, il Mulino, 2000, p. 95.

negotiations opened with the World Bank, which was available to finance further import needs arising from public investment programs. Since the loans by the World Bank were usually given directly to those operators investing and not the governments, the creation of a specific entity was due»[449].

Pasquale Saraceno, in turn, within a note contained in the introduction to his work titled *Ricostruzione e pianificazione*, set out the hypothesis according to which, among the original reasons for the extraordinary intervention, the need for foreign credit lines was primary: «concerning the difference between the prevailing expectations before the end of the war and the steering thoughts of the following policies it is worth reminding that this edition of the Cassa was not the result of an evolution of such thoughts, but rather of searching an apt instrument towards obtaining international loans: afterwards, the pressure of unresolved issues brought the Cassa on lesser inadequate positions for addressing the nature of such problems»[450]. Nonetheless, the combination of national and international interventions, as seen elsewhere, started a project of overall modernization able to ensure the progress of the Mezzogiorno while at the same time warranting the complementarity of Southern Italian interests with those of the rest of the country. All this was intertwined with the relevant decisions undertaken by the American economic leadership on the subject, which would not only bestow advantages to those areas interested by international interventions, but also grant undisputed benefits, both politically and economically, by means of financial tools and of a farsighted and wise development strategy.

Within such a context, it may be useful to examine the commitment and indications by the International Bank for Reconstruction and Development, itself a protagonist of the action of the Cassa per il Mezzogiorno, which adopted from the start a wide vision which leads to the understanding the deep roots and perspectives of the extraordinary intervention[451]. On this,

---

[449] G. Podbielski, *Venticinque anni di intervento straordinario nel Mezzogiorno*, cit., p. 38.

[450] P. Saraceno, *Ricostruzione e pianificazione (1943-1948)*, Bari, Laterza, 1969, p. 61.

[451] Leandra D'Antone specified the reasons for the establishment of the Cassa per il Mezzogiorno, as they were seen from a particular international angle having the United States of America and the World Bank as its base: «as it was the case with the Iri and the reform in 1936, the "meridionalist setup" of 1950 was conceived in exceptional circumstances, but survived long after them, having a hand in transforming "extraordinary" rules into structural elements of the Italian model of capitalistic development during the postwar period. The exceptional circumstances concerned politics first and foremost, especially the policies of the American government and of the World Bank towards reconstructing Europe and developing

Gabriele Pescatore referred to the model of the Tennessee Valley Authority, to treasure an overseas experience, reminding the American evaluations of the activities of the Cassa: «in my knowledge, no other federal projects of that kind were implemented, but I would like to underline that the activation of these interventions was entrusted to a State agency, namely the one based in Tennessee, with the overall aim to restrain and valorize the eponymous river, in order to improve the situation of several depressed agricultural areas, putting them back into an effective sphere of productivity. They were, after all, simple goals and interventions, all revolving around a single big project. I visited the concerned areas and the area involved, of course, into something great. However, [...] the Americans themselves, who followed closely the experience of the Cassa, were pleasantly surprised and filled with admiration for what we were doing in the Mezzogiorno, both for the variety and the sheer number of our goals, given also the several different areas of our work, from geology to demographics. The Americans were aware of the fact that we were working in the Mezzogiorno according to a clear setup and strategic planning as a base for the whole of the goal-oriented interventions within the overall Plan and its Programs. The Americans did also encounter our surprising competence in managing an activity featuring "work complexes" and their functional integration of all the chosen actions, with precious few chinks in the armor, into a strategic framework. Mr. Lilienthal and Mr. Clapp, President and Managing Director of the TVA respectively, during their visit to the Cassa's operational sectors were impressed, above all else, by the efforts made to integrate several different proposals, ranging from pure infrastructure to agricultural production, also featuring the possibility (then just an afterthought) to influence industrial development, within a unitary framework. Such features were all the more worthy since their Tennessee experience was based on a single big project, and not on a multitude of them integrated by sector and area»[452].

---

depressed areas all around the word. Into such a framework go also the particular interest shown by the American policymakers towards the Italian *Southern question* and the significant prestige Italy acquired on the international political stage by means of the action of the leaders of technical structures such as Mr. Menichella and Mr. Giordani, as well as the technocratic impulse Prime Minister De Gasperi gave his governance and his effective cooperation with Mr. Einaudi and Mr. Menichella, as well as the interest shown by the vast majority of the Italian entrepreneurial world for meridionalist public action» (L. D'Antone, *«Straordinarietà» e Stato ordinario*, cit., p. 595).

[452] G. Pescatore, *La «Cassa per il Mezzogiorno». Un'esperienza italiana per lo sviluppo*, Bologna, il Mulino, 2008, pp. 441-442.

The role of the IBRD had emerged even before the establishment of the Cassa and the actual start of the credit policies in the Mezzogiorno. Furthermore, right from the start, the presence of the Bank had taken on a double role, touching both the institutional relationships with the Italian authorities to manage credit lines and the more general ones, regarding the whole of the "system", themselves the base of a true intervention model, as promoted by the United States. As it was underlined: «The link with the World Bank must [...] be seen in light of two kinds of relationships: on one side, there was a historical and political link concerning the institutional integration between the Bank as the entity managing the international loans and the Italian government. On the other hand, another kind of relationship, concerning the system more than anything else and focused on the budding influence the Bank exerted on the institutions in the beneficiary countries, especially in the case of Italy, which, was very receptive of IBRD suggestions when building its institutions»[453].

The years between 1947 and 1949 represented a significant prologue to the following phase by means of the first contact between the International Bank for Reconstruction and Development and the Italian authorities (government and Bank of Italy); the first loan request by the latter amounted to $ 250 million but was refused also because it was totally unrealistic when compared with the effective availability of funds at the World Bank[454]. The missions by the IBRD began in this very period, in order to verify the true conditions Italy was in, so to effectively tackle problems and give educated and useful answers to the issues of financial support set up to solve them. However, even in those early years, an idea, typical of "impact loans" began to emerge[455], putting its emphasis not on the evaluation of single projects, but rather on an articulate development program in the Mezzogiorno. On this, it must be observed that the aforementioned program was suitable, more or less knowingly, to mediate between a free-market system, which was

---

[453] L. Paganetto, P.L. Scandizzo, *La Banca mondiale e l'Italia: dalla ricostruzione allo sviluppo*, cit., p. 102.

[454] See *Ibidem*.

[455] As Guido Carli recalled: «Once the Cassa per il Mezzogiorno was established, the IBRD agreed to the issues and indications Mr. Menichella put on the table and granted a series of loans, called "impact loans", precisely because they featured a residual effect on the Italian balance of payments and had not to be commensurated to any product. Experience showed that on one point Mr. Menichella was perfectly right: binding the aid to particular categories of goods would have warped such a process, favoring pressure by both exporters and importers on policymakers to steer credit flows on any given good; in other words, corruption» (G. Carli, *Cinquant'anni di vita italiana*, Rome-Bari, Laterza, 1996, p. 129).

mainly followed by the Italian economic policy, and a particular form of "supply-side Keynesianism"[456] such as the one set out by Pasquale Saraceno, aiming to promote the whole of a production system, rather than to simply raise demand in Southern Italy[457]. These traits, contradictory in themselves, arose from differences in inspirations concerning the internal economic strategy and its international references, which however succeeded in finding common ground both in implementing different tools supporting the catching up process in Southern Italy and in the convergence of potentially distant setups within the effective overall development experience of the country.

The role of the Bank, especially during the 1950s was vital in setting up the limits of such a "compromise" or, better still, to define and enhance the Italian model of economic growth[458]. Actually, an accurate examination of those IBRD documents dedicated to the issues of Southern Italy shows a peculiar, and somewhat new, combination of international and national elements. A sound supranational setup was also present, making Italy a special milieu to acknowledge confidence in, and begin the experimentation of, the new strategy of the extraordinary intervention. Furthermore, we have seen the costs and benefits of the loans granted by the International Bank for Reconstruction and Development to the Cassa per il Mezzogiorno, which highlighted, on one side, the birth of a technocratic structure, able to interact with the management of the Bank in implementing a program both

---

[456] See A. Lepore, *Cassa per il Mezzogiorno e politiche per lo sviluppo*, in VV.AA., *Istituzioni ed Economia*, edited by A. Leonardi, Bari, Cacucci, 2011, pp. 114-115.

[457] Mr. Saraceno expressed his viewpoint beyond all questions: «The Mezzogiorno [...] was a unique area whose problems might also be tackled with the typical tools of Keynesian analysis, as they allowed to see that supporting demand would not have brought a reprise in investments, but rather inflaction. Therefore, a direct commitment had to be set in forming capitals and therefore on supply, not on demand. To the results of an action supporting offer another supporting demand would have been ancillarily joined [...]. Anyway, it was reasoning around Keynes that the postwar new meridionalism was able to overcome the passionate viewpoints of the classical one and propose, albeit among a widespread unawareness, effective policies and tools for interventions» (P. Saraceno, *Politica Keynesiana e Mezzogiorno*, cit., pp. 540-541).

[458] Such a setup, in the case of Southern Italy, was focused towards the effort to «find a precise institutional model, an intervention method coherent with its model and inspired after successful interventions carried out in other countries»; by the same token, «industrialization was the final goal and at the same time an essential component, "underlying the chosen models and methods"» (L. Paganetto, P.L. Scandizzo, *La Banca mondiale e l'Italia: dalla ricostruzione allo sviluppo*, cit., p. 109).

balanced and effective in stimulating industrialization in Southern Italy; on the other hand, the persistence of several antinomies in the economic policies of Italy which made the balance between State interventions and market promotion an unsteady one. To all this, a lack of adequate support by the Bank during the shift from infrastructure-related policies to industrial initiatives is to be added[459].

Anyway, the opinion expressed by Barbara Curli may be agreed upon, when she underlined very clearly that: «The lack of attention historiography gave to the international dimensions of the extraordinary intervention on behalf of Southern Italy during the first half of the 1950s led to overlooking a vision of Italy as a "development laboratory", itself emerged in the postwar decade within those institutions tasked with fleshing out the new Western economic multilateralism. The interest shown for the Italian Mezzogiorno was one of the most meaningful moments during that season of "international dirigisme" instead. Such an interest was surely due to an idea of development planning typical of those optimistic years, featuring growth experiments and modernization as a series of "recipes" to be exported – from the United States to the European countries and from the industrialized to the developing and de-colonializing ones. However, the reflection on the Italian case included also other, less evident, aspects. First and foremost, development as a tool, being fundamentally strategic within the framework of international multilateralism and cooperation, fully regained the national dimension it apparently lost during the initial phase of the reconstruction emergency»[460].

The goal of economic and social growth in the Mezzogiorno, itself a cornerstone of SVIMEZ elaborations, connected to an international perspective by means of the IBRD, making the Casa a prototype development agency integrated within a complementary Italian nationwide vision, which saw Southern Italy as the true fulcrum of the Italian economic boom. Within such an encounter between relationships and opportunities, the concrete experimentation of "new meridionalism" choices was the effective mode of implementation of a complex, long-term strategy. Such a strategy was processed after the belief that the time had come, also by virtue of the national and international current situation, to heal the most grievous wound of post-unitary Italy and fully overcome the two totally different economic systems coexisting in the very same country. On the other hand, such beliefs were seen under a particular light from abroad, as distilled in the two main Bank goals: «on one side, to carry out its institutional tasks, whose detection

---

[459] See *Ivi*, pp. 105-107.

[460] B. Curli, *Energia nucleare per il Mezzogiorno. L'Italia e la Banca mondiale (1955-1959)*, cit., p. 317.

was somewhat perceived, however, as a problem; and on the other hand to become a credible entity operating on international capital markets»; and even if «the Bank leadership and the majority of its staff had mostly been recruited with the second goal in mind, more than the first», it came to pass that «the dynamics begun by Bretton Woods slowly brought the institutional goals to prevail on the international banking worries»[461].

Starting from such results, the International Bank for Reconstruction and Development committed itself to implement «a program for the extraordinary allocation of resources for a *series* of projects not directly built and evaluated by Bank staff, having the goal of tackling poverty in Southern Italy»[462]. Actually, the Mezzogiorno was seen by Washington as an important acting ground to preview new intervention instruments, during the shift from a strategy privileging the reconstruction of developed countries to a wider one, revolving around supporting the growth of yet undeveloped countries. Besides, during the 1950s, IBRD activity in Italy, a country it «treated like a sort of favorite»[463], anticipated the strategy to be used for developing areas in the following periods, trying to set up, implement and test a program, some projects and partners, as well as various financial procedures. All of this constituted a model to be used also within those contexts featuring remarkable differences compared to that of Southern Italy. However, the high degree of shared goals between Rome and Washington avoided Italy the so-called "conditionality clauses" among financial obligations; those clauses involved a conformity check between the sums granted and the objectives of the loan and usually enshrined within the agreements between the IBRD and those countries interested in development policies[464]. As a matter of fact, within the examined documents, after a rigorous control of the Italian conditions and of the foreseen usage of the loans on behalf of the Mezzogiorno, beyond punctual elucidations and criticism, emerged that the evaluation by the IBRD concerning the process of intervention, as well as the skills and the operability of the Cassa and the results achieved by the programmed measures and investments was largely favorable.

Truth be told, Leland Barrows, who, amongst other things, had the role of executive assistant for the Economic Cooperation Administration (ECA) in Europe from 1948 to 1953, underlined some differences between the Marshall Plan and further initiatives, as well as in the interventions carried

---

[461] L. Paganetto, P.L. Scandizzo, *La Banca mondiale e l'Italia: dalla ricostruzione allo sviluppo*, cit., p. 113.
[462] *Ivi*, p. 115.
[463] *Ivi*, p. 145.
[464] See *Ivi*, pp. 139-144.

out by the United States in undeveloped countries and the one carried out in Italy, a developed country "happening" to have a backwards region, reminding that: «Southern Italy has many economic and social problems like those in Greece and the rest of the Mediterranean littoral. In the Italian program we were dealing with Marshall plan procedures and resources and organization, and there were certain fundamental differences. There were no such things as projects and project agreements in the Marshall plan. The term "project", if I remember correctly, was reserved for any investment requiring the use of a million dollars worth of dollar-financed imports, or more. In other words, it had to be a major thing. Then we would look at those import requirements as a whole and try to evaluate the project. Otherwise, the resources that came in through the Marshall plan were entirely commodities or services, but mainly commodities, which moved through the normal channels of trade, paid customs duties, import taxes and the rest, and were distributed by sale. This gave rise, therefore, to a counter-part fund. The use of the counterpart fund might be negotiated to serve some social purpose like building housing. But it was only in that secondary stage that the Americans got into the question of what went on within the country in detail. Now, in Italy, as a matter of fact, the government was always responsive to the use of the counterpart funds for social purposes. Some of the money – counterpart money, a good bit of it – went into the Cassa per il Mezzogiorno, which was a special fund for the south, where the Italians themselves were doing the kind of development thing with technical assistance and everything else that Point Four would undertake to do. But our role was never as detailed as it is in the underdeveloped countries. We were dealing with a developed country that happened to have a backward region»[465].

---

[465] Harry S. Truman Library and Museum, *Oral History Interview with Leland Barrows*, by T.A. Wilson, Washington (DC), January 8, 1971, <https://www.trumanlibrary.gov/library/oral-histories/barrowsl>. The term "Point Four", indicated a technical assistance program for developing countries, presented by Harry S. Truman, the President of the United States of America, during his inaugural speech on January 20, 1949: such elimination was born of the fact that it was the fourth goal of the American foreign policy indicated during the aforementioned inaugural speech. On this issue, the following has been reminded: «Between October 1949 and January 1950 the Svimez men were busy collecting and elaborating data for a study upon the arrival of Rosenstein Rodan, himself a representative of the IBRD during the negotiations, with the task to bring news concerning the applicability of the "Fourth Truman Point" to Italy. The aforementioned study [...] detailed the "multiplicative" and "additional" effects on national wealth deriving from focusing expenditure policies for industrial investments in the Mezzogiorno. Keynesian theory was therefore adapted and reviewed in light

The documents issued by the IBRD show, anyway, the importance of the extraordinary intervention and its strict connection with the strategy of the Bank itself, providing an important wealth of data and of evaluations on the results achieved during the whole first period of the initiative, up to the end of the loans granted to Italy. From a general point of view, looking at the entire activity of the Cassa per il Mezzogiorno and not only at the part related to overseas financing, one may agree with the summary judgment, according to which «surely the Italian regional policy has not been unsuccessful; rather the income gap between Northern and Southern Italy has been, albeit slowly and unevenly, reduced»[466]. Such an outcome would have been impossible outside a "systemic" vision concerning the strategies

of the theory of "depressed areas". [...] It was the first opportunity to apply a theory to development policies all over the world» (S. Misiani, *I numeri e la politica. Statistica, programmazione e Mezzogiorno nell'impegno di Alessandro Molinari*, Bologna, il Mulino, 2007, p. 198). Finally, the interview to Mr. Barrows went on with another interesting evaluation about the influence of the USA on the Italian economy policy choices: «Because of the potential inflationary effect of counterpart expenditures, their use in Marshall plan countries was carefully controlled and required prior Washington approval. And in Italy, which, I believe, had been badly burned by inflation in 1948, there was a relatively conservative economist as President, and another conservative as Prime Minister, at least a part of the time I was there. They were not going to be pushed into what they considered to be a reckless monetary policy. So in supporting the use of counterpart funds for projects, we were pushing for a more adventuresome financial policy than the Italian government was willing to follow».

[466] P. Battilani, F. Fauri, *Mezzo secolo di economia italiana, 1945-2008*, Bologna, il Mulino, 2008, p. 287. The two authors described in one of the previous pages (p. 283), in a summarized form the relationships between the Cassa and the World Bank: «The international loans were the more important part of the credit lines set up by the Cassa per il Mezzogiorno: the World Bank (then still known as IBRD, i.e. International Bank for Reconstruction and Development) granted its first international loan in 1950, amounting to $ 10 million and other 338 were to be granted between 1953 and 1959. The Bank had proved its availability since 1949, provided that the Cassa were to be built after the model of the Tennessee Valley Authority, an entity that managed the agriculture and industrial development of the Tennessee Valley during the 1930s. Furthermore, the body to be established had to be trustworthy and to feature a strictly technical management. During the 1950s, the Cassa struck agreed seven loans with the Bank, amounting to a total of $ 348 million. The most consistent part thereof was given to financing power (92 million dollars), industrial (83 million) and irrigation (39 million) projects. The intervention by the Bank aimed to improve update or establish 42 industrial or energy plants. In 1959, the newly established European Investment Bank substituted the World Bank as an international lender. It's allegedly contributed to finance the Cassa, providing it to year after year with almost half of its total financial endowment, until its liquidation».

and the tools to be adopted in order to start a process of economic convergence, try and bridge the gap between the two halves of Italy and committing everyone involved to gradually solve the issue of Italian dualism. In fact, dualism had been the most grievous problem of Italy since the national unification. The capacity to combine the different and articulated reform tools that had been approved, together with the widening and the changing of some of the contents of the policies for Southern Italy within a sizeable system of long-term choices tied to development theories (which to some extent it anticipated and made true), was a cornerstone element for the evolution of the extraordinary intervention during the whole of the "golden age". In such a situation, the new paradigm of a country potentially able to walk towards a perspective of modernization and growth, while trying to overcome the social and economic imbalances of its previous history, was sketched.

In conclusion, a reference may be made to a both deep and original evaluation of the role carried out by the International Bank for Reconstruction and Development in the development of Southern Italy meridionalism, such as the one contained in the volume by Paganetto and Scandizzo, when it is claimed that «For many aspects [...] the program to develop the Mezzogiorno remains a cornerstone in the history of the World Bank. It allows economists to affirm their model of intervention, itself based on the fungibility of provided funds, without radically denying the need to link credit lines to high-priority, visible projects. It gives the possibility to finance an investment program within a vast region, by means of Keynesian indirect mechanisms, while launching the role of the Bank as a financer of development in a more refined and articulate way when compared with single projects. Finally, it supports from its early stages one of the guiding ideas, which were to dominate the action and internal contrasts of the Bank during further years. Such idea was tackling poverty, that is to say to embody, along with the Bank in Wall Street, an international agency striving to resolve the more dramatic issues concerning underdevelopment»[467]. During its first 15 years of life, the Cassa per il Mezzogiorno fully represented such a need, being the exemplary model within a single country. The interaction between the Cassa and the World Bank, also beyond the quantitative aspects of the loans, completed, with a refined financial mechanism, the framework of the extraordinary intervention, making it an advanced tool to implement an effective development policy. The relationship also pointed out the high-quality of the standards of intervention which could be implemented in the

---

[467] L. Paganetto, P.L. Scandizzo, *La Banca mondiale e l'Italia: dalla ricostruzione allo sviluppo*, cit., pp. 120-121.

Italian Mezzogiorno. Therefore, the outcomes of the Italian, but also international, strategy for Southern Italy from the beginning of the 1950s until the first half of the 1960s, when the opportunities offered by the loans of the International Bank for Reconstruction and Development ended, were extremely worthwhile for the whole of Italy, accompanying it along the way of the "economic miracle" and providing for the first, and maybe only time, an effective hope for the redemption and development of the whole Mezzogiorno.

Conclusions

The examination and interpretation of the World Bank documents in this volume is aimed at not isolating the relationship between the Cassa per il Mezzogiorno and the IBRD, but rather at putting it in the context of the Italian economic dualism and the policy mix activated by the Italian government for sustaining a balanced development of the whole Italian economy. The results of this research have been comforting and have opened new horizons for the interpretation of Italian economic events. It has also made clear the perspective within which the future of the Southern Italy macro-area is inscribed, something more complex than the classical North-South divide. Furthermore, the experience of the extraordinary intervention did not only concern almost half a century of Italian policy making, but it was also a good tool to interpret how policymakers implemented the ideas connected to the "new meridionalism", which appeared, especially in Pasquale Saraceno's approach, like a peculiar form of "supply-side Keynesianism". Moreover, this study has allowed to uncover the inner mechanisms of an original development model, itself based on the triangulation of interests between the United States, Italy and the Mezzogiorno. As a matter of fact, on the one hand we could see how the internal mechanism of the Cassa and of public intervention evolved through the implementation of a very articulated series of measures, starting with infrastructure projects and then continuing with the promotion of industrialization in Southern Italy. On the other hand, we could also appreciate the evolving relationship between the Cassa and the International Bank for Reconstruction and Development. We saw how the IBRD contributed to the goal of economic and social progress in Southern Italy not only by means of the loans, but also by designing and setting up a complex financing system accompanied by a long series of policy tools. These policy instruments were able to finance the most important productive initiatives, achieving this result – thanks to the wise engineering of every step, from the Bank to the borrowers and the firms – without squandering any resources. Thus, the Bank was able to maximize the opportunities for investments and their financial returns.

By means of these procedures, the project to modernize and develop the most backward part of Italy finally became a reality for a long but definite period of time. Such a goal had already been pursued before by attempting to industrialize some areas in Southern Italy. Early attempts were started by Giovanni Giolitti and Francesco Saverio Nitti, who opened a new path, anticipating those evaluations and initiatives which would mature within the "first IRI" and would finally be deployed, following the advent of the new meridionalism, during the reform season of the 1950s. However, the setup Nitti gave originally to the development projects had not been enough to stop the nascent regional gap which, in the absence of an organic strategy carried out by the Italian State for intervention in the Mezzogiorno, reached its historical peak just after the Second World War. Awareness of the critical point reached in the disparity in economic conditions between Northern and Southern Italy paved the way for an important public initiative. The risk that the gap could advance also during a new era of economic growth, in addition to the political pressure coming from both the national and international contexts, pushed in favor of the agrarian reform law and the provisions to establish the Cassa per il Mezzogiorno. Furthermore, well beyond the strict content of legislative norms, a fundamental feature to comprehend the success of the actions started in that phase was represented by the practical implementation of the reform program and the effective deployment of the extraordinary intervention. Therefore, during the 1950s, a pragmatic view for the growth of the Mezzogiorno and the Italian economy prevailed. According to this view, it was possible to recognize a reciprocity of interests between the two parts of the country and to successfully operate a mediation between the opposing strategies of Keynesian and conservative actors. This common ground was outlined by the connected approaches and initiatives undertaken by the World Bank and the Cassa per il Mezzogiorno. Within a context shaped by the birth of a new system of international regulations and by the intensifying relationships between the two sides of the Atlantic, the moment for reforms crossed national boundaries and gained a systemic dimension. This new dimension was able to give birth to an original prototype of economic growth policies and to begin overcoming the main historical contradiction in the development of Italy. The coincidence of this outstanding initiative with the Italian "golden age", rather than showing the dependency of a phenomenon from the other, revealed the importance and the good timing in choosing to implement the extraordinary intervention, pointing out the pro-cyclical features of the investments and of the grants by the Cassa. To summarize, the action carried out for the Mezzogiorno, albeit making the best of a positive economic cycle, succeeded in achieving significant macroeconomic results, by means of a high-impact model, built on a tight cooperation, 15 years long, between the Italian state and the financing authorities in Washington.

Therefore, the role of the World Bank was by no means marginal. It was a vital part the Italian strategy to develop its Southern regions instead. This shared vital presence by national and international institutions has been amply made clear in a piece that is worth to report here in its entirety: «The search for a national way to development, which may become a model for other countries becomes a dominating factor in the Italian national life. In such a search is placed the relationship of Italy with the international institutions and the World Bank, itself born from the Bretton Woods agreements, which reflected the will of the winning powers of the Second World War to take charge of a worldwide economic order by means of institutions open to market economies. The relation struck between the World Bank and the nascent national economic institutions appears as one based on an immediate and suitable correspondence of intent and initiatives. The aforementioned international institution does as a matter of fact operate, during its beginning years, in a slow growth scenario: its main goals do thus pertain to identifying autonomous models of development in single borrowing countries, where the contribution of the Bank could be used with maximum effectiveness. The Italian institutions, on their hand, and this is particularly true for the nascent Cassa per il Mezzogiorno and its constantly growing panoply of linked entities and committees, had a complex goal of economic and juridical affirmation, to be reached also by means of a special relationship with international partners. The World Bank, an entity which had already chosen professionalism and technology as the main tools to convey its development message and which focused on great infrastructure within the first phase of its action, seemed the ideal partner in this context. During the 1950s, the Italian institutions and the Bank struck a very satisfying relationship, based on reciprocal legitimation and, at the same time, on an almost specular development. The two bureaucracies, at the Bank and at the Cassa, despite their substantial differences, looked to each other as privileged interlocutors. As it would be the case with other countries, the World Bank considered the Cassa almost as its own creature. On the other hand, the Cassa was grateful for such an international acknowledgment, as it allowed to carry out an autonomous financial role (the Cassa negotiates and contracts debts with the Bank directly) as well as an executive one (the Cassa commits itself to complete works, in exchange for loans), allowing it to claim the role of a sort of "authority" for the Mezzogiorno»[468]. This description shows the way followed by the extraordinary intervention, after the good union between national and international interests, which came to a close only when the

[468] L. Paganetto, P.L. Scandizzo, *La Banca mondiale e l'Italia: dalla ricostruzione allo sviluppo*, cit., pp. 36-37.

International Bank for Reconstruction and Development, having ended the first phase of the financial strategies and of the policies for reconstruction and growth, shifted the focus of its action towards a single goal, i.e., the economic progress of underdeveloped countries. Such a shift was symbolized also by a change in the Bank's presidency, with the advent of George David Woods. The change, signaled by the end of the loans to Italy after fifteen years of cooperation, definitely turned the Bank into a "development institution".

This work also intended to accurately check the steps that brought about such a complex framework of cooperation. In order to achieve such a result, the most significant moments of the relationship between the Cassa per il Mezzogiorno and the World Bank have been examined, both by following the sources chronologically, and by identifying a common theme through the several events recorded in the documents. This is as a matter of fact the main value connected with studying the internal-use documents issued by the IBRD - as the basis for an innovative analysis of the Italian intervention in the Southern regions and the development of this international institution's strategies – also allowing to reconsider the cornerstone contributions made by personalities such as Paul Rosenstein-Rodan. The research has also added a detailed description of the starting phase of financing for Italy, an evaluation of the economic situation of the country, as well as the identification of the procedures by means of which the extraordinary intervention was started to such considerations. The topic of the evolution of the loans by the Bank has then been investigated, with a specific focus on the progress of the activities of the Cassa, to the initial infrastructural phase and its following shift towards industry, and to the condition of economic development in Southern Italy. Further attention has been dedicated to the second phase of international financing lines and their triggering a greater and greater inclination towards productive investments by the Cassa. The book has provided a specific examination of the first seven years of the extraordinary intervention, as well as the joint effort carried out by the IBRD and by the European Investment Bank for the growth of the Mezzogiorno. Finally, an analysis of the last phase of the loans granted by the World Bank has been carried out. This section of the book has focused on some relevant issues, such as the building of the Garigliano power plant, and the crucial question of the industrialization process in Southern Italy, with ample references to the role of the three special credit institutions. On this topic, the volume has identified a uniquely Italian economic development model, which originated from both the commitments by the International Bank for Reconstruction and Development and the Cassa per il Mezzogiorno.

The effort in researching such a complex topic has required identifying the interactions between various institutional actors on different levels, unified by the common goal of economic and social development of the territories of Southern Italy. The research has allowed not only to reconstruct an essential period of the Italian economic history in its connections with the global scenario, but also to pose some open-ended questions, and to design some paths for the present and future of this part of Italy. The end of the Cassa per il Mezzogiorno did not bring about a serene and balanced judgment on its experience. On the contrary, general criticism prevailed, unable to make a distinction between the propelling phase, which had achieved considerable results of the extraordinary intervention during almost a quarter-century, and a later regressive phase, during which this initiative suffered an involution and became an instrument for short-term assistencialist policies, a totally ineffective shadow of itself. Such a transformation was due to some structural reasons, which led to the closing of the Cassa and of each and every special initiative. On the one hand, the petering out of the "golden age" and the crisis of the Keynesian model brought about deep changes in the context where the most significant and durable convergence process between Northern and Southern Italy happened. On the other hand, the shift of the Italian institutional axis and the birth of the Regions added political pressure on the Cassa, leading to a decline of its "technocratic" role, and bringing about fragmented interests and particularistic visions. If to such reasons one does then add the disappearance from the Southern Italy scenario of that stimulating, balancing, and controlling factor represented by the IBRD, which – since the beginning of the extraordinary intervention up to half of the 1960s – had made a significant contribution in constructing a markedly original and innovative economic development model, then the reasons for an irredeemable decline may be more easily understood.

However, as is amply shown by the World Bank documents, the positive results of the extraordinary intervention should not be overshadowed by the crisis of the meridionalist reforms and the halting of the catching up process between the Mezzogiorno and Northern Italy. In particular, the early experience of the Cassa fully represents a unique period of the Italian unitary history when the North-South gap drastically decreased. Yet, during the most recent years, to the end of "special" development policies a new and disrupting element was added. This is the idea of an autonomous and self-reliant growth for the different areas of Italy, something that supersedes the need to solve the problem of backwardness in Southern Italy. Several cultural and political groups have sustained this argument, claiming the existence of a "Northern question". However, the local development policies which have been implemented after the end of the extraordinary intervention have not proved the soundness of this new approach. They failed to spur the local administrations towards taking responsibility for development and did not trigger a virtuous economic cycle, as they were supposed to do. On the contrary, these interventions in the Mezzogiorno triggered new harsh criticism on the vast squandering of public money, which was scattered among a thousand unproductive and patronage-oriented rivulets, instead of being focused on specific development projects. Therefore, the historical North-South divide came back with all its strength, widening, especially during the last decade, the inequalities and growth differentials between the two areas.

Such research clearly sets the relationship between the Cassa per il Mezzogiorno and the World Bank within an era that, after the destruction of WWII and the difficult reconstruction phase, would see Italy make use of a fundamentally changed global context and a new international competition scenario to leap forward in economic development. Hence, the research does not only provide results for historical interpretation, but it can also bring about new awareness of the current problems in the area. The positive reevaluation of the Cassa per il Mezzogiorno, at least during the considerable timeframe during which the Cassa kept its driving function and pushed onwards the productive modernization in the Southern regions, could have great importance. The aim is not to cultivate the idea of a return to the origins, back to a now unfeasible meridionalist view, but rather to recover the general value of a national policy. The main character of this policy was its ability of facing a critical situation, which could not to be left at the mercy of market forces, outside any kind of State-led interventions. However, faced with the need to reorganize economic strategies and to offer the country a new perspective, its most relevant character was the systemic approach. This consisted in identifying a general framework that, while it remained able to individuate specific strategies, was also able to realize a full complementarity between different advantages, interests and values, integrating each and every single intervention within a unitary development design. In this way, sixty years ago, the Cassa per il Mezzogiorno and the International Bank for Reconstruction and Development, the Italian government and the American authorities, created a mechanism unequaled in its coherence and effectiveness.

Within the current situation of deep crisis, which might pull Italy away from the frontier of global growth trends, the need for a new systemic vision is felt again. Reiterating the paralyzing contrasts between *bottom up* or *top-down* approaches to growth, in order to reopen the dilemma between centralized initiatives and autonomous territory responsibilities, has no justification, given the inharmonic and destructive forms they took in more recent years. The future of the Mezzogiorno can be built, given the new and harsh conditions of the era we live in, on a renewed attempt towards finally completing the process of economic and social unification of our country. To this end, one needs to keep an open approach towards the new challenges of today, given all the risks, but also the opportunities, connected with the process of globalization, and we should also consider the "Southern question" a fundamental component within European integration. Yet, one does not currently see on the horizon a new phase of development policy cooperation and coordination, rather the approach towards an evolution much more complex and articulated of the international scenarios than in the past. It is therefore necessary to build up awareness for the universal dimension of such issues and of the need to face them with new global regulatory tools and a strong drive towards not only financial recovering but also economic growth. On this topic, reprising national and European policies of development appears as a priority, given also the fact that the resources available are very limited and should be focused on selected targets, in order to enhance productive accumulation and innovation. At the same time, Southern Italy, by achieving a different awareness of its tasks and responsibility, may play a fundamental role in the process of consolidating (rather than denying) a European vision. Southern Italy may very well pose itself as a crossroads of relations and exchanges between the Mediterranean Sea, the Eastern countries and the rest of the continent. This also includes investing again to stimulate own cultural, scientific and economic excellence. The research of a project for the future of the Mezzogiorno may then proceed with renewed hope to find the way of a new "golden age", albeit not effortlessly, and not in a short time. This effort would mean for Southern Italy the opportunity to escape from the perspective of ultimate decline and, on the contrary, to try making the most out of its historical legacy as a protagonist of national and international institutions, which allowed overcoming a long period of difficulties, all the while decidedly heading towards the modernization process of Italy. Such a need is heartfelt even today.

Bibliography, Archives and Online Sources

Archive sources

ACS, *Archivi dello Sviluppo Economico Territoriale*, <https://aset.acs.beniculturali.it/aset-web/>.

ASBI, *Raccolte diverse, Relazioni e Bilanci*, pratt., no. 699.

Harry S. Truman Library and Museum, *Oral History Interview with Leland Barrows*, by T. A. Wilson, Washington (DC), January 8, 1971.

International Bank for Reconstruction and Development, Loan Department, *An Appraisal of the Development Program for South Italy*, L133/ Restricted, Archives/Records Center, Room HB1–001, Box 254–22, Nus Location 065–3–1, July 31, 1951.

International Bank for Reconstruction and Development, Department of Technical Operations, *Appraisal of Italian Industrial, Irrigation and Power Projects*, T.O.–84a/Restricted, May 24, 1955.

International Bank for Reconstruction and Development, Department of Technical Operations, *Appraisal of Italian Industrial, Irrigation and Power Projects*, T.O.–121a/Restricted, Archives/Records Center, Room HB1–001, Box 263–23, Nus Location 066–2–5, October 3, 1956.

International Bank for Reconstruction and Development, Department of Technical Operations, *Appraisal of Italian Industrial, Power and Irrigation Projects*, T.O.–162a/Restricted, February 19, 1958.

International Bank for Reconstruction and Development, Department of Technical Operations, *Appraisal of Italian Industrial and Power Projects*, T.O.–202a/Restricted, March 26, 1959.

International Bank for Reconstruction and Development, Department of Technical Operations, *Appraisal of the Senn Nuclear Power Plant – Italy*, T.O.–200/Restricted, September 4, 1959.

International Bank for Reconstruction and Development, Technical Operations Department, Public Utilities Division, *Italy. Cassa per il Mezzogiorno. Summary and Appraisal of Activities until June 1953*, T.O.–38a/Restricted, September 28, 1953.

International Bank for Reconstruction and Development, Department of Operations Europe, Africa and Australasia, *Cassa per il Mezzogiorno and the Economic Development of Southern Italy*, E.A.–51a/Restricted, May 20, 1955.

International Bank for Reconstruction and Development, Department of Operations Europe, Africa and Australasia, *Cassa per il Mezzogiorno and the Economic Development of Southern Italy*, E.A.–80a/Restricted, February 18, 1958.

International Bank for Reconstruction and Development, Projects Department, *The Development of Southern Italy. The Cassa per il Mezzogiorno and the Three Special Credit Institutes, Isveimer, Irfis and Cis. Italy*, T.O.–467a/Restricted, June 10, 1965.

International Bank for Reconstruction and Development, *Report and Recommendations of the President to the Executive Directors on the Proposed Loan for the Development of Southern Italy*, P–22/Restricted, Archives/Records Center, Room HB1–001, Box 935–01, Nus Location 099–1–2, October 5, 1951.

International Bank for Reconstruction and Development, *Report and Recommendations of the President to the Executive Directors on the Cassa per il Mezzogiorno Loan Application guaranteed by the Republic of Italy*, P–57/Restricted, Archives/Records Center, Room HB1–001, Box 935–01, Nus Location 099–1–2, September 28, 1953.

International Bank for Reconstruction and Development, *Report and Recommendations of the President to the Executive Directors on the Loan Application of the Cassa per Opere Straordinarie di Pubblico Interesse nell'Italia Meridionale (Cassa per il Mezzogiorno) guaranteed by the Republic of Italy*, P–85/Restricted, Archives/Records Center, Room HB1–001, Box 935–01, Nus Location 099–1–2, May 24, 1955.

International Bank for Reconstruction and Development, *Report and Recommendations of the President to the Executive Directors on the Loan Application of the Cassa per Opere Straordinarie di Pubblico Interesse nell'Italia Meridionale (Cassa per il Mezzogiorno) guaranteed by the Republic of Italy*, P–117/Restricted, Archives/Records Center, Room HB1–001, Box 935–01, Nus Location 099–1–2, October 3, 1956.

International Bank for Reconstruction and Development, *Report and Recommendations of the President to the Executive Directors Concerning a Proposed Loan for Southern Italy Development Projects*, P–152/Restricted, Archives/Records Center, Room HB1–001, Box 935–01, Nus Location 099–1–2, February 18, 1958.

International Bank for Reconstruction and Development, *Preliminary Report of the President to the Executive Directors on a Proposed Loan for Southern Italy Development Projects*, P–190/Restricted, Archives/Records Center, Room HB1–001, Box 935–01, Nus Location

099–1–2, March 25, 1959.
International Bank for Reconstruction and Development, *Report and Recommendations of the President to the Executive Directors on a Proposed Loan of $ 20 million to the Cassa for Development Projects in Southern Italy*, P–192/Restricted, Archives/Records Center, Room HB1–001, Box 935–01, Nus Location 099–1–2, April 13, 1959.
International Bank for Reconstruction and Development, *Report and Recommendations of the President to the Executive Directors on a Proposed Loan of $ 40 million to the Cassa for the Construction of a Nuclear Power Plant in Southern Italy*, P–204/Restricted, Archives/Records Center, Room HB1–001, Box 935–02, Nus Location 099–1–2, September 4, 1959.
International Bank for Reconstruction and Development, *Report and Recommendations of the President to the Executive Directors on a Proposed Loan to the Cassa per il Mezzogiorno for Industrial Financing in Southern Italy*, P–437/Restricted, June 11, 1965.
International Bank for Reconstruction and Development, *Minutes of the Twenty-ninth Special Meeting of the Executive Directors*, SM-29/Confidential, October 10, 1951.
International Bank for Reconstruction and Development, *Minutes of the Sixty-second Special Meeting of the Executive Directors*, SM-62/Confidential, October 6, 1953.
International Bank for Reconstruction and Development, *Minutes of the Ninety-third Special Meeting of the Executive Directors*, SM-93/Confidential, May 31, 1955.
International Bank for Reconstruction and Development, Department of Operations Europe, Africa and Australasia, *Creditworthiness of Italy*, E.A.–25a/Restricted, September 28, 1953.
International Bank for Reconstruction and Development, Department of Operations Europe, Africa and Australasia, *The Economy of Italy*, EA-71a/Restricted, July 16, 1957.
International Bank for Reconstruction and Development, Department of Operations Europe, Africa and Australasia, *Public Investments of Italy*, EA-71a/Restricted, Annex II, July 16, 1957.
International Bank for Reconstruction and Development, Department of Operations Europe, Africa and Australasia, *Current Economic Position and Prospects of Italy*, EA–94a/Restricted, April 13, 1959.
International Bank for Reconstruction and Development, Department of Operations Europe, *The Situation and Prospects of the Italian Economy. Report of a Mission to Italy (May-July and November 1964)*, EA–150a/Restricted, December 23, 1964.

International Bank for Reconstruction and Development, *Sixth Annual Report*, 10915, Washington (DC), 1950-1951.
International Bank for Reconstruction and Development, *Seventh Annual Report*, 10914, Washington (DC), 1951-1952.
International Bank for Reconstruction and Development, *Eighth Annual Report*, 10913, Washington (DC), 1952-1953.
International Bank for Reconstruction and Development, *Ninth Annual Report*, 10912, Washington (DC), 1953-1954.
International Bank for Reconstruction and Development, *Tenth Annual Report*, 2 voll., 10911, Washington (DC), 1954-1955.
International Bank for Reconstruction and Development, *Eleventh Annual Report*, 10910, Washington (DC), 1955-1956.
International Bank for Reconstruction and Development, *Twelfth Annual Report*, 10909, Washington (DC), 1956-1957.
International Bank for Reconstruction and Development, *Thirteenth Annual Report*, 10889, Washington (DC), 1957-1958.
International Bank for Reconstruction and Development, *Fourteenth Annual Report*, 10890, Washington (DC), 1958-1959.
International Bank for Reconstruction and Development, *Fifteenth Annual Report*, 10891, Washington (DC), 1959-1960.
International Bank for Reconstruction and Development, *Sixteenth Annual Report*, 10892, Washington (DC), 1960-1961.
International Bank for Reconstruction and Development, *Seventeenth Annual Report*, 10893, Washington (DC), 1961-1962.
International Bank for Reconstruction and Development, *Eighteenth Annual Report*, 10894, Washington (DC), 1962-1963.
International Bank for Reconstruction and Development, *Annual Report*, 20079, Washington (DC), 1964-1965.
International Bank for Reconstruction and Development, *Policies and Operations of the WORLD BANK, IFC and IDA*, Washington (DC), Report no. 11116, 1962-1963.
NARA, *Program Plans for Cassa – Fund for South. I-a 1950/51 Land Reclamation Program for Southern Italy*, from ECA Special Mission to Italy – to ECA Washington and OSR Paris, Despatch number D-157, 28 June 1958, RG. 469, Box 34, F. 8.
Rosenstein-Rodan P.N., *Preliminary report on the development program of Southern Italy*, Economic Department Report, no. E98, Washington (DC), The World Bank, 1950.
The World Bank/IFC Archives, *Oral History Program*, *Transcript of the Interview with Sydney Cope*, by R. Oliver, New York (NY), Columbia University, Oral History Research Office, August 9, 1961.

The World Bank/IFC Archives, *Oral History Program*, *Transcript of the Interview with Paul Rosenstein-Rodan*, by R. Oliver, New York (NY), Columbia University, Oral History Research Office, August 14, 1961.

The World Bank, Archives, *Eugene R. Black*, <https://www.worldbank.org/en/about/archives/history/past-presidents/eugene-robert-black>.

Online sources

Archivio Storico degli Economisti, Fonds: *Centro per gli studi sullo sviluppo economico - [Istituto: Associazione per lo sviluppo dell'industria nel Mezzogiorno - Svimez]*, <http://www.sie-ase.it/istituto-dettaglio.aspx?istituto=1390>.

International Bank for Reconstruction and Development, *IBRD Statement of Loans*, <https://documents.worldbank.org/en/publication/documents-reports/documentdetail/139951468336683147/europe-and-central-asia-and-middle-east-and-north-africa>, <http://documents1.worldbank.org/curated/en/139951468336683147/text/631380v30WP0SO0BOX361502B000PUBLIC0.txt>.

International Development Association, *What is IDA?*, <http://ida.worldbank.org/about/what-is-ida>.

The World Bank, *Projects & Operations*, *Country Lending Summaries*, <https://projects.worldbank.org/en/projects-operations/projects-home>, <https://inquiries.worldbank.org/knowledgebase/articles/894018-open-finances-country-lending-summaries>.

The World Bank, Archives, *First funding for Italy: Loan 0050 – Equipment for Development Project*, October 10, 1951, <http://docshare02.docshare.tips/files/26751/267519895.pdf>.

The World Bank, Archives, *Eugene Robert Black*, <https://www.worldbank.org/en/about/archives/history/past-presidents/eugene-robert-black>.

The World Bank, Archives, *George David Woods*, <https://www.worldbank.org/en/about/archives/history/past-presidents/george-david-woods>.

The World Bank, Archives, *Rosenstein-Rodan, Paul N.*, <https://oralhistory.worldbank.org/person/rosenstein-rodan-paul-n>.

Bibliographic references

VV.AA., *Vecchi e nuovi termini della questione meridionale*, Milan, Giuffrè, 1956.

VV.AA., *L'economia italiana dal 1861 al 1961*, Milan, Giuffrè, 1961.

VV.AA., *Cassa per il Mezzogiorno. Dodici anni 1950-1962*, 6 voll., Bari, Laterza, 1962.

VV.AA., *Cassa per il Mezzogiorno: interventi, agevolazioni fiscali e tariffarie per il Mezzogiorno: legislazione completa e coordinata*, Rome, Stamperia nazionale, 1966.

VV.AA., *Nord e Sud nella società e nell'economia italiana di oggi*, Turin, Fondazione Einaudi, 1968.

VV.AA., *Italy's intervento straordinario: an unexpected response to falling transport costs*, in *World Development Report 2009. Reshaping Economic. Geography*, Washington (DC), The International Bank for Reconstruction and Development / The World Bank, 2009.

VV.AA., *Federalismo e Mezzogiorno, a 150 anni dall'Unità d'Italia*, monographic issue, "Rivista giuridica del Mezzogiorno", no. 1-2, 2011.

Alacevich M., *Early Development Economics Debates Revisited*, in "Policy Research Working Paper", The World Bank, World Bank Archives and Development Economics Vice Presidency, no. 4441, 2007.

Alacevich M., *Le origini della Banca Mondiale. Una deriva conservatrice*, Milan, Bruno Mondadori, 2007.

Alacevich M., *The World Bank loans to Italy and the history of postwar development policies*, Working paper, New York (NY), Columbia University, 2009.

Alacevich M., *The World Bank's Early Reflections on Development: A Development Institution or a Bank?*, in "Review of Political Economy", vol. 21, no. 2, 2009.

Alacevich M., *Loan Interruptus: The World Bank, Reconstruction and Development in Italy, 1947-53*, New York (NY), The Italian Academy for Advanced Studies in America at Columbia University, Paper prepared for the Italian Academy Seminar Series, 2010.

Alvarez-Cuadrado F., *A Quantitative Exploration of the Golden Age of European Growth: Structural Change, Public Investment, the Marshall Plan and Intra-European Trade*, Montreal, McGill University, Department of Economics, 2005.

Amato G. (ed.), *Il governo dell'industria in Italia*, Bologna, il Mulino, 1972.

Amendola M., Baratta P., *Investimenti industriali e sviluppo dualistico*, Milan, Giuffrè, 1978.

Ammannati L., *Cassa per il Mezzogiorno e intervento straordinario. Origini e funzionamento di un modello di governo dell'economia*, Naples, Liguori, 1981.

Amorth A., *La struttura della Cassa per il Mezzogiorno e la funzione del Comitato dei Ministri per il Mezzogiorno*, Milan, Giuffrè, 1956.

Annesi M., *Rassegna di giurisprudenza sulle leggi per l'industrializzazione del Mezzogiorno*, Rome, Giuffrè, 1960.

Annesi M., *Aspetti giuridici della disciplina degli interventi nel Mezzogiorno*, Milan, Giuffrè, 1966.

Annesi M. (ed.), *Le leggi sul Mezzogiorno*, Rome, SVIMEZ, 1969.

Annesi M., Barucci P., Dell'Angelo G.G. (eds.), *Studi in onore di Pasquale Saraceno*, Milan, Giuffrè, 1975.

Arcelli M. (ed.), *Storia, economia e società in Italia, 1947-1997*, Rome-Bari, Laterza, 1997.

Archivio Storico Enel, *Il Nucleare in Italia*, text by Giovanni Paoloni, Rome, Eccigraphica, 2009.

Artioli R., *Il dualismo nelle economie industriali*, Turin, Editoriale Valentino, 1975.

Atti Parlamentari, Camera dei Deputati, *Discussioni*, Afternoon assembly of May 17, 1950, Intervention by M. Zagari.

Bank for International Settlements, Monetary and Economic Department, *Italy monetary and economic situation, 1949-1958*, Basle, 1959.

Barbagallo C., *La questione meridionale*, Milan, Garzanti, 1948.

Barbagallo F., *La questione italiana. Il Nord e il Sud dal 1860 a oggi*, Rome-Bari, Laterza, 2013.

Barone G., *Mezzogiorno e modernizzazione: elettricità, irrigazione e bonifica nell'Italia contemporanea*, Turin, Einaudi, 1986.

Barone G., *Stato e Mezzogiorno (1943-1960). Il "primo tempo" dell'intervento straordinario*, in *Storia dell'Italia repubblicana*, vol. I, "La costruzione della democrazia. Dalla caduta del fascismo agli anni cinquanta", Turin, Einaudi, 1994.

Barone G., *La Cassa e la «ricostruzione» del territorio meridionale*, in *Radici storiche ed esperienza dell'intervento straordinario nel Mezzogiorno*, Naples, Bibliopolis, 1996.

Barucci P., *Ricostruzione, pianificazione, Mezzogiorno. La politica economica in Italia dal 1943 al 1955*, Bologna, il Mulino, 1978.

Battilani P., Fauri F., *Mezzo secolo di economia italiana, 1945-2008*, Bologna, il Mulino, 2008.

Battilossi S., *L'Italia nel sistema economico internazionale: il management dell'integrazione. Finanza, industria e istituzioni (1945-1955)*, Milan, Franco Angeli, 1996.

Bauer P.T., Yamey B.S., *The economics of under-developed countries*, Chicago (IL), University of Chicago Press, 1957.

Bernardi E., *La riforma agraria in Italia e gli Stati Uniti: guerra fredda, piano Marshall e interventi per il Mezzogiorno negli anni del centrismo degasperiano*, Bologna, il Mulino, 2006.

Bevilacqua P., *Breve storia dell'Italia meridionale dall'Ottocento a oggi*, Rome, Donzelli, 1993.

Bianchi P., *La rincorsa frenata: l'industria italiana dall'unità nazionale all'unificazione europea*, Bologna, il Mulino, 2002.

Bini P. (ed.), *Il Mezzogiorno nel Parlamento Repubblicano (1948-1972)*, 5 voll., Milan, Giuffrè, 1976-1978.

Bonaduce M., Di Franco G., *Lo sviluppo del Mezzogiorno d'Italia: l'intervento della Banca Europea per gli Investimenti*, Palo del Colle, Tip. editrice Liantonio, 1974.

Bonelli, F. *Il capitalismo italiano. Linee generali di interpretazione,* in *Annali della Storia d'Italia*, vol. I, "Dal feudalesimo al capitalismo", Turin, Einaudi, 1978.

Bonoldi A., Leonardi A. (eds.), *Recovery and Development in the European Periphery (1945-1960)*, Bologna, il Mulino – Berlin, Duncker & Humblot, 2009.

Borghese M., Borghese N., *La Banca internazionale per la ricostruzione e lo sviluppo (BIRS) e la Banca europea per gli investimenti (BEI)*, Rome, Tipografia l'Editrice Finanziaria, 1961.

Bottiglieri B., *La politica economica dell'Italia centrista, 1948-1958*, Milan, Edizioni di Comunità, 1984.

Butalia B., *The Italian Mezzogiorno: development or decline?*, New Delhi, ABC Pub. House, 1985.

Cafagna L. (ed.), *Il Nord nella storia d'Italia*, Bari, Laterza, 1962.

Cafagna L., *Dualismo e sviluppo nella storia d'Italia*, Venice Marsilio, 1989.

Cafagna L., *Nord e Sud: non fare a pezzi l'unità d'Italia*, Venice, Marsilio, 1994.

Cafagna L., *Nord e Sud nella storia dell'Unità d'Italia*, in "Rivista giuridica del Mezzogiorno", no. 1-2, 2011.

Cafiero S., *La nascita della «Cassa»*, in M. Annesi, P. Barucci, G.G. Dell'Angelo (eds.), *Studi in onore di Pasquale Saraceno*, Milan, Giuffrè, 1975.

Cafiero S., *La questione meridionale*, Florence, Le Monnier, 1980.

Cafiero S. (ed.), *Il Mezzogiorno nelle politiche nazionali e comunitarie*, Milan, Giuffrè, 1982.

Cafiero S., *Tradizione e attualità del meridionalismo*, Bologna, il Mulino, 1989.

Cafiero S., *Questione meridionale e unità nazionale 1861-1995*, Rome, La Nuova Italia Scientifica, 1996.

Cafiero S., *Storia dell'intervento straordinario nel Mezzogiorno (1950-1993)*, Manduria-Bari-Rome, Lacaita, 2000.

Cafiero S., Marciani G.E., *Quarant'anni di intervento straordinario (1950-1989)*, in "Rivista economica del Mezzogiorno", no. 2, 1991.

Camera dei Deputati, *Relazione sulla attività di coordinamento (ai sensi delle leggi 18 marzo 1959, n. 101 e 26 giugno 1965, n. 717) depositata dal Ministro per gli Interventi Straordinari nel Mezzogiorno*, Rome, Istituto Poligrafico dello Stato, 1966.

Cairncross A., *The International Bank for Reconstruction and Development*, Princeton (NJ), Princeton University, 1959.

Campus M., *L'Italia, gli Stati Uniti e il piano Marshall*, Rome-Bari, Laterza, 2008.

Cao-Pinna V., *Le regioni del Mezzogiorno*, Bologna, il Mulino, 1979.

Carabba M. (ed.), *Mezzogiorno e programmazione (1954-1971)*, Milan, Giuffrè, 1980.

Cardini A., *Il miracolo economico italiano, 1958-1963,* Bologna, il Mulino, 2006.

Carillo M.R., Moro B., Papagni E., Vinci S., *Dualismo, nuove teorie della crescita e sviluppo del Mezzogiorno*, Bologna, il Mulino, 2008.

Carli G., *Cinquant'anni di vita italiana*, in cooperation with Paolo Peluffo, Rome-Bari, Laterza, 1996.

Carlyle M., *The Awakening of Southern Italy*, London, Oxford University Press, 1962.

Carreras A., *Lo sviluppo economico-industriale occidentale e il problema delle aree depresse*, in *Radici storiche ed esperienza dell'intervento straordinario nel Mezzogiorno*, Naples, Bibliopolis, 1996.

Cassa per il Mezzogiorno, *La Cassa per il Mezzogiorno. Primo quinquennio: 1950-1955*, Rome, Istituto Poligrafico dello Stato, 1955.

Cassa per il Mezzogiorno, *La Cassa per il Mezzogiorno*, Rome, Istituto Poligrafico dello Stato, 1960.

Cassa per Opere Straordinarie di Pubblico Interesse nell'Italia Meridionale, *Istituzione della Cassa per Opere Straordinarie di Pubblico Interesse nell'Italia Meridionale (Cassa per il Mezzogiorno): testo della legge istitutiva con le successive modifiche e integrazioni (legge 10 agosto 1950, n. 645; legge 22 dicembre 1951, n. 1575; legge 22 marzo 1952, n. 166; legge 25 luglio 1952, n. 949)*, [1952?].

Cassa per Opere Straordinarie di Pubblico Interesse nell'Italia Meridionale, *Che cosa è la Cassa: piano di investimenti, criteri di intervento, obiettivi*, Rome, Grafitalia, [1953?].

Cassa per Opere Straordinarie di Pubblico Interesse nell'Italia Meridionale, *Compiti e realizzazioni della Cassa per il Mezzogiorno*, Rome, Istituto Poligrafico dello Stato, 1956.

Cassa per Opere Straordinarie di Pubblico Interesse nell'Italia Meridionale, *Programma dodecennale degli interventi nel settore dell'agricoltura*, Rome, Istituto Poligrafico dello Stato, 1957.

Cassa per Opere Straordinarie di Pubblico Interesse nell'Italia Meridionale, *Primi rilievi sulle modificazioni della struttura industriale del Mezzogiorno*, Rome, Istituto Poligrafico dello Stato, 1958.

Cassa per Opere Straordinarie di Pubblico Interesse nell'Italia Meridionale, *Strutture e mercati dell'agricoltura meridionale*, Rome, Cassa per il Mezzogiorno, 1960.

Cassa per Opere Straordinarie di Pubblico Interesse nell'Italia Meridionale, *Iniziative industriali finanziate nel Mezzogiorno*, Rome, Cassa per il Mezzogiorno, 1960.

Cassa per Opere Straordinarie di Pubblico Interesse nell'Italia Meridionale, *Consuntivo del primo decennio della Cassa per il Mezzogiorno*, Rome, Tipografia della pace, 1960.

Cassa per Opere Straordinarie di Pubblico Interesse nell'Italia Meridionale, *La rinascita del Mezzogiorno e l'opera della Cassa*, Portici, Poligrafica e cartevalori, 1963.

Cassa per Opere Straordinarie di Pubblico Interesse nell'Italia Meridionale, *Raccolta leggi, decreti e circolari riguardanti la Cassa per il Mezzogiorno*, Rome, Arti Grafiche Labor, 1964.

Cassa per Opere Straordinarie di Pubblico Interesse nell'Italia Meridionale, *La Cassa per il Mezzogiorno*, Rome, Poligraf, 1972.

Cassa per Opere Straordinarie di Pubblico Interesse nell'Italia Meridionale, *Ricerche sugli effetti economici e sociali degli investimenti realizzati dalla Cassa*, [19?].

[Cassa per Opere Straordinarie di Pubblico Interesse nell'Italia Meridionale (Cassa per il Mezzogiorno), Centro Studi], *Cassa per il Mezzogiorno. Scopi e programmi*, Rome, A.BE.T.E., [1953?].

Cassese S., *Amministrazione speciale e amministrazione ordinaria per lo sviluppo del Mezzogiorno. Rassegna della legislazione*, Milan, Giuffrè, 1965.

Castronovo V. (ed.), *L'Italia contemporanea, 1945-1975*, Turin, Einaudi, 1976.

Castronovo V., *Storia economica d'Italia. Dall'Ottocento ai giorni nostri*, Turin, Einaudi, 1995.

Castronovo V., *L'Italia del miracolo economico*, Rome-Bari, Laterza, 2010.

Cenzato G., *L'industrializzazione del Mezzogiorno*, Naples, Unione degli Industriali di Napoli, 1954.

Cenzato G., *Situazione e prospettive per l'industrializzazione del Mezzogiorno*, Naples, Unione degli Industriali di Napoli, 1955.

Cenzato G., Guidotti S., *Il problema industriale del Mezzogiorno*, Milan, Stampa Strada, 1946.

Ceriani Sebregondi G., *Sullo sviluppo della società italiana*, Turin, Boringhieri, 1965.

Chenery H.B., *Structure and growth of the italian economy*, Rome, 1953.

Chenery H.B., *Politiche di sviluppo per l'Italia meridionale*, Rome, Giuffrè, 1962.

Chenery H.B., Kretschmer K.S., *Resource Allocation for Economic Development*, in "Econometrica", vol. 24, no. 4, 1956.

Chenery H.B., Syrquin M., *Patterns of development 1950-1970*, London, Oxford University Press, 1975.

Chwieroth J., *International liquidity provision: the IMF and the World Bank in the Treasury and the Marshall Systems, 1942-1957*, in D.M. Andrews (ed.), *Orderly Change: international monetary relations since Bretton Woods*, Ithaca (NY), Cornell University Press, 2008.

Ciocca P., *Il progresso economico dell'Italia: permanenze, discontinuità, limiti*, Bologna, il Mulino, 1994.

Ciocca P., *Ricchi per sempre? Una storia economica d'Italia (1796-2005)*, Turin, Boringhieri, 2007.

Ciocca P., Toniolo G., *Storia Economica d'Italia*, 3 voll., Rome-Bari, Laterza, 1999-2004.

Clark Carey J.P., Carey A.G., *The South of Italy and the Cassa per il Mezzogiorno*, in "The Western Political Quarterly", vol. 8, no. 4, 1955.

Clough S.B., *The economic history of modern Italy*, New York (NY) – London, Columbia University Press, 1964.

Cohen J., Federico G., *Lo sviluppo economico italiano, 1820-1960*, Bologna, il Mulino, 2001.

Compagna F., *La questione meridionale*, Milan, Garzanti, 1963.

Corbino E., *L'economia italiana dal 1860 al 1960*, Bologna, Zanichelli, 1962.

Cotula F. (ed.), *Stabilità e sviluppo negli anni Cinquanta*, 3 voll., Rome-Bari, Laterza, 2001.

Cova A., Fumi G., *L'intervento dello Stato nell'economia italiana: continuità e cambiamenti (1922-1956)*, Milan, Franco Angeli, 2011.

Crafts N.F.R., *The Golden Age of Economic Growth in Western Europe, 1950-1973*, in "The Economic History Review", vol. 48, no. 3, 1995.

Crafts N.F.R., Magnani M., *The Golden Age and the Second Globalization in Italy*, Rome, Banca d'Italia, "Quaderni di Storia Economica", no. 17, 2011.

Crafts N.F.R., Mills T.C., *Europe's Golden Age: An Econometric Investigation of Changing Trend Rates of Growth*, in "Centre for Economic Policy Research Discussion Papers", no. 1087, 1995.

Crafts N.F.R., Toniolo G. (eds.), *Economic Growth in Europe since 1945*, Cambridge, Cambridge University Press, 1996.

Cubel A., Sanchis M.T., *Investment and growth in Europe during the Golden Age*, in "European Review of Economic History", vol. 13, no. 2, 2009.

Cuoco L., *Il processo di sviluppo di un'area sovrapopolata: il Mezzogiorno d'Italia*, Milan, Giuffrè, 1971.

Curli B., *Energia nucleare per il Mezzogiorno. L'Italia e la Banca mondiale (1955-1959)*, in "Studi Storici", vol. 37, no. 1, 1996.

Curli B., *Ricostruzione e sviluppo. La Banca Mondiale e l'economia italiana, 1947-51*, in "Archivi e imprese", vol. 8, no. 15, 1997.

Curli B., *L'Italia e la Banca mondiale (1947-1959)*, in *L'Italia e le organizzazioni internazionali. Diplomazia multilaterale nel Novecento*, Padua, Cedam, 1999.

D'Aimmo A., *La politica della Cassa per il Mezzogiorno dal 1950 ad oggi*, Chieti, Kappa, 1989.

Daniele V., Malanima P., *Il prodotto delle regioni e il divario Nord-Sud in Italia (1861-2004)*, in "Rivista di Politica Economica", III-IV, 2007.

Daniele V., Malanima P., *Il divario Nord-Sud in Italia 1861-2011*, Soveria Mannelli, Rubbettino, 2011.

D'Antone L., *L'«interesse straordinario» per il Mezzogiorno (1943-1960)*, in "Meridiana", 1995, no. 24; now published in Id. (ed.), *Radici storiche ed esperienza dell'intervento straordinario nel Mezzogiorno*, Naples, Bibliopolis, 1996.

D'Antone L., *La «questione meridionale», gli aiuti internazionali e lo sviluppo economico dell'Italia*, in SVIMEZ, *L'Unificazione economica dell'Italia*, Bologna, il Mulino, 1997.

D'Antone L., *«Straordinarietà» e Stato ordinario*, in F. Barca (ed.), *Storia del capitalismo italiano dal dopoguerra a oggi*, Rome, Donzelli, 1997.

D'Antonio M., *Stato ed economia nel Mezzogiorno dagli anni '50 a oggi*, in VV.AA., *Il governo democratico dell'economia*, Bari, De Donato, 1976.

D'Antonio M., *Economia e politica dello sviluppo*, Turin, Giappichelli, 2006.

D'Antonio M. (ed.), *Il Mezzogiorno. Dall'intervento straordinario alla politica regionale europea*, Rome, I quaderni di "Economia italiana", no. 4, 2008.

D'Attorre P.P., *Anche noi possiamo essere prosperi. Aiuti Erp e politiche della produttività negli anni Cinquanta,* in "Quaderni Storici", no. 58, 1985.

Davis J.E., *The Economic Development of Southern Italy, 1950-1960*, Thesis, Madison (WI), University of Wisconsin-Madison, 1963.

de Carvalho O., *Desenvolvimento regional, um problema político: confronto de duas experiências, Cassa per il Mezzogiorno e SUDENE*, Rio de Janeiro, Editora Campus, 1979.

Degli Oddi Alfieri A., *Cassa del Mezzogiorno. Un decennio di attività*, Parma, La Nazionale Tipografia Editrice, 1967.

Del Monte A., Giannola A., *Il Mezzogiorno nell'economia italiana*, Bologna, il Mulino, 1978.

Del Monte A., Giannola A., *Istituzioni economiche e Mezzogiorno. Analisi delle politiche di sviluppo*, Rome, La Nuova Italia Scientifica, 1997.

Denitto A.L., *Istituti e dinamiche dei finanziamenti straordinari: l'Isveimer dalle origini agli anni del miracolo economico*, in *Radici storiche ed esperienza dell'intervento straordinario nel Mezzogiorno*, Naples, Bibliopolis, 1996.

De Rita G., Becchi Collidà A., Carabba M. (eds.), *Meridionalismo in crisi?*, Milan, Franco Angeli, 1966.

De Rosa L., *Lo sviluppo economico dell'Italia dal dopoguerra a oggi*, Rome-Bari, Laterza, 1997.

De Rosa L., *La provincia subordinata: saggio sulla questione meridionale*, Rome-Bari, Laterza, 2004.

Di Nardi G., *Politiche pubbliche e intervento straordinario per il Mezzogiorno. Scritti di un economista meridionale*, Bologna, il Mulino, 2006.

Di Taranto G., *Per una diversa interpretazione dell'intervento straordinario nel Mezzogiorno*, in "Nord e Sud", XXXI, no. 1, 1984.

Di Taranto G., *Italy and the International Monetary Fund. The beginning*, in "Review of Economic Conditions in Italy", no. 2, 2000.

Di Taranto G., *Italy and the International Monetary Fund: From Multiple Exchange-Rate System to Convertibility*, in "The Journal of European Economic History", vol. 35, no. 2, 2006.

Di Taranto G., *Guido Carli e le istituzioni economiche internazionali*, Turin, Bollati Boringhieri, 2009.

Di Vittorio A. (ed.), *Dall'espansione allo sviluppo: una storia economica d'Europa*, Turin, Giappichelli, 2011.

Eckaus R.S., *The North-South Differential In Italian Economic Development*, in "The Journal of Economic History", vol. XXI, no. 3, 1961.

Eichengreen B.J., *The European Economy Since 1945: Coordinated Capitalism and Beyond*, Princeton (NJ), Princeton University Press, 2007.

Einaudi L., *Il Mezzogiorno ed il tempo lungo*, editorial of the "Corriere della Sera", August 21, 1960, <http://www.luigieinaudi.it/doc/il-mezzogiorno-ed-il-tempo-lungo/>; now published in S. Zoppi (ed.), *Diciotto voci per l'Italia unita*, Bologna, il Mulino, 2011.

Esposito C., *Istituzioni Economiche Internazionali e Governance Globale*, Turin, Giappichelli, 2009.

European Investment Bank, Research Department, *The European Investment Bank and the problems of the Mezzogiorno*, Brussels, Weissenbruch Ltd., 1972.

European Productivity Agency, *Methods of industrial development: with special reference to less developed areas*, edited by A. Winsemius and J.A. Pincus, Paris, Organisation for Economic Co-operation and Development (OECD), 1962.

Faini R., *Cumulative process of de-industrialisation in an open region. The case of Southern Italy 1951-1973*, in "Journal of Development Economics", vol. 12, no. 3, 1983.

Faini R., Galli G., Giannini C., *Finance and development: the case of Southern Italy*, in A. Giovannini (ed.), *Finance and development: issues and experience*, Cambridge, Cambridge University Press, 1993.

Fanfani T., *Scelte politiche e fatti economici dal secondo dopoguerra ai nostri giorni. Cinquant'anni di storia italiana*, Turin, Giappichelli, 1998.

Fauri F., *Il Piano Marshall e l'Italia*, Bologna, il Mulino, 2010.

Felice E., *Divari regionali e intervento pubblico (1871-2001). Per una rilettura dello sviluppo in Italia*, Bologna, il Mulino, 2007.

Felice E., *Regional Development: Reviewing the Italian Mosaic*, in "Journal of Modern Italian Studies", vol. 15, no. 1, 2010.

Felice E., *Regional value added in Italy, 1891-2001, and the foundation of a long-term picture*, in "The Economic History Review", vol. 64, no. 3, 2011.

Frisella Vella G., *Storia ed economia nella questione meridionale italiana*, Milan, Giuffrè, 1966.

Froggio G.B., *La Cassa per il Mezzogiorno per lo sviluppo dell'Italia meridionale*, Rome, Ufficio Informazioni della Presidenza del Consiglio dei Ministri, 1961.

Fuà G., *Notes on Italian economic growth 1861-1964*, Milan, Giuffrè, 1965.

Fuà G., *Lo sviluppo economico in Italia. Storia dell'economia italiana negli ultimi cento anni*, Milan, Franco Angeli, 1974.

Galasso G., *Il Mezzogiorno: da "questione" a "problema aperto"*, Manduria-Bari-Rome, Lacaita, 2005.

Galasso G., *Meridionalismo e questione meridionale*, in "Rivista economica del Mezzogiorno", no. 3, 2011.

Galasso G., Romeo R. (eds.), *Storia del Mezzogiorno*, 15 voll., Napoli, Edizioni del Sole, 1986-1994.

Gallegati M., Stanca L.M., *Le fluttuazioni economiche in Italia, 1861-1995, ovvero, il camaleonte e il virus dell'influenza*, Turin, Giappichelli, 1998.

Gambino A., *La politica creditizia per lo sviluppo economico del Mezzogiorno,* Milan, Giuffrè, 1957.

Gattei S., *Evoluzione del divario Nord-Sud nelle condizioni civili e sociali nel periodo 1951-1987,* in "Rivista economica del Mezzogiorno", no. 4, 1989.

Gavin M., Rodrik D., *The World Bank in Historical Perspective*, in "The American Economic Review", vol. 85, no. 2, 1995.

Gerschenkron A., *Economic backwardness in historical perspective: a book of essays*, New York (NY) - Washington (DC) - London, F. A. Praeger, 1965.

Gesummaria M., *Piano Marshall e Mezzogiorno*, Atripalda, Mephite, 2003.

Giannola A., *Impresa manifatturiera e imprenditori del Mezzogiorno*, Napoli, Guida, 1986.

Giannola A., *Il Mezzogiorno nell'economia italiana. Nord e Sud a 150 anni dall'Unità*, in "Rivista economica del Mezzogiorno", no. 3, 2010.

Giannola A., *I cambiamenti dell'economia italiana alla luce delle ricerche promosse dalla SVIMEZ*, in "Rivista economica del Mezzogiorno", no. 3, 2011.

Giovannelli V., *L'organizzazione amministrativa dell'intervento straordinario nel Mezzogiorno*, Milan, Giuffrè, 1971.

Graziani A. (ed.), *L'economia italiana dal 1945 a oggi*, Bologna, il Mulino, 1972.

Graziani A. (ed.), *Crisi e ristrutturazione nell'economia italiana*, Turin, Einaudi, 1975.

Graziani A., *Lo sviluppo dell'economia italiana: dalla ricostruzione alla moneta europea*, Turin, Bollati Boringhieri, 1998.

Graziani A., Del Monte A., Piccolo D., Giannola A., Matrone L., *Incentivi e investimenti industriali nel Mezzogiorno*, Milan, Franco Angeli, 1973.
Gualerni G., *Ricostruzione e industria. Per una interpretazione della politica industriale nel secondo dopoguerra, 1943-1951,* Milan, Vita e Pensiero, 1980.
Gualerni G., *Economia aperta. Un approccio storico all'economia e politica industriale in Italia: 1860-1972,* Turin, Giappichelli, 1991.
Guelfi A., *La Banca Mondiale fra ricostruzione e sviluppo: il caso del primo prestito all'Italia, 1947-1951*, Ph.D. Thesis in "History and Theory of Economic Thought", Rome, Luiss, 2012.
Hildebrand G.H., *Growth And Structure In The Economy Of Modern Italy*, Cambridge (MA), Harvard University Press, 1965.
Hirschman A.O., *The strategy of economic development*, New Haven – London, Yale University Press, 1958.
Hirschman A.O., *Development Projects Observed*, Washington (DC), The Brookings Institution, 1967.
Holland S., *Capital versus the regions*, London, Macmillan, 1976.
Imbriani C. (ed.), *Mezzogiorno e meridionalismo. Tesi e confronti*, Napoli, Edizioni Scientifiche Italiane, 1987.
Jossa B. (ed.), *Economia del sottosviluppo*, Bologna, il Mulino, 1973.
Judt T., *Postwar: a history of Europe since 1945*, New York (NY), Penguin, 2005.
Kapur D., Lewis J.P., Webb R.C. (eds.), *The World Bank: Its First Half Century*, 2 voll., Washington (DC), Brookings Institution Press, 1997.
Killick J.R., *The United States and European Reconstruction 1945-1960*, London, Taylor & Francis Group, 2000.
King R., *The "Questione meridionale" in Southern Italy*, Durham, University of Durham, Department of Geography, 1971.
Kraske J., Becker W.H., Diamond W., Galambos L., *Bankers with a Mission. The Presidents of the World Bank, 1946-1991*, New York (NY), Oxford University Press, 1996.
La Francesca S. (ed.), *Iniziativa privata e sviluppo industriale del Mezzogiorno*, Milan, Giuffrè, 1979.
La Malfa U., *La politica economica in Italia, 1946-1962,* Milan, Edizioni di Comunità, 1962.
Lamont D.F., Purtshert R., *Managing foreign investment in southern Italy: U.S. business in developing areas of the EEC*, New York (NY), Praeger, 1973.
La Spina A., *La politica per il Mezzogiorno*, Bologna, il Mulino, 2003.
Leanza U., *Legislazione per il Mezzogiorno e Mercato Comune Europeo*, Rome, Giuffrè, 1963.

Lepore A., *La questione meridionale prima dell'intervento straordinario*, Manduria-Bari-Rome, Lacaita, 1991.

Lepore A., *Il dilemma del Mezzogiorno a 150 anni dall'unificazione: attualità e storia del nuovo meridionalismo*, in "Rivista economica del Mezzogiorno", no. 1-2, 2011.

Lepore A., *La valutazione dell'operato della Cassa per il Mezzogiorno e il suo ruolo strategico per lo sviluppo del Paese*, in VV.AA., *Federalismo e Mezzogiorno, a 150 anni dall'Unità d'Italia*, monographic issue, "Rivista giuridica del Mezzogiorno", no. 1-2, 2011.

Lepore A., *Cassa per il Mezzogiorno e politiche per lo sviluppo*, in A. Leonardi (ed.), *Istituzioni ed Economia*, Bari, Cacucci, 2011.

Lepore A., *L'impegno della SVIMEZ per il 150° anniversario dell'Unità d'Italia. Nuovi percorsi di ricerca per la storia e l'economia del Mezzogiorno*, in "Rivista economica del Mezzogiorno", no. 3, 2011.

Lepore A., *Il divario Nord-Sud dalle origini a oggi. Evoluzione storica e profili economici*, in VV.AA., *Elementi di diritto pubblico dell'economia*, edited by M. Pellegrini, Padua, Cedam, 2012.

Lunghini G. (ed.), *Scelte politiche e teorie economiche in Italia 1945-1978*, Turin, Einaudi, 1981.

Lutz V., *Italy. A study in economic development*, New York (NY), Oxford University Press, 1962.

Maddison A., *Economic progress and policy in developing countries*, London, Allen & Unwin, 1970.

Maraffi M., *Politica ed economia in Italia. La vicenda dell'impresa pubblica dagli anni Trenta agli anni Cinquanta*, Bologna, il Mulino, 1990.

Marciani G.E., *L'esperienza di riforma agraria in Italia*, Milan, Giuffrè, 1966.

Marciani G.E., *La spesa della Cassa e dell'Agenzia per il Mezzogiorno nei quarantatré anni dell'intervento straordinario*, in "Rivista economica del Mezzogiorno", no. 3, 1993.

Marelli L., *Sviluppo e sottosviluppo nel Mezzogiorno d'Italia dal 1945 agli anni 70*, Naples, Morano, 1972.

Marglin S.A., Schor J.B. (eds.), *The Golden Age of Capitalism: Reinterpreting the Postwar Experience*, New York (NY), Oxford University Press, 1990.

Marongiu G., *Aspetti giuridico-organizzativi*, in A. Parisi, G. Zappa (eds.), *Mezzogiorno e politica di piano*, Bari, Laterza, 1964.

Martellaro J.A., *The effects of the post-war economic development program in southern Italy, 1950-1960*, Thesis, Notre Dame (IN), University of Notre Dame, 1962.

Martellaro J.A., *Economic Development in Southern Italy, 1950-1960*, Washington (DC), Catholic University of America Press, 1965.

Marzano F., *Un'interpretazione del processo di sviluppo economico dualistico in Italia*, Milan, Giuffrè, 1969.

Marzano F. (ed.), *Incentivi e sviluppo del Mezzogiorno*, Milan, Giuffrè, 1979.

Mason E.S., Asher R.E., *The World Bank since Bretton Woods: the origins, policies, operations, and impact of the International Bank for Reconstruction and Development and the other members of the World Bank group: the International Finance Corporation, the International Development Association [and] the International Centre for Settlement of Investment Disputes*, Washington (DC), Brookings Institution Press, 1973.

Mazzocchi Alemanni N., *La depressione meridionale e la Cassa per il Mezzogiorno*, in *Problemi dell'agricoltura meridionale*, Naples, Istituto Editoriale del Mezzogiorno, 1953.

Mazzone M., *I sistemi di esecuzione delle opere pubbliche e la Cassa per il Mezzogiorno,* Rome, Jandi Sapi, 1978.

McGlade J., *Lo zio Sam ingegnere industriale. Il programma americano per la produttività e la ripresa economica dell'Europa occidentale (1948-1958)*, in "Studi Storici", vol. 37, no. 1, 1996.

Menichella D., *Stabilità e sviluppo dell'economia italiana, 1946-1960. Documenti e discorsi*, 2 voll., edited by F. Cotula, C.O. Gelsomino and A. Gigliobianco, Rome-Bari, Laterza, 1997.

Merusi F., *Disciplina e organizzazione dei finanziamenti pubblici nelle leggi per il Mezzogiorno*, Rome, Giuffrè, 1968.

Meti T.K., *Economic development of the underdeveloped region in Italy*, Dharwar, Karnatak University, 1969.

Milone F., *L'Italia nell'economia delle sue regioni,* Turin, Einaudi, 1955.

Milward A.S., *The Reconstruction of Western Europe, 1945-1951*, Berkeley (CA), University of California Press, 1987.

Monti S., Vinci S., *Mezzogiorno e sottosviluppo*, Naples, Loffredo, 1984.

Moro F., *Le spese dell'Agenzia per il Mezzogiorno per categorie economiche e per regioni*, in "Rivista economica del Mezzogiorno", no. 3, 1993.

Moro F., *L'avvio dell'attività della Cassa per il Mezzogiorno*, in SVIMEZ, *L'Unificazione economica dell'Italia*, Bologna, il Mulino, 1997.

Mosk C., *The political economy of the World Bank: The early years,* in "Journal of International Trade & Economic Development", vol. 19, no. 1, 2010.

Mountjoy A.B., *The Mezzogiorno*, London, Oxford University Press, 1973.

Muraca A., *La Banca Internazionale per la ricostruzione e lo sviluppo nella storia dell'intervento straordinario per il Mezzogiorno (1946-1960)*, PhD thesis in "Storia e Teoria dello Sviluppo Economico", Rome, Luiss, 2004.

Mutti A., Poli I., *Sottosviluppo e Meridione*, Milan, Mazzotta, 1975.

Myrdal G., *Economic Theory and Underdeveloped Regions*, London, Duckworth, 1967.

Napoleoni C., *Il pensiero economico del 900*, Turin, Einaudi, 1963.

Napoletano R., *Gabriele Pescatore il Grande Elemosiniere*, Naples, Edizioni Sintesi, 1988.

Nardozzi G., *Miracolo e declino. L'Italia tra concorrenza e protezione*, Rome-Bari, Laterza, 2004.

Novacco D., *La questione meridionale ieri e oggi*, Turin, ERI, 1976.

Novacco N., *Politiche per lo sviluppo. Alcuni ricordi sugli anni '50 tra cronaca e storia*, Bologna, il Mulino, 1995.

Novacco N. (ed.), *Problemi nazionali e meridionali nel pensiero e nell'impegno di Salvatore Cafiero*, Bologna, il Mulino, 2003.

Novacco N. (ed.), *Per il Mezzogiorno e per l'Italia. Un sogno ed un impegno che dura da 60 anni*, Bologna, il Mulino, 2007.

Oliver R.W., *International Economic Co-operation and the World Bank*, London, Macmillan, 1975.

Oman C.P., Wignaraja G., *The postwar evolution of development thinking*, Paris, Macmillan/OECD Development Centre, 1991.

Organisation For Economic Co-Operation and Development, Industry Committee, *Latest results and new features of official action in the Mezzogiorno (Italy)*, Paris, OECD, 1973.

Ortona E., *Anni d'America*, 3 voll., Bologna, il Mulino, 1984-1989.

Padovani R., *Le scelte della ricostruzione nel Sud Italia*, in G. Mori (ed.), *La cultura economica nel periodo della ricostruzione*, Bologna, il Mulino, 1980.

Padovani R., *Il Mezzogiorno nell'economia italiana a 150 anni dall'Unità*, in "Rivista economica del Mezzogiorno", no. 1-2, 2011.

Paganetto L., Scandizzo P.L., *La Banca mondiale e l'Italia: dalla ricostruzione allo sviluppo*, Bologna, il Mulino, 2000.

Parisi A., Zappa G. (eds.), *Mezzogiorno e politica di piano*, Bari, Laterza, 1964.

Pavarin A., *Lo sviluppo del Mezzogiorno. L'intervento dello Stato e il sistema bancario dalla nascita della Repubblica agli anni Sessanta. Una rassegna storiografica*, Rome, Editrice Apes, 2011.

Pellè L., *Mezzogiorno e Piano Marshall. La Ricostruzione dal 1947 al 1952*, Manduria-Bari-Rome, Lacaita, 2009.

Perrotta C., Sunna C. (eds.), *L'arretratezza del Mezzogiorno. Le idee, l'economia, la storia*, Milan, Bruno Mondadori, 2012.

Pescatore G., *L'attività della Cassa per il Mezzogiorno*, [Rome], Banco di Roma, [1957?].

Pescatore G., *Realizzazioni ed effetti del piano della Cassa per il Mezzogiorno*, Milan, Giuffrè, 1959.

Pescatore G., *Dieci anni di esperienze della Cassa per il Mezzogiorno*, Rome, Fausto Failli, 1961.

Pescatore G., *L'intervento straordinario nel Mezzogiorno d'Italia*, Milan, Giuffrè, 1962.

Pescatore G., *Menichella, l'intervento per il Mezzogiorno e la Banca Mondiale*, in D. Menichella, *Testimonianze e studi raccolti dalla Banca d'Italia*, Rome-Bari, Laterza, 1986.

Pescatore G., *La «Cassa per il Mezzogiorno». Un'esperienza italiana per lo sviluppo*, Bologna, il Mulino, 2008.

Pescosolido G., *Meridionale, questione*, in "Enciclopedia del Novecento", III Supplemento, Rome, Istituto della Enciclopedia Italiana, 2004.

Petri R., *Storia economica d'Italia: dalla Grande guerra al miracolo economico (1918-1963)*, Bologna, il Mulino, 2002.

Petriccione S., *Politica industriale e Mezzogiorno*, Bari, Laterza, 1976.

Piccinetti L., *The "Intervento Straordinario", its successor policies and the Political Economy of regional development in the Mezzogiorno: an anatomy of failure*, Master's thesis in "European Contemporary Studies" (MACES), Brighton, University of Sussex, 2000.

Pilloton F., *Effetti moltiplicativi degli investimenti della «Cassa per il Mezzogiorno»*, Milan, Giuffrè, 1960.

Podbielski G., *Storia dell'economia italiana 1945-1974,* Rome-Bari, Laterza, 1975.

Podbielski G., *Venticinque anni di intervento straordinario nel Mezzogiorno*, Milan, Giuffrè, 1978.

Presidenza del Consiglio dei Ministri, *L'intervento straordinario nel Mezzogiorno (1950-1984)*, Rome, Istituto Poligrafico dello Stato, 1986.

Pugliese A., *Esiste un filo di Arianna nello sviluppo del Mezzogiorno?*, Naples, Liguori, 2009.

Raitano G., *L'intervento straordinario per il Mezzogiorno e l'organizzazione del credito all'industria*, in SVIMEZ, *L'Unificazione economica dell'Italia*, Bologna, il Mulino, 1997.

Rigano A.R., *La Banca d'Italia e il progetto ENSI. Fonti per la storia dello sviluppo energetico italiano degli anni cinquanta nelle carte dell'Archivio della Banca d'Italia*, in "Quaderni dell'Ufficio Ricerche Storiche", Bank of Italy, no. 4, 2002.

Riviello C., *Dalla Cassa per il Mezzogiorno al nuovo intervento straordinario*, Bologna, il Mulino, 1988.

Rocco F., *Scritti e discorsi sul problema meridionale (1925-1953)*, Naples, Istituto Editoriale del Mezzogiorno, 1953.

Rodanò C., *Mezzogiorno e sviluppo economico*, Bari, Laterza, 1954.

Romeo R., *Breve storia della grande industria in Italia 1861-1961*, Bologna, Cappelli, 1961.

Rosenstein-Rodan P.N., *Problems of Industrialisation of Eastern and South-Eastern Europe*, in "The Economic Journal", vol. 53, no. 210-211, 1943.

Rosenstein-Rodan P.N., *The international development of economically backward areas*, in "International Affairs", vol. 20, no. 2, 1944.

Rosenstein-Rodan P.N., *Notes on the theory of the big push*, in H. Ellis, H. C. Wallich (eds.), *Economic development for Latin America*, New York (NY), St. Martin's Press, 1961.

Rosenstein-Rodan P.N. (ed.), *Capital formation and economic development*, London, Allen & Unwin, 1964.

Russell D., *The TVA idea*, Irvington-on-Hudson (NY), The Foundation for Economic Education, 1949.

Salvati M., *Economia e politica in Italia dal dopoguerra a oggi*, Milan, Garzanti, 1984.

Santillo M., *Il farsi di una classe dirigente per il Mezzogiorno. Lo start-up dell'intervento straordinario*, Naples, Edizioni Scientifiche Italiane, 2012.

Sapelli G., *Storia economica dell'Italia contemporanea*, Milan, Bruno Mondadori, 1997.

Saraceno P., *Elementi per un piano economico 1949-1952*, edited by the Centro di Studi e Piani Tecnico-Economici, the Technical and Economical Planning and Study Center, established by the CNR and IRI, Rome, Istituto Poligrafico dello Stato, 1948.

Saraceno P., *Lo sviluppo economico dei paesi sovrapopolati*, Rome, Editrice Studium, 1952.

Saraceno P., *Iniziativa privata e azione pubblica nei piani di sviluppo economico*, Rome, Giuffrè, 1959.

Saraceno P., *Ricostruzione e pianificazione (1943-1948)*, edited by P. Barucci, Milan, Giuffrè, 1974.

Saraceno P., *Il meridionalismo dopo la ricostruzione (1948-1957)*, edited by P. Barucci, Milan, Giuffrè, 1974.

Saraceno P., *Intervista sulla Ricostruzione, 1943-1953*, edited by L. Villari, Bari, Laterza, 1977.
Saraceno P., *Politica Keynesiana e Mezzogiorno*, in "Informazioni SVIMEZ", no. 11, 1976.
Saraceno P., *La questione meridionale nella ricostruzione post bellica, 1943-1950*, Milan, Giuffrè, 1980.
Saraceno P., *Gli interventi del primo IRI: dallo smobilizzo delle grandi Banche alla proposta di legge bancaria, 1933-1936*, in "Banca, borsa e titoli di credito", year XLIV, New Series, XXXIV, folio III, 1981.
Saraceno P., *Gli anni dello Schema Vanoni, 1953-1959*, Milan, Giuffrè, 1982.
Saraceno P., *L'intervento straordinario nel Mezzogiorno nella nuova fase aperta dalla crisi industriale*, in *Conferenza del Mezzogiorno ...La civiltà della ragione...*, Minutes of the Convention, Rome, Cassa per il Mezzogiorno, March 22-23-24, 1983.
Saraceno P., *Il nuovo meridionalismo*, Naples, Istituto Italiano per gli Studi Filosofici, 1986.
Saraceno P., *Sottosviluppo industriale e questione meridionale. Studi degli anni 1952-1963*, Bologna, il Mulino, 1990.
Saraceno P., *Studi sulla questione meridionale 1965-1975*, Bologna, il Mulino, 1992.
Saville L., *Regional Economic Development in Italy*, Edinburgh, Edinburgh University Press, 1968.
Sbrescia V.M., *Alle origini dell'intervento pubblico nell'economia meridionale: la Cassa per il Mezzogiorno a sessant'anni dalla sua istituzione*, in "Rivista giuridica del Mezzogiorno", no. 4, 2010.
Segré C., *Produttività e prezzi nel processo di sviluppo: l'esperienza italiana 1950-1957*, Rome, Giuffrè, 1959.
Segreto L., *Gli investimenti americani in Italia (1945-1963)*, in "Studi Storici", vol. 37, no. 1, 1996.
Silva F., Viesti G., *Il difficile sviluppo dell'industria nel Mezzogiorno*, Milan, Franco Angeli, 1989.
Spadavecchia A., *Regional and national industrial policies in Italy, 1950s-1993, Where did the subsidies flow?*, Reading, Henley Business School, University of Reading, 2007.
Spagnolo C., *La stabilizzazione incompiuta. Il piano Marshall in Italia (1947-1952)*, Rome, Carocci, 2001.
Spaventa L. (ed.), *Nuovi problemi di sviluppo economico*, Turin, Boringhieri, 1962.
Strangio D., *La rinascita economica dell'Europa. Dall'European Recovery program all'integrazione economica europea e alla Banca europea per*

gli investimenti, Soveria Mannelli, Rubbettino, 2011.

SVIMEZ, *Agevolazioni per l'industrializzazione e lo sviluppo economico del Mezzogiorno*, Rome, 1950.

SVIMEZ, *Statistiche sul Mezzogiorno d'Italia, 1861-1953*, Rome, 1954.

SVIMEZ, *Ricerche sullo sviluppo economico dell'Europa meridionale*, Rome, 1956.

SVIMEZ, *Agevolazioni per l'industrializzazione del Mezzogiorno*, Rome, 1960.

SVIMEZ, *Un secolo di statistiche italiane Nord e Sud, 1861-1961*, Rome, 1961.

SVIMEZ, *Il Mezzogiorno nelle ricerche della Svimez, 1947-1967*, Rome, Giuffrè, 1968.

SVIMEZ, *Gli investimenti industriali agevolati nel Mezzogiorno (1951-1968)*, Milan, Giuffrè, 1971.

SVIMEZ, *Un quarto di secolo nelle statistiche Nord e Sud, 1951-1976*, Milan, Giuffrè, 1978.

SVIMEZ, *Il Mezzogiorno e la politica degli aiuti*, edited by R. Padovani, F. Moro and L. Bianchi, in "Informazioni SVIMEZ", no. 1-3, 2001.

SVIMEZ, *150 anni di statistiche italiane: Nord e Sud 1861-2011*, edited by A. Giannola, A. Lepore, R. Padovani, L. Bianchi and D. Miotti, Bologna, il Mulino, 2011.

SVIMEZ, *Nord e Sud a 150 anni dall'Unità d'Italia*, Rome, Quaderni SVIMEZ – Special issue, 2012.

Sylos Labini P., *Problemi dello sviluppo economico*, Rome-Bari, Laterza, 1970.

Sylos Labini P., *Scritti sul Mezzogiorno (1954-2001)*, edited by G. Arena, Manduria-Bari-Rome, Lacaita, 2003.

Tamagna, F.M., *Sviluppo economico e intermediazione finanziaria: Il Mezzogiorno d'Italia, 1951-1972*, Milan, Franco Angeli, 1978.

Taviani P.E., *Il problema dello sviluppo e l'esperienza della Cassa del Mezzogiorno*, Florence, Le Monnier, 1972.

Temin P., *The Golden Age of European growth reconsidered*, in "European Review of Economic History", vol. 6, no. 1, 2002.

Temin P., *The Golden Age of European growth: A review essay*, in "European Review of Economic History", vol. 1, no. 1, 2006.

Toniolo G., *Le fasi dell'industrializzazione italiana e la crisi del 1971-72*, Padua, Cedam, 1972.

Toniolo G., *Europe's Golden Age, 1950-1973: Speculations from a Long-run Perspective*, in "The Economic History Review", vol. 51, no. 2, 1998.

Toninelli P., *Lo sviluppo economico moderno. Dalla rivoluzione industriale alla crisi energetica*, Venice, Marsilio, 2006.

Tremelloni R., *Storia recente dell'industria italiana*, Milan, Garzanti, 1956.

Trigilia C., *Sviluppo senza autonomia. Effetti perversi delle politiche nel Mezzogiorno*, Bologna, il Mulino, 1992.

United States of America, Mutual Security Agency, Special Mission to Italy for Economic Cooperation, *The structure and growth of the Italian economy*, Westport (CT), Greenwood Press, 1972.

Vaccaro R., *Intervento pubblico e Mezzogiorno*, Padua, Cedam, 1989.

Vaccaro R., *Unità politica e dualismo economico in Italia*, Padua, Cedam, 1995.

Valli V., *L'economia e la politica economica italiana dal 1945 ad oggi*, Milan, Etas Libri, 1982.

Van Ark B., Crafts N.F.R. (eds.), *Quantitative Aspects of Post-war European Economic Growth*, Cambridge, Cambridge University Press, 2007.

Vlora A.K., *Il significato geografico delle cifre: risultati dell'intervento della Cassa per il Mezzogiorno nell'Italia meridionale continentale tra il 1950 e il 1970*, Bari, Adriatica, 1974.

Vöchting F., *La questione meridionale,* Naples, Istituto Editoriale del Mezzogiorno, 1955.

Vonyó T., *Post-war reconstruction and the Golden Age of economic growth*, in "European Review of Economic History", vol. 12, no. 2, 2008.

Watson M.M., *Regional development policy and administration in Italy,* London, Longmans, 1970.

Webber M.J., Rigby D.L., *The golden age illusion: rethinking postwar capitalism*, New York (NY), Guilford Press, 1996.

You J.-Il, *The Bretton Woods Institutions: Evolution, Reform and Change*, in D. Nayyar (ed.), *Governing Globalization: Issues and Institutions*, New York (NY), Oxford University Press, 2002.

Zagari E., *La questione meridionale: la storia, le diverse interpretazioni*, Turin, Giappichelli, 2008.

Zamagni V., *Lo Stato Italiano e l'economia: storia dell'intervento pubblico dall'unificazione ai giorni nostri*, Florence, Le Monnier, 1981.

Zamagni V., *Dalla periferia al centro. La seconda rinascita economica dell'Italia (1861-1990)*, Bologna, il Mulino, 1993.

Zamagni V., Sanfilippo M. (eds.), *Nuovo meridionalismo e intervento straordinario. La SVIMEZ dal 1946 al 1950*, Bologna, il Mulino, 1988.

Zoppi S., *Il Mezzogiorno di De Gasperi e Sturzo (1944-1959)*, Soveria Mannelli, Rubbettino, 2003.

Zoppi S. (ed.), *Diciotto voci per l'Italia unita*, Bologna, il Mulino, 2011.